The Complete
Guide to the
Parables

The Complete Guide to the Parables

Understanding and Applying the Stories of Jesus

Dr. R. T. Kendall

Chosen Books

A Division of Baker Book House Co
Grand Rapids, Michigan 49516

Published in the USA by Chosen Books
a division of Baker Publishing Group
P.O. Box 6287, Grand Rapids, MI 49516-6287
www.chosenbooks.com

Published in cooperation with Sovereign World Ltd., England

Second printing, July 2004

Printed in the United States of America

Library of Congress Cataloging-in-Publication Data
Kendall, R. T.
        The complete guide to the parables : understanding and applying the stories
    of Jesus / R. T. Kendall
            p.   cm.
    Includes bibliographical references.
        ISBN 0-8007-9358-7 (paper)
            1. Jesus Christ—Parables. I. Title.
    BT375.3.K46 2004
    226.8'06—dc22
                                                            2003069648

To
Arthur, Pete,
O. S. and Graham

Contents

Preface

My final Sunday morning preaching series at Westminster Chapel—the parables of Jesus—is now the book you hold in your hands. It has been edited by Tim Pettingale and put into a readable form. This means that the final sermon as such that I preached at the Chapel is the closing chapter in this book, "The Parable of the Sheep and the Goats." I felt a lump in my throat—sheer sentiment and nostalgia—as I read through it, knowing once again it meant the end of an era that still makes me feel so unworthy that I was ever there.

I remember Dr. Martyn Lloyd-Jones telling me that he had postponed doing his Romans series for years because he was waiting to understand Romans 6. But I was forced to take a different approach. I always thought that if I understood the parable of the shrewd manager (Luke 16:1–12)—the most difficult of all (to me at least), I would have the courage to begin a series on the parables of Jesus. But I felt compelled to start them anyway—a scary venture indeed. Lo and behold, when it was time to treat this particular parable I felt that a wonderful breakthrough came!

During my time at the Chapel I developed a close friendship with four special men—Arthur Blessitt, Pete Cantrell, O. S. Hawkins and Graham Ferguson Lacey. We called ourselves the *Gang of Five*. We had such fun and fellowship—laughter and tears—in England and America. I dedicate most lovingly this book to these four highly esteemed friends and servants of Christ. "Iron sharpens iron," and they have refined me and blessed me more than they will ever know.

I pray that God Almighty will apply His Spirit to your mind and heart as you read, and that this book will make a significant difference in your life. God bless you all.

Dr. R. T. Kendall
Key Largo, Florida
www.rtkendallministries.com

Foreword

There are two reasons why I am always happy to recommend as widely as I can the writings of Dr. R. T. Kendall.

First, R. T. is original with the best kind of originality. His great strength is his willingness to rethink and dig deeper into Scripture. An original thinker is, strange to say, one who sticks close to the original data and builds on it, rather than basing his ideas on what others have been saying about the data. An original thinker does not build new stories onto a building that already has several floors. He goes back to the foundations and builds the first floor again. R. T. is made in such a way that he likes to go back to the Scriptures rather than back to what others have said about the Scriptures. Here he helps us to understand the parables that Jesus told by challenging us to look at them afresh and, rather than replacing our own thinking, helps us to think about them for ourselves. In this respect R. T.'s writing will help us more than a dozen others that flow in a more traditionalist mold.

Secondly, R. T. has a firm grasp on what I might call the "present tense" of Christian salvation—that is, the process of being progressively delivered from the influences of sin and Satan. Christian writers have tended to focus on the "past tense" of salvation (getting "saved" in the traditional sense of the term) and on the "future tense" of salvation (getting to heaven and being everlastingly rewarded). But the Bible spends a lot of its space on the present tense of salvation—and so does R. T.!

R. T.'s theology is outstanding because it is *preached* theology, church theology—it is the tried and tested Word of God applied in a popular manner. This is where theology should be—not in the hands of bishops in palaces, or monks in monasteries, or scholars in universities, but in the hands of preachers in touch with the people of God. I pray Jacob's prayer for this book and all of R. T.'s works: like Joseph's children, "Let them grow into a multitude in the midst of the earth."

Dr. Michael Eaton
Nairobi, Kenya
January 2004

Chapter 1

Why Parables?

The disciples came to him and asked, "Why do you speak to the people in parables?"

He replied, "The knowledge of the secrets of the kingdom of heaven has been given to you, but not to them. Whoever has will be given more, and he will have an abundance. Whoever does not have, even what he has will be taken from him. This is why I speak to them in parables: 'Though seeing, they do not see; though hearing, they do not hear or understand.'"

Matthew 13:10–13

Jesus spoke all these things to the crowd in parables; he did not say anything to them without using a parable. So was fulfilled what was spoken through the prophet: "I will open my mouth in parables, I will utter things hidden since the creation of the world."

Matthew 13:34–35

By way of introduction to this book, I want to ask two questions: First, why have I written about each of the parables of Jesus in this book? The answer is that one day it came to me out of the blue during my quiet time that I should preach on the parables. I can't say I was thrilled because at first I thought, *Oh no, I don't think I understand the parables.* I had never before had a great ambition to preach on them, although I always hoped to understand them, yet now I felt a *compulsion* to preach them. I had experienced this feeling once before, when the Lord drew me to the book of James. Although I felt that there were certain verses I didn't understand at all, the Lord compelled me to begin preaching on James, and as I did so, He gave me the revelation that was needed.

I preached on nearly all the parables during my time at Westminster Chapel, and now the series of messages I gave has been gathered together to form this book. As with the book of James, when I began preaching on the parables it was from a position of not claiming to understand fully all that God wanted to reveal. My prayer was that as we studied Jesus' teaching, we would be learning more about Him together. The parables appear in this book in much the same order that they occur in the synoptic gospels.

My second question is this: Why did Jesus use parables? We will discuss the answer to that question in the rest of this chapter, and it will lay the foundation for all that is to come.

A parable may be defined as a simple story that illustrates a profound truth. Telling parables was Jesus' main way of helping His followers grasp spiritual truths. He was building a bridge from the natural to the spiritual. It was Jesus' way of helping people to make the transition that each of us must make every day of our life—to move from the natural level of life to the spiritual level of life. Jesus revealed these insights through parables so that those for whom the truth was intended might know the meaning, but those for whom it was *not* intended would *not understand.*

To understand further Jesus' reason for teaching in parables, we will look at:

- The purpose of the parables
- The promise of the parables
- The paradox of the parables
- Three principles of the parables

The Purpose of the Parables

Jesus' disciples asked Him, "Why do you speak to the people in parables?" In answering that question, we may think that it was partly to encourage us to press on when we don't understand something— that the parables were designed to test our earnestness in seeking the things of God. That may be partly true, but I believe there are five key reasons why Jesus spoke in parables:

1. To Sow Seed

Jesus used the parables to sow spiritual seed. His teaching had a long-term purpose: to sow seed into people's lives that would later grow and bear fruit. Seeds take time to grow. Jesus didn't expect His followers to grasp everything He was saying in one go, so He allowed for a delayed understanding. He planted seeds in their minds that would grow and eventually explode when the time was right. In some cases it may have taken years until the understanding came—long after Jesus had gone— but the seed He had planted bore fruit all the same.

It is amazing to see this reflected in the Scriptures. Jesus spent three years with His disciples, personally teaching and training them. Yet even after three years of listening to Jesus' parables firsthand, they still didn't understand much of what He was teaching them until years later.

After Jesus was crucified and raised from the dead, He appeared to His disciples for a further forty days, and at the end of that time they still hadn't grasped the main point of why Jesus came! They asked Jesus, "Lord, are you at this time going to restore the kingdom to Israel?" (Acts 1:6). Jesus might have looked at them and said, "I can't believe you're asking Me that. I never said I was going to restore the kingdom to Israel. Whoever made you think that? What was my entire Sermon on the Mount all about? It was about the Spirit. What is the kingdom of heaven all about? It's about the Spirit!"

It may shock us to realize that there is much in our lives that we miss the point of too, but Jesus desires to sow seed into our lives through His teaching that will eventually bear fruit and bring understanding to us.

2. To Safeguard the Secrets of God

In answer to His disciples' question, Jesus replied, "The knowledge of the secrets of the kingdom of heaven has been given to you, but not to them" (Matthew 13:11). First of all, God let us in on a secret—that He has secrets! God can keep a secret, but He can also choose to reveal them to whom He wills. The parables were designed to unfold secrets to those whom He wanted to hear them and to hide secrets from those He didn't.

Why would God keep secrets? For three reasons. First, to keep the devil in the dark. For instance, God chose to obscure His plans for His Messiah to prevent the devil from interfering with them. No one ever understood the Old Testament prophecies about Jesus until they were fulfilled. No one could figure out how the prophecy regarding Bethlehem could be right, or why the Messiah was supposed to be brought up in Nazareth. The prophecies didn't make sense until after the events happened; then they were obvious. Parables are much like this. We read in 1 Corinthians 2:8 that "none of the rulers of this age understood it, for if they had, they would not have crucified the Lord of glory." Jesus' death to save people was God's best-kept secret. He sent His Son to die on a cross for our sins, but the powers of evil had no idea what was happening until it was too late.

God keeps secrets in order to keep those who are unspiritual, or "in the flesh," in the dark. Jesus said:

> This is why I speak to them in parables: "Though seeing, they do not see; though hearing, they do not hear or understand." In them is fulfilled the

prophecy of Isaiah: "You will be ever hearing but never understanding; you will be ever seeing but never perceiving. For this people's heart has become calloused."

Matthew 13:13–14

Jesus saw that hearts were hardened against God. God turned those people over to their own devices because they refused to listen to Him or His Son. He chose to allow them to follow their own desires, to turn from Him with calloused hearts.

God keeps secrets in order to reveal them at the proper time to those for whom they are intended. At the right time He unveils them to those whose hearts are seeking after Him. The power of God's Word is such that it can reach those at whom it is aimed and still be hidden from those who are not receptive to it. Parables are designed like this, to reach some and keep others in the dark. Jesus therefore makes a distinction between these two groups when explaining the reason for parables to His own close followers.

3. To Highlight the Sovereignty of God

The sovereignty of God has to do with His inherent right to either give or withhold mercy. God said to Moses in Exodus 33:19: "I will proclaim my name, the LORD, in your presence. I will have mercy on whom I will have mercy, and I will have compassion on whom I will have compassion." The apostle Paul repeats this in Romans 9:15 and concludes: "It does not, therefore, depend on man's desire or effort, but on God's mercy" (verse 16). Similarly, this truth is reflected in Jesus' teaching through parables. In John 3:8 Jesus described God's sovereignty, saying, "The wind blows wherever it pleases. You hear its sound, but you cannot tell where it comes from or where it is going. So it is with everyone born of the Spirit."

This means that you can't make the Holy Spirit do anything. You can't make Him save anybody. You can't make Him heal anybody. You can't make Him open anybody's eyes to the truth. Only the Holy Spirit can do that according to God's will and purpose. Some people believe that they can *make* God do things for them and so they continually try to force God's hand, but the parables reveal the sovereignty of God—they give an accurate portrayal of God's character and nature.

God gave a mandate to the prophet Isaiah that he may not have particularly liked. It was: "Go and tell this people: 'Be ever hearing, but never understanding; be ever seeing, but never perceiving'" (Isaiah 6:9).

What kind of mandate is that? Yet Jesus had the same mandate from God. It revealed His sovereignty.

4. To Survey the Teaching of Salvation

In the parables of Jesus you can view the whole panorama of salvation. They cover the entire spectrum of Christian experience, from initial conversion to Christ to the final consummation of all things when Jesus comes to earth for the second time. The parables even include the crucifixion of Jesus. At the time when Jesus spoke through these parables, it was unthinkable that such a thing could happen, but He foreshadowed His very death in this manner. The parables survey salvation—from conversion, through the work of the Spirit, to what happens when we die.

5. To Reveal the Spirit of God

Jesus revealed the work of the Spirit in all kinds of ways, some more obvious than others. The Sermon on the Mount is, in a real sense, an entire parable about the Holy Spirit. You may think, *But it doesn't even mention the Holy Spirit.* I know. Yet one of the most God-centered books in the entire Bible is the book of Esther, and it never mentions the name of the Lord anywhere. So if you understand the Sermon on the Mount, you'll understand that it's about Jesus' focus on the Holy Spirit, His revealing of the Spirit's character and work. Jesus' parables refer to the Kingdom of heaven. Whenever the Kingdom of heaven is mentioned, generally speaking, it is referring to the realm of the Spirit. Therefore Jesus is revealing what true spirituality looks like as it is lived out in the power of the Holy Spirit.

The Promise of the Parables

In Matthew 13:34–35, Jesus said an interesting thing. He drew attention to an Old Testament prophecy that foretold He would speak in parables: "Jesus spoke all these things to the crowd in parables; he did not say anything to them without using a parable. So was fulfilled what was spoken through the prophet: 'I will open my mouth in parables, I will utter things hidden since the creation of the world.'" Why did Jesus point that out? Because He wanted us to know that parables were foretold. The prophets had announced in advance that the Messiah would come speaking in parables. Jesus was saying, "Don't be surprised that I'm speaking to you in parables. This was foretold. This was promised long ago."

The prophecy even went on to foretell the *content* of the parables. Jesus was quoting Psalm 78:2 when He said, "I will utter things hidden from the creation of the world." The parables contain things that were previously hidden.

Let me ask you a question. When you read the Bible and you don't understand something when you first read it, what do you do? Do you close your Bible and say, "Well, I don't understand that"? If that's what you do, then you have just revealed how interested you are in understanding the things of God. But if you begin to seek God and ask Him about the things you don't understand, then a different dynamic comes into effect. You are now seeking God and asking for revelation, understanding and wisdom. That is why not even the most brilliant, intellectual mind in all the earth can simply "figure out" the meaning of the parables. You can have an IQ the equivalent of Albert Einstein's and still not understand the parables. Why? Because you need the Holy Spirit to *reveal* their meaning to you by His power.

Jesus showed His disciples that Old Testament prophecies were being fulfilled before their very eyes. What Isaiah said would happen, was happening. Jesus said, "Don't be surprised that you don't understand My parables. You weren't meant to. Understanding parables is a 'family' secret." You can react in one of two ways to His statement. You can either say, "Well, I'm outside the family, so that's it," or you can say, "Lord, I'd like to be in the family. Is there any chance You'd have mercy on me?"

The Paradox of the Parables

Third, we come to the paradox of the parables. The word *paradox* means "that which is contradictory yet true." We have already noted that those with hardened or calloused hearts "miss" the truths that are presented in the parables, but Jesus made an amazing statement in Matthew 13:12: "Whoever has will be given more, and he will have an abundance. Whoever does not have, even what he has will be taken from him." This is the paradox of the parables: The words that Jesus spoke serve to harden further the hearts of those who are unreceptive to them. Those outside the family of God who have calloused hearts are eventually "humiliated"—even that which they have is taken away and they are left with nothing.

But for those in the family of God, three things are true. First, they "hear." Jesus told His disciples in verse 16, "But blessed are your eyes because they see, and your ears because they hear." Not only do they hear, but they realize they are honored, because Jesus went on to say to them, "I tell you the truth, many prophets and righteous men longed to see what you see but did not see it, and to hear what you hear but did not hear it" (verse 17). And so the consequence is that those who are in the family are humbled that God should allow them to "see" and "hear." When you are outside of God's family, the consequence is humiliation. When you are inside the family, the consequence is humility. Outside the family, people are hardened; inside, they're honored.

Three Principles of the Parables

As we study Jesus' parables, three main principles will guide us. It will be useful always to have these in your mind as you study and absorb the truths that Jesus is imparting.

Principle 1
Not all parables point to the same truth. Some speak primarily about the work of the Spirit; some teach about eschatology—i.e., "last things"; some talk about our growth as Christians.

Principle 2
Often a parable will have only one basic truth in mind. We must not try to read more into a parable than we ought in order to make it speak about an issue, such as the second coming of Jesus or the judgment seat of Christ, when it might not be referring to that at all. Our aim must be to figure out the cardinal truth that Jesus wanted to illustrate.

Principle 3
Most important, we must never try to make a parable stand on all four legs! Not every detail of a parable has to have a meaning. When interpreting parables, be careful to keep the essential truth in mind, and don't try to build a major doctrine on what may be a secondary detail.

As we embark on this journey of exploring the parables together, I pray that God will help us to take hold of the essential ingredient—to hear what Jesus is saying to us by His Spirit and to understand and apply it to our lives. If God gives us a measure of understanding, then we are most blessed, most thankful, and we will give all the glory to Him.

Chapter 2

The Parable of the Sower

A farmer went out to sow his seed.
Matthew 13:3

The parable of the sower is one of Jesus' better known parables. In this book, I am attempting to address each parable in the order in which it appears in Scripture, yet one might argue that this parable is not the first. It could be argued that Jesus' first parable appeared during His Sermon on the Mount. As He reached the conclusion of His message, He said, "Therefore everyone who hears these words of mine and puts them into practice is like a wise man who built his house on the rock" (Matthew 7:24). Jesus then went on to recite the short parable about the wise and foolish builders.

In fact, much of Jesus' speech throughout His ministry contained fragments of parables. He used many vivid illustrations to get His point across to people. They occur throughout the gospel of Matthew long before chapter 13 and the parable of the sower. But so much of Jesus' speech was "parable-like" that we need to be selective. The parable of the sower is a good starting point because Matthew explicitly states that a parable is coming: "Then he told them many things in parables..." (Matthew 13:3).

One of the most interesting things about this particular parable is that Jesus said it was easy to understand: "Don't you understand this parable? How then will you understand any parable?" (Mark 4:13). Jesus was trying to reach people where they were. You could say that this parable was an "entry-level" parable; it was intended to be easily accessed. The parable of the sower is based around a farming illustration, and Jesus was speaking to a predominantly agricultural society.

Three things stand out about this parable:

- *It is easy to understand.*
- *It is elementary.* Jesus was giving us a simple teaching regarding the results of proclaiming the Word of God.

- *It is explained.* The good thing about this parable is that Jesus explains it. We might wish that Jesus had explained all of the parables, but He chose not to.

First, we are going to look at the general meaning of the parable. What did Jesus want to communicate to us through it? There are four basic takeaways from this parable:

1. Indiscriminate Recruiting by the Word
This parable implies that in God's Kingdom there is *indiscriminate recruiting by the Word.* All of us are meant to *recruit* disciples, and this recruitment is to be *indiscriminate.* This means we don't know whom God has chosen. We believe in the sovereignty of God, yes, that He has chosen people from the foundation of the world who are called "the elect." But *we* don't know who they are—only God knows. And although God knows who they are, He has instructed us to go out into *all the world* spreading the Gospel message. "Indiscriminate recruiting" means that we do everything we can to save everybody—the "indiscriminate offer of the Gospel," as John Calvin put it. Christ died for everybody so that we can say to anybody, "Jesus died for you." We don't discriminate. We don't sow seed only to those who we think may be one of God's chosen ones; we don't sow seed to only the middle classes; we don't sow seed only to those who share our political views; we don't sow seed only to those who belong to a certain racial minority or majority. In other words, the Gospel is "sown" to everybody.

2. Initial Responses to the Word
This parable also illustrates people's initial response to the Word. Interestingly, this parable only portrays positive responses to the Gospel. Wouldn't it be wonderful if this parable indicated the way it would always be, that no matter what, everybody said yes to the call to be saved? Standing alone, this parable might imply that everybody is going to say yes, but in fact it is only showing us the differences between the positive initial responses. It is leaving out the negative responses altogether. Jesus did not deal at all with any negative initial responses to the Gospel in this parable—He did that in other parables in which He described how the Gospel is rejected.

3. Individual Reactions to the Word
The parable identifies how different people react to the Gospel. Even though these people aren't rejecting it, some don't understand the

Gospel at all. So when Jesus gave the meaning in Matthew 13:19, He said, "When anyone hears the message about the kingdom and does not understand it, the evil one comes and snatches away what was sown in his heart." It shows that some can say yes when they hear the Word, even though they don't fully understand it. In some cases, then, it isn't that the Gospel is rejected; it's that the devil stole it away before the person had a chance to understand it.

The parable also tells us, according to Luke 8:13, that there are those who believe for a while, but in a time of testing fall away; and that there are those who believe for just a while, but "things" overtake them—the worries of life, riches and pleasures—and they subsequently fall away.

4. The Importance of Interpreting the Word Correctly

In the King James Version, 2 Timothy 2:15 reads, "Study to shew thyself approved unto God, a workman that needeth not to be ashamed, rightly dividing the word of truth." The fact that Jesus mentioned a group of people who, although they heard and received the Word, were overtaken by material things and worldly pleasures, highlights what a need there is for a sound understanding of God's Word.

Why Is This Parable So Important?

The parable of the sower is one of the most important parables. Why? Because it conveys important truths that are relevant to every generation. There are seven lessons to be learned from this parable that can help us to a greater understanding of the process of conversion and salvation.

▶ *1. We should never be surprised when people don't persevere.*
The Gospel is intended not only to change one's eternal destiny—from certain banishment to hell to an entrance into paradise—but to *change lives*. It's meant to result in permanent change, but we know for a fact that there are those who make a profession of faith and then months later, sometimes years later, drift away. This parable predicts that this will happen and warns us not to be surprised.

▶ *2. Nobody should be blamed when people don't persevere.*
Although there are clearly those who fall away, Jesus wasn't blaming anybody else for this. He didn't blame the person who sowed the seed if the one who heard the Word didn't persevere. He didn't blame the

church they attended, or any evangelist, preacher or teacher. Nobody else should be blamed.

▶ *3. Not everyone who makes a profession of faith is saved.*

Jesus made another interesting point that should also not surprise us: There will be some people who, though outward appearances seem to suggest they are saved, are not saved at all. This underscores the importance of discipleship—the teaching and training of those who make a commitment to Christ. We should not simply assume that because a person bows their head and prays, they are saved. We cannot perceive what is going on in another person's heart; only God can do that. Jesus used this parable to teach us this principle, namely, not all who make a profession of faith are necessarily saved.

▶ *4. We should never try to judge who is saved and who is not saved.*

Just as we should not assume someone is saved by their outward reaction, equally we cannot assume that they are *not* saved, Jesus taught us. I will never forget the story told to me by my friend Dr. D. James Kennedy. Jim is a pastor, but he is also an evangelist who has touched many people's lives. He told me about a dentist to whom he had witnessed during the early days of Evangelism Explosion. The dentist made a profession of faith, but Jim was convinced he had not really responded in his *heart*. The dentist's name was Dr. Freeman Springer. At one time he was our own dentist when my wife and I lived in Fort Lauderdale, so we knew him and heard both sides of the story.

Jim and his wife, Anne, called on the Springers and were invited in. The conversation that followed went something like this:

"Do come in."

"Thanks, it's nice to be here," Jim said. "You came to our church on Sunday, and you filled out a card."

"Well, yeah, we were glad to have been there."

And so Jim presented the Gospel and Freeman Springer just said, "Yes, yes, yes . . ." throughout the conversation. Eventually Jim invited the couple to bow their heads and pray.

"Yes," they immediately responded.

"Any questions?" Jim asked after they had prayed.

"No, thank you very much."

So Jim and Anne looked at each other and then showed themselves to the door. As soon as they were back in their car, Jim turned to his wife and said, "Well, there's a couple we'll never see again." It was all too easy. There was no emotion, no tears; he just kept saying yes. But I talked to Freeman Springer about it later and he said, "I knew they thought nothing happened, but the next morning when I opened the curtains and the light came in, I knew I had eternal life." Freeman became a member of the Evangelism Explosion team himself, and the last time I spoke to him, he had actually led over 75 people to the Lord! He became an amazing soul winner.

The point of the story is, never judge who is saved or who isn't saved. Hold your judgment. Sometimes the most promising person lets you down in a very short period of time, and sometimes when you think nothing has happened, you find that the seed was sown on good ground after all.

▶ *5. The truths contained in this parable will always be relevant.*
We must never think that we can render this parable redundant by "sounder" preaching. It will always be relevant. For example, years ago I belonged to a denomination that believed that no Christian, if they were really a Christian, would sin, because we're not supposed to sin. I used to ask the pastor at that church, "Why did Jesus give us the Lord's Prayer then, which says, 'Forgive us our trespasses as we forgive those who trespass against us'?" And he could never answer that question. We pray the Lord's Prayer over and over because we're always going to be sinners until we get to heaven. We cannot make the Lord's Prayer redundant. In the same way, no one can render the parable of the sower redundant, because despite hearing the best presentations of the Gospel, people will still make professions of faith that do not last.

▶ *6. A person's initial response to the Gospel need not be permanent.*
We should avoid what I call "permanentizing" people's first response to the Gospel. In other words, we should not assume that their initial manner of response is final. Take, for example, the person who hears the Word but does not understand it, and then the evil one comes and snatches away what is sown in his or her heart. We cannot say that that person cannot later be converted. The seed sown along the path may fall on good ground later. A false profession may be upstaged later by a genuine conversion. Don't make the mistake of *permanentizing* people's reactions.

▶ *7. The parable does not refer only to preaching to the lost.*
It can refer to a Christian who later fails to walk in the light. The parable of the sower therefore has other applications. Take the person whose heart is like the good soil that received the seed and who therefore had

a genuine conversion. Does that mean that he or she cannot also later on hear the message but have it stolen away? That can happen to a Christian. How many times have you looked forward to time spent in reading the Bible and you think, *Ah, I've got an hour.* Then the phone rings, or as you start to read, you're preoccupied with what you have to do when the hour is up. The devil robbed you! Or as you are praying, your mind begins to wander and before you know it, the hour is up. The devil came in with the cares of this life. The fact is, even those who have received salvation can later be like one of those described in the first three examples—it can happen to anybody.

Genuinely converted people, when they receive a new word from God, will often have a reaction just like the first three examples in this parable. Take tithing for instance. I've known people who have had a revelation regarding tithing and have started to tithe, but after six weeks or six months, something happens and they stop. Or take the teaching of total forgiveness. Some people, after hearing that they should always totally forgive others, say, "Yes, I will not hold grudges against people anymore." Then maybe two weeks later, they think of what someone did to them and worse, how they're going to get away with it, and they get all churned up inside again.

This doesn't mean that the person is not saved, but often when a Christian receives new revelation, they struggle to accept it and allow it to take root in their life. It indicates to us that there are some genuine Christians who lose their reward in heaven because of their conduct on earth. How could they lose their reward? Because although the Word of God fell on "good ground" in their lives initially, later when they heard preaching that demanded a tough commitment, they said, "I just can't do it." It doesn't mean they are not saved, but it could determine whether or not they receive their reward in heaven.

The Ministry of Proclamation

As well as highlighting the various reactions of people who hear the Word of God, the parable of the sower illustrates to us the fundamental need for preaching the Word—for proclaiming the message of the Gospel. Jesus was showing us that the *aim* of preaching the Word is to speak into the lives of both the unconverted and the converted. The *agenda* of preaching is the Gospel message. As Christians, we've got no other message! This is why I believe that regardless of what other factors are emphasized in the life of the Church—evangelism, worship, prayer—the preaching of the Word should be central.

Four Professions of Faith

Finally, I want to examine a facet of this parable that has been implicit in the preceding teaching—the mixed reactions of those who hear the Word. Each type of person who heard the Word of God reacted with a different kind of profession of faith.

1. The Supplanted Reaction

This describes a reaction to the Gospel in which the enemy manages to maintain control over the person hearing the message. Jesus said in Matthew 13:19, "When anyone hears the message about the kingdom and does not understand it, the evil one comes and snatches away what was sown in his heart." It shows us that there are those whom Satan succeeds in deceiving by keeping the person blind. Second Corinthians 4:4 confirms that "the god of this age has blinded the minds of unbelievers, so that they cannot see the light of the gospel." This is what the devil wants—to keep you from understanding, to keep you blind. As soon as a person makes a profession of faith, the devil is right there within hours, trying to snatch away the Word. The enemy is always trying to supplant what God might do in a person's life. That's the way Jesus put it. Jesus made it clear that such a person is not saved.

2. The Superficial Profession

This is a reaction to the Gospel that is enthusiastic and compliant. On hearing the message, some people will react with excitement and want to make an immediate commitment. However, Matthew 13:20–21 tells us, "The one who received the seed that fell on rocky places is the man who hears the word and at once receives it with joy. But since he has no root, he lasts only a short time. When trouble or persecution comes because of the word, he quickly falls away." Perhaps because this type of person reacts so quickly, they have not thought through the implications of their decision. They could be excited by what they've heard because they think it will be the answer to a personal problem they've been dealing with. Sometimes people will respond to the Gospel by coming forward at a church meeting and giving their life to Christ, but after that day you never see them again. It doesn't necessarily mean that they were insincere, but they made a quick profession of faith that turned out to be superficial. In Luke's account of this parable, he says that such a person will "believe for a while" (Luke 8:13).

3. The Stifled Profession

There are those who react positively to the Gospel but allow the message to be *stifled* by many competing worries and desires. Jesus said in Matthew 13:22, "The one who received the seed that fell among the thorns is the man who hears the word, but the worries of this life and the deceitfulness of wealth choke it, making it unfruitful." These people don't have a superficial reaction to the Gospel but gradually fall away over time as they allow many other concerns to crowd in. Jesus called it the "worries of this life" and the "deceitfulness of wealth." The Gospel message that the people received is closed out by the competition of worry about what people will think and is eventually choked by material cares.

4. The Solid Profession

Finally, Jesus described a fourth reaction to the Gospel: a solid profession of faith that lasts, in which the person hearing the Word receives it and allows it to take root in their life and grow to fruition. "The one who received the seed that fell on good soil is the man who hears the word and understands it. He produces a crop, yielding a hundred, sixty or thirty times what was sown" (Matthew 13:23).

This fourth example is surely the only one of these people who are really converted. Some scholars try to make the case that maybe one or two of the previous examples were also converted, that just because they had difficulty and didn't persevere doesn't mean they were not converted. Yet the Bible clearly states that they could not be saved. I agree that there are true Christians who fall, and the Bible makes an allowance for that, but that is not taught in this particular parable. We must remember that Jesus was not trying to prove *everything* that can *ever* happen in a single parable.

In this fourth example, the Holy Spirit is able to apply the Word that was sown effectively, creating life and giving those people the conviction that they are saved only by the blood of Jesus. They reach the understanding that a person can only be saved by the righteousness of Christ, and that lasts.

The parable of the sower is loaded with information and warrants further exploration on another level. We have already examined four basic reactions to hearing the Gospel message that are illustrated in this parable. To help us further understand Jesus' teaching in this parable, I want to identify three key words that occur throughout it: *identity, irony* and *inheritance*.

Identity

There are an additional three key words that need some definition. They identify the three main elements of the parable, and they are: *sower, seed* and *soil*. The word *sower* refers to a person who is a kind of herald—someone who announces the Gospel and proclaims the Word—a preacher. The preacher's job is to sow the *seed,* and this happens when a person preaches the Word and attempts to explain it to others. Someone who explains the Word is called a Bible *expositor*—in other words, he or she is trying to *expose* the Word so that others can see its meaning.

There are many possible types of sowers who preach the Word of God and sow seed. It may be a preacher *exposing* the revealed will of God in the Bible; it may be a prophet revealing the secret will of God through his or her spiritual gift; or it may be a pastor who is sowing seed continually. Each one is a herald of the good news of the Gospel.

The *seed* is the Word of God; it is what we hear. The Bible says that faith comes by *hearing* the Word of God. The Word is heard outwardly, but hopefully, and more importantly, it is heard inwardly. Jesus said that many are called but few are chosen. The message of the Gospel needs to be heard in a person's heart and not just in their head. When Jesus described those who hear but from whom the devil comes and snatches the Word away, or those who receive the Word with joy but have no root, or those whose seed fell among thorns and was choked, He was talking about those who heard outwardly but not inwardly. They receive the Word with their minds but not their hearts.

Jesus finished this particular parable by saying, "He who has ears, let him hear" (Matthew 13:9). Jesus was referring to those who would hear the Word and receive it in their hearts, who would persevere with it and eventually produce a fruitful crop.

A believing heart is the good soil that Jesus described. The *soil* is the fertile ground of a heart that hears, believes and applies the Word of God.

Can you say for sure that you belong to this fourth category of people? The Bible says that you can know! You can have a full and certain assurance of your faith. How can you know? There are two basic tests: first, you will have a godly fear and reverence for God. In Matthew 13:23 we read that "the one who received the seed that fell on good soil is the man who hears the word and understands it." What do you suppose caused that person to understand the Word? The Bible says that the fear of the Lord is the beginning of wisdom. A reverent fear of the Lord is a prerequisite for understanding, and an increasingly deep fear of the Lord is what will be produced in your life as you progress in your relationship with Him.

Secondly, you will bear fruit. Jesus taught that the person who receives the Word of God into good soil eventually produces a crop. There will be fruit produced as a result of the Word of God taking effect in your life. What is the fruit? The fruit will be *repentance, redirection* and *resolve*. Repentance is literally a change of mind. It is a process initiated by the Holy Spirit working in a person's life, bringing about a transformation inside. Repentance then leads to a redirection—a kind of spiritual U-turn. Your life was going in one direction and then the Holy Spirit leads you in a completely different direction. There will also be a new resolve—a commitment to persevere in your relationship with God, to honor God and obey His Word.

Irony

Jesus had something else to say through this parable that I call the *ironies of the parable*. I have only hinted at these in our discussion so far, but now I want to examine Jesus' words again from a slightly different angle.

The first irony is that the first three examples, as I said above, are not necessarily permanent. Although someone may have believed for a while before falling away, or believed but become choked with cares, they need not stay that way forever. They may well make a lasting profession of faith later on—they need not miss it forever.

Many of the Puritans held to a line of thinking that taught what was called the "temporary faith of the reprobate"—the word *reprobate* meaning to them "the nonelect." They taught that a person fell away from the faith because of the fact that they were predestined *not* to be saved, and that a person could temporarily *appear* to be saved. As far as they were concerned, the person who showed some sign of being converted but then fell away was regarded as reprobate and would never be saved—end of story. That view is quite wrong and completely unbiblical. A person who has responded to the Gospel and then fallen could be one of God's elect who will later respond and then persevere. No one should ever believe, *Well, I had my chance, and I failed. There's no hope for me.* That is the first irony—the first three examples are not necessarily permanent.

The second irony is that despite the failure of the first three examples to mature, the seed was still sown. This is so important to remember.

No harm was done to the person whose profession of faith did not last. We may be disappointed that the person didn't persevere, but a premature profession of faith may not be the end of the story. No harm is done to that person who made an enthusiastic commitment to Christ—it may help them to come to a solid decision to follow Christ later on. Let us not get locked into a system of thinking that tries to impose restrictions on what the Holy Spirit can or cannot do.

The third irony revealed in the parable is that a person who had a solid conversion—a genuine Christian who is saved—may later be like one of the first three examples. He or she may later have a "flash-in-the-pan" response to deeper preaching. This can happen when people hear preaching that demands a deeper commitment than perhaps they ever thought they'd have to give. Saved people struggle with issues. It may be a revealed truth that they are finding hard to accept, or it may be a struggle with forgiveness or with money—the point is that saved people can react like the unsaved people in the parable.

There's a fourth irony in the parable, which is this: A person solidly converted may lose his or her inheritance. Inheritance means "reward." We have already noted that a person whose initial response was superficial may later receive their reward when they are genuinely converted. Although a person may make a quick profession of faith and then not be seen again, they may eventually be converted, walk in the light and receive their reward. This is the irony—it demonstrates how so often the first may be last and the last may be first. The very people of whom we were perhaps critical because they didn't persevere can come through to a lasting faith and receive their inheritance. The last shall be first.

There is one final irony: Though we may know we are on good ground because of a true fear of God and a lasting response, we must never get our true assurance of faith from this. Why? Because our assurance of salvation is based on Jesus' blood, not our perseverance. We may well be aware of a fear of God—thank God for it—but we must never base our assurance on anything but Christ alone. "My hope is built on nothing less than Jesus' blood and righteousness."

Inheritance

Finally, I want to examine the inheritance that Jesus envisaged in the parable for those who believe. This is applicable to those people who responded to the Word of God with a prepared heart and have had a genuine conversion experience—the good soil. We have already seen that "fruit" is produced from a genuine conversion, but that is not the end of it. Ultimately there will be a reward given to those who have persevered in following Christ and have grown and matured in their faith. We are called to receive an inheritance. *Inheritance* is a New Testament word that simply means "reward." It means that when you die, you will not only go to heaven; you will also receive a reward at the judgment seat of Christ. I know of no greater motivation that this. The promise of a reward was partly what motivated the apostle Paul.

There are some who say, "I know I'm going to go to heaven, and that's good enough for me." But Paul said that we must all stand before the judgment seat of Christ and give an account of the things done in the body. You may feel ambivalent about it now, but I can tell you that when you stand before the judgment seat of Christ and give an account of your life, it will be an awesome moment.

The Bible tells us that there will be those who are saved like a person barely escaping through flames. They will be saved, but all their earthly deeds will amount to no more than a pile of ash and stubble, and they will not receive an inheritance.

There are three elements to an inheritance. First, there is a *refining* that takes place. Throughout your walk with Him, God seeks to refine you. The King James Version calls it *chastening.* It comes from a Greek word meaning "enforced learning." God chastens you as you walk in the light, and He exposes sin in your heart that you hadn't thought was there. If you are brought face-to-face with what you are really like, you may blush and think, *Oh, Lord, am I like that?* When God says, "Yes," you can either deny it, or you can ask for forgiveness and pray for God to change you. Any person who won't admit he's wrong, who won't say, "Please forgive me," is one who is not being refined.

Secondly, there is a *renewal.* To be renewed is to experience a fresh taste of glory. Paul described it as being changed from glory to glory. It is a moment when God may give you a special feeling in your heart that you're loved or a new insight or a great blessing. Sometimes that change is precipitated by a severe trial, but you come through it and God lets you know how special you are.

Thirdly, there is the *reward* itself. This is the ultimate way in which inheritance is fulfilled. The apostle Peter describes it as a "rich welcome" into God's eternal Kingdom. Every one of us is called to that inheritance. Let us continue to receive the Word of God into "good ground"; to walk continually in the light, trusting in the blood of Jesus. If you find that there is bitterness in your heart toward anybody, deal with it. If you find that your commitment is not what it once was, deal with it. It's okay because it means that God is still talking to you. Thank Him for anything He says. Take it with both hands. That is what Jesus wants us to take away from the parable of the sower. One day we will stand before Him and give an account of our life, and we will be glad that we walked in every bit of light God gave us.

Chapter 3

The Parable of the Mustard Seed

> If you have faith as small as a mustard seed ... nothing will be impossible for you.
>
> Matthew 17:20

Jesus was very fond of the mustard seed. He used it as a parable in Matthew, Mark and Luke, and He used it as an illustration in two other ways. In Matthew He used it when His disciples could not cast out a demon from a child: "I tell you the truth, if you have faith as small as a mustard seed, you can say to this mountain, 'Move from here to there' and it will move. Nothing will be impossible for you" (Matthew 17:20).

In Luke He used the same "mustard-seed faith" to refer to total forgiveness when He said to them:

> "If [your brother] sins against you seven times a day, and seven times comes back to you and says, 'I repent,' forgive him." The apostles said to the Lord, "Increase our faith!" He replied, "If you have faith as small as a mustard seed, you can say to this mulberry tree, 'Be uprooted and planted in the sea,' and it will obey you."
>
> Luke 17:4–6

According to Luke and Mark, when He introduced the parable of the mustard seed He said, "What shall we say the kingdom of God is like, or what parable shall we use to describe it?" (Mark 4:30).

I've always thought that was interesting. Was Jesus thinking aloud, scratching His head, wondering, *How shall I do this?* Or was He actually helping them to see that He had a task on His hands because they thought they didn't need any help understanding the Kingdom of God? Jesus knew exactly what they thought. It was His way of getting their attention and letting them know that they would have to make some major shifts in their thinking.

The whole time Jesus was on this earth, the issue that occupied His attention was the Kingdom of God and the Kingdom of heaven. His audience loved the idea of the Kingdom, but when they were thinking of the word *Kingdom,* they were thinking of the days of Samuel when Israel had said, "Give us a king! We want to be like other nations" (see 1 Samuel 8:5). God gave them a king at that time, and they paid dearly for it.

When the disciples thought of the coming king, they believed he would overthrow Caesar. Now that Jesus had come, they figured it wouldn't be long until this happened. Jesus spent three years trying to help them make the transition from natural understanding to spiritual understanding. The parables served as an entry point to the new and different; to reach people where they were and move them on to where they'd never been before.

There are so many parables because there are a multiplicity of ways in which the Kingdom of God can be described. The Kingdom that Jesus came to reveal was radically different from anything the disciples had thought of. Jesus' task was to lead them outside their comfort zones. I don't know if you've realized it yet, but the whole of the Christian life involves God leading us out of our comfort zones! Just as you begin to get comfortable with something, the next thing you know, God is leading you on to something new! In this life we are being made more and more like Jesus. When we get to heaven, it will all be comfort—no tears, no having to search your heart, no resisting the devil—but in this life, the very concept of being changed from glory to glory means being led out of our comfort zones. Jesus is happy to do that.

A Mustard Seed Is a Tiny Beginning

Jesus taught the parable of the mustard seed as a reminder to us not to be discouraged by slow or small beginnings. God loves to begin with what seems inconsequential. He loves to surprise us by doing things we could never have imagined. This is why the prophet Isaiah said of Jesus, "He grew up before him like a tender shoot, and like a root out of dry ground. He had no beauty or majesty to attract us to him, nothing in his appearance that we should desire him" (Isaiah 53:2).

And this is just the way God loves to do it. Take what seems to be an inconsequential moment, like meeting a person for the first time and exchanging a few pleasant words. Weeks later you realize that it was a pivotal event in your life: You met a person who turned out to be a very special friend perhaps. Just so, God loves to begin with what seems at first to be inconsequential.

Another reason Jesus told this parable was to show how God can take the most unlikely person and turn them into a sovereign vessel. Put another way, people who are rejected get God's attention. God loves to take someone who has been hurt, misunderstood or underestimated and turn them into a sovereign vessel that can change a nation. Did you know that the great Charles Haddon Spurgeon applied to study the ministry at Regent's Park College in London and was turned down? Talk about a skeleton in the cupboard of Regent's Park College! Similarly, G. Campbell Morgan, who was a minister of Westminster Chapel earlier this century, and who first gave the Chapel an international reputation, was rejected by the Methodists as a man who could not make it as a preacher. This is such an encouraging revelation if you have been looked down on, or passed over for a promotion or misunderstood by your pastor or by a church leader. God says, "Good, that's the kind I want."

This is also an important parable because it shows that God can take the most unpromising situation and turn it into triumph and glory. The greatest event in the history of the world was the most greatly underestimated event in the history of the world. If you had been at Golgotha on Good Friday, two thousand years ago, there were no CNN cameramen there, no one from *Time* magazine saying, "This is history in the making. We are privileged to witness this moment!" At the time it seemed to be nothing more than a very tragic, sad event that signaled that the hopes of many people had come to an end. Jesus was hanging on a cross, and the mob was saying, "He saved others ... but he can't save himself!" (Matthew 27:42). In hell the devils rejoiced, saying, "He's finished!" About that time Jesus Himself said, "It is finished," and the veil in the temple was rent from top to bottom (Matthew 27:50–51; Mark 15:37–38). A few weeks later Peter described Jesus as the One whom the builders had rejected as useless, but who had now become the capstone (Acts 4:10–11). God loves to do this—to take the most unpromising situation and turn it into glory!

Lastly, this parable shows how God can take the simplest and most elementary insight and turn it into a profound and life-changing testimony. The French writer Victor Hugo said, "Like the trampling of a mighty army so is the force of an idea whose time has come." And God does this with the mustard seed, just a little tiny seed that you can barely hold in your hand. God can take that little thought and make it grow and turn the world upside down.

We will look now at the purpose of the parable, the prophecy of the parable and the potential of the parable of the mustard seed.

The Purpose of the Parable

Talk of the "Kingdom" was a language with which Jesus' disciples were comfortable, although they were thinking along different lines than Jesus. So when He used the word *Kingdom,* He had to address their earthly viewpoint.

Kingdom, to the disciples, had always meant greatness and glory. They thought of the days of David and Solomon. They were aware of the prophecy of Haggai: "The glory of this present house will be greater than the glory of the former" (Haggai 2:9).

Every time Jesus performed a miracle, one of the disciples must have glanced at the Roman soldiers and thought, *It won't be long now till they'll be gone!* They eagerly awaited the day when the Roman soldiers and governors would be sent packing. To them the Son of Man was a godlike figure who would come with power, charisma, military genius and anything else that showed might.

In John 6 when Jesus fed the five thousand, the people said, "Surely this is the prophet who was to come into the world." Jesus, knowing that they would come and try to make Him king by force, withdrew again to a mountain by Himself (John 6:15). He had to be careful about performing miracles because people would get the wrong idea about what He had come to achieve. Perhaps the fact that Jesus often talked about the mustard seed should have given people a clue. They wanted to "think big" about their Messiah; in botanical terms they saw Him more like a cedar of Lebanon, representing beauty and grandeur, not the root out of dry ground about which Isaiah had spoken. And so the purpose of this parable was to help them to adjust their perspective and to begin to focus on eternal values. The people wanted everything to happen suddenly; they wanted it in the here and now. Luke wrote, "He went on to tell them a parable, because he was near Jerusalem and the people thought that the kingdom of God was going to appear at once" (Luke 19:11).

In a sense this is why Jesus told every parable—because He knew what people were thinking about the coming Kingdom. The parables presented new and radically different principles. The thought of having faith was an alien concept to most people at that time. Why would they need faith? Surely the Messiah would do everything for them. Why would they need to talk about trust? Why would they need humility? Why would they have to wait on God? Their Messiah was going to accomplish all these things for them. But Jesus said that small beginnings will lead you to God's own view of success.

Another purpose of this parable was to present an analogy of extreme variation. Jesus said, "Though it is the smallest of all your seeds, yet when it grows, it is the largest of garden plants and becomes a tree, so that the birds of the air come and perch in its branches" (Matthew 13:32).

The Bible, particularly the teaching of Jesus, is full of extreme variations: "Whoever humbles himself will be exalted" (Matthew 23:12). People had never heard anything like that taught before Jesus came along. "The greatest among you will be your servant" (Matthew 23:12). I'm sure that many people did not want to think along those lines! When Jesus talked about what would really give honor to God, He said:

> Unless a kernel of wheat falls to the ground and dies, it remains only a single seed. But if it dies, it produces many seeds. The man who loves his life will lose it, while the man who hates his life [literal meaning: to love less] in this world will keep it for eternal life. Whoever serves me must follow me; and where I am, my servant also will be. My Father will honor the one who serves me.
>
> John 12:24–26

Extreme variation is shown in this parable too. The smallest becomes the greatest. The way you become great is to become small. Jesus was saying that just as the mustard seed becomes the largest of garden plants, God can turn your inconsequential beginnings into a glorious ending. He can take a nobody and make them into a somebody.

There are issues implicit here. We're talking about *size;* we're talking about *success;* we're talking about *surprise*—about not being prepared for what God does; we're talking about *subtlety* in which something is understated and you realize later what is going on; we're talking about *slowness.* Are you unhappy that things aren't going quickly? Just wait, says Jesus. This is His strategy—His way of doing things.

The Prophecy of the Parable

In this parable Jesus was virtually announcing that a new order had already begun. Notice how He chose His words: "The kingdom of heaven is like a mustard seed, which a man took and planted in his field" (Matthew 13:31).

Jesus wanted to show His followers that a process had already begun—the Kingdom of God was indeed upon them. The seed was planted, and Jesus was making clear to them what His followers must expect. This parable can be seen as a prophetic word. In it Jesus prophesied several important principles that affect all who follow Him: "If anyone would come after me, he must deny himself and take up his cross and follow me." And again: "For whoever wants to save his life will lose it" (Matthew 16:24–25).

Have you ever noticed that that is exactly what happens? Whenever you do your best to protect yourself and make yourself invulnerable, you blow it every time. When you try to take things into your own hands, it never works. Instead, we have to "lose" our life to God in order to have life in abundance back! Paul wrote, "In all things God works for the good of those who love him, who have been called according to his purpose" (Romans 8:28).

It is not your job or mine to make things work together for good. That's God's problem. God makes it all work together for good. When we are in a situation that has become a mess, our human tendency is to see what we can do to make it work together for good. We try to pull strings or twist the arm of providence, but things just keep getting worse. It's the same when you've been misunderstood and want to clear your name. You want to do something that will make you look a little better. But 2 Corinthians 13:4 talks about Jesus being crucified in weakness. In His weakness He refused to try and make Himself look good. He was not allowed to say to anybody, "Look, when I go to the cross, don't panic." He wasn't able to look down and say to Mary Magdalene, who was sobbing her heart out, "Don't worry, Mary, this is for the salvation of the world!" No, He had to let her misunderstand Him. Instead Jesus said, "Whoever loses his life will find it." And God says, "Leave it to Me. I will make your righteousness shine as the noonday sun" (see Psalm 37:6).

The next prophesied principle is: "I tell you the truth, unless you change and become like little children, you will never enter the kingdom of heaven. Therefore, whoever humbles himself like this child is the greatest in the kingdom of heaven" (Matthew 18:3–4). And, "You know that the rulers of the Gentiles lord it over them, and their high officials exercise authority over them. Not so with you. Instead, whoever wants to become great among you must be your servant, and whoever wants to be first must be your slave" (Matthew 20:25).

The essence of this principle, summed up in those two verses, is that Jesus' way of doing things is often the *opposite* of ours. The reason Jesus chose to have fishermen and tax collectors as disciples was so that nobody could think anything great was going to happen. Today, when a Christian organization starts, the members get a high-profile Christian on the board so you know that this organization is safe and has credibility. Ever since Jesus chose fishermen and tax collectors, He's been calling people whom you'd think would amount to nothing. "Not many noble, not many mighty are called...." How many of us are gentry-bred or from the royal family? We're ordinary people, because that way no one could have any delusions about how important we are.

Jesus was speaking of a pattern that can be seen throughout Scripture. God loves to start small. Gideon had three thousand men, and God said, "That's too many." They got down to three hundred, and God said, "Now we can do it."

The planting of a mustard seed was exactly what happened when Jesus was dying on the cross. Nobody alive said, "Get ready for something big because Jesus is now on the cross." No. It was a day of disaster. Nobody was threatened when one hundred twenty disciples later began to pray that the Spirit would come down. Nobody worried about them because Jesus, their leader, was gone. Yet the Spirit of God came down on the Day of Pentecost, and the world was never to be the same. That's the prophesied purpose of the parable of the mustard seed.

But there is more. The mustard seed, once it becomes a tree, would never rival the majesty of an oak or a cedar of Lebanon. Jesus wants us to know that the growth of the Church, however visible, however much it will affect people's lives, will never look terribly grand in the world's eyes. Even if there's a great awakening, not everybody will be saved. In the great awakening in America, maybe up to 50,000 were saved—that was a small percentage of the population. In the Welsh revival maybe 25,000 were converted. Jesus was saying in this parable that His Kingdom is not of this world. God will do things in His own strategy, and He will do it in a subtle way. God will show how He can turn things around, but the Church, at its best, will always be despised. Any movement that God is in will be despised and opposed by the world, even in the best of times—even in times of revival. It will still be a plant; birds can come and perch on its branches, but it will never be a giant oak.

The Potential of the Parable

We come finally to the potential of this parable, which has an individual focus. Are you prepared to live the life of a mustard-seed planter? Can you agree to live by the prophetic principles and patterns that Jesus envisaged through this parable? It means the willingness to become nothing, to remain a nobody. You will wait to be vindicated, and you may wait a long time. Your strategy will be to let God bring success in His time. There must be a transparency to your life. To live like this, you will need true faith.

Once a child who was having seizures and who threw himself into the fire was brought to Jesus. The man said, "I brought [my child] to your disciples, but they could not heal him" (Matthew 17:16). Immediately Jesus healed the child, and His disciples wanted to know, "Why couldn't we do it?" Jesus said, "Because you have so little faith" (Matthew 17:20). Their faith wasn't even as large as a mustard seed. He said, "If you have faith as small as a mustard seed..." (Matthew 17:20). This lets us know that God isn't looking for us to have perfect faith but faith in a perfect God. It is not great faith He requires of us but faith in a great Savior. Once you focus on Him and know He is the One who turns things around, that is true faith. God is simply looking for true faith—a living faith. If it is real, it will grow. And the potential is this: "No eye has seen, no ear has heard, no mind has conceived what God has prepared for those who love him" (1 Corinthians 2:9).

Finally, Jesus used the example of the mustard seed when He applied the teaching of forgiving again and again (Luke 17:6). If a brother sins against you seven times a day, you still have to forgive him. The disciples struggled with that. It was okay if a man was sorry the first time. But then if he sinned against you again in the same way, and he said he was sorry again a day or two later, you would probably say, "Now, hang on a minute!" Jesus said, "If that happens, just keep on forgiving." We're talking about *total forgiveness*. The disciples responded to this by saying, "Increase our faith!" Jesus replied once again, "If you have faith as small as a mustard seed..." (Luke 17:5–6). Jesus was advocating the kind of faith that, when you are sinned against, says, "God, please let them off the hook. Bless them. Don't punish them." It is a place of faith. The faith of the mustard seed operates when you forgive. That's the planting of the seed: total forgiveness, true faith and a transparent focus.

Anyone who is willing to become nothing has already planted a mustard seed. Anyone who says, "I do forgive them," has planted a mustard seed. It doesn't necessarily mean that you should go to those who have hurt you and tell them that you've forgiven them, because they'll usually say, "I haven't done anything wrong." In 99 out of 100 cases of the people I've had to forgive, you could give them a lie-detector test about the situation, and they would pass—because they don't think they've done anything wrong! You've got to forgive them in your heart. They won't see it, but the moment you let them off the hook, get on with your life and ask God to bless them, you plant a mustard seed.

The process of the seed coming to fruition takes time, and we need to let it grow and allow God to do His work. There's a great question in Zechariah 4:10: "Who despises the day of small things?" There are always small days, inconsequential days when you think nothing is happening. The willingness to be nothing and not to despise the day of inconsequential beginnings sends a signal to heaven. God welcomes that and says, "Now I can work," and He does the rest because time is on His side.

Chapter 4

The Parable of the Yeast

What shall I compare the kingdom of God to? It is like yeast that a
woman took and mixed into a large amount of flour until it worked
all through the dough.

Luke 13:20–21

I wonder how many readers have ever eaten crackers along with their
breakfast bacon and eggs? A few years ago I was in Israel, right after
Easter, and it turned out I was in a Jewish hotel. It was Passover time. Of
course, one would never be served bacon in a Jewish hotel on any
morning, but they did have eggs and certain kinds of fish and cheese.
They also had matzo bread, which is a little like a cracker without any
salt. It is bread made without any yeast, which the Bible often refers to
as "unleavened." I tend to look forward to my breakfast, but it was
awful having to eat my eggs with unsalted crackers!

The concept of bread made with or without yeast was a familiar one
to Jesus' audience, so in this parable He talked about what yeast does
and used it to illustrate His point. The parable of yeast in Matthew
13:33–35 follows the parable of the mustard seed. They are similar in
their meaning and purpose, but with one significant difference. The
parable of the mustard seed refers to the Church in the world. It refers
to small beginnings, as in Galilee with the fishermen, although today
the Christian faith encompasses the globe. The parable of yeast, instead
of referring to the Church in the world, refers to the soul of a person
who is a believer. It refers to spirituality in the Church and how the
Gospel can change a person's life. It also refers to renewal of the Spirit
in the Church. And so, Jesus said, the Kingdom of God is like yeast that
a woman took and mixed into a large amount of flour until it worked
all through the dough.

The parable of the mustard seed refers to outward growth, but the
parable of the yeast refers to inward growth. The parable of the mustard
seed refers to the progress of the Church in society, but the parable of
yeast, to quote Donald Carson, refers to "intensive transformation"—

what goes on inside the Church and what goes on in the soul of a believer.

What is yeast? It is a kind of fungus used as an agent in baking and brewing, sometimes called "leaven." It produces fermentation in dough. The thing about yeast is that a little goes a long way; a tiny amount has the ability to permeate the whole. When yeast is added during the baking of bread, the result is that what would otherwise be just an unsalted cracker becomes an entire loaf of bread. It multiplies greatly.

In ancient Israel, bread made from wheat was the staple food of the time. Unless you were very poor, your bread came from barley. Bread was sometimes made in those days by keeping a piece of the fermented dough from the previous batch and mixing it with the new batch. Jesus used this parable because everyone present knew about this mysterious but powerful process of leaven at work, causing dough to rise and giving the most wonderful aroma and taste.

What does the parable of the yeast teach us? First, as with the parable of the mustard seed, it teaches us not to underestimate the potential of small beginnings in the Christian life. Second, the parable teaches us that when the Holy Spirit applies the Gospel, there is no limit to what can happen in a person's life. The Holy Spirit is like the leaven: He affects everything. Third, all these things happen even when we are not aware that we are being changed. The work is silent. Maybe you think, *I wonder if I am really growing spiritually? I don't think I am changing at all.* The truth is, wrote Paul, "It is God who works in you to will and to act according to his good purpose" (Philippians 2:13).

In this chapter I want to examine five things about yeast, how it applies to the Gospel and how it can change our lives.

The Paradox of Yeast

A paradox is something that is contradictory yet true. I am highlighting Jesus' use of yeast as an illustration of the Kingdom as paradoxical, because often in Scripture yeast has negative connotations—more so than positive ones. Jesus Himself said, "Be on your guard against the yeast of the Pharisees and Sadducees" (Matthew 16:6).

This simple statement is almost a parable in itself. When Jesus uttered these words, His disciples hadn't a clue what He meant. At first they took it literally and thought He was instructing them to guard against the yeast used in bread. Jesus had to spell out that He wanted them to guard themselves against the teaching of the

Pharisees and Sadducees, lest it spread through them in its subtle yet insidious way.

The apostle Paul also referred to yeast negatively: "Don't you know that a little yeast works through the whole batch of dough?" (1 Corinthians 5:6).

He was talking about getting rid of the "old yeast," referring to a sinful practice that was going on in the church at Corinth. "Get rid of the old yeast," Paul taught them, "so that you may become a new batch, without yeast, as you really are." Paul uses the analogy again in Galatians 5:9 to depict a negative, corrupting influence in the Church that must be removed.

In the Old Testament yeast is used both positively and negatively. For example, in Leviticus we read, "If he offers it as an expression of thankfulness, then along with this thank offering he is to offer cakes of bread made without yeast and mixed with oil, wafers made without yeast and spread with oil, and cakes of fine flour well-kneaded and mixed with oil" (Leviticus 7:12).

In Exodus 12, in the introduction to the Passover, the Israelites were commanded to eat bread made without yeast for seven days. And what is more, "For seven days no yeast is to be found in your houses" (Exodus 12:19).

Interestingly then, in this parable Jesus used the yeast to show something that is very positive.

The Presence of Yeast

The presence of yeast in flour is *alien* to its natural constitution. It is a foreign element that is introduced into the flour in the baking process in order to bring about a dramatic reaction. The yeast is radically different from the flour itself. This presents a picture of what it is like when we receive Christ. The pure Spirit of God comes from outside us, to dwell within us—we who are depraved sinners! How can the pure Spirit of God come into us like that?

The Holy Spirit is not native to man. He does not belong to man's nature. Before we could enjoy the Gospel, it was required that the blood of Jesus be shed on the cross. The blood precedes the Spirit coming to us. When the Spirit comes, He comes to convict of sin, righteousness and judgment. In order for us to receive the Gospel and enjoy fellowship with God through the presence of the Holy Spirit, we are given a new nature from above. It comes from outside of us; it has to be given to us, because we don't have it by nature. The Holy Spirit is introduced into us to bring about a radical change. And so it is with yeast—it is an alien subject.

Second, the yeast has an *auxiliary* function. In other words, it gives support and help. The yeast and flour need each other for the intended reaction to occur. Yeast and flour can exist without each other, but not if this intended reaction—the rising of the bread—is to come about. So the Holy Spirit can exist without us and we can exist without the Holy Spirit, but if a life is to be changed, the Spirit must come into us. We are helpless to change ourselves without the intervention of the Holy Spirit, just as flour is unable to transform its state without yeast. Deep inside every person is the need for God to come and dwell there by His Spirit and change us. As St. Augustine said, "Thou hast made us for thyself, our hearts are restless until they find their rest in Thee."

Third, it is not enough simply to put yeast into flour and wait for something to happen. The yeast has to be applied. This application is called kneading and is a process whereby the dough is pressed and stretched, ensuring that the yeast touches every part. Genesis 18:6 describes how Sarah did just that when she made bread for some angelic visitors.

Just as yeast must be applied, the Holy Spirit must apply the Gospel. We are agents of the Spirit. I am, in a sense, applying the Word as I speak and write—I am kneading the dough, stretching it and pressing it. This is what Peter was doing on the Day of Pentecost. He could have just preached the Gospel and sat down and said, "I've done my job." But he continued. He said, "Save yourselves from this corrupt generation" (Acts 2:40) and exhorted with many other words. The danger to those who believe strongly in the sovereignty of God is that they will say, "I have finished. There is nothing else I need to do now that I know Christ has saved me." But Peter continued to plead, and in this way the Holy Spirit is to be *applied* to our lives.

The Purpose of Yeast

The purpose of the yeast is not to destroy the flour. Instead it comes into the flour and changes everything. It communicates its own nature, which has a definite effect on the flour. It *communicates*, it *combines* and it *changes*. So it is with the Holy Spirit. He comes, and He communicates His nature to us. We could never have the grace of the Spirit unless the Spirit came and expressed that from within us. The grace of the Spirit brings love, joy, peace, long-suffering, meekness and so on; this is *communicated* to us—it is the Spirit being utterly Himself in us. It has nothing to do with our own temperament and everything to do with God. He takes what we are and through His Spirit working in us produces the fruits and gifts of the Spirit.

There has been a sad divorce in the Church today—a divorce between the Word and the Spirit. The emphasis of those who focus mainly on the Word is on sound teaching, expository preaching ministry, recovery of the doctrines of the Reformation, the God of Luther, Calvin, Edwards, Spurgeon and so on. What is wrong with that emphasis? Absolutely nothing. It is exactly right.

Those who focus mainly on the Spirit emphasize the gifts of the Spirit: signs, wonders and miracles—as seen in the book of Acts. Until there is a recovery of what was seen in the book of Acts, the world is going to take no notice of the Church. So what is wrong with that emphasis? Absolutely nothing. It is exactly right.

It is not that we need either one or the other but both. We need to emphasize both so utterly and completely that it is impossible to say which is emphasized more. We want to be utterly open and vulnerable to the Word and to the Spirit. We need churches that emphasize the Word and emphasize the fruits of the Spirit—love, joy, peace and so on (Galatians 5:22–23); churches that emphasize the gifts of the Spirit— words of knowledge, speaking in tongues, miracles and so forth (1 Corinthians 12). Often those who are on the "Word side" are a bit nervous about the gifts, and those who are on the "Spirit side" don't think it is too important to think about the fruit of the Word because the gifts are what is needed.

But if we allow the yeast to work—the Spirit who works through the whole dough—we will have both the gifts and the fruits. The Spirit working through us gives all that God wants us to be in Himself, which can be summed up as *holiness*. He gives a hatred for sin, a longing for Christ and a desire to see the glory of God manifest so that the world will see that there is a God in the heavens. The Spirit combines what He is with what we are, so that we might become that which we were destined to be. Darkness becomes light; confusion becomes order; numbness becomes feeling; apathy becomes longing; death becomes life. Things begin to happen!

The purpose of yeast is to communicate its own nature. Just as yeast doesn't destroy flour but changes it, so the Spirit doesn't destroy our faculties or abilities or personality but adds His own character to ours. We are afraid of Him taking over—what will I turn out to be? What will I look like? What will people think of me? But that is the fear of man and is not from God.

The Holy Spirit will not destroy you; He will change you and give you an aroma, a scent, a beauty, and He will use your abilities to exceed all you ever dreamed of. I plead with you: Do not be afraid of the Holy Spirit. The Holy Spirit is God; He is the God of the Bible. He doesn't destroy; He only changes.

The Process of Yeast

Yeast has certain properties that will highlight yet more characteristics of the Holy Spirit to us. These properties come into play as the *process* of the yeast working through the flour begins to happen.

► *It spreads.*

Jesus said, "What shall I compare the kingdom of God to? It is like yeast that a woman took and mixed into a large amount of flour until it worked all through the dough" (Luke 13:20).

The yeast affects the whole of the batch just as the Holy Spirit affects the whole of our being. To the degree that the yeast is applied, it does its work from beginning to end. So the Holy Spirit works in us to bring us to "completion." The work of the Spirit begins with effectual calling, it continues with the work called sanctification and it ends with glorification. It is the "golden chain" of redemption: "And those he predestined, he also called; those he called, he also justified; those he justified, he also glorified" (Romans 8:30).

And so, once the work of the Spirit begins to be applied in our lives, it spreads.

► *It is strong.*

Just a small amount of yeast affects a very large batch of dough. As with the parable of the mustard seed, the least measure of faith accomplishes God's purpose. You may feel that you are a weak Christian or that you have only a tiny amount of faith. But that's okay; the seed of faith is there, and God can use it, however small, to accomplish His work in you. As Paul would say, "Stir up that gift within you and fan it into flame." At present it may just be a glimmer, but with the breath of the Spirit it can become a raging fire.

► *It is secret.*

You can't always see what is happening when the yeast goes to work. You put dough into a dark place or into an airing cupboard, and you don't see what is happening. Its effect is seen at the end of the day. And so you may ask yourself, *Is God really doing anything in me? Is anything happening?* Paul would say yes: "We, who with unveiled faces all reflect the Lord's glory, are being transformed into his likeness with ever-increasing glory, which comes from the Lord, who is the Spirit" (2 Corinthians 3:18).

Though you may feel you are making no progress in your spiritual life, He who began a good work in you *will* perform it (Philippians 1:6). Maybe God is fanning the flame today. Maybe your life hasn't taken off as it should, but it can still happen. Open yourself to the Spirit, and don't worry about what you do or don't see. As John Newton put it when he looked across the breakfast table at his friend William Kelper, "I am not what I want to be. I am not what I ought to be. I am not what I hope to be, but thank God I am not what I used to be." The yeast, kneaded into the dough, has been working secretly, and you wake up one day and realize that God has been working in you.

► *It is silent.*

The work of the yeast makes no noise. Likewise, the secret work of the Spirit begins unconsciously. Did you know that regeneration is an unconscious experience? People will often quote the exact day and hour that they were saved, or *regenerated,* in Christ. All they are really telling you is the moment they *realized* they had been regenerated by Christ. Really the process had begun long before, subtly and unconsciously. The work of the Spirit to bring us to the point of salvation is like conception and eventual birth. A child is brought into existence in the womb and is eventually born, but the birth is preceded by the conception that took place nine months earlier. So it is with those born of God. It is a secret work, but at the end one comes to full assurance of faith in the love and praise of God. It is slow, and the work is gradual. You may wish it happened more quickly, but you have to let the yeast do its work.

► *It is savory.*

Paul said in 2 Corinthians 2:15, "We are to God the aroma of Christ among those who are being saved and those who are perishing."

There is nothing more wonderful than the smell of yeast in flour. I remember when I was a child we were at some people's house to eat fried chicken, and they put yeast rolls into the oven. We smelled those things and said, "Is there any chance we could have one?" The parents said yes. We ate so many of those rolls that we didn't have room for any chicken—and they had that all to themselves! I will never forget the smell and the taste of those rolls. The process of the Holy Spirit working in us begins to produce a wonderful fragrant aroma, and it is a pleasing thing to God.

The Power of Yeast

Jesus spoke in Luke 13:20 about the yeast being in a mixture. Yeast does its work when it is *mixed* with dough. The Spirit does His work when He becomes a part of our lives. How open are you to the Spirit? Each of us needs to come to the place where we can say, "Welcome, Holy Spirit," and we are prepared to allow Him to work in us. The yeast is the means by which the dough rises, and the Spirit is the means by which positive results are brought about in us.

There are two views of the Holy Spirit among evangelical Christians. One is that the Holy Spirit is simply the Third Person of the Trinity. Many hold to what is sometimes called a *soteriological* doctrine of the Spirit and that is all. The word *soteriology* refers to the doctrine of salvation; their view of the Spirit is simply that He applies the Word— the Gospel—that brings us to the point of salvation. That is the extent of their view.

The second view concerns the immediate and direct witness of the Spirit—the Spirit comes in to dwell, and you can feel Him. He is very real. There may be those readers whose view of the Spirit is purely soteriological—they believe the Gospel, and they are as saved as they will ever be. But they have yet to realize what happens when the Spirit comes in to bring change. How does yeast work? Who knows? I am not a chemist! No doubt others can explain it—but it just works. Greater still are the mysteries of God. I simply understand that the blood of Jesus, shed on the cross of Calvary and applied by the Spirit, gives us eternal life.

In the city of Chicago, one cold, dark night, a blizzard was setting in. A little boy was selling newspapers on the corner. People were inside, out of the cold, and the little boy was so cold that he really wasn't trying to sell many papers. He walked up to a policeman and said, "Mister, you wouldn't happen to know where a poor boy could find a warm place to sleep tonight, would you? You see, I sleep in a box, up around the corner there and down the alley, and it is awful cold. It sure would be nice to have a warm place to stay."

The policeman looked down at the little boy and said, "Well, I tell you what to do, you go down the street to that big white house and knock on the door. When they come out of the door, just say, 'John 3:16' and they will let you in."

So the boy did. He walked up the steps to the door and knocked, and a lady answered. He looked up and said, "John 3:16."

The lady said, "Come on in."

She took him in, sat him down in a split-bottom rocker in front of a great big fireplace and left. He sat there for a while and thought to himself, *John 3:16—I don't understand it, but it sure makes a cold boy warm.*

Later she came back and asked him, "Are you hungry?"

He said, "Well, just a little. I haven't eaten in a couple of days, and I guess I could stand a little bit of food." The lady took him into the kitchen and sat him down at a table full of wonderful food, and he ate and ate until he couldn't eat anymore. Then he thought to himself, *John 3:16—I don't understand it, but it sure makes a hungry boy full.*

She took him upstairs to a bathroom with a huge bathtub filled with warm water. He sat there and soaked for a while. As he soaked, he thought to himself, *John 3:16—I don't understand it, but it sure makes a dirty boy clean.* The lady came in and got him, took him to a room, tucked him into an old feather bed, pulled the covers up around his neck and kissed him good night. She turned out the lights. As he lay there in the darkness, he looked out of the window and saw the snow coming down on that cold night. He thought to himself, *John 3:16—I don't understand it, but it sure makes a tired boy rested.*

The next morning she came up and took him down again to the same big table full of food. After he ate, she took him back to the same old split-bottom rocker in front of the fireplace. She got a Bible, sat down and said, "Do you understand John 3:16?" "No, ma'am, I don't. The first time I ever heard it was last night when the policeman said to use it." She opened the Bible to John 3:16 and began to explain to him about Jesus. Right there in front of that fireplace, he gave his heart and life to Jesus. He sat there and thought, *John 3:16—I don't understand it, but it sure makes a lost boy feel safe.*

The yeast in the flour is a mystery. How does it work? All we know is that Jesus said the Kingdom of God is like that. A woman took the yeast and mixed it into a large amount of flour until it worked all through the dough. This is how the Spirit works when He comes in. Don't try to figure it out; just thank God it works.

Chapter 5

The Parable of the Hidden Treasure

The kingdom of heaven is like treasure hidden in a field.
Matthew 13:44

The parable of the hidden treasure is a short one containing two main points: First, a person discovers something tremendously valuable by chance, and second, that person sells everything he has in order to possess it. According to Jesus, this is exactly the way it is with the Kingdom of heaven.

In ancient times, in lands that were frequently ravaged by invading forces as Palestine was, people would often bury their treasured possessions to prevent them from being discovered. For whatever reason, however, they were not always able to go back to retrieve them. Sometimes the owners would die, and the treasure would lie hidden for years. The chances of someone later finding the treasure would have been fairly remote.

This parable introduces us to a man who was not very rich. We can assume that because of his great excitement in stumbling across the treasure. A rich man might have been quite pleased and then simply added it to what he already owned. But this man may have been a hired laborer who stumbled upon a jar filled with gold or silver coins, perhaps jewels, and then reburied the treasure because he had no rights to it. Had he been a dishonorable man, he could have simply taken it right then, but there were laws in those days in Palestine that governed the discovery of such riches. One ancient Rabbinical law said that if a workman came across such treasure, it would become the property of his master—that is, the owner of the field. However, the man was careful not to take the treasure, and he told no one about it. Instead he sold everything he owned and bought the field himself. He didn't want the field as much as the treasure, and being the legal owner of the field was the only way to get it. The treasure would be worth far more than the field ever was.

This parable deals with neither the legality nor the morality of the situation. We know that in a parable we must not take every minor detail and try to attribute biblical truth to it. It is a story, and the focal point of the story is the treasure—a treasure that was worth any sacrifice in order to possess it.

Why Is This Parable Important?

In this parable Jesus was really speaking about the value of the anointing. People use the word *anointing* frequently, but what does it really mean? Simply, the anointing refers to the power of the Spirit in a person's life. When you operate in the power of the Spirit, what you do comes easily. You don't have to worry about it, and you don't have to "work it up." There is no human effort or fatigue—it just happens. Another word that would describe the anointing is *understanding,* as in Proverbs 4:5: "Get wisdom, get understanding."

People in Jesus' day had a very foggy notion about the Kingdom of heaven. They could only think of the Kingdom of heaven in material terms—for example, they expected Israel to overthrow Roman rule when the Kingdom of God came in power. Jesus used such parables as this one to help people see things from a completely different perspective. He knew that they needed to make a major transition in their thinking, so He told one parable after another to show that He was talking about something altogether different from what they expected. In Matthew 13, Jesus said, "The kingdom of heaven is like treasure hidden in a field. When a man found it, he hid it again, and then in his joy went and sold all he had and bought that field" (verse 44).

The parable is intended to show us what a person is willing to do when he sees a way to have a true anointing. It is not explaining how to become a Christian; it is not showing us the way to be saved, because you can never buy your way into heaven. On this point the parable cannot be taken literally. You don't need literally to sell all your possessions when you come to Christ, because there are no such conditions. Salvation is a gift of God's grace, paid for by the blood of Jesus, that can only be accepted freely. Rather, this parable illustrates to us a person who has come to realize the value and the potential of the anointing.

The parable also shows the capability of the Kingdom of heaven to *give* the anointing and to excite a person enough to sell everything they own. People in ancient Israel had never heard of anything like this.

They were so wrapped up in their materialistic thinking that they could not understand the concept of the Kingdom "coming" to an individual. But Jesus was showing them that the Kingdom of God was about transforming individuals' lives, not about overthrowing nations.

Perhaps you haven't discovered what a desire for the anointing will motivate a person to do. There are people who have no concept of wanting something spiritually so much that they would give up anything and everything in order to get it. There are those who have no understanding of the possibility of having this kind of relationship with God, in which the Spirit of God comes in great power, giving you intimacy with the Lord as you never thought possible. However, if you realized the potential of such a relationship with God, you would be so excited by it that you would be willing to lose your head in order to have more of God!

The interesting thing is, it is possible to lose your head and keep it at the same time! You lose your head in your joy in knowing God and don't care if people think you are crazy. Yet you are probably at your sanest when you come to the place where you abandon all else but your desire for God. Once you have truly experienced the anointing of the Spirit, your money, reputation, love for the world, fear of what people will say and so on all pale into insignificance.

There is a third reason this parable is important. It shows the value of recognizing a once-in-a-lifetime opportunity and seizing it right away. In life, often two people can look at the exact same thing, but only one will recognize the value of it. Through His teaching, Jesus reminds us of the importance of being able to recognize that which is authentic; to learn to discern a key opportunity when it presents itself; to recognize history in the making. Such opportunities don't come every day and may never come again. The opportunity in question here is receiving the anointing of God. So in life, one has to possess the shrewdness to make a decision to do what it takes to get this kind of intimacy with God—a relationship of anointing, wisdom and understanding.

Has anything ever gripped you like this? Do you realize how your life could change if you were to be set on fire in this way? Consider the passage on faith from Hebrews 11—Abel, Enoch, Noah, Abraham, Sarah, Joseph, Moses, Samson, David—all these people, one individual at a time, were set on fire and did something no one had ever done before. A good way to understand Hebrews 11 is to keep this parable right next to it, because this is what happened to all of the individuals who are mentioned. Hebrews 11 is an example of those who "sold everything to get the treasure."

An Individual's Discovery

There are several things that I want to highlight about this parable. The first is that this discovery was *accidental*. The man in this parable wasn't looking for the treasure. It was not accidental in the sense that it was without cause or purpose, because there are no accidents with God. The point is that the discovery was sudden; it was unprecedented. It just happened, and one person's life was immediately changed. Take, for example, Saul of Tarsus. Saul was not on his way to a prayer meeting; he was on his way to kill Christians when suddenly he was struck down. He "lost his head" and made an unexpected discovery that radically changed his life. He wrote about the pedigree he had: "circumcised on the eighth day, of the people of Israel, of the tribe of Benjamin, a Hebrew of Hebrews; in regard to the law, a Pharisee; as for zeal, persecuting the church; as for legalistic righteousness, faultless" (Philippians 3:5–6).

Yet Paul continues: "Whatever was to my profit I now consider loss for the sake of Christ.... I consider everything a loss compared to the surpassing greatness of knowing Christ Jesus my Lord, for whose sake I have lost all things. I consider them rubbish, that I may gain Christ" (verses 7–8).

Suddenly Paul's past meant nothing to him. All his achievements now became "rubbish" compared to knowing Christ. What an incredible transformation; yet Paul was not expecting it to happen. As he traveled on the road to Damascus, he had no idea of what he was about to discover.

Similarly, Martin Luther made a discovery that transformed his life. Dissatisfied with what the Church was teaching him about trying to save his own soul, he came across the verse, "The just shall live by faith" in his Bible, and he wrote in the margin the words "only faith" in Latin. He had discovered the hidden treasure and was transformed. Before then, he had believed that one could only be saved by faith and works, and as a result he was always trying to work harder to prove that he had faith.

Martin Luther was a very conscientious man. He would go to confession and confess everything, but then come back an hour later having remembered one more sin that he hadn't confessed! When he saw that salvation was freely given by faith in Christ alone, he was never the same again, and the Church did not know how to handle him. They excommunicated him. Luther, however, held a ceremony in 1520 in the streets of Wittenberg, where he took the excommunication paper and burned it. In addition, he said, "That is not all; I am going to get married. I am going to marry Katie von Buhrer, and we are going to have babies and hang the nappies out in the front garden for the Pope to see." What made him act so rashly? Because he was *so* excited. You could say he lost his head. He had lost his head, and at the same time he was at his sanest. When you discover that which is truly authentic, you are prepared to lose everything else in order to gain it.

Incisive Discernment

The man who found the treasure grasped the significance of his find. In his joy he went and sold all he had in order to go and buy that field. At once he knew that he had found something very special. Some people don't see it at once; they see it a little bit later, but maybe just in time. Jacob was like that. He said, "Surely the LORD is in this place, and I was not aware of it" (Genesis 28:16). He realized that he had made an astonishing discovery, but he didn't get it right away—he realized it later.

On making the discovery, the man in our parable decided to guard his secret. When he found the treasure, he immediately hid it again. There will often come times in your life when the Lord will reveal something to you, but it is just for you. You are meant to keep it secret until God says it is time to share it with others. The Bible says, "The secret of the LORD is with those who fear Him" (Psalm 25:14, NKJV). The NIV reads, "The LORD confides in those who fear him." We see an interesting verse in Luke 2:51, which says that Mary treasured "all these things" in her heart. I believe that Luke was able to write the third gospel because he interviewed Mary after Jesus' death and she revealed insights that, until then, were known only to her.

No one except Mary would have known the things that Luke wrote about Simeon, Anna, the shepherds and Jesus as a twelve-year-old boy going to Jerusalem. These were a few things that Mary could finally reveal. She probably gave us one hundredth of one percent of what could be told, but she didn't tell anything until it was time to give just that little bit of information to Luke.

Sometimes God requires us to be willing to sit on things and not tell all that we know. Could you have tea with Her Majesty the Queen and never tell anybody about it? If it happened to you and you could tell no one about it, you would be miserable! One of my favorite stories is about a man who surprised everybody by letting them give him a knighthood. Knowing his personality, they said, "We are surprised that you accepted the knighthood. Why did you accept it?" "Well," he said, "it is very simple—nobody should turn down a knighthood unless he can keep quiet about it, and I knew I couldn't, so I accepted it."

What if God should share with you the equivalent of the secret of the atomic bomb—spiritually speaking? Maybe this is something just for you, because the secret of the Lord is with those who fear Him and He confides in those people. But what if that anointing from God depended on your keeping quiet? Few could do that. As soon as the Lord gives us a vision, we tend to want to share it with others—and not usually to bless them but because we want them to think we are great. That is why so little happens with people in terms of spiritual power. We can't be trusted with the secrets of God. But this man guarded the secret. He hid the treasure away, and he told nobody.

Protection of the Treasure

The man did not want anything to happen to this treasure. Consider these words: "*Guard* the good deposit that was entrusted to you—*guard* it with the help of the Holy Spirit who lives in us" (2 Timothy 1:14, emphasis added).

This idea of "protecting the treasure" highlights an interesting biblical paradigm—that of *antimony*. In essence it means that two things that are irreconcilable, and yet both true, are held together in tension. For example, Jesus is God, and Jesus is a man. Figure that out! God has chosen the number of people He would save from the foundation of the world, and yet He has told us to go out and try and save the whole world. They are irreconcilable principles that seem to oppose one another and yet both are true.

Similarly, we are justified by faith, and yet the Bible says that we can grieve the Spirit. We must therefore seek to "protect" the anointing of the Spirit on our lives. Just as the man discovered the treasure and then sought to protect it, so we must guard the spiritual blessings that God, in His grace, gives us.

About six years ago, I was sitting in our apartment, and the presence of the Lord came into that room. The old Nazarene preacher Uncle Buddy Robinson used to refer to such experiences as "receiving a chunk of honey in your soul." That day it happened to me—there are no words to describe it. It was so precious, and I wanted to guard it. How do you guard it? The Holy Spirit is described as being like a dove. A dove is a very sensitive bird that is very easily disturbed and frightened away. If you behave badly, then the divine Dove will fly away. If you shout at somebody, begin pointing the finger, begin to listen to something you shouldn't hear or say something negative, you grieve the Spirit. Instead, we should guard carefully the anointing of the Spirit.

An Instant Decision

Finally, we read that "in his joy [the man] went and sold all he had" (Matthew 13:44). The man's joy superseded everything else. He could have said to himself, *Now, I don't want to make a hasty decision right now. I need to cool down a little bit.* But no, this was a sudden decision. He didn't think, *I am going to ponder this.* In his joy he rushed out to sell all his possessions, buy the field and become the owner of the treasure.

In the New Testament, as soon as people were converted they were baptized. It was unusual for people not to be baptized almost immediately. Nowadays we say, "Well, let me think about this for a little bit." Some people have waited for years and still haven't been baptized. We are so afraid that we are going to do something we will regret, but New Testament believers, in the *joy* of their salvation, were baptized right then and never looked back.

The man made a sudden and shrewd decision. The point being made in this parable is that when you discover something authentic, you don't need to wait!

When Moses was a young man, he refused to be known as the son of Pharaoh's daughter. He chose to be ill-treated along with the people of God rather than enjoy the pleasures of sin for a short time (Hebrews 11:24–25). Many people must have told Moses he was stupid to behave in such a way, but Moses was making the best decision of his life because he had "seen" the treasure and had hidden it in his heart. Hebrews tells us, "He regarded disgrace for the sake of Christ as of greater value than the treasures of Egypt, because he was looking ahead to his reward" (Hebrews 11:26).

Imagine esteeming disgrace—it doesn't add up! Yet Moses knew that he had seen something. Though no one around him would understand what he was doing, he made a shrewd decision and guarded the secret. It was a sudden and strategic decision.

The man in this parable didn't want to own a field; he only wanted the treasure that lay hidden in that field. It was a sudden and strategic decision. It was also a *sacrificial* decision. Jesus said this man sold *all he had* to buy that field. The treasure—the anointing—is the greatest thing you can have. In the early part of my ministry, things would crush me, devastate me and get me upset so that I would be full of self-pity. I don't know when it was, but I woke up one day and realized that any time God in His mercy decided to visit me with the power of His Spirit, I should take hold of it with both hands.

What is it that means more to you than anything else? Is it your reputation, career, security, friends, respectability? What do you want that you don't have? What would you sell anything to get? Perhaps nothing. Jesus said that the Kingdom of heaven can so grip a person that they are prepared to sacrifice everything. Listen to these words:

> My son, if you accept my words
>   and store up my commands within you,
> turning your ear to wisdom
>   and applying your heart to understanding,
> and if you call out for insight
>   and cry aloud for understanding,
> and if you look for it as for silver
>   and search for it as for hidden treasure,
> then you will understand the fear of the LORD
>   and find the knowledge of God.
> For the LORD gives wisdom,
>   and from his mouth come knowledge and understanding.
>
>   Proverbs 2:1–6

> Wisdom is supreme; therefore get wisdom.
>   Though it cost all you have, get understanding.
> Esteem her, and she will exalt you;
>   embrace her, and she will honor you.
> She will set a garland of grace on your head
>   and present you with a crown of splendor.
>
>   Proverbs 4:7–9

Though it cost you all you have—get it.

Chapter 6

The Parable of the Fine Pearl

When he found one of great value, he went away and sold everything
he had and bought it.

Matthew 13:46

In the same way that the parables of the mustard seed and the yeast are similar in interpretation, the parable of the hidden treasure and the parable of the pearl are often interpreted by many people to be alike. No one can deny the similarity between the two, because both teach the idea of finding something of extraordinary value and selling everything in order to possess it. However, I believe that because Jesus told these two parables separately, He had a specific reason for doing so.

The parable of the fine pearl is found in Matthew 13:45–46. Jesus told of a merchant who was looking for something of great value. When he found it, he went away, sold everything he had and bought it. The item in question was a fine pearl. The King James Version refers to it as a "pearl of great price," while the New International Version calls it a pearl of "great value." The Greek phrase translated *great value* is used in only one other place in the New Testament—in John 12:3, which says, "Mary took about a pint of pure nard, an expensive perfume." The word translated *expensive* in that verse is the same Greek word.

The pearl then was apparently worth a great deal of money. The merchant obviously regarded it as being worth the equivalent of everything else he owned. He wanted it so much that he sold everything he had just to have that pearl for himself, and he got it.

There are two ways that one could view this parable. One interpretation could be that it is about our seeking after God, and I believe that is its primary meaning. But it could also illustrate the way in which God seeks us. He sees us as pearls of great value, so valuable, in fact, that He gave His one and only Son to die on a cross for us.

Although the main themes of this parable and the parable of the hidden treasure are the same, there are contrasts in the content. The parable of the fine pearl refers to a merchant, or businessman, while the parable of the hidden treasure refers to a poorer person, perhaps a laborer. The parable of the fine pearl refers to someone who is seeking, while the parable of the hidden treasure describes someone who wasn't looking for anything but who stumbled upon hidden treasure. The parable of the fine pearl refers to an "expert" who was looking for just that—fine pearls; he knew exactly what he wanted. The parable of the hidden treasure describes a person who was not an expert in anything, as far as we know. The parable of the fine pearl shows one man looking for one pearl, and he finds that one pearl. The parable of the hidden treasure shows a man who simply found hidden treasure. He would have been glad to have found anything at all in that field.

The parable of the fine pearl alludes to a search for a special relationship with God, not necessarily finding Christ the Messiah. Jesus was talking only to His disciples when He told this parable, but in earlier parables, He was addressing everybody. The message of the parable of the fine pearl is aimed at someone who already loves the Lord—a person who has come to know God and is seeking a special relationship with Him.

The parable also refers to the way people find this special relationship. Some seem to stumble upon it, like the man who found the hidden treasure in the field. You may think, *That's not fair! I have been looking, seeking and waiting on God, searching for a special and more intimate relationship with Him, and somebody else just stumbles onto it!* Like it or not, that is the way it is. This is why we will see in the parable of the vineyard that there are those who work all day long for their reward, and then others come to work at the eleventh hour, yet they receive the same wages. There are those who just stumble onto a special relationship with God, even though they weren't seeking it—God allows this to happen because of His sovereignty.

You may ask, "But what about those who have been waiting, seeking after and longing for a special relationship with God? What about those who say, 'How long, Lord? How long before this happens to me?'" This parable is for you.

Some people find a special relationship with God early in their Christian walk. In the early days of Methodism, an incredibly strong emphasis was placed on receiving the assurance of salvation. This emphasis was so strong that a person just wouldn't settle for anything other than the immediate witness of the Spirit. And by pursuing it, they received it. But there are other Christians who sometimes wait for years and years, or even a lifetime, before receiving this assurance. This parable refers to the time that it sometimes takes to find that special relationship with God. Perhaps you are among those who have waited a long time. You may have seen others find such intimacy with God, and you say, "Why does this happen to them and not me?" Let's be careful. God is sovereign, and He will have mercy on whom He will have mercy (see Exodus 33:19). Sometimes He gives this blessing to an immature Christian, while the most mature and knowledgeable are like the merchant—experts who know what they want and are seeking it.

As we have seen, the parable of the hidden treasure refers to somebody stumbling almost accidentally into a special relationship with God. But when it happened, they did recognize that it was something important; they knew the value of what they had discovered—to the extent that they sold everything in order to possess the treasure. The parable of the pearl, however, refers to a more sophisticated seeker—someone who is knowledgeable in the ways of the Lord and who longs for this special relationship with God, a relationship that, according to Jesus, is worth everything.

Areas of Expertise

A closer look at the text of this parable shows that it refers to three main elements. The first of these I call "areas of expertise."

Recognized Authority

The merchant was a recognized authority in his area of expertise. Others would have acknowledged him as a competent businessman. I don't know how much you know about the history of pearls, but in those days people paid divers to dive for oysters. Today we have oyster farms, but back then there were merchants who were known as pearl experts, and they were few and far between. When telling this parable, Jesus was assuming that there will be those in the Kingdom who are known as "knowledgeable" Christians. They are recognized as an authority in their area of expertise. They are godly people who know the Word and who know the Lord, but they don't yet have that special relationship with God through the Holy Spirit. Sometimes they know their Bibles better than those who *do* have a special relationship with God. Figure that one out! It is very possible that a person sitting in a church pew can know God with an intimacy that the pastor of the church doesn't know. The minister may know his Bible, church history and theology, but there may be a member of his congregation who doesn't know the Bible that well and certainly doesn't know Greek or any church history, but has a special relationship with God. The person in our parable was a recognized expert, but he was still seeking.

Refined Ambition

The second thing about the merchant was that he had a refined ambition. He was looking specifically for fine pearls. I don't know how many businessmen there were in ancient times who were so specialized. How many people do you know today who are like that in the Church? How many can say as David did, "One thing I ask of the LORD, this is what I seek: that I may dwell in the house of the LORD all the days of my life, to gaze upon the beauty of the LORD and to seek him in his temple" (Psalm 27:4)?

David's desire for intimacy with God exemplifies refined ambition— the narrowing of all your desires into one. If any of us were asked what our desires or ambitions were, we might say, "Well, there is this job I have got my eye on," "There is this amazing car ... apartment ... vacation..." and so on. The Bible says that "Out of the overflow of the heart the mouth speaks" (Matthew 12:34). What is it that you want most? Jesus says the Kingdom of heaven is a like a person whose area of expertise was in knowing what he wanted.

Recognizing the Authentic

One very important point about this merchant is that he recognized the authentic. Once he saw the pearl, he didn't have to go around asking for a second opinion: "What do you think of this—would you examine this pearl for me?" When a pearl is taken out of an oyster, it's ready. It can't be improved. There is nothing more you can do to it. Unlike other jewels that need to be polished, however, you wouldn't necessarily recognize it as being valuable unless you were an expert. The value of a pearl was determined first of all by shape; to be really valuable, it had to be perfectly round. It was also valued by the purity of its color; it had to be very white. Any yellowish color in it devalued the pearl. Its value was also enhanced by smoothness; it could have no scratches or roughness. And finally it was valued by size—the larger the pearl, the more valuable it would be. History tells us that Cleopatra had a pearl so large that, by today's standards, it would be worth millions.

The use of a pearl was for adornment but also, no doubt, for investment. Pearls symbolized finery, luxury and opulence. Jesus once used them as a figure of speech when He said, "Do not throw your pearls to pigs. If you do, they may trample them under their feet, and then turn and tear you to pieces" (Matthew 7:6).

This merchant knew a pearl of the highest value when he saw it. It is the same with the person who is seeking a special relationship with God. He knows what he wants, what he doesn't have, and he will recognize it when it comes.

An Active Expectancy

The second essential element of this parable is that it encourages us to have an *active expectancy.*

Many people are hungry for more of God, for a closer, more intimate walk with Him. Nothing saddens me more than the person who says, "I'm comfortable, thanks. I've got as much of God as I want." People who say that are like those who were described in the church of Laodicia. They think they have everything they want and that they have need of nothing. This parable is relevant for that person too. This is the person who knows the Bible in so many ways they could out-argue anyone in a theology debate. If that is you, would you be honest enough to admit there is something you don't know? You may have seen others who have that "something," and you wish that you had it too. They may not be as bright as you are or as intellectual, academic or learned as you, but they have something that you don't have. Maybe they stumbled onto it. It doesn't matter. God is sovereign. This is a word to challenge those of us who know our Bibles well—that is our area of expertise—but who know God Himself so little.

When Jesus talked about the merchant, He chose His words very carefully. Notice how He put it: "a merchant *looking* for fine pearls" (Matthew 13:45, emphasis added). A person who is always looking for more of God will be characterized by four qualities: openness, intimacy, insight and obedience.

Openness

What does it mean to be open? It means that when you are seeking God, you will not try to restrict the ways in which God will work in you. It means that you will not try to limit God by being selective. I taught the congregation at Westminster Chapel to pray for the manifestation of God's glory in our midst and an ever-increasing openness in us to the ways God might choose to manifest that glory. In fact, the Lord decided to visit that church in ways that did nothing to enhance its historic reputation! We might have hoped that God would have chosen a different way of manifesting His presence, but that was not what He wanted to do.

We must realize that we don't know everything. Most of us would love for God's anointing to fall within our comfort zone, but it rarely works that way. Openness means being willing to go where God tells us to go to get what we need. We can't enter the zone of God's glory without leaving our own personal comfort zone. Don't be someone who says, "If God shows up where I am, I'll believe it; but if I have to go outside my comfort zone, then I don't believe it's really God."

The person in Jesus' story was someone who had both expertise and openness. Some of us have the expertise but are not open. All of us need to develop that active expectancy. Even if you are getting older and it hasn't come yet, keep looking. Be like the widow who went back to the unjust judge and said, "'Grant me justice against my adversary....'" [Finally the unjust judge said,] 'Yet because this widow keeps bothering me, I will see that she gets justice'" (Luke 18:3, 5).

Jesus said, "How about being like that when it comes to seeking the Lord?" Be expectant and be open. Keep looking for pearls in the hope that one day you will find the pearl that comes only once in a lifetime.

Intimacy

Intimacy simply means a *close relationship*. Those who are seeking more of God will long for a greater intimacy with Him and will already have a level of intimacy that surpasses those who are complacent about their walk with God. I am attracted to people who have an intimate relationship with the Lord. The book of Acts tells us, "When they saw the courage of Peter and John and realized that they were unschooled, ordinary men, they were astonished and they took note that *these men had been with Jesus*" (Acts 4:13, emphasis added).

I would go hundreds of miles out of my way to talk to one person who has this kind of relationship with God. I am not talking about their knowledge of theology! I remember a lady in Tennessee who lived out in the country; she was known as Aunt Lily. Ministers would come from all over the area to have her pray with them. One day as Aunt Lily was out in the shed praying, she knocked over a lantern, and the hay all around her caught fire. I talked to a person who went to see her in the hospital just hours before she died. He said, "All she wanted to do was see how I was." Here she was, dying from unimaginable burns, and she wanted to know how someone else was. She was not an educated woman, but she had an incredibly close walk with the Lord.

When my mother was a little girl, she used to sit at the feet of another lady who was much like Aunt Lily. This woman lived in Springford, Illinois, and was ninety years old at the time. She used to say, "I have been serving the Lord so long that I can hardly tell the difference between a blessing and a trial."

The objective of intimacy is to know the Lord better than you know anybody else. Don't make the mistake of thinking that you have to know Him better than anyone else knows Him—that was Peter's problem. He thought he was the one who knew the Lord best. Those who think they know the Lord better than anybody else almost always will trip and fall eventually. Instead I am talking about knowing God so well that your knowledge of others is superficial by comparison.

Insight

Having an active expectancy also involves insight—the ability to understand true meaning. Did you know that the anointing is essentially insight? It is *wisdom,* and wisdom is best defined as knowing the next thing to do and then victoriously carrying it out. That describes the anointing of the Holy Spirit. Having the insight of the Holy Spirit enables you to make the right decisions that will take you toward your goal. It also gives you your identity—the self-awareness that God wants you to have about yourself and your purpose, the ability to know what He wants you to do with your life.

You may have spent years trying to live outside of your anointing, and so you may never have really found the real "you." You wanted to be like somebody else; you wanted a job you couldn't really do; you have been operating at your level of your own incompetence and may even be on the verge of a nervous breakdown. There are many who go through life like this without truly finding themselves.

But when you are open to God and know your objective for intimacy and insight, He shows you your true identity. The pearl of great value could be described as the discovery of your true identity in the Lord. When you have found your calling, you live within that identity and don't have to try to be someone else—you are free.

Obedience

There is such a thing as *active* obedience, as opposed to passive obedience, which is merely doing what you are told. Are you just waiting like the man with the hidden treasure? Do you say, "I will wait until I stumble onto it"? How much do you want God? The person who is passive in their obedience will probably go to their grave still waiting for something to happen. It is like the person who is brought up to be a strict Calvinist, and when he hears the preaching on predestination, says to himself, *Well, if I am one of the elect, it will happen to me, and if I am not, then it won't.* It doesn't seem to bother him either way.

In this parable Jesus was speaking about someone who has an active expectancy. It is active, not passive; attentive, not postponing; anticipating, not presuming. It does not assume or take anything for granted. There are those who say, "One of these days I am going to get around to seeking God more." One of these days . . . The days roll on, and nothing happens! Make a decision to seek God's face today.

Acquiring Excellence

The third and final element of this parable is that of *acquiring excellence.* It speaks of setting aside everything that is of secondary importance in order to take hold of the most excellent thing of all. By so doing, you accomplish four things:

▶ *1. You sell all.*
There is a period of self-evaluation in which you examine everything that makes up your life and has meant so much to you previously. You begin to say, "I have got to get rid of that! I am going to have this pearl of great value. These other things must go." In other words, you *sell* everything.

▶ *2. You surrender all.*
Once the things that have hindered you are gone, you have to choose never to allow those things to come in the way of intimacy with God again. That will mean self-denial. Even Christ denied Himself: "For even Christ did not please himself but, as it is written: 'The insults of those who insult you have fallen on me'" (Romans 15:3). And, "He died for all, that those who live should no longer live for themselves but for him who died for them and was raised again" (2 Corinthians 5:15).

Selling all and surrendering all, respectively, mean self-denial and forsaking self-esteem. Often that is the bottom line for us. *What will other people think of me?* I would urge you to think about your life and come up with the things that mean the most to you. If God were to say, "Sorry, that has got to go," be willing to surrender them and to forget about what others will think.

► *3. You sacrifice all.*

It is one thing to recognize a hindrance in your life and surrender it willingly to God, but another to let go of something that is particularly dear to you. There are two kinds of sacrifice. One is a grudging sacrifice in which we very reluctantly let go. The other kind of sacrifice is done with graciousness and cheerfulness. The apostle Paul said that one who gives should not do it grudgingly but cheerfully (see 2 Corinthians 9:7). To get this pearl, this intimacy, this insight, there cannot be a grudging attitude in your heart. You cannot grumble and say, "Well, I guess I am going to have to give this up," and the entire time you regret having to let whatever it is go. No, when you find out what it is that displeases the Lord—whether it seems good to you or not—you must *want* it out of there. Let it go in order to obtain this pearl of great value.

► *4. You secure all.*

By selling, surrendering and sacrificing, you actually secure everything! What exactly do you secure? Excellence. You receive something so marvelous that it cannot be improved on. The pearl cannot be improved. It needs no polishing, and it can't be cut—it is just perfect. With God, what you get in return for your sacrifice is always much more than what you lost. Jesus said, "Whoever wants to save his life will lose it, but whoever loses his life for me will find it. What good will it be for a man if he gains the whole world, yet forfeits his soul?" (Matthew 16:25–26). And, "Unless a grain of wheat falls to the ground and dies, it remains only a single seed. But if it dies, it produces many seeds. The man who loves his life will lose it" (John 12:24–25).

How true. You who are so afraid to step out of your comfort zone, are you going to be better off? No. You are going to miss out, and you will surely regret it. But Jesus continued, "The man who hates his life in this world [that means to love less] will keep it for eternal life" (John 12:25).

In Ephesians 3, Paul referred to "the unsearchable riches of Christ" (Ephesians 3:8). We cannot calculate what this means. He was talking about One "who is able to do immeasurably more than all we ask or imagine, according to his power that is at work within us" (Ephesians 3:20).

That is what God wants to do! Who knows what will happen when you narrow all your desires down to one refined ambition—the thing for which you are searching? You will sell everything to get it.

As I wrote at the beginning of this chapter, there are two ways of looking at this parable. One is to see that it is about us seeking God. The other is to see that it is about God seeking us. Guess what is true with the one who finds that pearl? You find out that God was behind your seeking all along, and you thank Him that He stayed with you, got your attention and caused you to want it above all else. So it was God seeking us after all.

Chapter 7

The Parable of the Fishing Net

The kingdom of heaven is like a net that was let down into the lake and caught all kinds of fish.

Matthew 13:47

In this parable Jesus explored a new theme. Here in Matthew 13:47–50, He taught that the Kingdom of heaven refers not only to the anointing of the Spirit but also to the sovereign right of Christ over all men. This parable has cosmic implications. In a few brief sentences, Jesus said the most important thing that can be said with regard to God's purpose on the earth. It relates to the Church's mission, the Church's mandate, the Church's message. In one breath Jesus showed what is the most essential element of the Kingdom.

Let me ask you a question. What will matter the most one hundred years from now? Think of what is on your mind. Maybe you are worried about something that needs to be done before the day is over. Perhaps you have an examination this week, and that is on your mind. You could give a thousand different answers. But one hundred years from now, only one thing will matter—whether or not you are saved. With this simple story Jesus brought people right to the heart of the matter. He highlighted the single most fundamental issue and decision we face in life and reminded us all of the most dreadful possibility—the possibly of being eternally lost. In this parable Jesus reaffirmed His view of hell.

Let me summarize for you what the parable of the fishing net teaches:

First, the net represents the application, or effect, of the Gospel. The fishermen are soul winners, and the fish are the people who are caught in the net. This is certainly a parable that the disciples would have immediately understood on one level, because they were fishermen. Nevertheless, Jesus went on to explain the parable because, on a deeper level, He spoke about the end of the age.

Second, not all who are caught in the net and brought into the

Kingdom through preaching and other efforts of the Church are eternally saved: "When it was full [that is, the net], the fishermen pulled it up on the shore. Then they sat down and collected the good fish in baskets, but threw the bad away" (Matthew 13:48).

Do you remember the seed in the parable of the sower? Some fell along the path, some fell on rocky places, some fell among thorns and some fell on good ground. Many people are brought into the Church, but not all of them are truly converted.

Third, we learn in this parable that there are ultimately only two categories of fish, or people: good and bad. When the Bible refers to "good" and "bad" in this context, it is not referring to a person's inner goodness, morality or worthiness. It is speaking about those to whom the righteousness of Jesus Christ has been imputed—that is what makes them righteous. How can you be sure you are a good fish, a "righteous" fish? It will not be your own personal worthiness or good works that is the deciding factor. It has entirely, totally, utterly and exclusively to do with whether the blood of Jesus has been applied to your life—whether your sins have been washed away and you have trusted in what Jesus did for you on the cross.

The bad fish refer to the wicked people. Who are they? They are not necessarily morally "bad" people, but they are those who did not trust in what Jesus did for them on the cross. They may have come into the Church for a variety of different reasons, but their lives were not changed. They never connected with Jesus' work on the cross. We are told that this is how it will be at the end of the age.

Finally, the parable teaches that the wicked are eternally lost. Jesus says that the angels will come and separate the wicked from the righteous and throw the wicked into the fiery furnace where there will be weeping and gnashing of teeth (Matthew 13:50). God will use the angels to separate the wicked from the righteous (Matthew 13:49). The angels are also described as ministering spirits that will minister to those who are the heirs of salvation (Hebrews 1:14). They will have a part in escorting the saved into paradise when they die, and they will have the task of escorting others to their everlasting doom. I wish it weren't so, but this teaching seems to have almost perished from the earth. Jesus' teaching here is so vital and so sobering.

The Cross and Salvation

However much you or I may feel the need for more anointing or for a special relationship with God, we must never forget our main purpose.

In this parable Jesus addressed the one thing that *really* matters. God sent His Son into the world to die on a cross for our sins.

It is wonderful when the anointing of God is apparent in our churches and everything is working as it should with a fresh injection of God's power. It is thrilling when this happens, but rather than simply enjoy it for ourselves, it must lead to people getting saved. If I understand correctly what happened on the Day of Pentecost, and I believe that I do, what made people want what Peter was talking about was not Peter's sermon. It was seeing one hundred twenty people around them beside themselves with joy and experiencing a taste of the supernatural. That is why they said, "What must we do? We want what they have got!" (see Acts 2:37). My desire is that we all experience God's supernatural power in our churches to the extent that we are on fire for Him and that all those who come in would long deep down to possess that same joy.

Our enjoyment of God's presence should lead people to Christ. We need to allow the power of God to work through us without any hindrance so that people will want what we have. And we must point them to Jesus on the cross—the only way to salvation.

Evangelism

The second reason this parable is important is that it shows the relevance of soul winning—or as Jesus put it, fishing for men. In Westminster Chapel in 1982, what initially broke the back of the hindrance of our traditionalism was evangelism. We went out onto the streets, and I began to give an appeal, not a "hard sell" or a twisting of arms but an opportunity for people to respond to the Gospel. Jesus likened soul winning to fishermen pulling the net up onto the shore. The Greek word used here describes a *dragnet*—this was a trawling net that was weighed down at the bottom with floats.

Some years ago, a boat was discovered at the bottom of the Sea of Galilee. It was dated back to approximately two thousand years ago. The people who discovered it are convinced that it is either the very boat used by Peter or one exactly like it, and it is now on display. Historians have determined that the net that the disciples used to catch fish would have been dragged through the lake between two boats or taken out by one boat that left the shore and swung around in a semicircle to catch the fish. Similarly, our evangelism, our preaching of the Gospel, is like trawling with a net that will catch as many men and women as possible.

Motives

People can be brought into the Church for many reasons other than conversion. For many, going to church may be the socially acceptable thing to do. People may go to church to meet with friends, or because they want to identify with high moral values or because of parental or other kinds of pressure. The point that Jesus was making in this parable is that the net can pull in people for reasons other than a true response to the Gospel. Jesus let us know that this isn't anything we should be surprised about. When we throw out the net and pull it in, not all will be "keepers," as we say when it comes to fishing. The Gospel can be transcended by other things that attract people to church—they may be there, but they are not saved.

The End of Times

This parable has obvious eschatological implications. The word *eschatology* means the doctrine of last things. This parable also refers to the second coming of Jesus.

> At that time the sign of the Son of Man will appear in the sky, and all the nations of the earth will mourn. They will see the Son of Man coming on the clouds of the sky, with power and great glory. And he will send his angels with a loud trumpet call, and they will gather his elect from the four winds, from one end of the heavens to the other.
>
> Matthew 24:30–31

Jesus indicated that, as in this parable of the fishing net, this is how it will be at the end of the age. The angels will come and separate the wicked from the righteous and throw them into a fiery furnace, where there will be weeping and gnashing of teeth. He was referring to the final judgment that is spoken of in Revelation:

> I saw a great white throne and him who was seated on it. Earth and sky fled from his presence, and there was no place for them. And I saw the dead, great and small, standing before the throne, and books were opened. Another book was opened, which is the book of life. The dead were judged according to what they had done as recorded in the books. The sea gave up the dead that were in it, and death and Hades gave up the dead that were in them, and each person was judged according to what he had done. Then death and Hades were thrown into the lake of fire. The lake of fire is the second death. If anyone's name was not found written in the book of life, he was thrown into the lake of fire.
>
> Revelation 20:11–15

That is what the apostle John saw in his vision, and it relates perfectly with what Jesus taught.

Good and Bad Fish

The bottom line is that not all who are caught by the net will be saved, and those not saved will go to hell. Are you saved or lost? Do you know with certainty that if you were to die today, you would go to heaven?

On October 31, 1955, I had a life-changing experience. It took place years after I was converted. I would call it the baptism of the Spirit, and I am certain that is the best term for it. But the greatest thing about it was that it gave me such an assurance of my salvation, and for the next few days I could think of only one thing: *I am not going to hell; I am saved. I will never go to hell!*

The Purpose of the Parable

A recurring theme in Jesus' teaching about the Kingdom was to show that the Kingdom is spiritual and not material. He wanted people to understand that the coming of God's Kingdom did not mean there would be an earthly king who would immediately vanquish all of their enemies. The Messiah was not going to overthrow Caesar because the Roman armies occupied the land that God had given to Abraham and his offspring. In fact, Jesus said that the Kingdom of God is "within you." It is spiritual, not material; eternal, not temporal. Jesus' audience could only think of a better life in the here and now; they had no concept of heaven where God would wipe every tear from their eyes, where there would be no more death or mourning or crying or pain (Revelation 21:4). They didn't think along those lines.

This parable also shows that the Kingdom will include the disobedient as well as the obedient, because Jesus said that the angels would come and separate the wicked from the righteous (Matthew 13:49). That will be at the end of the age. So fishers of men may "catch" those who are ultimately not acceptable to God. We should not be surprised when this happens.

The Perspective of the Parable

Elementary

This parable has an elementary perspective—that is, Jesus saves. That is why Jesus said, "Go into all the world and preach the good news to all creation" (Mark 16:15).

He who believes and is baptized will be saved. He who does not believe will be condemned, or damned. We must never lose sight of the simplicity of this. We need to warn people, to urge people to throw out the net, lest we forget this most elementary matter.

Ethnic

This parable also has an ethnic perspective. The Scripture says that they let down the net into the lake and it caught "all kinds of fish." The implication is that people of every color and creed will be brought into the Kingdom by the Gospel. Consider these words from the book of Revelation:

> After this I looked and there before me was a great multitude that no one could count, from every nation, tribe, people and language, standing before the throne and in front of the Lamb. They were wearing white robes and were holding palm branches in their hands. And they cried out in a loud voice:
>
> > "Salvation belongs to our God,
> > who sits on the throne,
> > and to the Lamb."
> >
> > Revelation 7:9–10

I long for the Church to mirror this ethnic perspective of Revelation, where people of all races intermingle and worship God together in unity. I used to think about this often when I led Westminster Chapel in London—a multiethnic metropolis like many other capital cities. I often thought of calling the Nigerian Embassy in London and asking them what percentage of Nigerians lived in London. Or what percentage of Indian, or Malaysian, or Scottish, or Welsh... Whatever that percentage was, I wanted to see it reflected in our church. Do you get the point? I don't want to see a middle-class church consisting of mostly professional people—I want to see the Church that Jesus envisioned: all kinds of people from every class and condition—the rich, poor, educated, uneducated, those who are sick, those who are healthy, the disabled, the hurting, the refined and the unrefined.

God wants every church to have a mix of cultures. Every class, every condition, every culture, every color—red, yellow, black or white; they are precious in His sight. Jesus loves the little children of the world! In these days when so many are looking over their shoulders to see who will be impressed by them, this parable reminds us of the ethnic perspective.

Evangelistic

We are called to be fishers of men. The net must go where the fish are. Spurgeon prayed, "Lord, send in Thine elect and then elect some more." This ministry of letting out the net is not the calling of the minister exclusively. It would be a sobering exercise for us all to watch a video of our lives up to this point and see the people we've met and how we did or didn't speak to them about Jesus. Do you carry pamphlets on your person to give away? When you have a chance, do you give somebody a tract? Maybe you are too shy to ask them if they are sure that if they died today they would go to heaven. If you can't do that, perhaps you could hand them a tract.

How often do you talk to people about the Lord? And how selective are you when you do? The point is, you can't be too choosy when you let the net down. You can't say, "I only do a very specialized kind of fishing." You can't cast the net and expect to bring in just one kind of fish. But there are churches that try! They only want one kind of fish. They look at you and the way you dress or the car you drive or your accent, and they say, "You will do nicely." In James 2:1–4 there were those who became snobs and only wanted a certain type in their church, but we are not supposed to be choosy. We are to let the net down and let God bring them in.

Eternal

The perspective of this parable is also eternal. Jesus said that this is how it will be when the angels come and separate the wicked from the righteous. He was talking about the end of the age. It means the end of this present Gospel era, in which people can still be saved through the preaching of the Word. This is why there is such urgency in the words, "*Now* is the time of God's favor, *now* is the day of salvation" (2 Corinthians 6:2, emphasis added).

There will come a time when it is too late to respond, and an angel will escort you to your doom. No amount of bribing or pleading along the way—"please, please, *don't*"—will be of any use, because the appointed time will have passed. *Now* is the accepted time.

At the end of the age, life as we know it will end. The dead in Christ will be raised, and there will be what Jesus called a "general resurrection." These are His words. We should not be amazed at this for a time is coming when all who are in their graves will hear His voice and come out. Those who have done good will rise to live, and those who have done evil will rise to be condemned. There will be no escaping, and the angels will be our escorts: "The time came when the beggar died and the angels carried him to Abraham's side" (Luke 16:22).

The angels will have the privilege of escorting believers to heaven, but another place awaits the unbelievers: "The king told the attendants, 'Tie him hand and foot, and throw him outside, into the darkness, where there will be weeping and gnashing of teeth' " (Matthew 22:13).

Each person will be examined to determine where they will spend eternity. In Jesus' day there were some fish that were ceremonially unclean and therefore should not be eaten; these would have been discarded by fishermen. Others would have been discarded because of their size. For various reasons they were all examined. In the same way, at the end of the age, everyone will be examined and, as Paul said, must give an account at the judgment seat of Christ for the life they have lived, good or bad (Romans 14:10–12). Here is a verse that I sometimes wish weren't in the Bible: "For there is nothing hidden that will not be disclosed, and nothing concealed that will not be known or brought out into the open" (Luke 8:17).

The only exceptions to this are those things that are under the blood of Jesus.

Punishment

Finally, I must refer to the punishment that is spoken of in this parable: "The angels will come and separate the wicked from the righteous and throw them into the fiery furnace, where there will be weeping and gnashing of teeth" (Matthew 13:49–50).

If the fiery furnace were to totally consume them so that they ceased to exist, there wouldn't continue to be weeping and gnashing of teeth. For those who hold to the doctrine of annihilation—that hell just means a "zap," as though you never existed—this verse contradicts your belief. I wish that it weren't true, but according to this parable, hell will last forever for unbelievers. Jesus didn't say they would weep and gnash their teeth because they are about to be thrown in, and then they will be obliterated. He said that they are thrown into the fiery furnace, and within the furnace there will be weeping and gnashing of teeth.

At this time, those who didn't trust in Christ in this life will become aware of God saying, "It is over." When the time of examination and then separation that Jesus spoke of comes, they will be separated from their loved ones, their parents, anyone who was special to them. Hell will be a lonely place. No one should ever glibly say, "Oh, well. I will have plenty of company!" It will seem as if you are the only one there. There will be a conscious feeling of rejection.

Sometimes we regret the things we do here in this life. I know a man who, thirty years ago, had the chance to buy a piece of property for five thousand dollars that is now worth one million dollars. He weeps and gnashes his teeth over that! But this is an even bigger life decision that you will regret—this is the one that really matters. This is the one in which, if you blow it, you will realize that you have blown it big time. You will be eternally lost.

Rolfe Barnard, an evangelist from North Carolina, used to say, "Ladies and gentlemen, the fires of hell and the blood of Jesus go together." One hundred fifty years ago, when the churches were full, they were always preaching about the blood of Jesus and the fires of hell. Now the churches are empty, and we don't preach much at all about the blood of Jesus and the fires of hell. Rolfe used to say, "The blood satisfies the justice of God. One drop will do. But the fires of hell do not satisfy the justice of God. That is why they *never* go out." *Now* is the acceptable time; now is the time to cast your net!

Chapter 8

The Parable of the Owner of a House

Every teacher of the law who has been instructed about the kingdom of heaven is like the owner of a house who brings out of his storeroom new treasures as well as old.

Matthew 13:52

The parable of the owner of a house is found in Matthew 13:51–52. There are a number of parables contained in this single chapter of Matthew 13, and like many other people, I had assumed that there were seven in total. A number of Bible commentators mention this fact. Often the seven parables are compared with and contrasted to the seven churches that are mentioned in the first chapters of the book of Revelation. But tucked away in these verses is an additional parable—the subject of this chapter.

After Jesus had taught the previous seven parables, He asked His listeners a question: "'Have you understood all these things?' Jesus asked. 'Yes,' they replied. He said to them, 'Therefore every teacher of the law who has been instructed about the kingdom of heaven is like the owner of a house who brings out of his storeroom new treasures as well as old'" (Matthew 13:51–52).

Here Jesus introduced a very short but completely new parable. He was applying all that He had just taught them. A few verses earlier, Jesus had quoted from Psalm 78 and said, "I will open my mouth in parables, I will utter things hidden since the creation of the world" (Matthew 13:35).

Matthew confirmed that Jesus spoke "all these things" (Matthew 13:34) to the crowd in parables. In fact, He did not say anything to them without using a parable. Now He used another parable that elaborated on everything He had just said.

What can this parable teach us? Several things. First, it teaches that what we have understood about the Kingdom of God must be taught to others. Jesus had just finished teaching His disciples using seven different parables. Now He was checking that they understood every-thing that He had taught and was encouraging them to teach others what they had learned. What we understand must be passed on to others.

Secondly, this parable teaches that there are levels of understanding about the Kingdom of God. When Jesus' disciples replied that they understood what He had taught them, He must have looked at them and thought, *Really?* He didn't, however, pass judgment on the depth of their understanding. He simply said, "Okay, if you understand, here is your responsibility."

When the disciples said, "Yes, we understand," they weren't trying to be pompous or arrogant. They were sincere, and no doubt they did understand more than the crowds who followed Jesus. Undoubtedly they understood more than they used to. Sometimes, when we understand more than we used to, we think that we have understood everything. If something becomes clearer to us, the danger is to then think we know it all. The disciples were on a pilgrimage, and they still had a lot to learn. The proof that they really *didn't* understand everything is shown later in chapter 15 when Jesus said, "Are you still so dull?" (Matthew 15:16). He knew that their understanding was actually quite limited—but because they understood a little, He said, "Therefore since you understand it, your responsibility is to *teach it."*

The third thing we learn in this parable is that Jesus implicitly upgraded the disciples' status. He called them "scribes and teachers of the law." Teachers of the law, or scribes as they were known in ancient Israel, were among the most learned men of their time. By inference, Jesus was actually bestowing this status upon His disciples. How could He do this? They were ignorant and uneducated. They were fishermen, and yet He included them as "teachers of the law"! The answer is that although they might not have been as erudite, as learned in the law and the Old Testament, as the other scribes of their day, they were actually miles ahead of them in terms of their spiritual understanding. That was Jesus' point.

Jesus knew that He had given them more learning in just a few weeks than the scribes had gained from a lifetime of study. You may already know this interesting verse in Acts: "When they saw the courage of Peter and John and realized that they were *unschooled, ordinary men,* they were astonished and they took note that *these men had been with Jesus"* (Acts 4:13, emphasis added).

They had the best Teacher of all.

Think of any new Christian whom you may know. There are some new Christians who, in a short period of time, seem to grasp an amazing amount and quickly become more mature than others who have been around for ages and who still don't seem to get it. It is astonishing. Jesus was saying to His disciples, "You are teachers of the law now."

Fourth, Jesus, by saying what He did in this parable, left the door wide open for the scribes, the proper teachers of the law of His day, to grasp His teaching. He made a blanket statement to include *"every teacher of the law who has been instructed about the kingdom of heaven"* (Matthew 13:52, emphasis added).

How many teachers of the law were going to listen to His instructions about the Kingdom of heaven? Not many. They treated Jesus with contempt. But Jesus was saying that there might be a scribe who would say, "I think I could listen to You and learn something." In such a case, Jesus said that any teacher of the law who had been instructed about the Kingdom of heaven was like the owner of a house who brought out of his storeroom new treasures as well as old. Should such a teacher come along and say, "I do need help. I want You to teach me some things," then he would have much, much more to share than what he had learned from the law in all his years of study. That is exactly what happened to Saul of Tarsus.

Saul was a man who was both a teacher of the law and who had been inspired by the Holy Spirit. He turned the world upside down. His life demonstrates that you have no idea how God could use you if you have great knowledge of the Bible and you are also open to the Spirit. Jesus left the door wide open for anyone like this to grasp His teaching and then pass it on to others.

This parable is an elaboration of Jesus' own words in Matthew 5:17, in which He declared that He had not come to destroy the law and the prophets but to fulfill them. Martyn Lloyd-Jones said that this was the most astonishing statement Jesus ever made—"I have come to fulfill the law!"

So what we have to teach now is the law, fulfilled by Jesus. That is why He said, "Every teacher of the law who has been instructed about the kingdom of heaven is like the owner of a house who brings out of his storeroom *new treasures* as well as *old*" (Matthew 13:52, emphasis added).

In this statement Jesus showed how, in His fulfillment of the law, the "old" teaching and His "new" teaching are in perfect harmony. In this verse, the word *old* is referring to Old Testament law, and the word *new* is referring to Jesus' teaching of the New Covenant. Jesus called this dynamic combination of the old and the new "treasure." He has used that word before: The Kingdom of heaven is like *treasure* hidden in a field, like a merchant looking for fine pearls, like a mustard seed. Now He was saying that understanding the harmony between the Old Covenant and the New Covenant is the treasure of the Kingdom.

Why Is This Parable Important?

I believe that this is one of the greatest parables Jesus ever spoke. Although it may seem to be insignificant upon first examination, it has far-reaching implications. It is important because it describes the need for both the Word and the Spirit. The Word *and* the Spirit—the dynamic combination of law and grace; the written Word and the power of God. It also highlights for us a number of other important truths.

We Have Much to Learn

This parable shows us that we all have much to learn. We too may answer yes to Jesus' question, as the disciples did. But the truth is that although we do have a limited understanding, we still have a great deal to learn. It is like peeling back the layers of an onion. We can't see everything immediately because much is hidden under the surface. There is still much that we need to grasp.

The Importance of Teaching

Jesus emphasizes the importance of receiving teaching. Teaching is important because it gives us a foundation from which the Holy Spirit can work. Do you remember the words of Jesus? He said when the Holy Spirit comes, He will "*teach* you all things, and bring to your remembrance all things that I said to you" (John 14:26, NKJV, emphasis added).

Jesus gave His disciples so much quality input that they must have thought, *I don't know how much we can remember of all of this*. It is like when you hear some great teaching and you think, *Oh, I really hope I can remember this*. Jesus was saying, "Don't worry, because when the Spirit comes, He will remind you of what you have learned."

When you have a solid foundation of teaching in place, God can use that when He moves through you by His Spirit. The Spirit can take what you have learned and use it to have a great effect. When the Spirit comes in great power, do you know who will be the sovereign vessels earmarked for use? It will be those who took the time to learn.

If you haven't learned anything, then there is nothing of which to remind you. If you are empty-headed when you hit the floor because somebody prays for you, you will be empty-headed when you get up! The Spirit will not create knowledge in your head; rather, He works to remind you of what you have already learned.

The Importance of Being Open

We learn in this parable that those who know their Bibles must still remain open to receive more knowledge and understanding. What do you suppose "more" is? Jesus called it the Kingdom of heaven. Jesus was saying, "You have learned the old; now become open to the new." The scribes of the day weren't open. Jesus said to His disciples and to us, "Don't worry; you are the new scribes." He is going to start with you. If only you will be open, look at what you could do. Don't be tempted to think you've got it all, as the scribes did. They rejected Jesus even though right under their noses Jesus Himself was teaching that they needed to be open to more. You see, there *is* more, and in this parable He said it was the Kingdom of heaven. It was all that the law anticipated, but they couldn't see it.

True Treasure

Jesus wants us to esteem the real value of this treasure. The "owner of a house" indicated a rich person. When we have the combination of the old and the new, we are *rich*. When we know our Bibles but understand we need the Spirit as well—this is true treasure.

Called to Teach Others

Every disciple is called to be a teacher of others, passing on the knowledge of the treasure of the Kingdom of God. Jesus said this implicitly, but let me say it right now: You are called to be a teacher. As the late Karl Barth said, every Christian is called to be a theologian. The book of Hebrews tells us, "Though by this time you ought to be *teachers,* you need someone to teach you the elementary truths of God's word all over again" (Hebrews 5:12, emphasis added).

The Bible warns us about becoming so dull of hearing that there is the possibility of not hearing God speak at all anymore. Don Carson referred to Jesus' disciples as "discipled scribes." They were disciples who had become teachers of the law, and in this they epitomized the Church to come.

The Old Is Imperfect without the New

Although Jesus did not directly use the word *covenant* in this text, it is clear that He was referring to the Old and the New Covenants. The word *covenant* is used when God makes an agreement based upon a condition. In our Bibles we refer to these agreements as the Old and New Testaments. Some suggest that we should have called them the Old and the New Covenants. Jesus taught that the Old and New Covenants were supplemental in nature. The word *supplement* means something that is added as an extra or to make up for a deficiency. From this parable we learn that the Old Covenant is imperfect without the New Covenant—and likewise, the new makes little sense without the old. The old and the new supplement each other.

It is interesting to note the order Jesus gave in this parable: "The kingdom of heaven is like the owner of a house who brings out of his storeroom *new* treasures as well as *old*" (Matthew 13:52, emphasis added). He begins with the new. The Greek literally reads, "new things and old things," in that order.

Although they are supplementary, we must always begin with the new. When Paul marched into Corinth, did he say, "I determined that when I came into Corinth I was going to teach you about the Mosaic Covenant"? Did Paul say, "I made a vow before I ever came that I was going to know nothing among you except the Ten Commandments"? Did he say, "Before you can ever be saved, you have got to be spoon-fed the law"? No. Paul said, "I resolved to know nothing while I was with you except Jesus Christ and him crucified" (1 Corinthians 2:2).

He begins with the new. It is called "new" because there was a long history that preceded what God did in Christ. This was a supplemental covenant.

The Old without the New

The second thing we can learn from this text is the stark contrast of the old without the new. All Jewish teachers looked back to the past. They could only conceive of sitting at the feet of Moses. To them the law was fulfilled within itself—they were blind to what the New Testament said should be the most obvious, namely, that the law always pointed beyond itself to something greater. This is the bottom line in the epistle to the Hebrews. The law is only a shadow of the good things that are to come: "For this reason it [the law] can never, by the same sacrifices repeated endlessly year after year, make perfect those who draw near to worship" (Hebrews 10:1).

Jesus was saying that the law itself implicitly showed that it was incomplete. It was pointing beyond itself. The same is true today when you have the Word without the Spirit. People who learn more and more of the Word, but do not have the Spirit, will find that although their knowledge increases, their lives don't change. It is so sad. Thirty-year-old babes in Christ—they have plenty of knowledge in their minds, but their lives don't change. Don't think the Word alone is sufficient. The Word without the Spirit will make people perfectly orthodox and perfectly useless.

Simultaneous Combination

The teachers of the law knew the Old Testament; they knew the law inside out. They were like people today who know their doctrine and can smell heresy a mile away. If a minister makes just one little mistake, they get their pens out and write it down, and they think it is a real find. To them it is the "pearl of great price" when they find something wrong. That way they can say, "Well, good job I heard that. I was beginning to think I might have to obey this teaching, but now I don't have to because of *this!*"

What God really desires for us is a *simultaneous combination* in which we receive both the Word and the Spirit with equal passion. God desires for us to be just as thrilled with the Word as we are with the Spirit; He wants us to get to the place where it becomes impossible to say which is more important to us. This was Jesus' objective for His followers. Jesus also knew that the teachers of the law needed a new purpose, a new aspiration. They needed to be instructed about the Kingdom of heaven. It was a rare scribe who would let himself be instructed in the Kingdom of heaven. And it is a rare Word person today who will truly allow themselves to be vulnerable to the Spirit. Very rare.

The scribes of Jesus' day needed a new openness because their thinking was so closed. They were locked into the law. Jesus posed a possibility to those who would be open. He said that they would be rich like the owner of a house who goes down into his store-house and brings up new treasures as well as old. New openness equals new ownership: they would be like the owner of a house full of treasure.

This is what happens when the truth becomes your own. The

apostle Paul was often criticized for using the phrase, "This is my gospel." Is it an arrogant thing to say—Paul talking about *his* gospel? This is what happens when truth becomes so precious to you—it becomes yours. Jesus said, "It is *yours.*" The simultaneous combination of the law and the Kingdom, the Old Testament and the New Testament, the Word and the Spirit has what I would call a sublime connection.

A Sublime Connection

As we have seen, the old and the new fit together. When the Holy Spirit eventually came upon these "discipled scribes," they saw the purpose and coherence of the simultaneous combination. It all fit together perfectly. The more you have of the Spirit, the more the Bible becomes precious to you, and you see that everything connects. It is amazing. There is nothing to convince you of the infallibility of the Bible like the combination of the Word and the Spirit. Those who only have the Spirit often don't believe in the infallibility of the Bible. But those who only have the Word don't realize what is out there for them to explore. Jesus said that it is like having a storeroom of treasure.

Spontaneous Combustion

A knowledge of the Word combined with the insight of the Spirit will bring about a *spontaneous combustion* in your life. This is the revelation of truth. When you are open to the working of the Spirit in your life, you will see things in the Word that you have never seen before. It is a refinement of truth. Paul commended Timothy: "Be diligent to present yourself approved to God, a worker who does not need to be ashamed, rightly dividing the word of truth" (2 Timothy 2:15, NKJV).

Dividing the word of truth means making a *rediscovery* of the truth. As Matthew wrote, "So was fulfilled what was spoken through the prophet: 'I will open my mouth in parables, I will utter things hidden since the creation of the world'" (Matthew 13:35).

Jesus was saying that although they had the law of the Old Covenant, there was much more to be discovered. This new revelation would also give them a fuller understanding of the Old Covenant. They would understand it in a completely new light. Jesus' point was that it had to be revealed by the Spirit. The simultaneous combination of the Word and the Spirit, the old and the new, would produce a spontaneous combustion.

Surprising Continuity

The new connects to the old. Fresh treasure will come from the deposit God has already given, namely, His Word. Whatever the rediscovery, it will show continuity, connection and coherence with what went on before. It will always be new, and it will always be fresh, but it will never be disconnected from the old.

What Martin Luther discovered in the sixteenth century seemed to be new truth, except that it wasn't new. He described Romans 3, 4 and 5, and he labored to convince people of everything the Bible taught in these passages as it had been revealed to him. The world was never the same again. There is still much more to be discovered. Did you know that the Baptist preacher John Robinson addressed the pilgrims in Plymouth in 1620, as they were getting ready to leave on the Mayflower, with the following words: "The Lord hath yet more light and truth to break forth from His Word"?

It is still true today.

Chapter 9

The Parable of the Wineskins

No one pours new wine into old wineskins.
Luke 5:37

At the end of Luke 5, Jesus, in response to a challenge regarding His disciples, told three short parables in succession—all illustrating a similar point. Jesus had been teaching the people by the Lake of Gennesaret that day, and later, after calling Levi the tax collector to follow Him as one of His disciples, He was relaxing at Levi's house at a banquet in His honor. The Scripture says that a "large crowd of tax collectors and others were eating with them. But the Pharisees and the teachers of the law who belonged to their sect complained to his disciples" (Luke 5:29–30).

The nature of the complaint was that Jesus' disciples seemed to be having too good of a time, eating, drinking and partying. The Pharisees compared the disciples' behavior to that of John the Baptist's disciples, saying, "John's disciples often fast and pray, and so do the disciples of the Pharisees, but yours go on eating and drinking" (Luke 5:33).

The first of the three parables in response to this remark occurred when Jesus asked, "Can you make the guests of the bridegroom fast while he is with them?" (Luke 5:34).

The second parable spoke of patching an old garment with new cloth (Luke 5:36), and the third about pouring new wine into old wineskins (Luke 5:37–39). These three parables are also mentioned in Matthew 9:14–17 and Mark 2:18–22, but there is a slight variation in Luke's gospel in which Jesus made a final comment: "No one after drinking old wine wants the new, for he says, 'The old is better'" (Luke 5:39).

So why are these parables told at this time, and how do they fit together? In essence, Jesus wanted to explain that the Kingdom was something *new* and *different*—different from anything that had ever come along before.

No doubt people had said the same about the ministry of John the Baptist. There was something radical, something new and different! Everyone from Judea had made their way down to the river Jordan and heard John the Baptist—his ministry shook Israel at the time. But right on the heels of John's ministry came the ministry of Jesus, and very quickly the ministry of John the Baptist became "old wine." That is how quickly things can change. When the new comes, often those who were in the middle of what God was doing yesterday will attack what God is doing today. Those who were in the center of what was happening yesterday usually want things to stay that way. At first, they had had to move out of their comfort zone to be a part of what God was doing, but now that they are used to where they are, they want to stay there, even when God has moved on. This is what was happening in Jesus' day, and He used these parables to describe it.

The ministry of John the Baptist was radical, but the ministry of Jesus even more so, and people weren't prepared for it. Jesus was saying to them, "Don't think you can stick the new thing I am bringing you on top of the old thing you've already got." That is the meaning of the parable of the garments. It is also the meaning of the parable of the wineskins. Both are making the same point.

In this chapter I want to examine three things: the *reason* for these parables, the *riddle* of these parables and the *relevance* of these parables.

The Reason for These Parables

John the Baptist's disciples were devoted to fasting and prayer. No doubt that was a *new* lifestyle for them. But people noticed that the followers of Jesus weren't doing any fasting, and they decided to challenge Jesus about it (Luke 5:33). Praying and fasting were highly respected, pious duties of the day. According to Luke 18:12, the Pharisees fasted at least twice a week. The fact that John the Baptist's disciples also fasted regularly may have given them a degree of respectability—at least in the eyes of the self-righteous Pharisees.

It was a well-known fact that there was a connection between Jesus and John the Baptist. Jesus had asked John the Baptist to baptize Him. John's attitude was that if his followers were really obedient, they would follow Jesus. The trouble was, there were many disciples who wanted to stay with John. It is amazing how a person can follow a strong leader and only take from that leader what he wants—no matter what else that leader might say. Did you know that John the Baptist still had disciples years and years later? It was evident when Paul came to Ephesus that the ministry of John the Baptist was still going on. But this wasn't John's wish.

According to Matthew, John's followers were the ones to raise the question, "Why is it that we fast and pray and your disciples don't?" These were the differences between Jesus' followers and those of John. And Jesus told these parables to answer that question.

The Riddle of These Parables

I have referred to this section as the *riddle* of these parables because Jesus' words here require some unraveling. The first parabolic riddle He posed reveals the purpose of fasting. Jesus said, "Can you make the guests of the bridegroom fast while he is with them? But the time will come when the bridegroom will be taken from them; in those days they will fast" (Luke 5:34).

So, Jesus was saying that people will fast when they don't have the Lord there and they are saying, "Lord, where are You?" With that in mind, Jesus was saying, "It would be ridiculous for My disciples to fast now, because they have Me with them. . . . Later, when I'm not around and they desperately need My presence, they will fast."

So, in response to the allegation that Jesus' disciples should fast, He turned the complaint on its head. "Wait a minute," Jesus said, "Why is it that *you* fast?" The point of His riddle is that people don't fast when they have what they want—they fast when God has been hiding His face; they fast when they are not sure if they are pleasing God and they need to know; they fast to get God's attention; they fast to see His face. The fundamental reason for fasting is to try to achieve what you don't have, hoping God will give it to you.

Jesus called Himself the Bridegroom. This was the first time in the gospel of Luke that Jesus used the language of Zion. The Bride of Christ is the Church, and Jesus is the Bridegroom. It was the first time He called Himself that, and it is also possibly the first time that He implicitly pointed to the fact that one day He would leave them. He told them that the time would come when the Bridegroom would be taken from them—and at that time they would fast.

In Acts 3, when Peter and John were on their way to their set time of prayer, they encountered a crippled man, and they realized that God was going to heal him. Peter stopped and took the crippled man by the hand. What if John had said at that time, "Peter, wait! In just a few minutes we have to be at the Temple." Wouldn't that have been a stupid thing to do? We need to be sensitive to what God is doing every moment and respond accordingly.

One Friday evening, Arthur Blessitt addressed the young people at our church.[1] When he had finished, we went out from the church to do door-to-door evangelism. On the way, Arthur saw three young people standing on the sidewalk. I have often wondered what might have happened had those three people not been standing there. Arthur went right up to them and started talking about Jesus. After a few minutes, two of them seemed to be interested, but I said, "Arthur, we have got to go and start on our route for the door-to-door evangelism." He replied, "Just a minute, Dr. Kendall," and continued to lead two of them to the Lord. I should have been impressed, but all the time I was thinking, *We have got to get going!* Eventually two of the young people prayed with Arthur. The third didn't but remained standing there. Then Arthur pulled out some literature to give them that explained what had just happened to them: You have become a new person, your life has changed, your friendships have changed, you should start reading your Bible and so on. And all the time, I was looking at my watch.

When we finally got going, would you believe it? Arthur stopped again and began talking to someone else, and minutes later he was praying with them as well! Sensing my impatience, Arthur finally said to me, "I don't know where this street is that you want to go, but you don't need to leave the steps of your church." At that moment, the new wine was poured into what had quickly become a new wineskin, and my life was never the same again! Right under my nose there had been something immediate that God wanted to do. The lesson I learned was that when God is doing something, I must obey Him right then and there.

One Saturday morning, Arthur met with forty men to pray for revival in Phoenix, Arizona. The first prayed, then the next, then the next and so on. Arthur was the seventh in line, and when they came to him, he also prayed a prayer for the city. Arthur said, "Then I noticed out of the window there was a restaurant across the street. I got up, walked out of the meeting, went across to the restaurant, walked inside the door and asked, 'Does anybody here want to be saved?'"

The waitress across the counter said, "I do." He went right over to her, shared with her the Gospel and led her to the Lord.

When he had finished, he asked, "That church across the street—do you ever go there?"

"No," she said.

"Do you ever see any of their members?"

"Yes. They come in here for lunch after the morning service on Sundays."

"Have any of them ever talked to you about Jesus?"

"No."

"Have they ever invited you to come to church?"

"No."

"How long have you worked here?"

"Many years."

Arthur went back to the prayer meeting where they were now to the fifteenth person praying. He said, "Stop your praying. God has answered your prayer." He then told them what they needed to do.

Sometimes it is easier just to pray for revival! But when it comes to actually doing something, many Christians will say, "Oh no, not that!"

In the second riddle, Jesus gave the picture of someone patching a torn piece of clothing. He pointed out the folly of patching an old, damaged garment with a piece of new cloth or fabric. In Matthew's account, Jesus said that this would ruin the old garment (Matthew 9:16). In Luke's account, He said that you would ruin both the new one and also the old (Luke 5:36). After being washed, the new patch would shrink and tear away from the stitching. The new piece of cloth would be torn and ruined, and the old one would still be no good.

John's disciples had begun the discipline of praying and fasting through their association with him. They had continued this pattern after initially leaving their comfort zones and were, no doubt, now quite used to it. They probably enjoyed it and wanted to get others to do it as well—especially Jesus' disciples, with whom they had a natural connection. But Jesus called these pious duties an "old garment." He told them, "You can't combine the old with the new. It just won't work—you will ruin both!"

In the third riddle, Jesus used the image of wineskins. He made the point that it was not practical to put new wine into an old wineskin. Why? People generally used animal skins to hold wine since at that time there was no such thing as a bottle. A new wineskin had to be used to hold recently made wine because the wine would change in character and expand as it fermented. The wineskin had to be pliable and able to expand along with the wine.

Older wine, of course, had already fermented and would not undergo any further chemical changes. The process was complete, and the alcoholic content was stable. Ten, or even a hundred, years later, it will still have the same constitution. But if new wine was stored in old wineskins, the result would be disastrous. The expanding wine would burst the skins. The wineskin would be destroyed, along with the wine.

Jesus was saying that you cannot have it both ways. Don't think you can pour My new wine into your old wineskins. By old wineskins He meant old structures, traditions and comfort zones. The new wine was the new work of the Spirit that was upon them. The two do not mix.

The Relevance of These Parables

God Works within a New Wineskin

In the same way that Jesus knew that new wine could only realize its potential in a new wineskin, so we must welcome the new things that God wants to do in our lives. Again, this calls for an ever greater openness to the Spirit.

Being Changed from Glory to Glory

Jesus was not only telling a parable, He was also setting a pattern for future behavior—the kind of behavior that is required of all of us in an ever-increasing measure. As Paul said in 2 Corinthians 3:18, we are being changed from glory to glory by the Spirit of the Lord. We are ever crossing over from the old to the new—from the natural to the supernatural. But in order for this to happen, we must continually cooperate with the Holy Spirit as He seeks to transform our old wineskin so that new wine can be poured in. Even after we have been changed into glory, we will still want to be changed into more glory, and that will continue. That is the meaning of being renewed.

There are saved people who will go to heaven when they die, but who have had a small glimpse of being changed into glory and that was enough for them. They are like the followers of John the Baptist who, when John the Baptist said, "He must increase and I must decrease," said, "No, we want to stay with you, John."

The Christian faith has not been designed to create a new, superior kind of comfort zone in which we can remain unchanged. It has been designed to create new hearts that are continually being renewed, like the new wine that stays in process but is not fully aged. The Bible calls this process *sanctification.* We will never be sinless and perfect in this life, but we are being changed. We are being made more like Jesus, but we are not yet totally like Him.

If we don't walk in the light, our personal relationship with God is not right, and so when the new wine comes, we will say, "Oh, I don't like this. I want the old." You know, there are two kinds of Christians: those who stay in their comfort zones and those who are willing to keep moving out of their comfort zones. The latter type is in the process of sanctification.

We Need Structures

Every new generation of believers needs new structures in order to continue God's work. Let me tell you a principle of the Great Reformation in the sixteenth century: The Church was reformed but was always reforming. Reformed believers today often don't like the second part of that sentence. They are already reformed, thank you very much, end of story. But the principle of the Great Reformation was that the Church was reformed but was always reforming—always learning, always developing, always responding to God's fresh revelation. That is why Jonathan Edwards taught that the task of every generation is to discover in which direction the sovereign Redeemer is moving and then move in that direction.

We Resist New Wine

Jesus made a shrewd observation about human nature: "No one after drinking old wine wants the new, for he says, 'The old is better'" (Luke 5:39).

This is the way we human beings are. Something has got to happen to us that will change our tastes. I understand that those who are connoisseurs of wine (which I am not) develop a certain taste. They get used to the taste and aroma of a certain quality of wine, and when they are presented with a young, or new, wine, they don't want it. So it is in the Church when "old" Christians are presented with new wine— a new style of worship perhaps, or new songs. When Isaac Watts wrote, "When I Survey the Wondrous Cross," they said, "We don't want this." The Church at that time had as much trouble getting past hymns that didn't directly quote Scripture as anybody in the twenty-first century has ever had adjusting to a chorus they have never heard before. There are those who don't want a new style of worship; there are those who don't want a new way of preaching, teaching or witnessing—they don't want anything different. They say, "The old is better!"

Jesus, however, was not teaching that we should do completely away with the old. He said, "Do not think that I have come to abolish the Law or the Prophets; I have not come to abolish them but to fulfill them" (Matthew 5:17). In other words, He was saying: "Do not think that the old has no value." As Paul said, "What advantage then has the

Jew? ... Much in every way! Chiefly because to them were committed the oracles of God" (Romans 3:1–2, NKJV).

So, this passage is not saying that the old has no value. Neither is it saying to throw away all of our traditions. (Paul wrote in 2 Thessalonians 3:6, "Stick to the traditions I have given you.") But Jesus was saying, "When it comes to the Kingdom of heaven, change is here to stay." Changing will be God's way until we get to heaven, because both we and the Church are not perfect yet.

To sum up the relevance of this parable:

- *New wine requires new wineskins.* The Holy Spirit is the new wine, we are the wineskins and we must change to accommodate Him.
- *New wine calls for new structures.* Instead of doing it the same old way after years and years, we must be open to new patterns of worship, praise and prayer, and we must always have an expectancy of God's doing something new.
- *Moving with God means a continual moving out of our comfort zones.* As we need new wineskins to receive God's ever-refreshing new wine, so we will be made continually uncomfortable by the requirements of, for example, bringing the Word and the Spirit together.

The message of this parable is applicable to three further issues:

The Coming of God's Spirit
On the Day of Pentecost, the mockers said, "They are full of new wine" (Acts 2:13, NKJV). New wine was not grape juice. It was wine that was still being fermented, but it could be tasted and drunk, and it was intoxicating. For three years, Jesus prepared the disciples for the new wine of God's Spirit.

The Changing of God's Strategy
Jesus knew He wouldn't always be there to tell the disciples every little thing they needed to know. This is why Paul said to the church at Philippi, "Work out your salvation with fear and trembling" (Philippians 2:12). Jesus was saying, "I won't be there to answer every little question, but if you hear what I say, you will get it right. I will be giving instructions from the right hand of God." The key is to listen to God. If you will take the time to wait on Him and listen to what He says to you, you will not be taken by surprise when the new wine comes and God begins to do a new thing. God's strategy is always changing, but if you listen to Him carefully, even though there may not be an exact precedent for what is happening, He will always show you what to do.

Commending God's Sovereignty

The bottom line is, whatever the Holy Spirit wants you to do, do it. If He says don't do it, then don't do it. We must always respect the sovereignty of God. Sometimes He will tell us to do a certain thing, and at other times He will forbid us from doing a certain thing. He has reasons for both that He doesn't always choose to divulge to us. We can never outgrow what God said to Moses: "I will have mercy on whom I will have mercy, and I will have compassion on whom I will have compassion" (Exodus 33:19).

Developing a New Wineskin

Some things just don't go together. You don't fast when you don't need to. What God is doing today may be different from what He did yesterday. To develop a new wineskin, you have to leave your comfort zone like Samuel did. God said, "Quit mourning for Saul. I have rejected him. Be on your way, and go to the house of Jesse" (see 1 Samuel 16:1).

"But, Lord, Saul will hear about it and kill me!"

"Sorry, that is what you have got to do."

Sometimes we have to do painful things. You can't have your cake and eat it too! No one tears a patch from a new garment and sews it onto an old one. You can't follow both John the Baptist and Jesus at the same time. We have to leave what God has been doing previously and move into what He is doing now.

We all have ways of justifying our own particular comfort zones. But our duty is to be new wineskins for the glory of God. Do you really think the old is better? "Do not say, 'Why were the old days better than these?' For it is not wise to ask such questions" (Ecclesiastes 7:10).

Do you insist on saying that the old is better? It is possible that my own ministry at Westminster Chapel will be seen as little more than developing a new wineskin. If so, it is worth it all. Don't be afraid of people who say, "Hey, they are drunk on new wine!" I can tell you that when you develop a new wineskin, you can take in the new wine, and you can cope with the mocking and the criticisms when they come your way.

Chapter 10

The Parable of Kingdom Abuse

> From the days of John the Baptist until now, the kingdom of heaven
> has been forcefully advancing, and forceful men lay hold of it.
>
> Matthew 11:12

In this chapter we are gong to address two statements that Jesus made
in Matthew 11. The first, found in verse 12, is *almost* a parable. It
certainly uses enigmatic, symbolic language that is a little puzzling,
and in my opinion, it should be treated as a parable. The second
statement can be found in verses 16 through 19. We will look at both of
these statements and see how they fit together to provide instruction
on the subject of Kingdom abuse.

Neither of these two passages is particularly easy to interpret. The
first is translated two different ways in the New International and the
King James Versions of the Bible: "From the days of John the Baptist
until now, the kingdom of heaven has been forcefully advancing, and
forceful men lay hold of it" (Matthew 11:12, NIV). And, "From the days
of John the Baptist until now the kingdom of heaven suffereth
violence, and the violent take it by force" (KJV).

These two translations bear very little resemblance to each other.

The second parable reads as follows:

> To what can I compare this generation? They are like children sitting in
> the marketplaces and calling out to others: "We played the flute for you,
> and you did not dance; we sang a dirge, and you did not mourn." For John
> came neither eating nor drinking, and they say, "He has a demon." The
> Son of Man came eating and drinking, and they say, "Here is a glutton and
> a drunkard."
>
> Matthew 11:16–19

These two passages are closely linked together, as we will discover as we
go on.

Some 23 years ago, when we were still using the King James Version,
one of our church members came to me and asked me what Matthew

11:12 meant. I was ashamed to have to admit that I didn't know, but I have been thinking about it ever since! Five years ago I went on a mission to research just about every view that has ever been put forward concerning this verse. Then, about three years ago, I had what I felt was the first breakthrough in my understanding of it. *Just maybe,* I thought, *I might have it!* I hope that I do not seem insensitive to an opposing view, but I am comfortable with the position I now take: I believe Jesus was saying that the Kingdom of heaven had already come into their midst, and what should have thrilled ancient Israel had instead been met with violence.

At the beginning of this chapter, Matthew 11, John the Baptist was imprisoned. The captive John began to have a few doubts about Jesus, as is expressed in verse 3: "Are you the one who was to come, or should we expect someone else?" Having remarked earlier that Jesus was the Lamb of God who takes away the sin of the world (see John 1:29), it is hard to imagine that later John would say, "Are you really the one?"

It ought to have thrilled ancient Israel when they saw John the Baptist come along. But his lifestyle confused them, and they said, "He has a demon" (Matthew 11:18). Then when Jesus came along and His disciples continued to eat and drink rather than fast, they said, "Ah, He is a wine bibber; He is a glutton and a drunkard" (see Matthew 11:19). Jesus said, "You know, this generation are just like children. They play their games; they call out: 'We played the flute, but you didn't dance.' And then they say, 'Let's play funeral. We sang a dirge, and you were supposed to cry, but you didn't cry. We are going to take our toys and go home.'"

Everyone thought that when the Kingdom came, Israel would be thrilled, but instead there were all kinds of problems. There was persecution, even from those who were on the "right" side. Even those on the right side practiced violence.

These two parables go together: first, because they both refer to the Kingdom of heaven; second, because both are Jesus' observations about the Kingdom of heaven and third, because both show the reaction of people to the arrival of the Kingdom of heaven. Jesus said that this reaction to the Kingdom had been occurring since John the Baptist came, and now it was continuing.

Similarities and Differences between the Parables

Both of these parables show how people react to the Kingdom of God. They demonstrate both a *nonverbal* and a *verbal* reaction. The first parable shows a nonverbal reaction: People take the Kingdom by force; they push it. The second parable reveals a verbal reaction: what people say about the Kingdom.

Second, both parables demonstrate the appearance of the Kingdom; they indicate that the Kingdom of God has indeed arrived—something about which many were unsure at that time. Jesus had begun His ministry, and the Kingdom of heaven had been at hand, but now we know that it had *arrived* because Jesus said, "Go back and report to John what you hear and see: The blind receive sight, the lame walk, those who have leprosy are cured, the deaf hear, the dead are raised and the good news is preached to the poor" (Matthew 11:4–5).

You would have thought that these sort of occurrences would have made everybody happy. They show the advancement of the Kingdom and the inroads it had already made into the life of ancient Israel. But the main theme of these parables is the *abuse* of the Kingdom. The first parable shows Jesus making an observation about the overreaction of people on a nonverbal level. In the second parable He made an observation of people's overreaction in what they said: "John the Baptist has a demon," "Jesus is a drunk" and so on. In the first parable, violence is done to the Kingdom by the way people react, and in the second, the Kingdom is abused by what people say.

Why Are These Parables Important?

These verses reveal to us Jesus' shrewd observation about people—both His followers and His persecutors. We learn that we shouldn't be flattered by loyal supporters who will go too far. Often the followers of a strong man will try to outdo what the man himself did.

Jesus taught that we should not be dismayed by these two kinds of persecution, verbal and nonverbal. He revealed how people often justify whatever position they take on an issue. They said John the Baptist had a demon because he was so strict in his living. They said he had a demon because his disciples fasted all the time. But when Jesus and His disciples ate and drank, the people said, "Here is a glutton and a drunkard" (Matthew 11:19). People will find a way to justify whatever they insist to be true.

Lastly, this parable is important because it shows that throughout the centuries, people have not changed! People are still the same today—entrenched in their views and holding to every excuse under the sun to justify themselves. If widespread revival were to come, this is still the way people would be. Those who dig in their heels would find something wrong with what was happening and then find a way to justify their views.

The Kingdom Suffers Violence

Let me take a moment to take another look at the first enigmatic saying, and explain why I choose to take the "violent" interpretation of the King James Version. Matthew 11:12 is openly acknowledged by every Bible scholar I have come across as one of the most difficult verses in the New Testament. The reason for this is that the translation depends on how you look at a particular Greek word, *biossytie,* and whether it is in the middle or passive voice. If it is expressed in the middle voice, it can be translated "has been forcefully advancing," and the NIV has it right. But if it is expressed in the passive voice and is translated, "the kingdom suffers violence," then the KJV has it right. Whichever way you translate it, the meaning is still not crystal clear!

If you were to accept the NIV as being the most accurate translation, then Jesus was saying that what was taking place was a good thing. The best of God's people should be *forceful* people, laying hold of the Kingdom. This verse is used by certain people to motivate their followers to roll up their sleeves and get on with it. I may be wrong, but I suspect that nearly every charismatic interpreter of the Bible will take this verse to refer to something that we *ought to do.* They will say that Jesus was not just stating a fact about the Kingdom of heaven forcefully advancing, but He was saying that His people need to advance it *in a forceful way.* The result is that people will say, "We have got to make things happen. We are too passive. The world is going to hell, so we have got to get on with it—roll up our sleeves and forcefully go into Satan's territory." Personally, I like that attitude. I can understand it, but I don't need that verse to motivate me in that way. I think such an interpretation causes something to be missed that is very precious.

The interpretation of this verse in the KJV gives a very different emphasis. If you accept this translation as accurate, then Jesus was saying that what had been happening was *not* good—that the Kingdom was being attacked. People at that time were being put in prison: John the Baptist was in prison, and the Kingdom of heaven was suffering violence. In this interpretation, the phrase refers to the way people *abuse* the Kingdom, not only through an actual attack but by the over-zealousness of those who are on the "right" side.

Few verses in the New Testament have caused as much controversy as this one. Allow me to explain why I believe that the KJV translation is correct—that what was happening was not a good thing.

The Notion of Force

The NIV rendering brings a notion of force that is contrary to the biblical emphasis. If you take the view that the Kingdom of heaven is forcefully advancing, you will play into the theology of those who believe that the Church should be involved, for instance, in politics. Some Christians use this verse to justify forcefully advancing the Kingdom in that sphere of society. This verse might have even appealed to the Crusaders. Richard the Lionheart was given that name because he claimed to represent the Lion of the Tribe of Judah. He went out to kill the Muslims, and his victory actually took place just north of Capernaum—the very place where Jesus had stood and said, "Blessed are the peacemakers; blessed are the meek" (Matthew 5:9, 5). The result has been unending hostility from Islam toward the Christian faith; they have never forgotten the Crusades. Are we truly to believe that this is how the Christian faith is to advance? " 'Not by might nor by power, but by my Spirit,' says the LORD Almighty" (Zechariah 4:6).

The NIV rendering creates a notion of force that is contrary to everything else that Jesus taught. That is the first reason that I don't believe Jesus was saying that this idea of force was a good thing.

Violent Men

The second reason is that the Greek phrase that is translated, "forceful men lay hold of it," is a phrase that means, almost everywhere else in the Bible, "violent" in a negative sense. The NIV chose the word "forceful," but the KJV called them "violent" men. If you were to trace the Greek use of this word in Hellenistic literature, almost every time it indicates something that is forceful but also violent—and in a negative way. It would be strange for Jesus to now use that word to describe what He wanted His followers to do. I believe we should read it this way: the Kingdom of heaven is suffering violence, and violent men are seizing it. And that certainly cannot be a good thing.

In Revelation 5, the apostle John wrote:

> And I saw a strong angel proclaiming with a loud voice, Who is worthy to open the book, and to loose the seals thereof? . . . And one of the elders saith unto me, Weep not: behold, the Lion of the tribe of Juda. . . . And I beheld, and, lo, in the midst of the throne . . . stood a Lamb as it had been slain.
>
> Revelation 5:2, 5–6, KJV

This is the One who died on a cross for our sins. As Paul said, Jesus was crucified in "weakness" (2 Corinthians 13:4). Note also that the whole context of Matthew 11 is about the Kingdom being abused. John the Baptist was in prison, and he was discouraged (Matthew 11:2).

Jesus Opposed Force

Jesus was opposed to the use of force. What Peter did in Matthew 26:51 would certainly seem to fall into the category of "taking the kingdom by force," but Jesus would not allow it. Do you remember what Jesus said to His betrayer?

> "Friend, do what you came for." Then the men stepped forward, seized Jesus and arrested him. With that, one of Jesus' companions [we know it was Peter because it is mentioned in John's gospel] reached for his sword, drew it out and struck the servant of the high priest, cutting off his ear. "Put your sword back in its place," Jesus said to him, "for all who draw the sword will die by the sword."
>
> Matthew 26:50–52

"The sword" was not Jesus' way. Archbishop William Temple made this comment: "When the Church picks up a sword, it cuts people's ears off." It is not surprising then that Muslims will not listen to the Gospel today. We have cut their ears off, and they don't want to hear. They are biased; they hate us; and all because of one who said, "I will show them."

Let me ask you a question. Suppose I went up to someone, put a pistol to their head and said, "You are going to be baptized and become a Christian!" and they said, "OK, OK! Don't shoot!" Do you think they would really be saved? Or what if I forced people to pray the sinner's prayer at the end of every Sunday night service? Would you think those people were really saved? "Using the sword" was the approach that Constantine took in 315 A.D., and the Roman Empire was suddenly "converted" by a legal act. Christianity was never the same again.

Jesus told a second parable on the heels of the first to show the callous manner in which people had reacted to John and to Himself. Are we really to believe that Jesus was saying this is a good thing? That this is the way to be motivated? Any exegetical scholar surely would say that that is an odd interpretation.

Nonverbal Abuse

This type of "Kingdom abuse"—nonverbal persecution—comes, first of all, from enemies to the faith, but the Kingdom can also be "abused" by its followers. How could that be? Generally, it is caused by those who overreact, who think they are doing God a favor but do not realize that their actions are counterproductive. I would call those followers foolish. Whatever wisdom is, they don't seem to have it.

I'll give you an example. Back in 1982 when we first started our evangelistic ministry at Westminster Chapel, some people took "Jesus stickers" and put them on store windows up and down Victoria Street. The owners came out and said, "What on earth are these things?" When they realized that the stickers were related to our ministry, they were not happy, and it did not make us look good. Those stickers were counterproductive to what we were trying to do—reach them with the Gospel message. Instead, we were suffering violence. There were those among us who went too far, and even the dean of the cathedral was not blessed. He wrote me a letter, asking me to explain.

You have foolish people such as this and also what I call the "flakes"—empty-headed, shallow people who embarrass everybody else! Often the greater the sense of the power of God in a place, the more the "flakes" will be right in the middle of the action! I can't explain why this happens, but I do know that it gives others an excuse to ignore the good things that God is doing. It provides ammunition for the critics. People said, "Here is John the Baptist and he has a demon," and then Jesus came, doing the opposite, and they criticized Him too. It gives people one more excuse to not accept the Gospel.

The foolish, the flakes and the fanatics—the overly zealous ones, like Richard the Lionheart—have done great damage to the Church over the years. Remember: Whenever the Church picks up the sword, it cuts people's ears off. Jesus was saying that this is not the way we ought to behave.

Verbal Abuse

Jesus then continued in the same context: "To what can I compare this generation?" (Matthew 11:16). He went on to talk about overreaction by verbal abuse: "They are like children sitting in the marketplaces and calling out to others: 'We played the flute for you, and you did not dance'" (Matthew 11:16–17).

People had overreacted to John the Baptist's ministry and then they did the same thing to Jesus. They automatically became opponents, and they found a reason not to have to accept Jesus. Jesus said this kind of reasoning reminded Him of spoiled children. Bible scholars tell us that in those days children played games in the open air, often right in the marketplace. Sometimes they would pretend that they were at a wedding. One would play the flute, but the others wouldn't dance like they were supposed to. The flutist would get angry: "Come on, you are supposed to dance! I will play it again. Dance! Oh, you don't want to play. Well, how about funerals? Would you like to play funerals? Well, if you want to play funerals, you have to cry now." It is child's play. Jesus told them, "That is what is going on here." The abuse of the Kingdom occurred by their outspokenness, by their obstinacy and by their obsession.

The people to whom Jesus was referring were fickle, like children, switching immediately from playing weddings to playing funerals. It showed their churlishness; they were being spiteful, surly and spoiled.

Are we like this? One preacher may speak in our church, and people say, "He preaches too deep. Let's get somebody in who tells a few more stories." But then others say, "No, he's too shallow. He's too simple for my taste." So another preacher comes in, but he is too serious. When they bring in somebody else who perhaps gets people laughing, then others say, "Oh, you shouldn't make people laugh. Humor is deadly." When people criticized Spurgeon for his humor in the pulpit, Spurgeon's reply was, "If you just knew how much I held back!" You can't please everybody.

There will always be someone who is not happy. It is impossible to please those whose hearts are not in tune with what God wants to do. This is why we need to pray for the manifestation of God's glory, along with an ever-increasing openness to the way in which He chooses to turn up—so that we don't miss it. We must not be like those who criticized John the Baptist or those who criticized Jesus. We must not be changeable, churlish or childish—immature adults, reacting to the Kingdom and playing games.

The Way Things Are

How can we apply these verses in such a way that they are edifying to our lives? Jesus was stating a fact about the way things are, and I think we can learn the following from what He taught:

Revival Does Not Solve All Problems
We can have a very romantic view of revival and say, "Oh, if only revival would come." But revival in and of itself will not solve all our problems. What it will do is bring a new set of problems we have never had before.

The Supernatural Does Not Solve All Problems

Suppose we pray for and receive the healing presence of God? Suppose God gives us more power in prayer and anybody who prays sees people delivered because God invests the power? That wouldn't solve all the Church's problems either. Jesus said, "Go back and report to John what you hear and see: The blind receive sight, the lame walk, those who have leprosy are cured, the deaf hear, the dead are raised, and the good news is preached to the poor" (Matthew 11:4–5).

You may say, "If that happened where I live, the entire town would believe that there is a God." Don't bet on it! They'll find something to doubt. Seeing the supernatural will not solve all problems in ministry.

Problems from within the Church Will Always Occur

Even those who are on the right side of the issue can create problems. It's not just the world looking for a chance to persecute. Those who act unwisely in the Church give our critics all the ammunition they need. Why is this relevant? Because if people's hearts aren't truly changed, then they are going to react in a certain way, and you cannot, by logical reasoning, or even by putting a miracle before their eyes, cause them to change their minds. A man convinced against his will is of the same opinion still. You may say, "Look, here is a person who was obviously demon possessed and now that person has been set free." They will scratch their heads and say, "Well, how do you know?" If people's hearts aren't right, it will always be that way. So revival often results, sadly, in the Kingdom being abused. But just because that frequently happens, do not stop praying for revival—revival will bring greater glory to God than persecution, because people will be saved. Just be ready for the negative as well as the positive.

Chapter 11

The Parable of the Uprooted Plant

Every plant that my heavenly Father has not planted will be pulled up by the roots.

Matthew 15:13

I am reminded of a church where once a man was shouting, "Hallelujah!" during the sermon, and the chief usher went over to him and said, "Shh." But the man continued calling out loudly, "Amen! Glory to God!" Once more the chief usher tapped him on the shoulder and said, "Shh!" The man protested, "But I've got religion!" The chief usher answered dryly, "Yes, but you didn't get it here."

Matthew 15 contains two short parables. The first occurred when Jesus responded to yet more allegations from the Pharisees regarding His disciples' conduct. The Pharisees had complained because the disciples did not wash their hands before eating, thus breaking "the tradition of the elders" (Matthew 15:2).

After turning the allegation on its head and pointing to their own hypocrisy, Jesus then addressed the crowd of people before and said, "What goes into a man's mouth does not make him 'unclean,' but what comes out of his mouth, that is what makes him 'unclean'" (Matthew 15:11).

Peter took Jesus to one side and said to Him, "Do you know that the Pharisees were offended when they heard this?" (Matthew 15:12). And so Jesus answered with a second parable, saying, "Every plant that my heavenly Father has not planted will be pulled up by the roots" (Matthew 15:13).

Before we continue, it is worth exploring the context of the Pharisees' complaint. These teachers of the Law came to Jesus and asked, "Why do your disciples break the tradition of the elders?" This tradition they referred to was an oral one, passed on from generation to generation by word of mouth. For many years this is the way it was always done, and so it became almost like law. In 1545 the Council of Trent issued an edit to put Scripture and tradition on the same level. That is virtually what had happened in this case. They were referring to an oral tradition that was still very much observed. And Matthew 15:2 shows how seriously the Pharisees took it.

Everyone in that day knew about the tradition, and everyone observed it, but Jesus didn't play their game. Jesus said that it was an obstructive tradition because it nullified the Word of God. In other words, it hindered people from the pure Word of God and kept them from the truth.

Jesus took some time to answer their question, eventually answering it by addressing the crowd of people in general. Before doing that, He had some things He wanted to say to the Pharisees. He began by referring to the fifth commandment, "Honor your father and mother," and He showed them how they were perverting the original commandment. He said, "You know how you take money that should go to your parents, and you call it *korban* (meaning a gift devoted to God) and give it to the temple? You nullify the fifth commandment by this tradition, yet you have the nerve to ask Me about this meaningless tradition of washing hands?!" It was at that point that Jesus, for the first time as far as we know, called the Pharisees hypocrites: "You hypocrites! Isaiah was right when he prophesied about you: 'These people honor me with their lips, but their hearts are far from me. They worship me in vain; their teachings are but rules taught by men'" (Matthew 15:7–9).

The fact that Jesus then turned His back on the Pharisees and simply addressed the crowd must have infuriated them even more! They, after all, were the ones who had all the questions. Elijah did the same when he got all the prophets of Baal together but decided to address the people instead of the prophets (1 Kings 18:30).

Why Is the First Parable Important?

The Danger of Tradition
We learn in the first parable about the danger of tradition. The passage of time teaches us that not all traditions are bad, although often the word *tradition* connotes something that is an anachronism—an out-of-date relic of a bygone era. The word *tradition* is sometimes used in a very positive sense in the New Testament. But the danger that Jesus was highlighting here is that we must not assume that every teaching, or tradition, that is handed down to us is the pure Word of God. Just because "we've always done it that way," don't assume that is what the Bible actually teaches!

Head Knowledge and Heart Knowledge

This first parable also shows the difference between *head knowledge* and *heart knowledge*. Jesus recalled the words of Isaiah: "These people honor me with their lips, but their hearts are far from me" (Matthew 15:8).

This was Jesus' description of the Pharisees. Head knowledge means having good doctrine—right doctrine—but heart knowledge is a hunger for God.

We also learn that we must see for ourselves what the Bible actually says without man's interference. What goes into a man's mouth does not make him unclean, but what comes *out* of his mouth *does* make him unclean. This shows Jesus' doctrine of man and sin. His doctrine of sin is based on what comes out of the mouth. This is also Jesus' basis for conviction of sin—that is, conviction for sin comes when you begin to see what is truly going on in your heart, not when you break some religious rule. Many people are experts at seeing what is wrong with everybody else, but when it comes to self-examination and feeling a real conviction or remorse over what they themselves are like inside, they are blind.

The Tongue Reveals the Heart

This parable shows how the tongue reveals the heart. Later in Matthew, Jesus said, "Out of the overflow of the heart the mouth speaks" (Matthew 12:34).

What comes out of a man's mouth makes him unclean. Paul Cain, a father in the prophetic ministry, always says, "God offends the mind to reveal the heart." Well, God also allows the tongue to reveal the heart. Jesus said, "I tell you that men will have to give account on the day of judgment for every careless word they have spoken" (Matthew 12:36).

Read that verse just before you go to bed and see if you sleep very well! Think about having to give an account on the day of judgment for every careless word you've spoken. Jesus then went on to say, "For by your words you will be acquitted, and by your words you will be condemned" (Matthew 12:37).

God will allow the tongue to reveal the heart.

Why Is the Second Parable Important?

"Every plant that my heavenly Father has not planted will be pulled up by the roots" (Matthew 15:13). This second parable shows that not everything that exists was put there by God. You may see a person in authority and say, "How did he get there?" You may see people who have a high profile in the Church and appear to be speaking for God, but their actions don't reflect the truth. Here Jesus let us know that not everything that exists was put there by God.

This parable also shows that what may be highly regarded by people may be despised by God. Jesus said this even more clearly in Luke: "For what is highly esteemed among men is abomination in the sight of God" (Luke 16:15, NKJV).

It also makes the point that if God is not the architect and builder of what exists, it will eventually come to nothing: "Unless the LORD builds the house, its builders labor in vain" (Psalm 127:1).

The Priority of the Heart

The theme of the first parable in Matthew 15:11 is *the priority of the heart*—the issue is what is clean and what is unclean. The Hebrew word *kosher* refers to those foods included in ancient Israel's dietary laws set out in Leviticus 11 and Deuteronomy 14. The kosher foods were those that were designated as "clean."

Not only were the Jews concerned about what went into the stomach, but the washing of hands before they ate was also very important. In those days, they didn't have any cutlery. You have no doubt eaten pita bread at some point. That is the way they ate, scooping food into a pita and eating it with their hands. The idea that we should wash our hands before we eat is something we have all been taught from our mother's knee—except for one little point: "The Pharisees and all the Jews do not eat unless they give their hands a *ceremonial* washing" (Mark 7:3, emphasis added).

There are good practical reasons for washing your hands before eating—especially if you have been fixing the car or working in the yard. But the Pharisees and the Jews had lost sight of the practical purpose for their hygiene, and they had turned it into a ceremony that had, in turn, almost become a superstition.

When Jesus said, "Do you want to talk about what is clean and what is unclean?" they no doubt thought He would be referring to certain types of foods; but Jesus said, "What goes *into* a man's mouth doesn't make him unclean. What comes *out* of his mouth is what really makes him unclean." The Pharisees were concerned about what went *into* a person, but Jesus was concerned about what came *out*.

He didn't bother to explain His words further. It was a rather extra-ordinary thing to say, and no doubt it puzzled many of the Pharisees.

Some people, however, must have understood Jesus' inference because the disciples said to Jesus, "Do you know that the Pharisees were offended when they heard this?" (Matthew 15:12).

Jesus' reference to the mouth was deliberate and essential to His point. He wasn't talking about regurgitation; He was making the point that who a person *is* affects what he *says*. What a person says will reveal what he or she is really like. This theme runs all the way through the Bible with numerous warnings about watching the words that come out of your mouth. Take the book of Job. Here was a man who was self-righteous right down to his fingertips. When God eventually got through to him, he said, "I [will] put my hand over my mouth" (Job 40:4).

Recognizing this principle and the importance of purity of speech, David wrote, "May the words of my mouth and the meditation of my heart be pleasing in your sight, O LORD, my Rock and my Redeemer" (Psalm 19:14).

James explained that it is the tongue that makes the difference to the direction of our lives: "Out of the same mouth come praise and cursing. My brothers, this should not be" (James 3:10).

Having set forth the issue about what is clean and unclean, and then provided the imagery—that it is not what goes in but what comes out of our mouths that is important—Jesus finally gave the interpretation. He did so because His own disciples asked what the meaning of the parable was (see Matthew 15:15).

The Natural and the Spiritual

What Jesus presented in His interpretation was an analogy—a comparison between the natural and the spiritual. The Pharisees were thinking only on a natural level: what goes into the body, what goes into the stomach. But Jesus was thinking on a spiritual level about what comes out of the mouth—indicating the state of a person's spiritual well-being. The two are at cross-purposes. The "stomach" refers only to the physical. Jesus put it like this: "Don't you see that whatever enters the mouth goes into the stomach and then out of the body?" (Matthew 15:17).

The Greek literally reads, "cast into a latrine." Jesus was giving a very literal analogy between the stomach and the heart. The heart refers to the seat of the personality, the seat of the affections. It turns out that what He meant by "mouth" was not the regurgitating of what one has eaten but what is said, which comes from the heart.

Behind all of this, then, is an assumption: that the heart is essentially evil. Earlier, in the Sermon on the Mount, Jesus had said the following: "If you, then, though you are evil, know how to give good gifts" (Matthew 7:11).

Jesus' Doctrine of Sin

"The heart is deceitful above all things and beyond cure" (Jeremiah 17:9).

Consider also the words of the apostle Paul: "There is no one righteous, not even one; there is no one who understands, no one who seeks God. All have turned away, they have together become worthless; there is no one who does good, not even one" (Romans 3:10–12).

Does this surprise you? The Bible teaches a certain thing about mankind. David, the psalmist, said, "They go astray as soon as they are born, speaking lies" (Psalm 58:3, NKJV).

You don't have to teach a child to tell a lie. We can recall when our kids were just a year or so old, they would say no even when they knew the answer was yes. We come from our mother's womb speaking lies. Telling a lie is the easiest thing in the world. You don't need an Oxford degree to learn how to tell a lie. David said, "in sin my mother conceived me" (Psalm 51:5, NKJV).

The point is that we are all sinners. Do you believe that man is basically good and nice? You will find that because of God's common grace to all men, there is a nice side to all of us. Think of someone like a Mafia godfather, for instance. He may love his grandchildren dearly, yet he has done all kinds of evil, wicked things. If you saw him holding his grandchild, not knowing about those other things, you would think, *He looks like such a good man.* You might find that people like this even give money to the church once in a while. In our society God has given us policemen, firemen, doctors and nurses—these are all part of God's common grace to humanity. There are those who are raised up to do things for the poor, and you might try to say that this shows that man is basically good. But Jesus was saying, "Let Me tell you what is unclean..." Cleanness or uncleanness comes from the heart of a person. Paul continued in Romans 3:

> Their throats are open graves; their tongues practice deceit. The poison of vipers is on their lips. Their mouths are full of cursing and bitterness. Their feet are swift to shed blood; ruin and misery mark their ways, and the way of peace they do not know. There is no fear of God before their eyes.
>
> Romans 3:13–18

Jesus was giving a lesson on what man is really like. In fact, James put it like this: "The tongue also is a fire, a world of evil among the parts of the body. It corrupts the whole person, sets the whole course of his life on fire, and is itself set on fire by hell" (James 3:6).

Think of the phrase, "All hell broke loose." That often happens because of the tongue. If you are in some sort of trouble today, chances are it is because of your tongue. Again David exhorted, "Set a guard over my mouth, O Lord; keep watch over the door of my lips" (Psalm 141:3).

This is why Jesus said that what comes out of the mouth makes a man unclean. But He then went further: "For out of the heart come evil thoughts, murder, adultery, sexual immorality, theft, false testimony, slander" (Matthew 15:19).

How do these things get out of the heart? Through the mouth. Let me give you an example. Sexual temptation often begins when a person *says* something. That is how you get a person's attention. The tongue is a fire that can be used to say something that will ignite the other person: "When tempted, no one should say, 'God is tempting me.' ... But each one is tempted when, by his own evil desire, he is dragged away and enticed" (James 1:13–14).

You are tempted when you are drawn away by your own lust and out of that lust you begin to speak. It is what you say that does it. The outlet is the tongue, and, said James, "No man can tame the tongue. It is a restless evil, full of deadly poison" (James 3:8).

So Jesus made His case. He took a long time to answer their question. Eating with unwashed hands does not make a man unclean.

It is amazing how people who want to be religious cling to their little ceremonies, their religious rites, in order to get a pious feeling. Are you content with certain traditions that give you a "religious" feeling? Do you feel good when you go to church? Have you come to see what you are really like inside, or have you come just to feel good about yourself? Have you come to terms with what you are really like? What are you doing about it?

You may say, "Hey, nobody is perfect." You can certainly take that attitude, or you can say, "God, help me. I am sorry. Help me to change inside." Some, when they are shown to be sinners, become defensive. They say, "How dare you talk to me like that?" Others say, "God, I am sorry."

Repentance is a change of mind as well as a change of heart. Where before you thought one way, now you think another. Thank God that Jesus died on the cross for all of our sins. We have all sinned and come short of the glory of God, but the blood of Jesus washes away all sin. God gives us a life of repentance—we don't become perfect, and yet we are perfected little by little. We can say as John Newton did, "I am not what I ought to be, I am not what I hope to be, I am not what I will be, but thank God I am not what I used to be." Little by little, you can see that God is perfecting you through conviction of sin.

The Biggest Put-Down

Now let's examine the connection between the two parables. Jesus went on to say, "Every plant that my heavenly Father has not planted will be pulled up by the roots. Leave them; they are blind guides. If a blind man leads a blind man, both will fall into a pit" (Matthew 15:13–15).

When Jesus talked about "every plant," He was referring to the scribes and the Pharisees—the teachers of the law who were antagonistic. It was Jesus' answer to the disciples who were worried. You may be surprised to learn that they were worried. The disciples said, "We think You should know that You have offended the Pharisees." They were concerned because more than likely they respected the Pharisees. The Pharisees were highly respected members of society, and the disciples, at this stage, weren't really much farther on in their walk with Jesus than when Peter had seen Jesus transfigured. Peter had wanted to put Jesus right alongside Moses and Elijah, and he had thought he was elevating Jesus by offering to build a tabernacle for them. The disciples still didn't see exactly who Jesus was. At this stage in their development, they still had respect for the Pharisees—after all, these were important religious men. It is the same as us respecting certain ministers of the Gospel. Human nature seems consistently to look at others with great respect and not realize that they are not actually worthy of such admiration. Because the disciples had such respect for the Pharisees, they panicked a bit when Jesus offended them, and they wanted to be certain of exactly what Jesus had said to upset these teachers of the law.

Now Jesus had a rather delicate thing to do. This is the way Donald Carson put it: "Our Lord must now disillusion His rather naïve disciples as to the reliability of these Pharisees and teachers of the law as being spiritual guides." I also have to face this problem once in a while. I will pray a covenant prayer that I will speak blessings into people's lives and speak evil of no one, but then I will hear a negative comment made by, say, a particular bishop or some other highly respected clergyman.

People who have always had such respect for the clergy then come and say, "What do you think of this?" Well, I don't want to say anything that is going to make anybody look bad, but at the same time I must always warn against any false teaching. This is the fine line that Jesus also had to walk. And that is the reason for His answer being given as a parable: "Every plant that my heavenly Father has not planted . . ." It was the biggest put-down Jesus had yet made with regard to the Pharisees. In one stroke He basically said, "God didn't put them there. My Father hasn't planted these Pharisees; therefore they will be pulled up by the roots."

In Israel there were many references to the idea of being planted (Psalm 1:3; Isaiah 60:21). This was a parable that described the way Israel tended to see herself—as God's plant. But Jesus said, "I have to tell you that the Pharisees are not God's plants." In fact, John the Baptist had said as much (see Matthew 3:9). Jesus said in Matthew 8, "But the sons of the kingdom will be cast out into outer darkness. There will be weeping and gnashing of teeth" (Matthew 8:12, NKJV).

Jesus made two statements regarding the Pharisees:

▶ *1. Let them be.*
He didn't say how they got there; He just said that they weren't planted by His Father. Then He referred to their effect: "Leave them; they are blind guides. If a blind man leads a blind man, both will fall into a pit" (Matthew 15:14).

So He said, "Just leave them. Neither join them nor punish them. God will deal with them." "It is mine to avenge; I will repay" (Deuteronomy 32:35). It is only a matter of time, said Jesus, before their folly will be made manifest.

▶ *2. They will come to nothing.*
When Jesus said, "Every plant that my heavenly Father has not planted will be pulled up by the roots" (Matthew 15:13), there is a certain paradox that He was giving. Some people have asked the question, "If we can't make revival come, can we stop it?" I am afraid that we can. In fact, here is the paradox: If God isn't in what we want to do, nothing will make it happen. But if He is in what we perhaps do not want to do, we still have the ability to stop it.

I can think back to a move of the Holy Spirit in our church that was so precious. I can tell you now that if we hadn't been motivated to move outside of our comfort zone, we wouldn't have received this blessing. It's true that if God isn't in what we want to do, we will never be able to make it happen. So if you fear that what has been going on in your church recently is not of God, don't worry. It will eventually come to nothing. But if He *is* in what is going on, by your actions you can still hinder its progress greatly. It is a scary thought. Our traditions can nullify God's Word, the same thing as quenching the Spirit. We can worship God with our minds and be sound in our doctrine but still have cold hearts. The only way forward from that place is if God makes us hungry. Pray that He will do that in your life in an ever-increasing way.

Chapter 12

The Parable of the Two Debtors

Now which of them will love him more?
Luke 7:42

The parable of the two debtors is the story of a moneylender who was owed money by two people who couldn't pay, and yet he forgave them both (Luke 7:36–50). Jesus told the story and then immediately followed with the question, "Now which of them will love him more?" (Luke 7:42). I believe I am right in saying that every one of us needs to be much hungrier than we are right now—hungry for more of God: more of His presence, more of His grace. We all need to be hungrier for the nature of God to be manifested in us, so that we will care more about the plight of others. My ministry is, in essence, an effort to make people hungry—which is what Jesus was trying to teach in this particular parable.

When I was a little boy, sometimes my parents would let me stay at my grandmother's house. She was always sweet to me, like most grandparents are. One weekend, I was at her house, and I was dreading going to school the next day because there was going to be a really difficult exam that I wasn't ready for. When I woke up, I said, "Grandma, I am sick."

She said, "Ah, well, that means you won't be able to go to school today."

"I am afraid I won't," I replied. That is when I made my mistake. "What's for breakfast?" I asked.

Grandma immediately said, "I'll fix you breakfast while you get ready for school."

"No, I am sick."

"Well," she said, "if you have got a good appetite, there's not much wrong with you."

I have learned over the years that that principle is also true spiritually. If a person has a good appetite, there is not much wrong with them! For reasons I cannot explain, God has made me hungry for Him.

113

I can't take any credit for that; I don't even understand it. Perhaps it was the prayers of my mother, my father, my grandmother or my church. I wish I could make other people hungry. The desire of my heart is to bring people to a place where they don't care what other people think of them because they are sold out for God. That has become my mission in life.

The Occasion of the Parable

An Invitation

This parable begins with an invitation. Jesus accepted an invitation from a Pharisee named Simon. He was obviously not a Pharisee who was hostile toward Jesus in the same way others were, but he was a Pharisee nonetheless. Perhaps he sat on the fence when it came to judging Jesus' ministry. It is rather well known that Jesus kept company with sinners. It is perhaps less well known that He also kept company with Pharisees. I find that very interesting. There is good reason to accept an invitation to reach out to people with whom you don't always agree. As believers, we ought to mix with people a little bit—to have nonbelieving friends and acquaintances. Jesus was given an invitation, and He accepted it.

An Intrusion

To intrude means to join in without being invited. We see this taking place in Luke 7:37 when a woman broke into this social occasion completely uninvited. Jesus and Simon weren't meeting in secret, so word had gotten out, and this woman had decided that she needed to meet Jesus. The text describes her as a woman who had lived a sinful life. Many scholars say that she was a prostitute, which may well be true. No sooner had she arrived than she began to weep at Jesus' feet. Some would call this a manifestation of the Spirit. People show their love for the Lord in different ways. When the Spirit comes, some weep, some cry, some fall on the floor, some shake, some put their hands in the air, some go quiet and have a deep inner peace. This woman started crying. Then her tears fell on Jesus' feet, and she began to wipe the tears with her hair.

An Imagination

When the Pharisee who had invited Jesus saw this, he said to himself, "If this man were a prophet, he would know who is touching him and what kind of woman she is—that she is a sinner" (Luke 7:39).

Simon began to imagine and to speculate. This shows that he wasn't quite sure about Jesus. He was, I believe, a fence straddler and hoped that he wouldn't have to get off the fence onto the side of Jesus. This "chance" event had turned into a test—how would Jesus react? Would He realize what kind of woman He was dealing with? Surely this interruption would show whether Jesus was the genuine article or not. Simon must have thought to himself, *Ah, I am going to get off the hook! This Jesus doesn't know what I know about this woman. If He really were a prophet, He would know who she is! But since He doesn't know who she is, then I don't have to follow this man.*

It is amazing, isn't it, how we can want to get off the hook if we possibly can? Something may grip us a little bit, provoke us, even hook us, and we begin to think, *Oh no, it looks like I am going to have to do this if I follow the Lord. But, wait. Maybe I can find a way out.* Some of my church parishioners look for reasons not to attend the services on a Sunday night because they don't like the style of the service. One lady used to avoid the evening meetings because people put their hands in the air when they worshiped the Lord, and she didn't want to do that. She even came to me with a Bible verse, saying, "I have found a Scripture that shows that I don't have to do it (put her hands in the air)." She said, "The Bible says that you only do it when you pray, not when you sing." As if God wouldn't like it if you did it when you sing! Do you think He is in heaven, saying, "Stop it, stop it! You're singing! You are supposed to be praying when you do that!"

The point is that there are people who look for anything to get them off the hook. If we can find something that will play to our self-pity, we will. If we can find something that will enable us to feel a little self-righteous, we will. If we can find any reason not to get out of our comfort zone, we will. And so the Pharisee found it: "If this man knew who she was, then I would believe He is a prophet. He obviously doesn't know."

The Irony

The irony is this. Not only did Jesus reveal that He knew all about the woman and her past, but He even knew what the Pharisee was thinking! He was going to show that He knew the woman and that He knew Simon as well. Neither was Jesus going to let Simon off the hook, and so He presented this parable in order to challenge his thinking. After telling the parable, Jesus asked Simon which of the two men in the story would love the moneylender more—the one whose debt of five hundred denarii was canceled, or the one whose debt of fifty denarii was canceled. Simon was beginning to get the picture: "Jesus knows who the woman is, and He also knows what I am thinking!"

"Simon replied [having to hide the disappointment in his voice], 'I suppose the one who had the bigger debt canceled' " (Luke 7:43).

"You've got it right," said Jesus.

Why Is This Parable Important?

Jesus' point was that some people show more love for God than others and there is usually a reason why. Some people have a greater hunger for God than others—perhaps because they are very needy or for a whole host of other reasons. People's devotion to Christ can be affected by their backgrounds, especially their childhood. My father tells me that when my mother was pregnant with me they were in a church in Indianapolis, listening to a preacher named C. B. Cox. As he was preaching, my father was so moved by the sermon and by the spirit of the man that he put his hand on my mother's stomach and prayed, "Lord, make my boy (I don't know how he knew I was going to be a boy!) a preacher like that man."

So I had a head start! But other people have a devotion to Christ because instead of having had a head start, they fell into sin and got terribly mixed up. Maybe they had even sold and abused their bodies like the woman who came to Jesus, and then they were blessed, converted and delivered. Many of these people never get over this miracle and are grateful to God their entire lives. It was like that with Saul of Tarsus—he never got over being saved, and it was especially meaningful to him because he knew what he had been like in the past.

This parable also shows that Jesus is never put off by the way people show their love. The woman's behavior was not very sophisticated, if you ask me—to allow her tears to fall on His feet. Some people I know would have said, "Get away from me!" especially when she began to wipe His feet with her hair. But Jesus was not put off by that. He is never put off by anybody who cries out to Him.

Do you remember blind Bartimaeus who shouted, "Jesus, Son of David, have mercy on me!" (Mark 10:47)? The crowd told him to be quiet, but Jesus came over and healed him. He is not put off by the way we worship Him when He sees our heart. Would to God that we wouldn't be put off by the way other people worship either! It may be that they are hungrier than we are or have more reason to be grateful to God than we do.

In this parable we can see that the most needy are often the ones who get Jesus' attention. It has been said that those who have greater manifestations of the Spirit in their lives may actually be the neediest. Maybe there is something to that. It may not be necessarily true in all cases, but it could be sometimes—which is all the more reason why we should be careful in our comments about spiritual manifestations. As Jesus said, "It is impossible that no offenses should come, but woe to him through whom they do come! It would be better for him if a millstone were hung around his neck, and he were thrown into the sea" (Luke 17:1–2, NKJV).

Be very careful, my friend, how you react to someone who is under the power of the Spirit. They may not react as you would. But you could be quenching the Spirit, and that is one of the greatest dangers in life. However, hungry people don't easily get offended.

The Object of the Parable

Why did Jesus tell this parable? Well, He told it partly to let Simon know that He knew the woman's past but also to let Simon know that He knew Simon! After telling the parable, Jesus posed a question: Both men had their debts canceled—which of them would love the man more? That is the point. Jesus canceled our debt. Which of us will love Him more?

Degrees of Guilt

I was converted when I was six-and-a-half years old, on an Easter Sunday morning. I could not tell you why I did it, but I went to my dad and mother in tears and said, "I want to be a Christian." Well, Dad had the presence of mind to say, "We don't have to wait until he gets to church. Let's kneel down right now." So we knelt down by my parents' bedside, and I began to sob. I thought of the sins I had committed—mainly sassing my parents, being naughty and answering back. I felt convicted of those sins like they were the worst sins in the world. And then I felt forgiven. I was six-and-a-half years old, and it was April 5, 1942. I remember it so well.

There are those like me who come to faith early on, but there are others who don't come to Christ until much later in life. I remember talking to a man who was converted under my ministry at Lauderdale Manors Baptist Church. His name was George. He was out in front of the church one evening with tears rolling down his cheeks. I asked, "What is the matter?"

"Nothing is the matter. I'm happy," he replied.

I said, "I'm glad to hear it, but you are crying!"

"I know! I'm just asking myself, why did I take so long?" He was fifty years old.

I thought, *Man, that is old!* But I did reassure the man, "George, some people *never* see it!"

People can be converted at any age—young or old. Some sin more than others, some sin longer than others and some sins are worse than others—the law makes this clear. There are categories of sin and various punishments for them. But if the Holy Spirit touches you, you ought to be able to say, "Great as any; worse than many." That is how we should see ourselves.

In the ancient law there were what were called sins of weakness and ignorance. They were covered by the atonement that was made by the priest on the Day of Atonement. But some sins were not covered by that sacrifice. They were called presumptuous sins. Those who had committed these sins were put outside the camp. The sin addressed in this parable falls into that second category. You see, this woman was a "first-class" sinner! In other words, had the law really been administered at that time (and, by the way, it wasn't), she would have been outside the camp. So, the parable reveals that there are degrees of guilt.

Demonstration of Grace

One denarius was a coin that was worth about a day's wages. "One owed him five hundred denarii, and the other fifty. Neither of them had the money to pay him back, so he canceled the debts of both" (Luke 7:41–42).

I wonder how the one felt who only owed fifty? That fifty denarii probably felt like a lot until he found out about the guy who owed five hundred! Maybe he thought, *Ha! Look at him. I could have gotten away with a lot more!* Or take a person who hasn't sinned very deeply but who meets a person who has been a great sinner and whose sins have been forgiven. The first might think, *All the fun you got to have, and I didn't get any of it.* That is often the feeling when such a situation occurs.

All we really know is that in one stroke, God forgave us all. Whatever the debt, it was paid. Whatever the sin, it was forgiven. We could also assume from this parable that Jesus was contrasting the sins of the woman with that of Simon. There is a little hint that the woman's sin was the equivalent of the five hundred denarii and that Simon's sin was the fifty. We may be surprised to find that Jesus even held out hope for Simon.

Here is another irony of the parable. Simon was the one who should have loved the most. He was very fortunate indeed to get included at all since God hates self-righteousness. Jesus said, "I have not come to call the righteous, but sinners" (Matthew 9:13).

Depth of Gratitude

"Neither of them had the money to pay him back, so he canceled the debts of both. Now which of them will love him more?" (Luke 7:42).

Our thankfulness will almost always be in direct proportion to our awareness of sin. Whether we have committed a serious sexual sin or a minor sin of "ignorance," we should realize what it means for God to forgive this. This has to do with our ability to remember what Jesus has done for us. Do you remember the leper who was cleansed and later came back to thank Jesus? Jesus immediately asked, "Where are the other nine?" (Luke 17:17). What was it about that leper? He wanted to thank Jesus. The ability to remember isn't necessarily about having a good memory; it is about being seized with gratitude and hunger for God.

Jesus obviously used the five hundred denarii in His parable to accommodate the common consensus regarding the morality of the day. It has always been like that, hasn't it? People immediately think that sexual sins are automatically the worst. But Jesus had less trouble with the woman's sin than He did with Simon's. It was self-righteousness that He had the bigger issue with.

If I understand the God of the Bible, then He has great mercy for those who have physical weaknesses, such as a temptation toward sex. He has great sympathy for this but much less sympathy for the self-righteous. It is true, like it or not. He hates self-righteousness more than He does sexual immorality. (The trouble with sexual immorality is that it brings disgrace upon the name of God; that is what makes it so bad—it is always scandalous.) The Pharisee, if only he knew it, needed to see that God was being especially gracious to him to let him be included in the parable at all. As Paul said, "Not many mighty, not many noble, are called. But God has chosen the foolish things of the world to put to shame the wise, and God has chosen the weak things of the world to put to shame the things which are mighty" (1 Corinthians 1:26–27, NKJV).

This means that any aristocrat in the Church should feel singularly blessed because they are an exception. So in this case, both had reason to be grateful—both the woman *and* the Pharisee.

Jesus' Observations

Jesus made some observations in this parable. He turned toward the woman and said to Simon, "Do you see this woman? I came into your house. You did not give me any water for my feet" (Luke 7:44).

Isn't that something? Did you know that providing water to wash one's feet was a common courtesy in the ancient Middle East? It was the first thing that any good host would provide. But the Pharisee neglected to do that.

Then Jesus said, "You did not give me a kiss, but this woman, from the time I entered, has not stopped kissing my feet" (Luke 7:45). Jesus was speaking of a kiss on the cheek that was customary, as we do it today—it was cheek to cheek, and you were supposed to act like you were glad to see the person. Simon didn't do even that. And Jesus went on, "You did not put oil on my head, but she has poured perfume on my feet" (Luke 7:46).

Who loved Jesus more? Was it the Pharisee or was it this woman? Who loved the most? Who was the hungriest? Who was willing to move heaven and earth to show gratitude? It was the woman.

Notice the contrast to the Pharisee—he offered no water for Jesus' feet, "but she [a sinful woman] wet my feet with her tears and wiped them with her hair" (Luke 7:44).

The Pharisee was afraid to be too nice to Jesus. The Pharisee gave no kiss; the woman kissed Jesus' feet. The Pharisee gave no oil; the woman took expensive perfume and poured it over His feet. The point is that Jesus accepted these evidences of affection and devotion. He wasn't embarrassed; He wasn't put off. He didn't say to Simon, "I am sorry about this. There are people out there who do this." Oh no. He affirmed her to the hilt.

What was the conclusion of the matter? "Therefore, I tell you, her many sins have been forgiven—for she loved much. But he who has been forgiven little loves little" (Luke 7:47).

Her love for Christ was in proportion to her gratitude, in proportion to her hunger—she wanted to be as close to Jesus and have as much of His attention as she could. Those people who are saved but just barely—maybe they don't have any "past" and they are not as grateful, not as hungry, as the others.

Conviction

When you are convicted of your sin, it becomes everything to you—like when I was six-and-a-half years old and felt that my sin was the worst in the world. I had another "epiphany" in 1963 when I first discovered John Newton's hymn: "In evil long I took delight, unawed by shame or fear, 'til a new object struck my sight and stopped my wild career." John Newton was referring to his life of debauchery before he was a Christian. When I read that, I saw my own self-righteousness. I felt so ashamed of my quickness to point the finger and my attempts to straighten everybody else out; that became as wicked in my eyes as any sin you could imagine. The point is that if the Holy Spirit comes upon us, we will begin to see ourselves as the one who has had the five hundred denarii wiped off in one stroke. We are convicted.

How Hungry Are You?

To be fair and completely balanced, I must mention two other kinds of motivation that illustrate how hungry we are. One is the desire to see God work. How much do *you* want to see Him work? If you take the view, "Well, if He works, then it's fine with me, but let *Him* do it; He is sovereign"—that is quite complacent.

The other motivation is a strong desire for the best gifts of the Spirit. There are some who think that the real test of spirituality is "love, joy, peace, patience, kindness, goodness, faithfulness, gentleness and self-control" (Galatians 5:22). Those are the *fruit* of the Spirit. We need to seek the *gifts*. But if we have the gifts of the Spirit with a smug little look on our faces and believe that is what matters, our pride will make God sick. Do you earnestly covet the best gifts? How much do you want them? How hungry are you?

I will close this chapter with a question that we all should consider very carefully. Suppose that God works in proportion to our hunger and our gratitude. Suppose that is the basis of how He determines to work in a church. Suppose He goes from one church to another, asking, "How hungry are they? How grateful are they?" Suppose He comes to *your* church, looks over the congregation and asks, "How hungry are they?" What would the answer be? Suppose He looks at each individual. Suppose He looks at *you*. He wants to know how hungry you are. If that was the prerequisite, the condition for His getting involved in your life, what would be the result?

Chapter 13

The Parable of the Signs and the Yeast

> You know how to interpret the appearance of the sky, but you cannot interpret the signs of the times.
>
> Matthew 16:3

> Be on your guard against the yeast of the Pharisees and Sadducees.
>
> Matthew 16:6

Matthew 16:1–12 contains two parables that quickly follow one another. The first of these parables (found in Matthew 16:1–4) was directed to those outside the family of God and was given as a response to the Pharisees and Sadducees who were testing Jesus.

"You know how to interpret the appearance of the sky, but you cannot interpret the signs of the times," Jesus said (Matthew 16:3). Then He answered their demand for a sign with these words: "A wicked and adulterous generation looks for a miraculous sign, but none will be given it except the sign of Jonah" (Matthew 16:4).

Anyone can learn how to interpret the weather, Jesus said, but you are scholars, learned men, and you still can't tell what is really important.

The second parable followed immediately and was directed privately to those within the family—Jesus' own disciples. It was a reference to the ones who were testing Jesus. Jesus warned them, "Be on your guard against the yeast of the Pharisees and Sadducees" (Matthew 16:6).

Jesus was still talking in parabolic language, but His disciples mistakenly took what He said at face value. They were thinking on a natural level and assumed that He was talking about literal, physical bread. But Jesus was using an analogy, and so He rebuked them. He said, "I have already shown you what we can do if we have a problem with bread!" "Don't you remember the five loaves for the five thousand, and how many basketfuls you gathered? How is it that you don't understand that I was not talking to you about bread?" (Matthew 16:9, 11).

After this, however, He didn't say what He really meant; He just warned them a second time about the yeast. On this occasion, because Jesus didn't interpret the parable for them but left them to figure it out for themselves, they eventually came to the meaning on their own. They realized that He was being sharp in His criticism, and, being the great teacher that He was, He didn't continue to spoon-feed them. He simply said, "Figure it out"—and they did.

How the Two Parables Connect

United against Jesus

These two parables show how people who oppose each other fiercely can unite if they have a common enemy. In England, supporters of two local soccer teams might be sworn enemies, yet when it comes to supporting the national team against a team from another country, they will suddenly be united! Once they were enemies, but then suddenly they closed ranks. It is human nature. Once you find a common enemy, the people you were formerly against suddenly become your friends.

Whenever the Lord Jesus comes on the scene, He has a way of uniting and dividing. It has happened throughout Church history that whenever the Spirit comes down in power, people will both unite and divide. When a new move of God's Spirit comes, often people who previously had nothing to do with another person suddenly find common ground in uniting against that move of God. Others are amazingly united by the same move of the Spirit and find a new depth of fellowship together. To those who love what God is doing, the fellowship is sweet and wonderful. But it can also divide those who had been close friends before. It is amazing how people can be very close friends on a natural level, but then when the Spirit comes, they might not be close anymore. Jesus said:

> Do not suppose that I have come to bring peace to the earth. I did not come to bring peace, but a sword. For I have come to turn a man against his father, a daughter against her mother, a daughter-in-law against her mother-in-law—a man's enemies will be the members of his own household.
>
> Matthew 10:34–36

Likewise, the Pharisees and the Sadducees hated each other. The Pharisees were separatists, and they emphasized the law. They loved to be seen by men and were more numerous than the Sadducees. They strutted around, were readily identified by their clothes and wanted everything to be done in a certain way. They were ritualistic and loved the law. They loved order and wanted things to be as they always had been. The Sadducees, on the other hand, were rationalists, and they were a minority. They denied the supernatural. They didn't believe in angels, they didn't believe in the resurrection of the dead and they considered the prophets of the Old Testament to be second class—they only accepted Moses. Yet these two hostile factions suddenly found some common ground when it came to opposing Jesus. Suddenly they were united against Him.

This phenomenon happened again in Luke 23:12 when Herod and Pilate became friends. Before that time, they had been enemies. It is amazing how a common enemy will unite those who were once opposed to each other.

It is incredible that the people were asking Jesus for a sign. Never mind that He had just miraculously fed five thousand people with a few loaves and fish and then later fed another four thousand people. Everyone knew about those miracles, and yet still they asked for a sign—this time a sign from heaven! They were thinking of what Elijah had done (see 1 Kings 18:36–38), and they wanted Jesus to call down lightning or thunder from heaven.

Spiritual Blindness

This shows how spiritual blindness can keep a person from seeing the obvious. God may be powerfully at work, and yet some will just not see it; they will still want evidence that what is going on is of God. The trouble is that those who need signs like this when God is working right under their noses are usually insatiable in their need for "proof."

One of the most melancholy stories to come out of the Welsh revival was that of a British couple living in India who heard that revival had broken out in Wales and decided to come home to see it. They left India, landed at Southampton, came up to London and saw old friends who asked them, "What are you doing back in England?"

"Oh," they said, "we're going to Wales."

"Why would you want to go to Wales?" the friends asked.

"Well, we have heard that revival has broken out in Wales."

These friends were people the couple knew and respected, but the reply came, "It is Welsh emotionalism, nothing more. Just Welsh emotionalism." The couple believed their friends, got back on a boat at Southampton and went back to India—they never got to see what God was doing!

These parables show that a person may be able to see what is obvious on a natural level and yet still be spiritually blind. The Pharisees and Sadducees could interpret the appearance of the sky but not the signs of the times. Just because we can see on a natural level doesn't mean we have vision on a spiritual level. People may be very bright—historians or philosophers, architects or experts in languages—and because they have such a high intellect, they assume that they will automatically be able to understand the Bible as well. But then they read the Bible and it makes no sense to them.

People who are naturally very intelligent can miss out on the most important thing in life. They will not see themselves as sinners. As the Scriptures say, "The god of this age has blinded the minds of unbelievers, so that they cannot see the light of the gospel" (2 Corinthians 4:4). But they never see it that way because they can only think on a natural level. If people don't accept what is there to be believed, they will not get what they claim they want. Jesus said, "A wicked and adulterous generation looks for a miraculous sign, but none will be given it except the sign of Jonah" (Matthew 16:4). Or as Jesus said in the book of Luke, "If they do not listen to Moses and the Prophets, they will not be convinced even if someone rises from the dead" (Luke 16:31).

Even those closest to Jesus can lapse into thinking on a natural level and still need to be taught. Those who were closest to Jesus were the ones who misunderstood Jesus' warning in Matthew 16:6 because they were thinking on a natural level. Jesus was thinking on a spiritual level, and so the disciples need to be taught again. It is a reminder that we are all still learning. We all can miss the obvious.

Some years ago I preached on Philippians and spent about four weeks on a single verse. Then later I preached on it again. Just recently I gained a renewed understanding of this verse. My point is that we are all still learning. Usually God doesn't drop insight into our heads like a penny dropping into a machine. Instead He requires us to think and to think hard; He would prefer that we come to it ourselves rather than having to spoon-feed us.

Those Outside the Family

The first thing to see in the parable given to those outside the family (Matthew 16:1–4) is that they tested Jesus. The Greek words used in this phrase can also mean "tempted Him." They *tempted* Him by asking Him to show them a sign from heaven. All of the other miracles that

Jesus performed they saw as having some kind of natural explanation, and they wanted a sign "from heaven." Despite the differences between the Sadducees and Pharisees, they both wanted to see Jesus' downfall. The fact that they wanted to be rid of Him shows how hardened they were to everything God was doing. God was powerfully at work, and they couldn't even see it. They were not able to make any sense of it.

A good example of this takes place in John 6, when the most nonsensical question was put to Jesus. They asked, "What miraculous sign then will you give that we may see it and believe you?" (John 6:30).

Just before this they had wanted to make Jesus their king because He had fed the five thousand with two fish and five loaves of bread (John 6:15). But the more they got to thinking about it, the more they began to say, "This miracle is not enough." They were hardened to what God was actually doing.

Gene Phillips, my father's pastor, once told me a story of being in a service where there was the greatest demonstration of the Holy Spirit he had ever seen. But the pastor of the church was making fun of it; he just wasn't into it. The pastor whispered to Gene, "Do you want to get up and speak now or would you like a little more 'stir'?" Brother Phillips said, "My heart sank; it was like a dart that went right through me. Here was the glory of God on the people, and all the pastor could say was, 'Do you want a little more "stir"?' He didn't see it as a demonstration of the Spirit."

It is a sad moment when God turns up and we just see it as a "stir," as "Welsh emotionalism" or the equivalent.

A Simple Illustration
What was Jesus' tactic in dealing with this attitude? This time He didn't ask them any deep theological questions. Sometimes Jesus dealt with the Pharisees by asking them a really hard question, but this time He didn't. He just used a simple illustration (Matthew 16:2–3). Why did He do this?

A Question of Priorities
The first reason is because the "spiritual" was at the bottom of their priorities. They were much more concerned with the temporal than with the eternal. Jesus used the weather as an illustration. The weather is temporal—if you don't like it, hang on for a few hours and it will change. Jesus was telling them that something powerful was happening

right in front of their eyes, but it wasn't like the weather. The Son of Man was on the scene. All that had been prophesied by the Old Testament prophets, starting with Moses, was now being fulfilled right before their eyes. He said, "Amazing! You scholars, you can predict the weather a little bit, but you cannot interpret the signs of the times" (see Matthew 16:3). The issue that was at the bottom of their priorities was the most important. They needed to open their spiritual eyes and see what was taking place—the fulfillment of Scripture right in front of them. They couldn't see it because the spiritual was at the bottom of their priorities.

Lack of Discernment

Perhaps another reason that Jesus refrained from posing a deep theological question was because of their limited perspective. They wanted a sign from heaven—yet that was what they already had. God had come to earth; the Word was made flesh—and all right before their eyes. That is why Jonathan Edwards taught us that the task of every generation is to discover in which direction the Sovereign Redeemer is moving and then to move in that direction—because it can be missed.

I never will forget meeting the church warden of Holy Trinity Brompton in London. I had heard what was going on at that church (people falling on the floor and laughing) and had said from my pulpit that it was not of God. Some weeks later, the warden asked to see me because he wanted to be sure himself whether or not it was of God. I went with all kinds of ammunition to warn him against what was going on, but I realized while he was talking that I was wrong. I thought of those who had opposed Jonathan Edwards; they had their reasons. I thought of those who had opposed the Welsh revival; they, too, had their reasons. For myself, I simply thought, *I don't want to be on the wrong side.* Just before all this broke out at Holy Trinity, we had started a prayer covenant at my church. We agreed that we wanted the manifestation of God's glory along with an ever-increasing openness to the way He chose to show up. That meant being willing to say that we were wrong. I suddenly realized that I had been wrong! It is not fun to go to the pulpit in front of your entire congregation and admit you have been wrong, but I wanted to make it right quickly, for the worst thing on earth is for God to be at work and for us to just call it a "stir."

In this parable God was at work, but they were still saying, "We want to see a sign from heaven." So the issue was their perspective, but their perspective was colored by their prejudice.

Prejudice

When we are prejudiced and don't want to believe in something, we can generally find a good reason not to. I knew a man who opposed Evangelism Explosion in Fort Lauderdale many years ago, and he was thrilled to discover anything negative about it that he could. He was pleased to be able to say, "We can forget about E.E. now. Did you know that Jim Kennedy is an amillenialist?" Now that means that you don't know whether there will be a millennium or not, or you think that the millennium spoken of in Scripture is just figurative or symbolic. Most evangelicals in America are premillenialist, which this man was. I had to say to him, "You know, I think that maybe I am an amillenialist myself. So where does that leave me?" The point is that we will look for any issue that lets us off the hook so that we won't have to believe the truth. Both the Pharisees and the Sadducees were sufficiently uncomfortable with Jesus so that they came together against Him. "We ought to test Him," they agreed, but of course, they were already prejudiced against Him.

A Wicked and Adulterous Generation

After His illustration, Jesus said, "A wicked and adulterous generation looks for a miraculous sign" (Matthew 16:4). They were adulterous because they had been unfaithful to God's covenant. Jesus then said, "If you believed Moses, you would believe me" (John 5:46).

The Pharisees were believers in Moses. Even the Sadducees, though they didn't particularly like Isaiah or Jeremiah, championed Moses. That's why Jesus used this phrase. He put it in a slightly different way in John 8: " 'If you were Abraham's children,' said Jesus, 'then you would do the things Abraham did. As it is, you are determined to kill me, a man who has told you the truth that I heard from God. Abraham did not do such things' " (John 8:39–40).

The point is that they were rightly called a wicked and adulterous generation because they were unfaithful to God's covenant.

Always Looking for Miraculous Signs

This is the way to know a wicked and adulterous generation. Even though everything is right in front of their eyes, they still want something more. They are still not convinced, and they look for miraculous signs. Calvin put it like this:

> He does not call them an adulterous generation simply because they seek a
> sign, for God sometimes allows this for His own people. Gideon needed

a sign, and so Jesus is not categorically rejecting the need for a fleece or confirmation, but the reason He said that to them is because they had set up to provoke God. They weren't accepting anything that was going on and they were insatiable. And so they would not have believed more signs when they did not yield to the testimony of scripture.

Actually, they would never have accepted a sign from Jesus. There was just no way Jesus could come up with what they wanted. They were too threatened to accept Him.

The Decree

Jesus said, " 'None will be given it except the sign of Jonah.' Jesus then left them and went away" (Matthew 16:4).

Now this is very interesting. Mark's gospel says nothing about this sign of Jonah. Mark simply wrote that there would be no sign and that then Jesus left them. Matthew wrote that there would be no sign except for the sign of Jonah. Is the Bible contradicting itself? I come to the Bible with the conviction that the Holy Spirit wrote it. God would not deceive us in His Word, and the Bible does not contradict itself. Some liberals might say, "This is wonderful! We don't have to believe the Bible now. We can see that it contradicts itself." There are people who work overtime to show that the Bible contradicts itself because that way they don't have to believe it.

So if the Bible does not contradict itself, what do you suppose the sign of the prophet Jonah is? There are two elements to this sign.

Repentance or Resurrection

Jonah asked a generation to repent. They repented and turned from their ways, and God spared them. So you could say if you are looking for a sign, that it would be that they must repent. They repented at the preaching of Jonah, but he hadn't given them a sign.

There is another way of looking at it, and that is that the only sign they would receive was the resurrection. Later on Jesus said, "For as Jonah was three days and three nights in the belly of a huge fish, so the Son of Man will be three days and three nights in the heart of the earth" (Matthew 12:40). So some say the sign was the resurrection of Jesus.

However, when Jesus was raised from the dead, He didn't appear to the Sadducees and Pharisees, or to Herod (Herod was included because he also had hoped to see a sign). No, Jesus appeared only to believers who were already in His "family." This was something that was to be believed in the heart and that would change lives. And so Jesus said, "No sign will be given."

Those inside the Family

Now Jesus turned His attention to those closest to Him. Having denounced the Pharisees and Sadducees, He had some words of caution for His disciples.

Watch Out for the Yeast

Jesus didn't say, "Beware of the *teachings* of the Sadducees and Pharisees," because He would actually have agreed with much of their teaching. Often those who oppose what God is doing don't necessarily have wrong doctrine. Jesus would have agreed with the Sadducees and not the Pharisees on certain rules of conduct that they derived from the interpretation of Scripture. But He would have agreed with the Pharisees and not the Sadducees when it came to their views of the supernatural—their belief in angels and the resurrection of the dead. Jesus had some common ground with both groups.

Instead of disagreeing with their doctrine, Jesus told His disciples, "Be on your guard against *the yeast* of the Pharisees and Sadducees" (Matthew 16:6, emphasis added).

Jesus had earlier referred to yeast in a good sense (Matthew 13:33). But this time He was using yeast as a metaphor, a parable, in a negative sense. In Luke 12:1 He called the yeast of the Pharisees "hypocrisy." In the ancient law, yeast was often referred to in a negative way: "Do not offer the blood of a sacrifice to me along with anything containing yeast" (Exodus 34:25). And, "Every grain offering you bring to the Lord must be made without yeast" (Leviticus 2:11).

The apostle Paul also referred to yeast in a negative way:

> Don't you know that a little yeast works through the whole batch of dough? Get rid of the old yeast that you may be a new batch without yeast—as you really are. For Christ, our Passover lamb, has been sacrificed. Therefore let us keep the Festival, not with the old yeast, the yeast of malice and wickedness, but with bread without yeast, the bread of sincerity and truth.
>
> 1 Corinthians 5:6–8

Elsewhere Jesus referred to the yeast of the Pharisees and Herod. The Bible refers to Herod's disposition to believe only if signs that compel faith are produced (Luke 23:8). In other words, he refused to believe unless he saw a sign that would make him believe. This is called the "yeast of Herod."

Jesus' Method of Teaching

It is very interesting to learn from the teaching methods of Jesus. If you are a teacher and you want people to grasp what you teach, then you can certainly learn from Jesus. He used several techniques to communicate His message.

He Rebuked

Sometimes when Jesus queries us in such a way as to rebuke us, we may think, *Well, what else could we have thought?* Maybe we feel that the slap on the wrist is unfair. So what if the disciples thought Jesus was annoyed because they hadn't brought any bread? But Jesus said, "You have such little faith." I have thought a lot about that rebuke. The angels, when they appeared to the disciples after Jesus ascended into heaven, asked, "Why are you looking up into heaven?" The disciples might well have responded, "Well, where would you be looking if you had seen Him go up to heaven?" The point is that there is often a better way of looking at things. We sometimes think, *Why would the Lord rebuke me for this?* The answer is invariably, first, because we need it, and second, because of our unbelief. I ask God every day not to let me be found in unbelief. I don't want to be found unbelieving.

So Jesus reprimanded His disciples (Matthew 16:8). He told them that they should have known better. Often they just wanted Jesus to spoon-feed them and tell them every little thing, when He wanted them to learn to think for themselves. If we are not careful, we will become dependent on the words that others say and not ever learn to think for ourselves. It is not a good teacher who says to his students, "You believe what I say, and that is enough." That is not good teaching.

In the Florida Keys, there are pelicans that are always hanging around fishing boats. Before there were ever fishing boats, the pelicans had to go find their own food, but in certain parts of the Keys, they don't ever go out looking for food because the fishing boats will throw the scraps to them. Consequently, they never have to work for their food. We can become like that—we often want Jesus to tell us every little thing. Jesus was saying, "No, that's not the way."

Did you ever notice that when Jesus talked to the two men on the road to Emmaus, He actually rebuked them? "How foolish you are, and how slow of heart to believe" (Luke 24:25). That is the way our Lord often gets our attention. He rebukes.

He Reminds

"Do you still not understand? Don't you remember the five loaves for the five thousand, and how many basketfuls you gathered? Or the seven loaves for the four thousand, and how many basketfuls you gathered?" (Matthew 16:9–10).

Reminding us of what we clearly know is a great way to teach. When we are reminded of what we already know by a good teacher, then we can get a pretty shrewd idea that it is very important.

He Reveals

"How is it you don't understand that I was not talking to you about bread?" (Matthew 16:11).

Jesus revealed a little. He didn't tell them everything, but He said just enough to get them to think. Then they would want to know what He was talking about. He said to them, "You figure it out. I am *not* talking about bread."

I remember something I heard many years ago as a young Christian, from Dr. Samuel Young who was the general superintendent of the Church of the Nazarene. I didn't understand it at the time, but I was so gripped by it that I wrote it down and I have thought about it many times since. He said, "Sometimes God gives hints instead of directions." In other words, we want every little thing explained to us in great detail, but He will just give us a hint and say, "Work it out." Here Jesus revealed only what He *didn't mean* in order to get His disciples to think for themselves. Instead of explaining His precise meaning, He gave them a head start on working it out.

A number of years ago I had the feeling that God wanted me to start getting up at 5 A.M. each day to pray. My hero in those days was John Wesley, and I had read that he used to get up very early every morning to pray, so I started following his example. I noticed that when I got up at five o'clock, by a quarter past I would have fallen back asleep, and I would sleep until eight o'clock on my knees! I prayed, *Lord, if You are in this, You wake me up at five o'clock. If You wake me up, then I'll get up.* Well, I went to bed and forgot about the matter. I went to bed, slept and then suddenly found myself bright-eyed and wide-awake. I looked at the clock and, sure enough, it was 5 A.M. I got up and prayed for the next two hours, and it was wonderful. The next night I prayed, *Lord, do it again*. The next day I slept until eight o'clock! He only did it once. He gave me a hint that's what He wanted *me* to do.

He Repeats

"Be on your guard against the yeast of the Pharisees and Sadducees" (Matthew 16:11).

Jesus said the same thing in Matthew 16:6. Repetition shows that God means what He said the first time! Jesus often prefaced His remarks with the word *verily* or *truly*. He was saying, "Watch out—what I am about to say is doubly important!" For this parable the eventual breakthrough came in verse 12 where Matthew wrote that the disciples finally understood: "Then they understood that he was not telling them to guard against the yeast used in bread, but against the teaching of the Pharisees and Sadducees" (Matthew 16:12).

Whenever a person comes to me to ask for baptism, I will say to them, "Do you know for sure if you were to die today that you would go to heaven?" Usually they will say yes. I then ask, "Well, if you were to stand before God (and you will), and He were to ask you (and He might), 'Why should I let you into heaven?' what would you say?"

Someone came up to me not long ago, seeking to be baptized, and responded in this way to my questions: "I have really started to live for the Lord and turned over a new leaf, and nothing is like it was." I said, "Well, now, look, there is nothing I want to do more than to baptize you, but you are not giving me what I want to hear." He asked, "What is it you want to hear?" I said, "If I tell you, you'll say it, and that won't be good enough. I am not going to tell you." He was a little hurt, and he missed getting baptized, but he came to me later and said, "I have got it! It's because Jesus died for me." I said, "Isn't it better that you came to it on your own?" He agreed. That is the way Jesus taught.

The Yeast

Let's take a closer look at the yeast of the Pharisees. They preferred to ignore the obvious signs around them and continue to ask for just one more. There were three things the Pharisees and the Sadducees had in common.

Hypocrisy

Jesus said that the yeast of the Pharisees was hypocrisy (Luke 12:1). They were playing a game.

Hardness

They refused to accept Jesus' teaching. One of the worst things in the world that can happen to a Christian is to become hard.

I talked to a preacher about four years ago who at one time believed in all the gifts of the Spirit and was right on the cutting edge. Something happened, I don't know what, but he backpedaled and now has become anti-everything of the Spirit. At that time in our own lives, my wife was miraculously healed, and words of knowledge were given that were exactly accurate. I thought, *This poor man. Something has happened and he has become bitter.* I asked him not to become hard. It can happen. When you become hard, you may have a smile on your face, you'll still sing hymns and you'll still love great preaching, but nothing can get through to you.

Being Harmful

This is why Jesus warned the disciples to be on their guard against the yeast—it is something that can get inside the body and then just spread right through it. The teaching of the Pharisees and the scribes was sterile and lifeless. It was also subtle. In other words, asking for a sign may have seemed to be reasonable. The trouble was that the person who did that would never get enough. Their teaching was also sinister. If you listened to them for long enough, you would completely miss what God had said and done.

The Effect of the Yeast

Forecasting the Familiar

What was the effect of the yeast of the Pharisees? I call it *forecasting the familiar.* In other words, they were only concerned with what could be explained on a natural level. Jesus observed, "So, when evening comes, you say it will be fair weather. Oh, really? Where did you get that? That's brilliant!" Jesus was mocking them with faint praise. People who are opposed to the Holy Spirit can't think spiritually. The effect of the yeast is to keep people thinking on a natural level.

Fostering Fear

The Pharisees and Sadducees fostered fear. They had a way of making statements that made others fearful. But "God has not given us a spirit of fear, but of power and of love and of a sound mind" (2 Timothy 1:7, NKJV).

The Pharisees and Sadducees must have lived in the fear and bondage of breaking the law, and they wanted to make sure that everyone else did too!

Finding Fault

They were always critical and always looked for something wrong. People like this are afraid that if they encourage others, then those people will go on beyond them. They will say something to slow others down by being critical. The result is that others are kept from seeing what God is really doing. People are brought to such unbelief that they don't expect to see anything happen, and yet God wants to do big things!

"No eye has seen, no ear has heard, no mind has conceived what God has prepared for those who love him" (1 Corinthians 2:9). We have seen very little, just a little drop, of what God desires to do among us. God gives us a tiny bit to see how we react. We will see extraordinary things.

Recently there came across the Internet something that Tony Campolo said:

> When it comes to being led by the Spirit, sometimes there is a lot of fun to be had. Several years ago I was invited to speak to a small Pentecostal college located near Eastern College [where he teaches]. Before the chapel service, several of the faculty members took me into a side room to pray with me. These men prayed long, and the longer they prayed the more they leaned on my head. They prayed on and on and leaned harder and harder. One of them kept whispering, "Do you feel the Spirit, do you feel the Spirit?" To tell the truth, I felt something right at the back of my neck, but I wasn't sure it was the Spirit. One of the faculty members prayed at length about a particular man named Charlie Stultzvoes. He prayed on and on for this guy who was about to abandon his wife and three children. I can still hear him calling out, "Lord, Lord, don't let that man leave his wife and children, you know who I am talking about, Lord. You know who I am talking about—Charlie Stultzvoes, he lives down the road about a mile on the right hand side in a silver house-trailer."
>
> I thought to myself, with some degree of exasperation, "God knows where he lives, what do you think you are doing? What is God doing? Sitting up there in heaven saying, 'Man, would you give me that address again?'" Following the Chapel talk I got into my car and headed home. I was getting onto the Pennsylvania turnpike when I saw a young man hitchhiking on the side of the road. I picked him up. As we pulled back onto the highway, I introduced myself. I said, 'Hi, my name is Tony—Tony Campolo—what is your name?' He said, 'My name is Charlie Stultzvoes.' I didn't say a word. I drove down the turnpike, got off at the

next exit, turned around and headed back. When I did he looked at me and said, "Hey Mister, where are you taking me?" I said, "I am taking you home." He said, "Why?" I said, "Because you just left your wife and three children, right?" He said, "Right, right!"

I drove off the turnpike and onto a side road straight to his silver house-trailer. When I pulled into the driveway, he looked at me in astonishment and said, "How did you know I lived here?" I said, "God told me. You get into that house-trailer because I want to talk to you and I want to talk to your wife."

He ran into that mobile home ahead of me. I don't know what he said to his wife, but when I got into the house-trailer her eyes were as wide as saucers. I sat them down and said, "I am going to talk and you are going to listen." Man, did they listen! During the next hour I led both of them to a personal relationship with Jesus. Today that guy is a Pentecostal preacher down south.[1]

When the Spirit leads, there are all kinds of surprises in store. And they come when we will accept what God gives us. Sometimes we have to accept His rebuke—a slap on the wrist. But the Lord wants us to think for ourselves and trust in Him. When we do, then the breakthrough will come, and it will be worth waiting for.

Chapter 14

The Parable of the First Among Equals

And on this rock I will build my church.
Matthew 16:18

In Matthew 16:18–19, there are some words of Jesus that I would like to examine. As we have seen, not all of Jesus' illustrations were obvious parables, but there were significant things He had to say that were parabolic in nature. In this passage, there is a metaphor and sort of parable in verse 18 and an enigmatic saying in verse 19.

Jesus prefaced these verses with a question to His disciples: "Who do people say the Son of Man is?" (Matthew 16:13).

Why did Jesus ask a question like that? I am certain of at least one thing: He did not ask because He was actually trying to discover what people thought of Him. Remember that any time God asks us a question, He is not looking for information! He asks questions to get us to think about our situation and so that a truth may be revealed to us. Jesus wasn't trying to build up His self-esteem by fishing for a secondhand compliment or some other kind of affirmation. He wasn't trying to develop an objectivity about Himself by finding out what people said. (Although some people often try in this way to find out what others think of them. If two or three people say much the same thing about you, then it is probably pretty close to the truth.) In fact, as we will see, Jesus was actually preparing the way for one disciple in particular to emerge as the leader—to be first among equals—and it turned out to be Simon Peter.

Why Is This Parable Important?

First, this parable shows how Jesus can gently engineer a conversation to achieve a particular purpose. Second, it proves an interesting point that some scholars have argued over—namely, that Jesus did in fact refer to Himself as the "Son of Man." Some Bible scholars contend that

Jesus only ever referred to "the Son of Man" in the third person singular, as if He Himself were looking for the Son of Man. This was the teaching of Rudolph Bultmann in Germany and some of his followers. Here we see that this theory is nonsense because in Matthew 16:13, when Jesus asked the question, He was obviously referring to Himself as the Son of Man. Third, these verses are important because they show that the Lord is not interested in what the uncommitted masses say about Him, only what His own followers feel about Him. He is only concerned about what His committed followers think. So He introduced this section by saying, "What do people say about me?" But then He asked, "Who do *you* say I am?" (Matthew 16:15, emphasis added).

The *you* here is in the second person plural. He was not just looking at Peter; He was still talking to all of the Twelve. But it was only Peter who spoke up and said, "You are the Christ, the Son of the living God" (Matthew 16:16).

Jesus responded by saying,

> Blessed are you, Simon son of Jonah, for this was not revealed to you by man, but by my Father in heaven. And I tell you that you are Peter, and on this rock I will build my church, and the gates of Hades will not overcome it. I will give you the keys of the kingdom of heaven; whatever you bind on earth will be bound in heaven, and whatever you loose on earth will be loosed in heaven.
>
> Matthew 16:17–19

We must get to the bottom of the meaning of Jesus' words here. For example, is Peter himself "the rock," or is Christ the Rock and the Church is built upon Christ Himself? Is it Peter's confession that is the rock? Was the power to "bind on earth" given to Simon Peter only? And how does this relate to us today?

Peter's Confession

A Voluntary Confession

First of all, Peter's confession was testimonial. Peter volunteered to give his testimony. All twelve of the disciples had the same opportunity. Matthew might have spoken up, or Thomas, John or James; but it is only Peter who spoke. This shows that God does reward those who will speak up when the Lord is asking for something. Yet we will see later that Peter could take no credit for this. The same is true of those who develop a hunger for God. Those who come forward will be the ones that God will bless, and yet the hunger itself we can take no credit for.

Perhaps you know the story of D. L. Moody who, as a young minister, was sitting on the platform when he heard another preacher say, "The world has yet to see what God can do with one man utterly and totally resigned to Him." D. L. Moody spoke up and said, "I propose to be that person." So it is a matter of saying, "That's me!"

A Theological Confession

Peter's background was not theological. I am sure that all fishermen have the *potential* to be theologians, but Peter was not. Nevertheless, when he was questioned, he gave Jesus an answer loaded with theology! "You are the Christ; You are the Messiah; You are God's Anointed One." It just goes to show that you don't have to understand everything when you start out as a Christian. God can make any of us theologically minded when the Spirit reveals things to us.

A Trinitarian Confession

Referring to the Son of Man as "the Son of the living God" showed that Simon Peter was edging toward a most profound truth, the bedrock of Christian thinking—the Trinity. The word *trinity* is never used in the Bible, but nonetheless there is overwhelming evidence to support the doctrine of the Triune God. The moment you say, "Jesus is the Son of the living God," you are there. Those who deny the Trinity are those who deny the deity of Jesus. That is the heart of the matter. Take Islam, for instance. Muslims will talk about Christians having three Gods, not one. The only question to put to a Muslim is, "Will you confess that Jesus is the Son of God?" They won't. Once you confess that Jesus is the Son of God, you are automatically a Trinitarian.

A Truthful Confession

Why was it truthful? Because Jesus *is* the Son of God. Peter's saying that didn't suddenly *make* Jesus the Son of God. Peter was stating what was already true. It was Peter's testimony, yes, but it was also objectively God's Word. We read at the end of 1 John, "And we are in him who is true—even in his Son Jesus Christ. He is the true God and eternal life" (1 John 5:20).

So it was the beginning of Christian understanding when Peter made this confession. It is what Muslims cannot say and still remain Muslim; it is what Jehovah's Witnesses cannot say and remain Jehovah's Witnesses.

A Turning-Point Confession

Nothing would ever be the same again after Peter uttered those words. And Jesus affirmed what he said: "God has revealed this to you, Simon, and now all twelve will see this to be the case. Nothing will be the same again" (see Matthew 16:17). In one stroke Jesus had been affirmed by Peter as the Messiah—the One whom the Jews had awaited, the One whom Moses spoke of and the One whom the prophets foretold. Nothing would be the same again. Not only that, He is the Son of God Almighty, the Son of the living God!

Peter—God's Choice

First among Equals

What emerges from this account is that Peter had been chosen by God. There were various opinions in response to Jesus' question, "Who do people say that I am?" (see Matthew 16:13): "They replied, 'Some say John the Baptist; others say Elijah; and still others, Jeremiah or one of the prophets'" (Matthew 16:14).

I would remind you that Jesus used the second person plural in the following question: "'But what about *you?*' he asked. 'Who do *you* say I am?'" (Matthew 16:15, emphasis added).

Presumably any of the others could have been "chosen," but it was Peter who actually was. Why Peter? Was it his personality? Was it his temperament? Was it his intelligence? Was it his education? Jesus said, "Blessed are you, Simon son of Jonah, for this was *not revealed to you by man, but by my Father in heaven*" (Matthew 16:17, emphasis added).

This was not something Peter thought of on his own. No one had whispered the answer in his ear beforehand. It was revealed to him by the Father in heaven. God was behind it. This did not mean that Peter was the only one of the Twelve who comprised God's elect, for all of the disciples were chosen, with the exception of Judas Iscariot. (The reason we know that Judas Iscariot was not included is because of Jesus' comments in John 17:12.) All eleven, then, were chosen, but Peter was the first among equals.

Like it or not, there always seem to be an elect within the elect. It is almost certain that around five hundred people were present when Jesus said the words, "I am going to send you what my Father has promised; but stay in the city until you have been clothed with power from on high" (Luke 24:49).

He appeared to more than five hundred people after being raised from the dead (1 Corinthians 15:6), yet just one hundred twenty were there when the Spirit came down (Acts 1:15). Those who just come forward and volunteer like Peter did—they are the elect within the elect. Jesus said to Peter, "Blessed are you." The word *blessed* here means "happy," and the word *happy* comes from a Greek word that means "lucky." It is so sad that a perfectly good word like this has been stolen by the world, and now we are afraid to say the phrase, "you are lucky." But Jesus said it to Peter! Peter was to have a responsibility that would exceed that of the other disciples.

A Surprising Choice

As far as we know, Peter had no training for his new role. It thrills me to see how a new convert can, within a very short period of time, learn so much. Some grow so much faster than others, some absorb things more quickly than others and some show more devotion to Christ than others. Some are hungrier than others. Yet here God, who knows the end from the beginning, chose a man who at a crucial moment would deny Christ. *Surely this was a bad choice?* we might be tempted to think. But I actually think God did this to encourage all of us. We have all let the Lord down, and yet He stays with us. I am glad God chose Peter. He chose Peter because He can choose us. Even when Jesus said, "Before the rooster crows, you will disown me three times!" (John 13:38), He still gave comfort: "Do not let your hearts be troubled. Trust in God" (John 14:1).

So God stays with such a choice.

A Strategic Choice

All that was happening was part of a divine strategy. Because God chooses you, you will do things that you never thought possible. Look at the language in the books of 1 and 2 Peter. This was a fisherman! Who would have thought he could ever write like that? Here was a man who preached the inaugural sermon of the Church on the Day of Pentecost with such power, irrefutable wisdom, logic and knowledge of Scripture that thousands came to Christ. God can do that with you as well!

A Sovereign Choice

There is only one explanation for this—the Holy Spirit. God the Father made the choice. The first thing Jesus said was that Peter was blessed because His identity was revealed to Peter by God. There was no way Peter could go around to the other eleven claiming to be especially clever or knowledgeable. Jesus made the situation clear, and Peter could take no credit for it. But it was God who chose Peter, as Jesus confirmed, "All things have been committed to me by my Father. No one knows the Son except the Father, and no one knows the Father except the Son *and those to whom the Son chooses to reveal him*" (Matthew 11:27, emphasis added).

It was a sovereign choice involving the entire Trinity. The Father had made the choice, Jesus made the choice and, according to John 6:63, the Holy Spirit also made the choice.

What we are seeing then is that Jesus' original question was a sovereign "setup" to reveal what God was going to do next. Whenever God comes to us and questions us, it is not because He is looking for information or because He doesn't know what is going on; it is because He wants to bring us to the point where we will see His glory.

The Call of Peter

"Blessed are you, Simon son of Jonah, for this was not revealed to you by man, but my Father in heaven. And I tell you that you are Peter, and on this rock I will build my church, and the gates of Hades will not overcome it" (Matthew 16:17–18).

A Pun

The first thing to see about this verse is that Jesus used a play on words. It was not the occasion when Peter was given his name—that had already happened. Jesus had called Simon "Peter" in Matthew 4:18 and 10:2. Probably the first occurrence is recorded in John: " 'You are Simon son of John. You will be called 'Cephas' (which, when translated, is Peter)" (John 1:42).

The Aramaic word used here is *caphor* or *cephas,* which means "massive rock." The Greek word *petros* also means rock. Jesus uses a pun, which you wouldn't know unless you understood the original language. He said, "You are *petros,* and on this *petra* I will build My Church." *Petros* was Peter's name, and *petra* means rock: "You are the rock, and on this rock (i.e., Peter) I will build My Church."

Many of us Protestants overreact to the extreme manner in which Roman Catholicism has embellished this. We're afraid to say that perhaps Jesus really meant Peter himself, that Peter was the rock on which Christ would build His Church. We say the rock must be Christ, or the rock is the "revealed truth." We say Jesus called Peter "blessed" because God revealed the truth to him. We get defensive, and we look for a way out.

Perhaps you would be encouraged to know that, were it not for Protestant reactions against the extremes of Roman Catholic interpretation, it is doubtful whether many would have taken the rock to be anything or anyone other than Peter. This text is saying nothing about Peter's successors. It's certainly saying nothing about his infallibility because nobody else thought he was infallible. In Acts 11 Peter was held accountable by the whole Church when, in effect, they said, "You had better tell us what you mean." Also in Galatians Paul said, "When Peter came to Antioch, I opposed him to his face, because he was clearly in the wrong" (Galatians 2:11).

There was nothing there about infallibility or exclusive authority. All Jesus was doing was to show that Peter, being the first to make this formal confession, would be greatly used in the early Church. He dominated the first part of the book of Acts. He preached the inaugural sermon. He was first among equals.

Remember that our faith is built upon the foundation of the apostles (plural) and prophets with Christ Jesus Himself as the chief cornerstone.

A Promise

"You are Peter, and on this rock I will build my church, and the gates of Hades will not overcome it" (Matthew 16:18).

Here Jesus revealed what was going to happen. God began with Peter on the Day of Pentecost, and we begin to see how He would use a man who had earlier denied Christ. Peter began to preach with great power. The Church here is not an anachronism but a reference to the assembled people of God. The Greek word *ecclesia*, "called out", does not refer to a building but to the people of God.

Jesus also predicted here what *wouldn't* happen. The word *Hades* means death. The word *gates* refers to the strength of Satan. So the Church will not be defeated by the hosts of darkness. In a word, the Church cannot die. Never believe for one minute that the Church can die! God has never left Himself without a witness, and it is amazing to see His sense of humor at times. Voltaire said that one day the Bible would be extinct and that no one would ever be able to find a copy. Yet on the day of Voltaire's death, the British Museum paid two million pounds to obtain a manuscript that had been discovered on Mount Sinai. On that very day, Voltaire's writings were worth about twenty cents! God loves to do things like that. He will always have the last word. Even when the Church appears to pass behind a cloud and Satan appears to be triumphing, don't believe it! God sees the end from the beginning—the elect will be saved, and the Church will flourish. The Church is going to flourish again in Western society. It will happen.

"The gates of hell will not prevail against the Church" was a promise. No doubt when Peter denied the Lord, some cynic said, "Oh, where is the promise now?" At the lowest ebb, it may appear that the outlook is hopeless, but in no time God turned Peter around, and He can do it again today.

A Principle

"The gates of Hades will not overcome it. I will give you the keys of the kingdom of heaven; whatever you bind on earth will be bound in heaven, and whatever you loose on earth will be loosed in heaven" (Matthew 16:18–19).

Now, the Church and the Kingdom are not the same thing, but neither are they unrelated, and they are certainly not opposed to each other. The word *church* refers to the people of God. The word *kingdom* refers to the power of the Spirit—the rule of the Spirit. Christ rules His Kingdom through the Holy Spirit. To the degree that the Holy Spirit in us is *not* grieved, the Kingdom flourishes. To the degree to which we grieve Him, the Kingdom diminishes.

This verse says that what is bound on earth will also be bound in heaven. The person with the keys, therefore, has the power to exclude or to permit entrance. Was this given exclusively to Peter? The answer is no, because Jesus said it again in Matthew 18:18, after He was raised from the dead. This time He said to all the disciples, "If you forgive anyone his sins, they are forgiven; if you do not forgive them, they are not forgiven" (John 20:23).

The implication was that authority such as this was given to all. There is no evidence here at all for priestly absolution. We are not saying that the priest has the power to forgive sins just because he is a priest.

Let me show you how this authority should be carried out by all who claim to be disciples of Jesus:

▶ *Preaching in the Spirit.*
This is proclaiming the Gospel. We accomplish "binding and loosing" by proclaiming a Gospel that has already been given. We are not forcing heaven to comply; our task is to be faithful to Jesus' words. We can assure a person or withhold assurance depending on whether that person complies with the Gospel. When we, as ministers in the Spirit, pronounce with authority whether a person is fit to be baptized, we are

carrying out what Jesus said. To some people we say, "Sorry, we cannot baptize you." Similarly, there is a place for saying to a person, "You are saved." Why? God has given us the authority to say that because they meet the conditions of the Gospel.

▶ *Prophesying in the Spirit.*

A prophetic person who is in the Spirit can set a person free in a way in which that person could never have been set free before. God is not bound by what a person says, but if what is said is under the anointing, God may choose to set someone free through a prophetic word.

I will never forget, as long as I live, when Paul Cain stood in the pulpit at Westminster Chapel, looked down and called out a lady in the congregation. He had no idea who she was, but under the anointing, he called her by her name and quoted an address to her. He said that at this particular address God had showed her something, and she was afraid that it wasn't as God had said. A few weeks before, her husband had died, but someone had led him to the Lord in the hospital before he died. This lady had begun to doubt it because her husband had been drugged at the time, and she was afraid that because of that, his conversion hadn't been genuine. She was so discouraged and had pleaded with the Lord that she would be able to see her husband, Sam, in heaven. She saw a Bible on the table, opened it and said, "Lord, give me something." Her eyes fell on the words, "Samuel with the Lord" which made her very happy. But later she reasoned that it was a children's Bible, not a proper Bible, and she was down again. Nobody knew this until Paul called her out by name, gave her the address and said, "It was there that God showed you something and you were afraid it wasn't God, but it was." She will never doubt it now. What is loosed on earth is loosed in heaven because of prophesying in the Spirit.

▶ *Praying in the Spirit.*

This is when you pray consciously in the will of God. "If we ask anything according to his will, he hears us. And if we know that he hears us—whatever we ask—we know that we have what we asked of him" (1 John 5:14–15).

This is praying in the Holy Spirit—when you know you are praying in the will of God. It shows the force of prayer. It shows the need to be in the Spirit when you pray, because like it or not, God is only going to answer what is His will. It is our duty to find out His will and pray in His will. Prayer doesn't twist God's arm, but if it is in the Spirit, it reveals what God has already decided is right for us—what you bind on earth will be bound in heaven, and what you loose on earth will be loosed in heaven.

I want a closer walk with God. I want a greater touch from Him on my life. Peter was the first to be given this promise and authority, but he wasn't the last. We all have an opportunity to get in line! As D. L. Moody said, "I am going to be like that." This is a word extended to everybody, whether you are a fisherman, a tax collector, a solicitor, a nurse, a taxi driver, a deacon or a minister. But this word is given only on the condition that we confess what Peter confessed—that we bow to the sovereignty of God, that we uphold this given Gospel, not changing or adding to it, and that we pray in the Spirit.

Chapter 15

The Parable of Childlike Religion

Unless you change and become like little children.
Matthew 18:3

Jesus said in Matthew 18:3–4, "I tell you the truth, unless you change and become like little children, you will never enter the kingdom of heaven. Therefore, whoever humbles himself like this child is the greatest in the kingdom of heaven."

These words of Jesus were given in response to the disciples' question, "Who is the greatest in the kingdom of heaven?" (Matthew 18:1).

The disciples had also argued about this in Mark 9:33—an occasion when they had been debating the issue on the road and Jesus later challenged them about it—and again in Luke 9:46–48. In Matthew's account, the disciples just seem to have blurted out the question, prompting Jesus to call over a small child to illustrate His reply.

The issue of "who was the greatest" seems to have been so important to the disciples that they thought about it at the most inappropriate moments. We know, for instance, that when Jesus revealed He was going to be betrayed, killed and then raised to life, the disciples were filled with grief. Yet their grief didn't last too long, because in no time they were asking this question again! Something even more amazing occurs in Luke 22 when they were gathered around what was to be the Last Supper. Jesus was speaking of being betrayed and teaching the disciples to remember Him through the communion meal. It was an awesome, somber moment, and yet "a dispute arose among them as to which of them was considered to be greatest" (Luke 22:24).

Imagine thinking about that at such a time!

These twelve men who were chosen to be the famous disciples should have been incredibly grateful just to be numbered among "the Twelve." But it wasn't enough—they wanted more. In Matthew 20, even the mother of Zebedee's sons came to Jesus and asked this favor of Him: "Grant that one of these two sons of mine may sit at your right and the other at your left in your kingdom" (Matthew 20:21).

Later in Mark's gospel, the text implies that it was probably the two sons themselves who had prompted their mother to ask such a question (Mark 10:35), because we are told, "When the ten heard about this, they were indignant with the two brothers" (Matthew 20:24). No wonder!

Isn't it amazing how pride gets in and we say, "If I can just attain this level, I will be happy"? Perhaps there was a time when you said, "If I could just live in this one place, get this one job, I will be so happy I won't want anything ever again...." Then you get there and you want more. The person who makes their first million wants a second million. Those who are the most unworthy and later get to be in a better place think, *This is marvelous,* but they still want more. So being among the Twelve wasn't enough for the disciples. They wanted to be the greatest among the Twelve.

Listen! "The heart is deceitful above all things and beyond cure. Who can understand it?" (Jeremiah 17:9).

The human heart is a mystery, but God knows it only too well. So Jesus was probably not surprised when the disciples asked, "Who is the greatest in the kingdom of heaven?"

Jesus responded to this kind of question in two different ways. In both responses He used metaphors, if not parables. For example, in Matthew 20 He responded this way: "You know that the rulers of the Gentiles lord it over them, and their high officials exercise authority over them. Not so with you. Instead, whoever wants to become great among you must be your servant, and whoever wants to be first must be your slave" (verses 25–27).

Second, Jesus uses the parable of childlike religion:

> He called a little child and had him stand among them. And he said: "I tell you the truth, unless you change and become like little children, you will never enter the kingdom of heaven. Therefore, whoever humbles himself like this child is the greatest in the kingdom of heaven."
>
> Matthew 18:2–4

It is impossible to know from the Greek text exactly how old a "little child" would be, but the child was obviously quite young, perhaps kindergarten age or even younger. It is very important to note here that Jesus was *not* implying that children are without sin. Psalm 58:3 says that we come out of our mother's womb speaking lies, that is, born in sin. You don't have to teach a child to lie, and any parent knows that children can be horrible to each other and say awful things. I talked to someone recently who has been bruised their whole life, not because of something a parent said to them but because of what another child said to them in the playground years earlier. So Jesus wasn't saying that children are without sin; rather He was saying that there is something about a child that needs to be emulated in our adult lives.

Why Is This Parable Important?

An important factor in this parable is that, surprisingly perhaps, it shows the place of children in Jesus' teaching. In Matthew 19:13, little children were brought to Jesus for Him to place His hands on them and pray for them, but the disciples rebuked those who brought them. Jesus, however, overruled their decision and said, "Let the little children come to me, and do not hinder them, for the kingdom of heaven belongs to such as these" (Matthew 19:14).

In Matthew 21:15, on Palm Sunday, we are told that when the priests and the teachers of the law saw the wonderful things that Jesus did and the children shouting in the temple area, "Hosanna to the Son of David," they were indignant. You can imagine some of the adults witnessing this and saying to one another, "How can these children know what they are saying? Rebuke them! Stop it!" But Jesus saw things differently. " 'Do you hear what these children are saying?' they asked him. 'Yes,' replied Jesus, 'have you never read, *From the lips of children and infants you have ordained praise"?'* " (Matthew 21:16, emphasis added).

This parable shows how Jesus' followers, then and now, tend to underestimate children. The disciples did. They didn't grasp the importance of reaching out to children, and they assumed that Jesus would be too busy to bother with them. Jesus, however, overruled His disciples immediately, which lets us know that God sees children differently than many of us do. It is a rebuke to those who under-estimate the place of children in His Kingdom.

The old adage, "Children should be seen and not heard," is not biblical. The Christian psychologist Clyde Narramore has many times shown that the worst thing you can do to a child is make him feel unimportant. Instead, we should bring children out and let them talk. Dignify their questions, and they will grow up with a more positive self-image.

One of the things I cherish is thinking back to when I lived in Ashland, Kentucky. My dad would let me sit in the living room or at the table with visiting preachers and evangelists and ask questions. It shaped me. I wouldn't be here today were it not for that. I was con-verted when I was six-and-a-half years old. Jonathan Edwards was converted when he was four. Never underestimate what God can do with children. I have often thought, and still do think, that when revival comes, children, even the youngest, will be right at the center of it. But you can expect people to be indignant about that when it happens.

The main reason, however, that this parable is important is because it gives us an insight into what true greatness is. Two concepts of greatness are given in this passage. The way the disciples viewed greatness—as in, power and prestige—and the way Jesus viewed greatness. Jesus said that when an adult can humble himself and become like a child, that is true greatness.

The Request for Greatness

"Who is the greatest in the kingdom of heaven?" Because of the parallel accounts of this passage in the other gospels, we know what the disciples really meant by "greatness" when they asked Jesus this question. They were thinking of being highly honored and admired by everyone they knew. They were assuming that the characteristics of greatness were prestige and power, and therefore they expected to be highly esteemed by their peers as a result. They were not thinking of servanthood or putting their own needs last!

I don't know if you have ever attended a class reunion. I get invitations every five years to come back to Ashland to the class of 1953—usually in the summer when I can't be there. I always send them my apologies. One of the reasons people want to go back to revisit the past is to show off—especially in front of those who gave them so much trouble all those years ago! Back when I was in school, everyone wanted to be the greatest; they wanted to be remembered for some outstanding achievement. Jesus' disciples were no different.

Now, the question is, was the disciples' question inappropriate? Was it a vain request? Who *was* the greatest in the Kingdom of heaven? Jesus didn't rebuke them for wanting to be great. As a matter of fact, God uses ambition. Martin Luther used to say, "God uses sex to drive a man to marriage, ambition to drive a man to service, fear to drive a man to faith." Dale Carnegie, the author of the best-seller *How to Win Friends and Influence People,* said that the strongest desire of a human being is the desire to feel important.

That is what was at the bottom of this request—the disciples wanted to be at the top! Peter had already been affirmed as first among equals, but now James and John wanted to get in on the action too—they wanted one of them to be at the right hand of Jesus and the other at His left hand in heaven (Mark 10:35). This lets us know that the author of the fourth gospel had a lot of ambition and pride. Reading between the lines of the New Testament epistles, we can see that the apostle Paul had a rather huge ego too, but God can still use people like that.

Many years ago I read a verse in Ecclesiastes that had a great impact on me: "I saw that all labor and all achievement spring from man's envy of his neighbor" (Ecclesiastes 4:4). The Bible lets us know that the main reason people want to excel is so that others will notice and say, "Ooh, boy, that is something amazing!" That is why we do it.

You may say, "Well, I am not that way." Maybe the Bible got it wrong in your case, but for the rest of us, that is the way it is. All our labor and all our achievement spring from man's envy of his neighbor. "Some people are born to greatness, some achieve greatness, some have greatness thrust upon them," said Shakespeare. But the kind of greatness that Jesus had in mind is different. The definition that He had in mind is to be great in God's eyes.

In Daniel 10 we read the words, "Daniel, you who are highly esteemed" (Daniel 10:11). Daniel had favor in God's eyes because he made a choice. His choice was to refuse to do what was popular, what his peers were pressurizing him to do, and to seek greatness in God's eyes by humbling himself in obedience.

You too have a choice to make—do you want other people to think you are great, or are you willing to be great in the eyes of God alone? John 4:44 says, "How can you believe if you accept praise from one another, yet make no effort to obtain the praise that comes from the only God?"

The step forward for people like us who may want to be seen as great by people, but should want to be seen as great by God, is to become like a child.

Requirements for Greatness

Jesus knew exactly what was behind His disciples' request for greatness, but nevertheless He didn't rebuke them. Instead He took the opportunity to teach them the requirements for greatness. There are three principles contained in Jesus' teaching.

To Change

The King James Version says, "Except ye be *converted,* and become as little children" (Matthew 18:3, emphasis added).

The word *conversion* in Scripture is used in more than one way.

Sometimes people get into a theological straightjacket and believe that conversion can only mean that first experience when you come to God. But conversion is something that is ongoing. This is why we are all being changed from glory to glory by the Spirit of the Lord (see 2 Corinthians 3:18). The New International Version puts it this way: "Unless you change..." Although they were disciples, they still needed to change. Do you? Or are you one of those who say, "I got everything I need at conversion"? I look at some people and think, *God have mercy on us if you got it all at conversion! Is this the most we have to look forward to?*

From personal experience and Scripture, I can tell you, you didn't get the fullness of everything God has for you at conversion. But you did get the potential to receive all of that fullness. Paul began his letter to the Corinthians by saying, "You have been enriched in every way" (1 Corinthians 1:5), and yet he ended chapter 12 by saying, "Covet earnestly the best gifts" (1 Corinthians 12:31, KJV). He began his letter to the Ephesians by saying, "You have got it all" (see Ephesians 1:3), but then at the end he wrote, "Be filled with the Spirit", there is more (see Ephesians 5:18). All believers live in this paradox of having received the full potential of every good thing in Christ and yet having to change and be transformed day by day.

To Conform

Notice how Jesus continued. He said we must *become* like little children. That means we must make certain adjustments. The old saying "You can't teach an old dog new tricks" can be true of so many people because they get set in their ways. They know it all, they have heard it all and they say, "I haven't changed in thirty years—glory to God." It must make the angels blush! Rather than accepting the status quo, we need to conform. The factor that will determine your willingness to make adjustments as you get older will be your motivation. It comes down to this: How much of God do you really want?

Jesus said, "Unless you change ... you will never enter the kingdom of heaven" (Matthew 18:3).

Why did He say that? I think it was because He was so sure it would be an enticement to them. He was sure that they were desperate for the reality of God the Father and would do anything to have it. Are you hungry enough to have such a high level of motivation? Will you swallow your pride, go outside of your comfort zone and cease to be motivated by a spirit of fear?

We know the disciples were born again, yet now Jesus said that unless they changed they wouldn't enter the Kingdom of heaven. What did He mean by that? He meant the same thing that Paul and Barnabas meant when they said, "We must go through many hardships to enter the kingdom of God" (Acts 14:22).

Paul recognized that although he was living by the power of the Spirit and was being used mightily to advance God's Kingdom, he still needed to be continually transformed. He still needed to change. We are being changed to inhabit a realm where the Spirit isn't grieved—to gain an intimacy with the Father.

To Condescend

"Therefore, whoever humbles himself like this child is the greatest in the kingdom of heaven" (Matthew 18:4).

To *condescend* means "to lower yourself"; that is, to humble yourself. There are two ways of coming into a measure of humility. One is to be humbled, and the other is to humble yourself. Have you ever asked God to give you more humility? That is a serious request! What if God were to say, "Hmm, I wonder if he really means that? Let's see . . . "!

Many years ago, in 1956, I heard a sermon on Philippians 2:5 preached by Dr. Hugh Benner, general superintendent of the Church of the Nazarene. It was about having the mind of Christ. The text said:

> Who, being in very nature God, did not consider equality with God something to be grasped, but made himself nothing, taking the very nature of a servant, being made in human likeness. And being found in appearance as a man, he humbled himself and became obedient to death— even death on a cross!
>
> Philippians 2:6–8

He made the point that Jesus submitted Himself to the worst possible shame for the honor and glory of God. I was so moved by that sermon that I got on my knees and prayed, *God, I surrender myself to the worst possible shame.* I meant it. The angels must have looked at each other and said, "I wonder what the Father is going to do about that?" You see, when you pray a prayer like that, if it doesn't get answered in the next two hours or the next two days, you forget about it. But three or four years later, I found myself hearing about my peers who were pastoring nice churches—one had even become a national evangelist. When people asked, "Where is R. T. these days?" I could imagine the answer: "Oh, you haven't heard about R. T.? He's out knocking on doors and talking to strangers." I was selling vacuum cleaners door-to-door while all the others were preaching and enjoying the acclaim of men. People would come up to my father and say, "How is R. T.?" and he would say, "Well, pray for R. T." It was awful.

Being humbled may be the next step forward, but the better way is to humble yourself. You have to become vulnerable. You resist the temptation to say something that would make yourself look a bit better. Jesus was crucified in weakness. He who put the planets into space was now listening to men say, "He saved others but he couldn't save himself" (see Matthew 27:42). He heard it all, but He didn't try to justify Himself—He allowed Himself to be crucified in weakness.

The Resemblance of Greatness

Unpretentious

Why did Jesus select a child to illustrate His point about greatness? Because there are certain characteristics of childlikeness that He wanted us all to learn. First, children are unpretentious—they haven't learned to take themselves too seriously. To be unpretentious is an exceedingly rare quality in the human race, but children naturally have it. They don't know any other way to be. They don't have to learn to lie, they don't have to learn to lose their temper, but they do have to learn to be pretentious. Most children when they become older and enter their teenage years develop a smugness. They learn that either from their parents or from their peers. They learn to strut about who they know, how much they know, how "cool" they are and so on. Or perhaps they feel the need to create a mystique about their personality out of a desire to make others envious. It all boils down to pretentiousness.

Pete Cantrell always says that the greatest liberty is having nothing to prove. A child has nothing to prove. Perhaps the most astonishing thing about Jesus is that He was unpretentious—there was not a trace of arrogance; He didn't try to impress anybody. I am amazed when I read the fourth chapter of John. Jesus went to a well in Samaria. He met a Samaritan woman and asked her, "Will you give me a drink?" (John 4:7). He was the Son of God, and He was a Jew—but He didn't say so. He was completely unpretentious, and the woman was stunned. Jesus is looking for unpretentiousness in us—for us to be childlike in our estimation of ourselves and in our dealings with others.

Unsophisticated

A child is unsophisticated, naive and uncomplicated. To be sophisticated is to be shrewd and worldly-wise. One gains these traits through learning and experience. The Greek word *sophia,* from which we get the word "sophisticated," means "wisdom which we are commanded to have." But the danger with having wisdom is pride. That is why the King James Version says, "Don't be wise in your own conceits." The apostle Paul put it like this in 1 Corinthians: "Brothers, stop thinking like children. In regard to evil be infants, but in your thinking be adults" (1 Corinthians 14:20).

Children haven't yet picked up ways of thinking the worst about other people. They are naive and gullible. Why do you have to say to children, "Don't take candy from a stranger?" Because otherwise they will take it—they will listen and accept openly. This is what Jesus is after—for us to openly trust our heavenly Father. He wants us to be unpretentious, unsophisticated, unprejudiced.

A small child hasn't learned class distinction, cultural gaps or social or racial prejudice. A child brought up playing with a person of another race or color doesn't even know it is a "problem" until some adult says, "You shouldn't be talking to him or her." We learn these prejudices, but with a child there is no social or cultural prejudice. He or she just accepts everybody the way they are.

A child is not ambitious. He is largely unaffected by praise and flattery. It doesn't go to his head. Ambition must be taught one way or another. When we do learn it, that's when rivalry and jealousy appear—they are linked to ambition, and they can be the reason we want to control our circumstances. A child has not learned these pitfalls.

A child is not self-conscious. A child will cry openly in front of people. He or she doesn't worry what people will think. This is why when revival comes and the Spirit of God comes down, people are only conscious of God and not worried what other people think of them.

A child obviously is very self-centered, but Jesus meant in this passage that an adult must become *like* a child again: utterly trusting and not suspicious. We must learn to expect anything from God and nothing from ourselves.

The Reason for Greatness

Do notice that it is greatness in the Kingdom of heaven that Jesus was talking about (Matthew 18:4)—not greatness in the Church. There is a difference between the Kingdom of heaven and the Church. I repeat: they are not disconnected, but neither are they the same. You can be in the Church and be a deacon and be "great," but in the Kingdom of heaven you may be nothing. Or you can be in the Kingdom of heaven and be "great," but you do nothing in the Church that would cause anyone to think you are great. The same goes for the minister. I can be great in terms of my profile but be the least in the Kingdom of heaven.

The essence of what Jesus was after was to show us that we must always let God be in control. If we humble ourselves and let God do what He wills with us, then He can do all the promoting and make us "great." Joseph could be trusted to be the prime minister of Egypt because he had totally forgiven his brothers who betrayed him. He had reached the bottom of the pile and surrendered to God. Once he had been truly humbled, God could use him. There is nothing sadder than to see small men scrambling for power; small people starved of recognition. But you can be trusted with power and prestige if you are childlike before God.

Dr. Martyn Lloyd-Jones used to say that the worst thing that can happen to a man is to succeed before he is ready. It is a truly great person who does not let success and admiration go to his head. Winston Churchill said that the price of greatness is responsibility. But when small people get power, they love it too much. They luxuriate in their power and forget the needs of others.

What Jesus is after is that we come to a place where we are willing to unlearn so much that has become a part of us and shed any baggage that fights against the Spirit. He wants us to come to the place where our only ambition is to be great in the Kingdom of heaven on God's terms, so that, like Daniel, the Father will call us greatly esteemed.

Chapter 16

The Parable of the Unmerciful Servant

Therefore, the kingdom of heaven is like a king who wanted to settle
accounts with his servants.

Matthew 18:23

This parable is one of the most soul searching that Jesus ever told. In
Matthew 18:21–35, Jesus told the story of a servant who was forgiven
an incalculable debt by his master because he had no ability to pay.
This same man was also owed a sum of money, very small by comparison, by a fellow servant, who also could not pay back what he
owed. One might expect that a man who had been overwhelmingly
forgiven such a massive debt of his own would be so grateful that he
would want to pass on the blessing and forgive his own debtor in the
same way. But this does not prove to be the case. We are told that
the man who had been forgiven the great debt grabbed his own debtor
and began to choke him, demanding his money back. He then had the
man thrown into prison until he could repay all he owed.

However, this is not the end of the story. Word of this servant's
incredible ingratitude got back to the king who had so freely forgiven
him. He said, " 'I canceled all that debt of yours because you begged
me to. Shouldn't you have had mercy on your fellow servant just
as I had on you?' In anger his master turned him over to the jailers
to be tortured, until he should pay back all he owed" (Matthew
18:32–34).

Like it or not, the bottom line of this parable is as follows: "This is
how my heavenly Father will treat each of you unless you forgive your
brother from your heart" (Matthew 18:35).

First, we need to clear up what this parable is *not* teaching, because
some have misinterpreted it. Jesus is not teaching us that we will lose
our salvation if we do not forgive. If it meant that, then everybody
would have lost their salvation a long time ago. The reason we know

that we do not lose our salvation due to unforgiveness is because the Bible makes it clear that we are saved by *grace alone,* not by works. Neither does this parable show that we *keep* our salvation by forgiving. Why? Because again, this would suggest that salvation was achieved in some way by our own works (see Ephesians 2:8–9; Romans 11:6).

Even though that is the case, I can tell you that there is no greater "work" than totally forgiving others. The nearest you get to a work that is pure in God's eyes is when you totally, unconditionally forgive another person. Jesus Himself confirmed this:

> Bless those who curse you, pray for those who mistreat you.... If you love those who love you, what credit is that to you? ... Love your enemies, do good to them, and lend to them without expecting to get anything back. Then your reward will be great, and you will be sons of the Most High.
>
> Luke 6:28, 32, 35

If you do this, Jesus said, then your reward will be great. People often ask me, how do you know that you can expect a reward in heaven? This is one of the few places in the Bible where you can examine the facts for yourself. If you observe the conditions laid down in this verse, then you can certainly expect to receive a reward.

I believe that the greater the hurt you have to forgive, the greater the anointing will be on your life here on earth, and ultimately, the greater the reward you will receive in heaven. At the moment, you may not appreciate the need to forgive or its eternal implications. Perhaps you have been wounded and the hurt is still very immediate. Perhaps you have to forgive an infidelity or something someone did to your children. Perhaps you have to forgive a parent for an unthinkable thing they did to you. Maybe you've been walked over, lied about, lost your job or didn't get what you were promised. Those things hurt. When you are in the middle of it, you cannot appreciate that forgiveness is a blessing in disguise. But just as you cannot out-give the Lord when it comes to finances (and you can't, by the way), you cannot outdo the Lord when you forgive. He notices. He knows the things we have to do, and He will bless us in ways we can't imagine when we forgive unconditionally.

As well as the promise of a great reward for those who forgive, there is also a stern warning for those who don't forgive. It doesn't mean that we will lose our salvation or that we won't get a second chance to forgive, but this parable does provide a clear model for how we should behave. It reveals much about God's nature and how He feels about unforgiveness.

We Are Forgiven

First, Jesus used this parable to underline for us the fact that we have been forgiven an incalculable debt. In His parable He stated that "a man who owed [the king] ten thousand talents was brought to him" (Matthew 18:24). Ten thousand talents was a huge amount of money at that time. Then we read, "Since he was not able to pay, the master ordered that he and his wife and his children and all that he had be sold to repay the debt" (Matthew 18:25).

Well, that's the way they did things in ancient times. Since clearly the debt would never be paid, neither would these people ever have their lives back. The servant was now going to lose his wife, his children and all his possessions. Since he had reached rock bottom, the servant embarked on the only course of action left open to him. He fell on his knees and begged his master for mercy.

At this point, the king took pity on the servant and did exercise mercy. Jesus was showing us that God is rich in mercy. He is so merciful that He is even prepared to forgive a debt of incalculable proportions. We will not know until we get to heaven just how awful sin is and how deeply offensive it is to God. Each time we look at ourselves, just like peeling back the layers of an onion, we see more that's not right and confess it to the Father, asking to be forgiven. But when we get to heaven, we will begin to understand how vast our debt really was. God knows what He has done in each one of us. He knows exactly what He has had to forgive of all of us. It is an immeasurable debt, yet He has just wiped it clean.

We Must Be Merciful

Jesus clearly taught that, just as God is rich in mercy toward us, we need to show mercy to others (see Luke 6:36). Our human tendency is to think that we have not needed forgiveness for much but that what others have done to us is awful. The Bible puts this into perspective. Whatever "they" have done to you or me, it is nothing compared to what we have done to God. Therefore God expects us to show mercy just as He has shown mercy to us. It is inconceivable and unjust that we should demand that others "pay" when God has let us off the hook. So when you, having been forgiven, go to another person and start pointing the finger—forget it! Whereas love keeps no record of wrongs (see 1 Corinthians 13:5), you *are* keeping a record and calling attention to a misdeed while God has let *you* off the hook. He doesn't like it when we behave in such a manner.

God Hates Ingratitude

The unmerciful servant was an ungrateful man. He didn't appreciate what the king had done for him; otherwise he would have behaved very differently toward his fellow servant. God knows about all that we have done, and all things are laid bare before Him. Because we, too, know all that we have done in our disobedience toward God and how we have wounded others, we should be incredibly grateful that God is prepared to wipe the slate clean. Would you be willing for all there is to know about you to be flashed on a movie screen for everyone to see? Are you so proud of your life that you could say, "I don't care what people know"? The truth is that we would never want a soul to know the whole truth about our misdeeds, if we could help it. Never! Yet God knows both our open sins and our secret sins, and He is prepared to forgive them. This should produce in us a very grateful heart.

Ingratitude forgets, while gratitude remembers to say thank you. At the Lord's Supper, Jesus said, "Do this in remembrance of me" (Luke 22:19). So we should pause to be thankful when we hold the cup in our hands and see the fruit of the vine that symbolizes His precious blood. Through that cup, God says, "You are okay—My blood has made you that way." Choose to remember; choose to be thankful.

The forgiven servant chose to forget. "But when that servant went out, he found one of his fellow servants who owed him a hundred denarii. He grabbed him and began to choke him. 'Pay back what you owe me!' he demanded" (Matthew 18:28).

God Holds Us Accountable

God will hold us to account when we do not forgive. He doesn't cancel our salvation, but He does, nevertheless, deal with us. I could write a personal testimony at this point, but I won't, because I would have to tell you too much about myself that I wouldn't want you to know! A lot of people say that I am open and transparent, but I am not! I can tell you, however, that I have learned that Jesus meant it when He said, "Do not judge, or you too will be judged. For in the same way you judge others, you will be judged, and with the measure you use, it will be measured to you" (Matthew 7:1–2).

If you judge someone else, it doesn't mean you are going to lose your salvation, but it does mean that with "the measure you use, it will be measured to you"—God will deal with us the same way we have dealt with others. The list concerning how God could deal with us when we won't forgive is endless. It could be more, and often is, than the loss of our anointing. It could be more, and often is, than the loss of our fellowship with Him. God has a way of sending a clear signal to those who have been so graciously forgiven and then start pointing the finger at others. God says, "I can't believe you are doing that!" If God doesn't deal with you over unforgiveness here on earth, then He certainly will at the judgment seat of Christ. "If you are not disciplined ... then you are illegitimate children and not true sons" (Hebrews 12:8).

The Lord chastens those whom He loves. If He doesn't chasten us, then we are not true children. If we are not children of God, then we are not saved, and God will just send us to hell. But if we are saved, we will be dealt with at the judgment seat of Christ.

Repeated Forgiveness

This parable is not just about forgiveness but *repeated* forgiveness. It is often necessary to forgive the same person for multiple offenses. To truly experience the Kingdom of heaven on earth means that we must live in a realm where we do not grieve the Holy Spirit. In order to not grieve the Spirit, we must have a clear conscience when it comes to the issue of forgiveness. The chief way we grieve the Holy Spirit is by not totally forgiving what others have done to us. We cultivate a bitter spirit if we remain angry and upset. We say, "How dare they do that to me—and they are getting away with it!" But God says, "Hang on a minute. Aren't you getting away with a lot yourself?"

Even though we may "forgive" others for offenses against us, sometimes we still hold a grudge. We refuse to release just a tiny bit of offense that says, "I can't trust them as I used to." In truth, we are still holding onto a fragment of unforgiveness, and this does not please God. The point of this parable is: We have to keep on forgiving and forgiving completely.

People will continue to do bad things. People are people. We hurt others all the time ourselves and don't even know we have done it. It is not a case of my forgiving you for yesterday; I have also got to be prepared to do it today—and tomorrow. Forgiveness is a choice. We make a choice to forgive or not to forgive. God made a choice to forgive, and it will take eternity for us to unravel in our minds what it meant for Him to send His Son into the world to die on a cross. We will never understand it; we can only say, "Help me to understand it; help me to take it in...." God made a choice to forgive, and we who have been forgiven make a choice to forgive—or to punish; to forgive, which pleases God and ensures the Spirit isn't grieved, or to punish, which arouses God's anger.

The Occasion of the Parable

This parable arose from a question that was posed to Jesus by Peter: "'Lord, how many times shall I forgive my brother when he sins against me? Up to seven times?' Jesus answered, 'I tell you, not seven times, but seventy-seven times'" (Matthew 18:21–22).

Peter made an assumption here that he *should* forgive. He had been around Jesus long enough to know that this was at the heart of Jesus' teaching. But in ancient times, among the rabbis, there was a consensus that a brother might be forgiven for a repeated sin three times, but not four. Literally, if a person committed the same sin against you a fourth time, you didn't have to forgive him. That was the consensus. Perhaps Peter thought that he was going to score some points with Jesus by magnanimously suggesting that a person could be forgiven up to seven times. But then Jesus responded by saying, "Not seven times, but seventy-seven times."

It is hard to know if the Greek is saying "seventy-seven" or "seventy times seven," which would be four hundred ninety. In reality it makes little difference which is correct. Jesus' point was that forgiveness should not be measured in that way. When He said "seventy-seven times," He meant, "There is no limit."

"True forgiveness," Jesus contended, "is unconditional, however great the offense."

Sometimes what you have to forgive is great. No one would deny that. What people do can be so awful that sometimes we think we are justified *not* to forgive. We get up a kind of "buddy-buddy" relationship with God where we think we are hearing Him say, "Most people would have to forgive that, but you and I know that what you have gone through is so horrendous that I will waive it in your case. It is OK for you to be bitter." And we say, "Thank You, Lord, I appreciate that. I knew that You were going to say that to me."

Forgiveness is unlimited, it is universal and it applies to all who have hurt us personally. It can change your life. Peter thought he was saying something really great. He wasn't prepared for what Jesus said in return.

The Way of Forgiveness

Let's examine the way of forgiveness as illustrated in this parable. Forgiveness is several things:

A Desire

"The kingdom of heaven is like a king who wanted to settle accounts with his servants" (Matthew 18:23).

The parable begins with a desire—the king wanted to settle accounts. He made a choice. Isn't it good that God wants to settle accounts with us? The moment Adam and Eve sinned in the Garden of Eden, God could have ceased His involvement and let the whole human race be born into sin, die and go on to hell. But He wanted to be involved with us—He chose to do it. It was His desire.

A Debt

"A man who owed him ten thousand talents was brought to him" (Matthew 18:24).

Don Carson says, "Jesus may simply be using hyperbole (an exaggeration) to make clear how much the heirs of the kingdom have really been forgiven." Whether He was or not, the truth is that our debt is astronomical. One of the great effects of encountering the glory of God is that you suddenly see your sin for what it is. I am all for laughter, joy and jumping up and down or falling on the floor, but if at the end of the day you don't see your sin, something is not right. The glory of God will eventually make you see your sin.

A Demand

"Since he was not able to pay, the master ordered that ... all that he had be sold to repay the debt" (Matthew 18:25).

In those days, you could do that. What the king demanded is what the law allowed. If a person could not pay, then they forfeited their entire lives. God gave the law to Moses at Mount Sinai, but no one has ever been able to fully keep it. Jesus announced that He would keep it, and He did. The law demands that we be punished, but Jesus fulfilled the demands of the law, and He paid for our shortcomings.

A Warrant

A warrant is the authority or authorization to forgive. It begins with a cry for mercy. "The servant fell on his knees before him. 'Be patient with me,' he begged, 'and I will pay back everything'" (Matthew 18:26).

That is exactly the way we are—we ask God for mercy. We say, "God, be merciful to me a sinner." But mercy can be given or withheld, and justice would be done in either case. So the king had to choose whether to be merciful or not. He didn't have to be merciful. Remember God once said to Moses, "I will have mercy on whom I will have mercy, and I will have compassion on whom I will have compassion" (Exodus 33:19).

That hasn't changed. Let us never forget it. The holiest and most godly, whoever he or she may be, when they come to the throne of grace will ask only for mercy. That means none of us have any bargaining power. You can't rush into the presence of God, snap your fingers and expect God to jump—you must ask for mercy.

The Continuity of Mercy

"The servant's master took pity on him, canceled the debt and let him go" (Matthew 18:27).

Jesus said on the cross, "It is finished." Those words are translated from the Greek phrase *tettalestii,* which was a colloquial expression in the ancient marketplace meaning "paid in full." The blood canceled the debt. The warrant to forgive has to do with the *continuity* of mercy. That means once you receive it, you are to pass it on. Can you imagine how the world would be changed if every person who was forgiven immediately began to forgive others, so that everyone who was saved forgave anyone who had ever grieved them? This is what God wants—He expects us to pass it on. We have been authorized; we have a warrant to forgive.

The Possibilities of Forgiveness

This parable shows the possibilities of forgiveness—and they are endless. Every one of us will have stories to tell. The greater the thing you have to forgive, the greater the opportunity for reward in heaven. There will be degrees of reward. You could, at this moment, be on the verge of "blowing it" because you think, *This is too much. I can't forgive—I am not going to do it.* But listen! Take it with both hands and just write it off. Pray that they never get caught. "But they are not dealt with," you say, "I can't do that." Fine—then your reward won't be great.

The Principles of Forgiveness

Forgiving means that you let the person completely off the hook. That means not telling anybody else what they did. It means not allowing them to be afraid. In other words, don't send them on a guilt trip. If you set out to make people feel guilty, then you haven't forgiven them. When God forgives us, He doesn't give us a spirit of fear but the Spirit of *Abba* Father—we can just crawl up onto His lap and love Him and be loved. He wants us to feel good. He doesn't say, "Oh, by the way, I guess you know what I have forgiven you for?"

When you have totally forgiven a person, also give them the opportunity to forgive themselves if possible. In other words, do nothing to contribute to their feelings of guilt—no pointing of the finger. Let them save face. Do you know what it is for God to let you save face? I do. He hasn't told other people the things I have done. He has let me save face. I don't deserve to have been a minister for all these years, but God has let me save face. He is good. Has He let you save face? That is the way God is. Do you know He protects us from our deepest secrets? We have all got skeletons in the cupboard. It is always tempting to yank someone's skeleton out and say to others, "Well, I'll tell you what I know about them!" God doesn't do that.

Most of the time the people who have hurt you shouldn't even have a clue that you have forgiven them because it happens in the heart. Then you pray for them. When you pray for them, you don't just pray, *Lord, I commit them to You.* And you do *not* pray, *Lord, deal with them.* You don't wait for the phone to ring with news that so-and-so has had an accident and will be paralyzed for life, and then say, "Oh, praise the Lord; God did that for me."

What if God decided to deal with *you?* I believe that one of the main reasons people lose their healing is that they become bitter. There is a close connection between healing and forgiveness. Bitterness could be the thing that blocks your healing. It doesn't mean that all who need to be healed are bitter. I am not saying that, but in many cases that is the situation.

The Purpose of Forgiveness

The purpose of forgiveness is twofold. First, it is to show graciousness because God has been gracious to us. Second, it is to show gratitude—that you remember what God has done for you. The next time a person hurts you, instead of sending them on a guilt trip, just remember that God doesn't do that to you. The next time you start to say, "I am going to tell everyone what I know about you," remember that God doesn't tell other people what He knows about you. The next time you want them to squirm and to be embarrassed, remember that God has let *you* save face.

We have all failed in the matter of total forgiveness. You may not have realized it, but this parable describes every single one of us. But we can change. You may say, "I have blown it. I have been so bitter; I have been so angry. I haven't been very forgiving, and I have said all these terrible things." All you need to say is, "Lord, thank You for this parable. I am sorry for what I have said and done. Lord, You told Peter that he should forgive 77 times, and so, Lord, would You forgive me again? I am sorry."

Begin today.

Chapter 17

The Parable of the Good Samaritan

A man was going down from Jerusalem to Jericho, when he fell into
the hands of robbers.

Luke 10:30

The parable of the Good Samaritan is one of the most well-known and
popular parables in the Bible. It occurs in Luke, but it does not appear at
all in any of the other synoptic gospels. Luke's gospel seems to show a
particular interest in the underdog and the downtrodden. It may be
that, for this reason, Luke was keen to include it.

This parable highlights how interested Jesus was in looking after
the neglected. He wanted to come to the rescue of the very people
whom most others would despise. The unlikely hero of this story is a
Samaritan. The Samaritans were certainly unpopular with everyone,
but they were hated most of all by the Jews.

Envisage for a moment someone whom you don't particularly like.
Be honest enough to admit that there are one or two people you can
think of. It could be someone whose sexual orientation really offends
you. It could be a person whose way of going about things always rubs
you the wrong way. It could be someone who has hurt you or your
children. It may be someone whose theology is off center. Whoever it
is, you just don't like them. Generally speaking, if you were in some
kind of trouble, they would probably be the last person from whom
you would want to receive help—wouldn't they?

The ancient hostility between Jews and Samaritans went back over
eight hundred years. Sometimes this happens with nations. The French
and the English have never gotten along well, and much hostility has
passed between them. The Indians and the Pakistanis have always been
at odds with one another. Similarly, Jews and Samaritans did not mix.

Back in 2 Kings 17:24–41, we read the story of Hoshea, the last king
of Israel. Hoshea was the "straw that broke the camel's back" in his
unfaithfulness to God. The Assyrians were able to take over Samaria

because the Israelites had sinned against the Lord. Then we read that "the king of Assyria brought people from Babylon [and other places] and settled them in the towns of Samaria to replace the Israelites" (2 Kings 17:24).

The land of Samaria was just north of Jerusalem and south of Galilee. It is not difficult to see why the Samaritans were hated by the Jews. They were made up partly of the ten tribes of Israel and partly of the descendants of the people who had settled in Palestine from Assyria. They had intermarried, and so the Jews considered them to be semiforeign and semipagan, although in reality the Samaritans were probably more Jewish than anything else. Naturally, there were clashes between the Samaritans and the Jews over the years. Luke prepared the way, in a sense, for this parable because he recorded that Jesus and His disciples went through a Samaritan village where the people wouldn't welcome them (Luke 9:51–56). James and John asked, "Lord, do you want us to call fire down from heaven to destroy them?" (Luke 9:54). But Jesus rebuked them, and they continued on to another village. Remember also how shocked the disciples were in John 4 when they found Jesus talking to a Samaritan woman? Certainly the stage was set for the parable of the Good Samaritan.

Two Questions

Jesus gave this parable in response to two questions from a teacher of the law: " 'Teacher,' he asked, 'what must I do to inherit eternal life?' " (Luke 10:25).

In response to this first question, Jesus basically said, "You should know; you're the expert" (Luke 10:26). Here was a teacher of the law— not a solicitor or barrister who dealt in the Mosaic Law but one who knew the religious, moral law. This man wasn't looking for information; he was trying to test Jesus. In response to Jesus' answer, he quoted from two Old Testament passages: "Love the Lord your God with all your heart and with all your soul and with all your strength" (Deuteronomy 6:5). And, "Love your neighbor as yourself" (Leviticus 19:18).

Jesus, as always, upheld the law and said in response, "You have answered correctly . . . Do this and you will live" (Luke 10:28).

Maybe the man didn't like the idea of this being turned around and focused on him. It seems so, because he squirmed and looked for a loophole: "And who is my neighbor?" (Luke 10:29).

I am sure that he didn't really want to know who his neighbor was! Many times people will ask questions, but they don't really want to know the answers. People will often ask a question when, truthfully, they just want to make a point. People did this to Jesus often. Despite that, however, Jesus took the opportunity to teach some important principles about godliness and responded with the parable of the Good Samaritan. As we continue on to examine Jesus' teaching, keep in mind that this parable was an answer to the man's question, "Who is my neighbor?"

The Priest and the Levite

Jesus told of an ordinary Jew who was traveling from Jerusalem to Jericho. It was a journey of around twenty miles, a journey with a steep descent into Jericho from Jerusalem, which is about two thousand five hundred feet above sea level. It was a treacherous journey then, and still is not an easy journey today, even with a fairly good road. You still see Bedouins all over the area, and you wouldn't want to travel that way alone. It is a dangerous part of Israel, and Jesus' story was a plausible one.

When we read Luke 10:30–35, we see how even the clergymen of the area avoided a fellow Jew in distress. The man had fallen among thieves and was in trouble. They had taken his money, beaten him and left him for dead. Not long after that, some other people passed by: first a priest and then a Levite. The priests, responsible for the worship and sacrifices at the Temple, were among the most prestigious people of the time; they were the ones who upheld the law. The Levites assisted the priests in all the Temple duties, including providing music and maintaining the security of the building; so they too were well aware of the requirements of God's law. Both of these people witnessed what had happened, but they act as if they have not. Despite recognizing the plight of the Jew, both the priest and the Levite pass by on the other side of the road.

You sometimes find people like this in the ministry today. They are more interested in liturgy than in people, more interested in "the ministry" itself than in actually helping people. They love the prestige, but they don't want to get their hands dirty. Many who aspire to go into the ministry today see a bit of glamour and maybe some prestige in the public profile, but they don't realize that to be a minister you have to be a real person.

I remember someone who came to see me because he felt called to preach. Immediately I doubted it, but I asked him why he thought this was the case. He said, "I just know that I am." I said, "Well, come out as part of one of our evangelistic teams, because that is a good place to test

your calling. Let's see if you can talk to people about the Gospel."
"Oh," he said, "I could preach to thousands, but not to just one or
two." I responded, "Well, Jesus said that he that is faithful in that
which is least, is faithful also in much" (Matthew 25:21). That man
never came back to me again.

The clergymen in Jesus' parable didn't want to have anything to do
with the person who was in real trouble and hurting. Then a Samaritan
turned up and did what the priest and the Levite would not.

Why Is This Parable Important?

What can we learn from Jesus' teaching in this parable? First, He
showed how surprising people can come from out of the blue to do
what God's people should be doing. People whom we think are bad can
actually be very, very good. People whom we think are very good can
be very, very bad. The "bad guy" should have been the Samaritan,
because he was the one the Jews hated at the time. Here was a character
who had probably turned away from the God of Israel and intermarried
with the Assyrians. But he turned out to be the "good guy." The good
guys should have been the priest and the Levite, but they were not so
good. Isn't it just like Jesus to tell this parable? It is a typical upside-
down story told to reveal the hypocrisy of the day.

Second, the parable is about pride and prejudice. People were
prejudiced against the Samaritans. This refers to social prejudice, racial
prejudice, sexual prejudice, cultural prejudice and theological prejudice, all of which are still relevant today. And the pride? People don't
want to give glory to someone who doesn't take their party line. We
don't want someone to be a good example who has never been a hero
in our minds. It goes against our thinking. We all have our heroes, and
we want to see them do better and better. There are even those who
won't accept help unless it comes from someone they respect. It's a bit
like saying, "If I ever get saved, I want to be prayed for by Billy Graham,
not some evangelist on the street!"

However, we should be willing to receive and learn from anybody.
I am amazed when I read Romans 1:14–15, where Paul wrote that he
was a debtor to the "wise and the unwise"—that he was obligated to
them, bound to them. Over the years I have had to admit that I could
learn from people that maybe I wouldn't have invited to preach at
Westminster Chapel.

A number of years ago, we were in the Florida Keys on vacation, and
Hurricane Andrew came through. We were without electricity for three

days, so we just sat and talked. I couldn't fish; we couldn't do anything. My friend and I were just sitting there reading together. My friend read to me from a particular book, and I said, "That's good; read that again." He read it again, and then I asked, "Who said that?" When he told me whom the quote was from, I thought, *Oh my goodness, I can't believe he could say anything that good!* I realized then that my heart had been wrong. I hadn't wanted to learn anything from this particular person, because at one time the man had spoken out against me, and I knew that. In fact I was upset that my friend was even reading a book by him—although he did not know that I had been hurt by him. When I didn't know who the author was, I thought it was a good comment. But when I found out who it was, suddenly I didn't like it. This attitude was wrong.

Are you willing to accept "help" from anybody? This Jew was half dead and couldn't even speak. If he had had a choice, he might have said, "*You* are not going to help me. I would rather die than have you help me." Are you like that?

Third, the parable shows that your "neighbors" may not be the people you hoped they would be. When I was growing up in Ashland, Kentucky, I used to think that my "neighbor" was the one who lived next door to me, or maybe across the street. When you think of a neighborhood, you think of the cluster of houses right next to you. But you see, most neighborhoods are made up of the same kinds of people, and you can adjust to them, especially when it comes to loving your neighbor as yourself. But this parable widens that concept—it widens the scope and definition of the word *neighbor.* Jesus defined our neighbor as one whom we hoped would never qualify for the title because, just maybe, that person could make a contribution to help us!

This is also an important parable because its interpretation has an intentional ambiguity—that means that Jesus gave it a double meaning on purpose. Having told the story, Jesus said to this teacher of the law—this expert who didn't really want the answer, " 'Which of these three [the priest, the Levite or the Samaritan] do you think was a neighbor to the man who fell into the hands of robbers?' The expert in the law replied, 'The one who had mercy on him.' Jesus told him, 'Go and do likewise' " (Luke 10:36–37).

Now this statement has fascinated Bible scholars, because it is hard to say exactly who Jesus was saying we should be like. The "neighbor" was the Samaritan. Notice that the teacher of the law couldn't even bring himself to say the word *Samaritan!* Instead he said, "The one who had mercy on him." That shows the depth of his hostility. The intentional ambiguity is that Jesus wants us first of all to be *like* the Samaritan in our actions, but He also wants us to *love* the Samaritan. We should learn from him, *and* we should love him. Jesus says to us that the "Samaritan" is our neighbor, and we have to love our neighbor.

An Old Interpretation

Let's look more closely at the interpretation of this parable. You might find it a bit amusing to know the way in which the early Church interpreted it. One method of understanding the Bible is through *allegory*. In the early Church, starting with Origen (c. 185–254 A.D.) through to St. Augustine (354–430 A.D.), most biblical interpretation was by allegory. This is how they interpreted the parable of the Good Samaritan.

First, they reasoned that the man in the parable who fell among thieves was Adam, because Adam fell. He fell in the Garden of Eden just as this man fell among thieves. Jerusalem, because of its altitude level, represented heaven. Jericho was the world—the man went "down" into Jericho. The robbers were the powers of darkness. The priest represented the law. The Levites represented the prophets. The Good Samaritan was Jesus. The wine, because we read that the Samaritan treated the man's wounds by pouring oil and wine on them in Luke 10:34, referred to the blood of Christ, and the oil was the Holy Spirit. The Samaritan brought the man to an inn, which referred to the Church. The Samaritan said to the innkeeper, "Look after him, and when I return, I will reimburse you" (Luke 10:35)—that supposedly referred to the second coming of Christ.

This may seem really quaint to us now, but that is what they preached in the early Church. Later, when the Reformation came with Luther and Calvin, not only did they turn the world upside down by their teaching of justification by faith alone, but they made the preaching of the Word central to the Church, and so the whole style of preaching changed. They rejected the allegorical interpretation of the Bible and said, "There is another way: apply it." I am of the tradition of Calvin, the Reformed tradition of understanding the way to interpret this parable. And I think it is the right way.

Practical Godliness

This parable is mostly about us, not about Jesus. When Jesus said, "Go and do likewise," He was saying those words to all of us. How should we interpret it? First of all, it is about *love* and not about the *law*. Those who live by the law, as the priest and the Levite did, can be very cold. There are exceptions to this of course. I am not saying categorically that this is the way people act who are strong on the law. But often this is the case. They love those two thousand verses of legislation, and they want to apply them somehow. Sometimes those who are the most legalistic have no heart. Often you find that those who are strong in the law have marriages that are shattered.

Let's set aside the law for a moment and think about those who can be very open to the Holy Spirit. They also can get really uptight if others are not open to the Spirit. What I want to know is, would they help a person who is on the side of the road with a flat tire? Would they give that person a lift in their car? Would they come to the rescue? Sometimes these believers are too spiritually minded to be of any earthly use.

I knew of a lady some years ago who had a habit of pointing the finger at other people and highlighting their deficiencies. Someone once suggested to her that, since she always passed right by a certain person's door on the way, she could give that person a ride to church. She went ballistic at the idea that she should have to stop and pick anyone up, showing an incredible lack of grace. In this parable Jesus gave a lesson in practical godliness that many of us need to hear. Jesus had a straightforward way of delivering a message that can make us feel very uncomfortable with ourselves. He said that it is all about *love* not *law*. It is about taking risks. Love takes risks.

What about the Samaritan? What was it he did? For one thing, he accepted an inconvenience, whereas the Levite and the priest avoided it and went by on the other side. The Samaritan went to where the man was. Listen to Paul's testimony in 1 Timothy: "May the Lord show mercy to the household of Onesiphorus, because he often refreshed me and was not ashamed of my chains. On the contrary, when he was in Rome, *he searched hard for me until he found me*" (2 Timothy 1:16–17, emphasis added).

Some of us make a halfhearted attempt to emulate godly concern like this. Had we been in this position, we may well have said, "Sorry, Paul, I did try to find you, but I couldn't track you down." But Onesiphorus *searched hard* until he found Paul.

The Samaritan accepted the inconvenience and showed pity. He went to where the Jew was and looked to see what he could do for him

(Luke 10:33). Listen to this and learn what it means: "I desire mercy, not sacrifice" (see Hosea 6:6; Matthew 9:13; Matthew 12:7).

The fact that Jesus quoted Hosea twice in the gospel of Matthew means that this is more than just an unguarded comment. He said, "If you had known what these words mean, 'I desire mercy, not sacrifice,' you would not have condemned the innocent" (Matthew 12:7).

This is what we see here in the parable—a man who showed mercy. He showed pity, and it cost him something. He went down, put the man on his own donkey, brought him to an inn and took care of him. It cost him money as well as time and inconvenience. He took out two silver coins and gave them to the innkeeper so the man could stay there for several days and recover. Some scholars say it was possibly for 24 days. What about the priest and the Levite—upstanding church members—those who were known to be godly? They were very cautious and calculating. Just like them, our rationale today often is, "We don't know how they are going to spend the money, so let's not give it to them."

We insist on being careful, so we sometimes say, as the teacher of the law did, "Who is my neighbor?" Jesus gives us the answer—and it makes us all so uncomfortable. The priest and the Levite were looking for a reason not to get involved. We look for anything that will excuse us and think, *Thank You, Lord, I don't have to do it after all.* We look for ways in which we can avoid responsibility. We act like we don't see the needs, and yet we still go to church, sing the hymns, love the sermon, go out and eat and go home and feel good.

It is easy to pray and not act. We had a sweet Welsh brother who used to come to our prayer meetings in the old days, and every week he would say, "Lord, send in thine elect." Quite so—send them in—but let's not forget to go out and get them! When Jesus said, "Go and do likewise," He meant that He wants us to learn from the Samaritan and do what he did. Perhaps, just as the Jew would have hated the Samaritan, you too can sometimes be selective because of prejudice. Maybe you wouldn't want to help, or be helped by, a person who had a different color skin than you. Maybe you would be offended if someone who was openly gay came to your assistance when you were in trouble. But Jesus said, "Be willing." It doesn't matter what someone's skin color, social status or sexual orientation is, we are often called to give help to or receive help from those with whom we least wish to be identified. Maybe God wants us to humble ourselves and affirm and love the disenfranchised of society. That sounds like Jesus to me.

Humility and Gratitude

The parable is not just about service; it is also about humility. Service means giving your time, your energy and your money. Humility, in this sense, is about graciousness, about accepting help from someone with whom you wouldn't normally associate. Whereas previously you wouldn't have wanted that person to help you, you are now willing to accept help from wherever it comes.

It is also about gratitude. As Paul said, "I am a debtor both to . . . wise and to unwise" (Romans 1:14, NKJV),

Gratitude is a key to the biblical doctrine of sanctification. The best way to understand sanctification is through gratitude. Sanctification is holy living, and the process by which we become more holy is gratitude. Your sanctification doesn't help you to get to heaven, in case you are wondering, but sanctification says, "Thank You, Lord, for saving my soul." So here, in your gratitude, you can learn from the Good Samaritan. You want to be like him who says, "God, look what You did for me—thank You!" You are going to love the person who wants to help you.

Jesus—The Good Samaritan

So "goodness" is the main intent of this parable. That is why we refer to the *Good* Samaritan. Remember how Peter put it in Acts when he was talking to the house of Cornelius? He said that Jesus "went around *doing good*" (Acts 10:38, emphasis added). Using the ancient allegorical method, Jesus is the *epitome* of the Good Samaritan.

The challenge for each of us is to affirm those whom Jesus wants us to help or whom Jesus wants to help us. Are you so proud as to say, "I can make it very well by myself"? God sent Jesus to die on a cross to do for you what you couldn't do for yourself. Never say, "I can get by on my own, thank you very much." You are saved by affirming the One who did for you what you couldn't do for yourself.

Learn from the Good Samaritan and love him, because Jesus makes it clear that he was the true neighbor—and this keeps us humble.

Chapter 18

The Parable of the Rich Fool

The ground of a certain rich man produced a good crop.
Luke 12:16

The parable of the rich fool is found in Luke 12:13–21. We read there that it was precipitated by someone in the crowd who asked Jesus to help him sort out his financial wrangle with his brother. He asked Jesus to make his brother share his inheritance with him! It was an unusual request. Jesus declined to get involved with the matter, saying, "Who appointed me to be the arbiter or judge between you two?" Following this comment, He turned to the crowd and issued a warning: "Be on your guard against all kinds of greed; a man's life does not consist in the abundance of his possessions" (Luke 12:15).

Jesus then went on to tell this parable. The story was about a rich man who had such a good crop harvest that his barns couldn't contain it. He thought to himself, *I'll tear those old barns down and build some new, bigger barns. I'll store all my grain there and have plenty to live off for years. I can take life easy now; eat, drink and be merry.* However, this was not to be. Jesus said that God rebuked the man, saying, "You fool! This very night your life will be demanded from you. Then who will get what you have prepared for yourself? This is how it will be with anyone who stores up things for himself but is not rich toward God" (Luke 12:20–21).

Why Is This Parable Important?

The first thing we should notice from these Scriptures occurred before the parable was told. Consider the man in the crowd who sought Jesus' help. Here we have a man who simply wanted to use Jesus' power to help him get his own way. It shows how people sometimes prefer to use God without having any interest in God Himself. That is, they have no interest in His Kingdom, honor or glory. They use God because they want to get something out of Him—a bit of advice perhaps, or some other kind of help. That is all the man in this parable wanted—he wanted Jesus to tell his brother what to do. This came directly after Jesus had said, "When you are brought before synagogues, rulers and authorities, do not worry about how you will defend yourselves or what you will say, for the Holy Spirit will teach you at that time what you should say" (Luke 12:11–12).

Wow, what a word! Imagine someone then saying, "Teacher, tell my brother to divide the inheritance with me" (Luke 12:13).

This man hadn't listened to a thing! All that was on his mind was, *I will get this man's advice.* I know what it is to preach my heart out, and then, when I think I have preached a powerful word, someone will come into the vestry and their first question will be, "I don't know whether to take this job or the other job, and so I am going to do what you tell me to do." They haven't listened to a word I've preached! Sometimes I have to say, "I am your pastor, not your solicitor."

In addition to illustrating how people often want to get something from God, this parable answers the question, "Of what does life consist?" The answer, in case you wondered, is that this life is a preparation for the life to come. We should spend every minute of every day thinking of the life to come, for we can take nothing with us when we die. "Naked I came from my mother's womb, and naked I will depart" (Job 1:21). Or as Paul put it to Timothy, "We brought nothing into the world, and we can take nothing out of it" (1 Timothy 6:7).

The parable also shows the danger of financial blessing. Often when we receive a material blessing, we tend to want even more. Jesus depicted such a man here. He was blessed by a massive harvest and immediately he thought, "This is what I'll do. I will tear down my barns and build bigger ones, and there I will store all my grain and my goods" (Luke 12:18). That is the danger of financial blessing.

We also learn here about the danger of presumption, because this rich fool said to himself, "I have many years left, I am going to take life easy—eat, drink and be merry" (Luke 12:19). The presumption was that he had plenty of time left.

Jesus also was teaching the importance of being rich toward God: "This is how it will be with anyone who stores up things for himself but is not rich toward God" (Luke 12:21).

Has it crossed your mind that you need to be rich toward God? There is a great deal of uncertainty about life and death. None of us knows how much time we have. One day we will die, and after death there will be a judgment. That is why this life is a preparation for the life to come. The only question is, where will you be a hundred years from now? Will you be glad that you did what you did a hundred years before?

Finally, this parable is important because it gives us the description of a fool, and we can learn from this model—we can learn how not to think and behave in order to avoid being a fool.

Family Division

There are a number of things I want us to learn from this parable. The first issue it raises is that of division in the family. Luke 12:13 shows that there was a family quarrel taking place between two brothers. Nearly all of us know what it is like to be involved in a family squabble. Many, if not most, family quarrels have to do with money.

Many years ago, while driving from Florida back to Ashland, Kentucky, my own family (my grandmother, aunts and uncles and my dad) had the biggest family quarrel I have ever heard in my life. It had to do with their inheritance. I couldn't believe it. It is amazing how people think they are not attached to money until they discover that someone might be dying. Then they wonder what's in the will!

Graham Lacey used to tell about the wealthy man who died. His executor called everybody into the solicitor's office, and the will was read. "First, to my brother John I give all of my stocks and bonds. To my sister Mary I give all my property. To my other sister, Helen, I give all my cash in all my banks. And to my brother Harold, who always said I wouldn't mention him in my will—hello, Harold!"

A Request

The incident that occasioned this parable began with a request: "Tell my brother to divide the inheritance with me" (Luke 12:13).

Here is a person who was manipulating Jesus without any interest in what really mattered. Does Jesus' response surprise you? "Man, who appointed me a judge or an arbiter between you?" (Luke 12:14).

Why did Jesus refuse to answer the man's question? The Jews thought that the Messiah's Kingdom was an earthly kingdom, and Jesus wanted to be careful not to further this error. If He had gotten involved with this dispute, it would have opened the way for many more. Word would have spread: "Oh, if you want good legal advice, here is our earthly Messiah. He will give you wisdom." Jesus wasn't going to go down that road.

A Rebuke

It is true that if we acknowledge God in all our ways, He will direct our paths (Proverbs 3:6). We all know what it is to ask God for wisdom in the details of our lives, and the Lord is happy to give that wisdom—on one condition: that He is already first. "Seek first his kingdom and his righteousness, and all these things will be given to you as well" (Matthew 6:33).

Those who are gripped only by "things" don't qualify to bring God into their lives on the details. We need wisdom to know what God would have us do in life. I have known people who have prayed and fasted about the lottery, asking God to give them just the right numbers. I know of one person who was given a "word of knowledge" that he was going to win it. He is still waiting. Perceiving this attitude, Jesus issued a rebuke: "Watch out! Be on your guard against all kinds of greed; a man's life does not consist in the abundance of his possessions" (Luke 12:15).

This parable shows the subtlety of the love of money. As the apostle Paul said: "For the love of money is a root of all kinds of evil. Some people, eager for money, have wandered from the faith and pierced themselves with many griefs" (1 Timothy 6:10).

Be careful that you are not in a state of grief because of money. The love of money is very subtle.

Richness Toward God

Jesus gave this parable to show what it will be like for anyone who lays up treasures for himself and is not rich toward God (Luke 12:21). The apostle Paul tells us how to be rich toward God: "Command those who are rich in this present world not to be arrogant nor to put their hope in wealth, which is so uncertain, but to put their hope in God, who richly provides us with everything for our enjoyment" (1 Timothy 6:17).

Here's how to be rich toward God.

- Don't be arrogant.
- Don't trust in money.
- Enjoy life without being selfish.
- Be rich in good works.
- Be generous.

"In this way they will lay up treasure for themselves as a firm foundation for the coming age, so that they may take hold of the life that is truly life" (1 Timothy 6:19).

Divine Favor

"The ground of a certain rich man produced a good crop" (Luke 12:16).

This man was the beneficiary of common grace. This is a phrase we use often, perhaps without knowing what it means. Common grace is what God does for you even if you are not a Christian. Your mind, your intelligence, your job, the good things in life, the fact that we have a fire brigade, a police service, hospitals and so forth—these are all God's provision in the realm of common grace. This is divine favor. If there is financial blessing, God has given it. It doesn't mean that you are worthy of it, even if you have worked hard. Others have worked just as hard as you but don't necessarily have what you have. You may say, "Ah, it is because I am clever." But there are other people just as clever as you, and they don't have what you have. "Every good and perfect gift is from above, coming down from the Father of the heavenly lights, who does not change like shifting shadows" (James 1:17).

God is not against people having money. Some people can be trusted with it. If you are a Christian and can be trusted with wealth, you are unusual. Most of us cannot be trusted with much, because although we say we can be good stewards of it, God knows us better than we know ourselves. Has God blessed you? Are you rich toward God? It could be that you have it both ways. The proof that God has blessed you in this sense may be a good income, good health and general happiness. The proof that you are rich toward God is found in the points that Paul listed in 1 Timothy 6:17. I could also add a couple of things.

Tithing

Do you tithe? To my mind, tithing is the fairest scheme in the world. A rich man pays the same amount for a pound of minced beef as a poor man. A rich man pays the same amount for his newspaper as a poor man. But tithing is a percentage—10 percent. When you get to heaven, you may have many regrets over how you used your money, but you will not regret anything you gave to God.

I was named after a man called R. T. Williams. He had a friend who was a businessman and who had made a million dollars. The man had given one hundred thousand dollars to the church and had receipts to show it. This was back in the 1920s when a million dollars was a lot of money! Eventually, however, the man went bankrupt—he lost it all. Members of his family said, "Don't you wish now that you hadn't given any to the church?" "Oh no, you have got that wrong," he said. "That is the only thing I kept." That is being rich toward God.

The Priority of Your Time

How much time do you spend with God? How much do you pray? How much do you read your Bible? If you don't know your Bible, it is because you don't read it. You should read at least a chapter a day. If you read four chapters a day, you will get through the whole Bible in a year. Spend time with God, and spend time with your family. You won't get those years back. When you get to heaven, the proof that you were rich toward God will be that you had your priorities right on earth.

A Distorted Focus

The rich man thought to himself:

> "What shall I do? I have no place to store my crops." Then he said, "This is what I'll do. I will tear down my barns and build bigger ones, and there I will store all my grain and all my goods. And I'll say to myself, 'You have plenty of good things laid up for many years. Take life easy; eat, drink and be merry.'"
>
> Luke 12:17–19

The man had a completely distorted focus. He could have turned to God and said, "Lord, You have blessed me enormously. What shall I do with this abundant harvest? What would You have me do with all this extra grain?" But the man did not look to God. His focus was entirely self-centered.

His Thoughts

Notice how the verse reads: "He thought *to himself,* 'What shall *I do?*'" (emphasis added). We read in Proverbs that "for as he thinks in his heart, so is he" (Proverbs 23:7, NKJV). And the psalmist confirms, "In his pride the wicked does not seek him; in all his thoughts there is no room for God" (Psalm 10:4). "The LORD knows the thoughts of man; he knows that they are futile" (Psalm 94:11).

The man looked only to his own desires. He didn't thank God for blessing him with an abundant harvest in the first place, and he had no thought of God afterward.

His Tactics

The man made plans to tear down his barns and build bigger ones in which he could store all his extra grain and his goods (Luke 12:18). But listen to this: "Many are the plans in a man's heart, but it is the LORD's purpose that prevails" (Proverbs 19:21). "There is no wisdom, no insight, no plan that can succeed against the LORD" (Proverbs 21:30).

God said to him, "You fool! This very night your life will be demanded from you. Then who will get what you have prepared for yourself?" (Luke 12:20).

The person who says, "I have many things; I will store up all my goods," has only one treasure—it is his earthly treasure. Jesus said, "Where your treasure is, there your heart will be also" (Matthew 6:21).

The Tragedy

His focus was so distorted. He thought he would have "plenty of good things laid up for many years" (Luke 12:19).

He thought his life expectancy was "many years." Maybe that is the way you feel. Listen to what James says:

> Now listen, you who say, "Today or tomorrow we will go to this or that city, spend a year there, carry on business and make money." Why, you do not even know what will happen tomorrow. What is your life? You are a mist that appears for a little while and then vanishes. Instead, you ought to say, "If it is the Lord's will, we will live and do this or that." As it is, you boast and brag. All such boasting is evil.
>
> James 4:13–16

Perhaps you have taken for granted that you have many years to live. Maybe you think, *Well, I am young.* I recall an incident that happened when I was a boy. I used to have a job delivering newspapers. One day at the end of my paper route, I arrived home, and my mother came rushing out to meet me. "Have you heard about Patsy?" she asked. I replied, "No." She said, "Oh, it's awful; she has just been killed." Patsy was a sixteen-year-old girl. Only the day before, during a church service, the visiting preacher had said, "I cannot dismiss the service this morning, because I believe there is someone here whom God is calling to Himself. I believe that this is the last call that this person will ever receive." It was a very dangerous thing to say, but he was an eighty-year-old man and had accumulated a lot of godly wisdom. When he spoke these words, Patsy had scoffed openly. My mother had watched her during the service and said, "I watched her chewing her gum and laughing. Eventually she left the building and was angry." It was the morning service, and she didn't come back for the evening service. The next day while she was out walking, a car careened onto the sidewalk and killed her, just like that. I never will forget it. To those who think they have a long time to live, God says, "You fool!" "For what profit is it to a man if he gains the whole world, and loses his own soul?" (Matthew 16:26, NKJV).

The tragedy in Jesus' parable is that God said, "This *very night...*" (Luke 12:20, emphasis added). In all his thoughts and calculations regarding his "plenty of years," the man had forgotten that there is "a time to be born and a time to die" (Ecclesiastes 3:2).

Furthermore, God said, "Then who will get what you have prepared for yourself?" (Luke 12:20).

Consider also the following:

> I hated all the things I had toiled for under the sun, because I must leave them to the one who comes after me. And who knows whether he will be a wise man or a fool? Yet he will have control over all the work into which I have poured my effort and skill under the sun.
>
> Ecclesiastes 2:18–19

We come into this world naked, and naked we will leave it (Job 1:21). What does it profit us if we gain the whole world and yet lose our own souls (Matthew 16:26)? What really matters to you at the end of the day?

God's Prerogative

It is God's privilege to call somebody a fool. Only He has the prerogative to do so. You may recall that in the Sermon on the Mount, Jesus warned the people against calling anyone a fool: "But anyone who says, 'You fool!' will be in danger of the fire of hell" (Matthew 5:22).

God, however, can do this because He knows all things. We may call someone a fool, but we never know all the facts. Usually when we say, "You fool," it is because we are angry, and having lost our temper, we want to make the person feel second rate. When God used this phrase in Jesus' parable, He was speaking to a person who should have known better. He was saying, "You did not have your priorities right." It is God's prerogative, just as it is His prerogative to give life and take it away.

Like it or not, God knows how long we will live. We can try jogging, eating health foods or taking vitamins, but at the end of the day, our days are numbered. God knows; it is His prerogative to know. Jonathan Edwards resolved to live every day as if that day would be the day of the second coming of Jesus; we should live this way also.

God's Provision

The rich fool thought that God's provisions were his own. They were not. God gives to whom He chooses. Notice how the man put it: "I will tear down *my* barns.... I will store all *my* grain and *my* goods" (Luke 12:18, emphasis added).

The resources we have actually belong to God. That is why I earlier emphasized the importance of tithing. God in His grace only lays claim to a tenth of all that He allows us to have. If you use the other ninety percent in a way that you know will please Him, then you are laying up treasures in heaven and being rich toward God.

The Fool

Luke 12:18–20 gives us a clear description of what a fool looks like. There are four main points in the passage about the fool.

He Forgot the Giver

First, in thinking about the gift, the man in this parable forgot the Giver. He thought to himself all about what he would do, and he forgot about God. The trouble was not that he had things; the trouble was that the things had him. We should constantly be reevaluating our priorities with regard to our possessions. Our priorities can often be seen reflected in our church life. For example, why is it that twenty percent of the people do eighty percent of the work? Are you are in that twenty percent or not? Does it bother you? How much time do you give to God? Assess your priorities.

He Forgot the Helper

The fool forgot that he didn't achieve everything he had by himself. It is a terrible thing when people forget those who have really helped them.

He Forgot His Own Soul

While thinking of his body, he forgot his soul: " 'And I'll say to myself, "You have plenty of good things laid up for many years. Take life easy; eat, drink and be merry.' " But God said to him, 'You fool! This very night your life will be demanded from you. Then who will get what you have prepared for yourself?' " (Luke 12:19–20).

The fool had only made provision for his physical needs. A satisfied stomach is not necessarily a satisfied spirit. As St. Augustine put it, "Thou hast made us for Thyself, our souls are restless until they find their rest in Thee."

Once a man said to his friend, "I hear that George died. How much did he leave?" His friend replied, "Everything!"

He Forgot the Next Life

Lastly, while thinking of this life, the fool forgot the next. John Wesley's famous retort to his critics, those who laughed at the early Methodists, was, "Our people die well." Do you know for certain, if you were to stand before God today, that you would go to heaven? If you stood before God, and you will, and He were to say to you, and He might, "Why should I let you into My heaven?", what would you say? What are your priorities? Where is your life going?

A Demonstrable Forecast

This parable ends in a prophecy from Jesus. He said, "This is how it will be with anyone who stores up things for himself but is not rich toward God" (Luke 12:21).

Jesus was saying that this is how it will be with anyone who thinks about himself and forgets the Giver: anyone who, while thinking of himself, forgets others; anyone who, while thinking of his body, forgets his soul; anyone who, while thinking of this life, forgets the next. Do not think that this rich fool couldn't be you. "The heart is deceitful above all things and beyond cure. Who can understand it?" (Jeremiah 17:9).

We think we are detached from temporal things, until the crunch comes; then we realize the grip they have on us. This is the way it will be with everyone.

Do you need to hear this word? Do you feel trapped right now as you are reading? Do you think, *You don't need to talk to me like that?* Perhaps God is doing you a favor. How would you feel if God said, "You fool, this is your day"? No further warning, just—"This is your day."

If God has succeeded in getting your attention, then thank Him. It could be that somewhere down the road, you will wish you could roll the clock back to this moment. God does not give us warnings to make us feel bad over our failures. We all have our regrets. It is what we do from this point on that counts. God doesn't give such a warning to make you feel bad. Rather He says there is a better way to live—it is to know that you are being rich toward Him.

Chapter 19

The Parable of "Just Waiting"

Be dressed ready for service and keep your lamps burning.

Luke 12:35

You also must be ready, because the Son of Man will come at an hour when you do not expect him.

Luke 12:40

Luke 12:35–48 contains two parables. Scholars have often referred to them as "the waiting parables" because they are concerned with issues of waiting for the Lord in some respect. They urge us to remain in a state of preparedness because Jesus might return at any time. That is the main thrust of the parables here, although I believe there are five possible applications.

The Second Coming

The primary meaning of these parables almost certainly is the second coming of Jesus. In Matthew 24 we see almost an exact repeat of the first parable given here in Luke 12, and in Matthew 24:45–51 there is the overlapping of the second parable from Luke 12:39–48. The parables in Matthew 24 clearly confirm the context of the second coming of Jesus.

Waiting for the Lord to Turn Up

However, if you read only Luke's account of Jesus' teaching, not knowing about the parables in Matthew's gospel, you wouldn't necessarily apply it to the Second Coming. It may therefore be possible that Jesus was not specifically referring to His second coming when He told these parables in Luke 12. He could have been speaking of the times in our lives when we are simply waiting for the Lord to "turn up." This fits perfectly with the covenant prayer we made at Westminster Chapel some years ago, which says we pray for "the manifestation of God's glory among us, along with an ever-increasing openness to the way He chooses to turn up." Sometimes in life we are praying for the Lord to come into a situation. We pray and we wait. Jesus was teaching that while we are waiting, we must not be idle, but we must remain dressed and ready for service and keep our lamps burning (Luke 12:35).

Between the Times

This parable may also be interpreted to mean "the time between the times." What did Jesus mean? He was referring to the seasons of God's presence. There are certain times when, for reasons beyond our reckoning, God is hiding His face. At certain times in life, though you may have known God's presence and His power in marvelous ways, you find yourself in a valley with no explanation, waiting for Him to come again and show His presence. When God hides His face, He usually gives us no warning. Sometimes a new Christian discovers this before he or she has been told about it. Nobody meant to withhold that information, but when a person is converted, you can't tell them everything at once. It is only a matter of time before someone suddenly feels like they are all alone and wonders if anything ever really happened in the first place. God just doesn't seem to be around.

The Lord once left Hezekiah to test him, to see what was in his heart (see 2 Chronicles 32:31). Are you in a period when God is hiding His face? Are you waiting for God to answer your prayer? If so, you are between the times. So what are you to do? Jesus said, "Be dressed ready for service and keep your lamps burning" (Luke 12:35).

And whatever you do, don't give up. *Do not give up!*

The Lord's Assessment

There is a fourth way that this parable may be understood. God has a way of using "waiting" periods to assess the state of our heart. Sometimes we will receive the Lord's assessment after being commissioned by Him regarding a certain work. The assessment of our lives and deeds will ultimately take place at the judgment seat of Christ. We must all stand before Him and give an account of the things done in this life, whether they be good or bad (see 2 Corinthians 5:10). At that time there will be no arguing—and everyone will see it happen. That's the ultimate way this will take place, but while we are still here on earth, God also has ways of doing this. It may be at the end of a trial—a trial you think will never end—and then it's over and you get a verdict from the Lord on whether you did all right. Did you retain your dignity, or did you murmur, complain and grumble all the way through? If you did complain or murmur, you are no better off at the end.

When I think of the years and years I knew nothing about the teaching of dignifying a trial, it's terrifying! How I could have grown instead of just complaining. But there *is* such a thing as learning to dignify a trial, so that when it eventually ends, you will have learned something. Then the Lord comes in and says, "Good, well done," and it is a wonderful feeling. This can also occur at the end of an era, whether long or brief—God will step in and let you know in no uncertain terms how you did. If you haven't experienced that, it may be because you didn't do so well and you got no conscious report card from the Lord. God wants you to know of this possibility, that even prior to the judgment seat of Christ you can hear God say, "Yes, you have done OK." There is nothing that can be compared with that!

Satanic Attack

These parables can also be interpreted as relating to satanic attack. While going about our normal, everyday lives, there sometimes comes a "sudden," unexpected attack. Something happens very quickly and takes you by surprise, just as Jesus implied when He said, "You also must be ready, because the Son of Man will come at an hour when you do not expect him" (Luke 12:40).

Believe it or not, behind many so-called "satanic" attacks lies a sovereign God who instigated the whole thing. "Then the LORD said to Satan, 'Have you considered my servant Job?' " (Job 1:8). Job endured a long period of harassment for which the devil was the only possible explanation. But the devil had been given permission by God to attack Job. With a satanic attack, as with the Second Coming, you often will get no warning. It just comes, and you are shaken and think, *What on earth is going on?* Job didn't know at the time that the devil was attacking him, and yet God instigated it.

Do you know that God has always used the devil to do His dirty work? Yet we are told that like a roaring lion, the devil prowls about, and you never know when he is going to attack (1 Peter 5:8). He may even come as an angel of light (2 Corinthians 11:14).

Why Is the First Parable Important?

The first parable (found in Luke 12:35–40) shows that we need to be ready and watching both when the devil attacks and when God shows up. If you are ready and watching, you will be blessed by God. "It will be good for those servants whose master finds them watching when he comes. I tell you the truth, he will dress himself to serve, will have them recline at the table and will come and wait on them" (Luke 12:37).

What an incredible picture! It shows how open we must be to the way in which God chooses to show Himself. How open and ready we are will be determined by whether we are found watching and what our reaction is when He comes. You may say, "When great revival comes, I'll know it. Then I'll be ready." You are wrong. If you miss or show contempt for the little raindrops falling along the way, when the authentic great revival does come, you will miss it entirely. Or you may see it but you won't be able to enjoy it. You will be like the five foolish virgins who said, "Give us some of your oil" (Matthew 25:8), and it will be too late. Don't say, "At the next move of the Spirit, I'll go along with it." He who is faithful in that which is least will be faithful also in much (see Matthew 25:21).

The reward for waiting and for being ready, as well as the consequences of not being ready, are demonstrated here in this passage (Luke 12:35–40). Zechariah was not ready when his prayer was answered (Luke 1:18). The shocking thing is that you can ask God to do something and then forget about it, so that when God answers, you are not ready for it. If you had told Zechariah that his wife, Elizabeth, would be pregnant with a boy, but that he would not be thrilled when it happened, no doubt he would have strongly disagreed. But because Zechariah wasn't ready, he got into an argument with an angel! Can you imagine anything so dumb as to argue with Gabriel? But Zechariah said, "No, there has got to be something wrong here; my wife is too old." He missed it! He was struck dumb, and so he couldn't enjoy the fulfillment of the prophecy. If you are ready, the Lord Himself will bless you, and you will recline at the table while He waits on you. But if you are not ready, the consequences will be horrendous.

A Command to Be Ready

"Be dressed ready for service and keep your lamps burning" (Luke 12:35).

This is a command to work. Far from doing nothing while we wait on

God, we are to be busy. To be ready for service means to be prepared to be used at any moment. You never know when your particular gift will be needed. Don't sulk and say, "They don't need me," because all of a sudden God may say, "I need you now." You will find yourself taken unaware—"Who, me? I'm not ready."

There came a time when the pharaoh of Egypt had a dream that no one could interpret. Joseph was ready. Maybe no one needs your talent yet, but when there is a knock on your door, will you be dressed and ready for service? God may knock unexpectedly and say, "I need you, and I need you now." Keep your lamp burning.

To whatever context you align this parable, it always refers to the anointing. Oil in those days was used primarily for fuel, not for cooking. It refers to the oil of the Spirit, indicative of light and warmth. We must keep the anointing at an optimum level. Keep your relationship with the Spirit at a peak, even if God is hiding His face and you think, *What is the use of trying to dignify this trial?* Keep your anointing at an optimum level so that when you hear the knock, you are ready. This parable is a command to work. Waiting on God is anything but laziness or inactivity. When God says, "Wait," He means for us to work in the interim.

A Command to Watch

"It will be good for those servants whose master finds them watching when he comes" (Luke 12:37).

This passage tells us that we must stay awake. The slave mentioned in Psalm 123:1–2 stayed in the background, but he was always in sight of his master. He only looked at one thing—his master's hands—because he didn't want to miss any cue. If the master raised a finger, the slave would be right there. That is what Jesus was instructing us in this parable.

In Jesus' time, wedding celebrations took place at night; that is why they needed to keep their lamps burning. The bride would wait for the groom to come to her house. Then they would have the ceremony with its rituals, followed by the festivities. Weddings would mean a long procession in the streets, sometimes lasting for hours. Jesus was talking here about someone who had been invited to such a wedding—there was no telling when he would get home. Perhaps he would be away a long time, but when he finally did get home, he wanted his servants to be wide awake. He didn't want to have to knock on the door and wait in the dark. You see, the danger was that those servants would fall asleep after several hours. "Keeping awake" is a better translation than the word *watching*. Don't say you will wake up when God shows up. You won't—you will sleep on and miss it all.

A Command to Wait

Purposeful Waiting

Waiting for God, then, is a purposeful waiting, a prepared waiting, even "aggressive waiting"—waiting with eager expectation because at any moment God may turn up. "Like men waiting for their master to return from a wedding banquet, so that when he comes and knocks they can immediately open the door for him" (Luke 12:36).

Waiting on God is not aimless waiting. You are waiting because God may turn up, and this is just the way He does things. And if God turns up, you will be glad you waited.

Positioned Waiting

The servants should have been positioned right by the door. If they were at the other end of the house when their master's knock came, they would not hear it. If they were several yards away, they might hear it, but by the time they arrived to open it, the master would say, "You were supposed to be ready." Positioned waiting means being near the door. It is the way Elisha was when he knew that Elijah was going to be taken to heaven. Elijah teased Elisha and said, "I am going to go to Bethel, you wait here." "Oh no, I am going with you," said Elisha, "I am not going to let you out of my sight" (see 2 Kings 2:1). He wanted the double anointing. Be positioned so that as soon as you hear Him knock you can swing the door open.

It Will Be Good

"It will be good for those servants whose master finds them watching when he comes. I tell you the truth, he will dress himself to serve, will have them recline at the table and will come and wait on them" (Luke 12:37).

This is an extraordinary verse; there is hardly another verse like it in the New Testament. It is interesting that Jesus repeats it. *"It will be good for those servants . . . even if he comes in the second or third watch of the night"* (Luke 12:38, emphasis added).

How good will it be? Well, if God says "good," then it's very good. He created the earth, He created the stars, He created the heavens and

He called it all "good" (Genesis 1). All things work together for good (Romans 8:28). Here Jesus says it will be good for those servants whose master finds them watching when He comes. He says it twice, so it will definitely be worth waiting for.

Why Is It Good?

A Rich Reward

> God is not unjust; he will not forget your work and the love you have shown him as you have helped his people and continue to help them. We want each of you to show this same diligence to the very end, in order to make your hope sure. We do not want you to become lazy, but to imitate those who through faith and patience inherit what has been promised.
>
> Hebrews 6:10–12

Later the writer to the Hebrews said, "So do not throw away your confidence; it will be richly rewarded" (Hebrews 10:35).

A Role Reversal

When the master returns and is pleased to find his servants waiting faithfully, he rewards them in a most unusual way. Jesus says the master will dress himself to serve and will wait upon the servants. The nearest parallel we have of this is in John 13:5 where Jesus washed His disciples' feet, drying them with a towel that was wrapped around Him. On that occasion, Simon got very nervous about what Jesus was doing and was uncomfortable with the role reversal. Yet, this is what God wants to do. You cannot out-give the Lord, you cannot out-praise the Lord, you cannot outdo the Lord, and when you are ready He will serve you. This means restoration and rest. Maybe you have wanted to know what it is like to enter into God's rest. Here's how: Be dressed and ready, and don't try to figure it out with your head. Don't try to figure it out theologically. One day you will just enter into a rest, and your soul will be flooded with glory—there will be warmth, joy and peace, and you will say, "I never knew this was possible!"

Jesus Gives Caution

Look again at verse 38. There are two cautions given in this verse. First, you may find you wait a long time. In the story of the calming of the storm, it wasn't until the fourth watch of the night (around four o'clock in the morning) that Jesus turned up (Matthew 14:25). Luke said it might have been the second or third watch of the night—so it might have been midnight or it might have been two o'clock in the morning. Second, we remind ourselves of the fact that we just do not know when He will come. "You also must be ready, because the Son of Man will come at an hour when you do not expect him" (Luke 12:40).

But there is also a parable within this parable. Jesus said, "Understand this: If the owner of the house had known at what hour the thief was coming [He changed the metaphor], he would not have let his house be broken into" (Luke 12:39).

If I were to tell everyone to show up at a particular time for a prayer meeting because the glory of God was going to come down, everyone would be there. But if I said, "Come and pray for hours; God may come or He may not," not many people would actually show up. Jesus spoke of a thief coming. This is what Peter referred to when he said, "The day of the Lord will come like a thief" (1 Thessalonians 5:2).

Why Is the Second Parable Important?

After the first parable Peter asked, "Lord, are you telling this parable to us, or to everyone?" (Luke 12:41).

Jesus answered his question with the second parable. This parable refers mainly to Christians in positions of responsibility. However, it refers not only to being awake and ready but also to being found *obedient* when the master comes (Luke 12:43). The emphasis in this parable is upon the horrendous consequences of *not* being ready. In the first parable the master was away for a few *hours*, but in the second the master was absent for *many days*. This parable demonstrates the possibility of a long time elapsing before the Lord comes back suddenly and gives an assessment of the kind of work we are doing. But like so many of the parables of Jesus, it also has an intentional ambiguity—a double meaning on purpose—in that it can apply equally to the lost.

This second parable shows the responsibility of leadership. All of us have been given something to do by God. We have to take that responsibility seriously and understand the horrendous consequences that will occur if we are found to have behaved irresponsibly when the Lord turns up (Luke 12:46). We have the potential to abuse the responsibility given to us.

Like the parable of the rich fool in the previous chapter, this parable reminds us that it is dangerous to assume that we have plenty of time. The arrival of the master will be completely unexpected. We will be held accountable in accordance with our own anointing and gifts:

"From everyone who has been given much, much will be demanded; and from the one who has been entrusted with much, much more will be asked" (Luke 12:48).

If you have been greatly gifted, you are therefore greatly responsible. Jesus also said, "That servant who knows his master's will and does not get ready or does not do what his master wants will be beaten with many blows" (Luke 12:47).

This parable is one of the rare occasions when we are given a theological basis for various levels of punishment. There are some who think that if you are saved, you are simply saved, and if you are lost, you are simply lost. No rewards among the saved, no degrees of punishment for the lost. However, the saved will have levels of reward, but there may be levels of punishment as well. The great William Perkins, a Puritan in the seventeenth century, reckoned that this parable showed there would also be degrees of punishment in hell, because Jesus said, "But the one who does not know and does things deserving punishment will be beaten with few blows" (Luke 12:48).

There are those who haven't heard the Gospel. But for those who have the Gospel (and have therefore been given much), much will be demanded. We are talking about levels of reward and levels of punishment.

Responsibility

When Peter asked at whom the parable was aimed, Jesus answered, "Who then is the faithful and wise manager, whom the master puts in charge of his servants to give them their food allowance at the proper time?" (Luke 12:42).

There is something interesting here in the original Greek. The *manager* is later called the *servant*. The word for *servant* here is *doulos,* which means "slave." In ancient times a bond-slave, a *doulos,* had no rights of his own. This is what we are as Christians. The apostle Paul referred to himself as a bond-slave of Jesus Christ. So the manager referred to here is also a bond-slave. It is like the church leader or shepherd in the following text:

> Be shepherds of God's flock that is under your care, serving as overseers—not because you must, but because you are willing, as God wants you to be; not greedy for money, but eager to serve; not lording it over those entrusted to you, but being examples to the flock. And when the Chief Shepherd appears, you will receive the crown of glory that will never fade away.
>
> 1 Peter 5:2–4

That is the promise given to someone like myself if I please the Lord in the way I preach, pastor and live. I may be the shepherd, but I am a bond-slave first. We are all in this together. This comes out again in the following passage: "So then, men ought to regard us as *servants* of Christ and as those entrusted with the secret things of God" (1 Corinthians 4:1, emphasis added).

Winston Churchill said that the price of greatness is responsibility. For whom are we responsible as servants? For one another. For some of us it is a greater responsibility than for others. Peter's job was to feed the flock. Mine is to be a good pastor. I will be judged by how I prepare, what I say and the spirit in which I say it. Even if I were to fool people, I can't fool God. None of us are off the hook; we are all bond-slaves, and we are all our brother's and sister's keeper.

In the ancient East, slaves were stewards of the property of their master, the owner. A steward not only had charge of the property, but he was also responsible for the administration of the household. That is what Jesus was talking about here, yet He too was a bond-slave or steward in this parable.

Requirements

"From everyone who has been given much, much will be demanded" (Luke 12:48).

Talents

You have a certain level of intelligence, an intellectual capability, that comes from God. If you think your IQ increased when you became a Christian, you are quite wrong. You are what you are because God made you that way. If your church organist wasn't a Christian, he would still be able to play the organ. As a Christian, he would perhaps say that the Lord helps him, but he still has a natural God-given talent. It is good to hone whatever talents we have and offer them to the Lord in service.

Training

Some people are born to privilege and have a very good education. There is a class system in every country. Like it or not, that is the world in which we live. It is a wicked world. But if you have been given much, then much will be demanded of you.

I come from the hills of Kentucky, and for many years our slogan (back when there were only 48 states) was "Thank God for Arkansas"—

Kentucky was number 47 in educational standards, and Arkansas was number 48! Then I moved to England. Talk about having an inferiority complex! I was working beside people in Oxford who were the first in their graduate classes. You cannot imagine how overwhelming that was. By the grace of God I got through it, but with it their great training came responsibility.

Let us move on to a spiritual level. Being given much in this context refers to the amount of "light" or revelation we have received. Jesus said that the servant who knows his master's will and doesn't act accordingly will be punished (Luke 12:47). God knows how much teaching we have had. Some of us have almost been overtaught; we have been given a great deal of light. God knows whether or not we have walked in that light. He knows whether your life has been renewed because you walked in the light, whether you welcomed the Holy Spirit and whether the Word and the Spirit have had an equal impact on you. He also knows if you are one of those who only likes to be intellectually challenged. You want to hear teaching, but it makes no impact in your life. Life may not be fair, but God is fair. He knows how much we know. You cannot be too ignorant of how you will be judged when you realize how much you actually know—and how good God has been to you. God takes into account our liabilities and our strengths and weaknesses.

"Everything is uncovered and laid bare before the eyes of him to whom we must give account" (Hebrews 4:13). God sees how our minds work. He also knows how much we rationalize. We can wear a mask, but at the judgment seat of Christ the masks will be taken off. God will say, "I know what you are thinking."

What do you suppose God requires of you? Given your background, your knowledge and your intelligence, and given the light that God has shed upon your path—how much do you suppose God requires of *you?*

Readiness

"It will be good for that servant whom the master [the owner] finds doing so when he returns" (Luke 12:43). What was Jesus talking about in this verse?

He was talking about the manager—the servant who had been given responsibility. In the first parable, the servant only had to stay awake. But the readiness in this parable refers to the servant being found "on the job," working when his master returns. He has been in charge of the domestic running of the house while the master has been away.

The whole estate is in the hands of this *doulos,* this servant-manager who has been given a higher profile and a higher responsibility.

Jesus posed a question. Suppose that the master was away a *very* long time and the manager became careless? Suppose he began to mistreat the fellow servants under his care? What if he got drunk and treated them with no respect (Luke 12:45)? Jesus said that this was a very dangerous thing. Do you know that this was exactly what happened when Moses went up to Mount Sinai? Moses took so long to come down from the mountain that the people gathered around Aaron and said, "Come make us gods who will go before us. As for this fellow Moses who brought us up out of Egypt, we don't know what has happened to him" (Exodus 32:1).

God often functions like that. Sometimes it seems as though He goes away on a long trip or journey. He has told us what to do, and He says, "Get on with it. I'll be back." Sometimes He seems to be gone an awfully long time, and we don't know what has happened to Him. In Jesus' parable, the wicked and unfaithful manager used his master's prolonged absence as an excuse to abuse his fellow servants (Luke 12:45). However, "the master of that servant will come on a day when he does not expect him and at an hour he is not aware of. He will cut him to pieces and assign him a place with the unbelievers" (Luke 12:46).

How dare a manager and servant abuse his responsibility like this! Sometimes it happens. Take the ministry for example. A minister can let his authority go to his head or begin to take himself too seriously. Perhaps he abuses his responsibility by the way he talks to those under him—intimidating or frightening other people. God doesn't like this kind of behavior. Perhaps you feel it is good if those who work for you are afraid of you so that you can keep their attention, keep them on their toes. Is that the way you get respect? It is not Jesus' way. This is a word that applies to all of us in varying degrees.

For me, being ready means being faithful to that which has been entrusted to me. If I am not true to God, then I am not being true to those in my church. I have to live the kind of life before God that will be a blessing to others. This means being faithful to the Word of God. According to Peter, it also means not being greedy. It is easy for a minister to focus on a way to get ahead financially. I have seen it happen over the years, and I have seen ministers lose their anointing because of it. I have committed myself to God never to let money have anything to do with my decision making. "For the love of money is a root of all kinds of evil" (1 Timothy 6:10).

Readiness consists of being wide awake so that no matter what time the Lord shows up, we are found conducting the affairs of His household with loyalty, faithfulness and dignity. How do we apply this? Jesus could return at any moment. God could manifest His glory at any time in such a manner that all of us would know we were getting an assessment from the Lord. God has His own means of judging the value of our stewardship. He could do it at any moment. The way He does it will make it all too clear to us what He thinks. How would you feel if it happened right now?

Reward

Jesus goes on to speak of the rewards of being a faithful steward. "I tell you the truth, he will put him in charge of all his possessions" (Luke 12:44).

Jesus was talking about the manager who is faithful and wise. If I am faithful and wise and am doing what God wants me to do, then I will get a promotion. This means that God is going to do something for me. I will receive a greater responsibility. Perhaps it is nothing that can be seen on the outside, but He may give me a greater anointing or a greater sense of His presence. According to this second parable, when the Lord turns up and we are ready, we will receive a promotion. We will be given more power and maybe in some cases more prestige. When the owner of the house returns and finds the manager doing a good job, he puts that manager in charge of all his possessions. God will do that with us. We will receive a spiritual promotion on earth. We will be given power and increased anointing, and then at the judgment seat of Christ, we will receive what Paul calls the prize (Philippians 2:14).

Retribution

In the most solemn part of this parable, Jesus referred to the retribution that will fall upon the irresponsible manager: "The master of that servant will come on a day when he does not expect him and at an hour he is not aware of. He will cut him to pieces and assign him a place with the unbelievers" (Luke 12:46).

The Unexpected Arrival

Would you be shocked if revival came? Some of us would be thrilled, and some of us would be shocked. After the shock, those people would feel shame. The master of the servant will come on a day when He is not expected, and He will assign some a place with the unbelievers.

The book of James says, "Friendship with the world is hatred toward God" (James 4:4). If you become a friend of the world (that is, if you act like a person who has not been converted), you will force God to treat you as an enemy, and you will be assigned a place with the unbelievers. There will be shock, shame and suffering. In Matthew Jesus said, "He will cut him to pieces and assign him a place with the hypocrites, where there will be weeping and gnashing of teeth" (Matthew 24:51).

How can this refer both to the lost and to the saved? You, as the saved, will have a realization of what could have been yours. I remarked to a man recently about what God could do with his great gifting—he had been given much—but he wouldn't listen to me. One day he will get the shock of his life when he sees that God was reaching out to him. There will be weeping and gnashing of teeth because punishment is given out according the degree of light received (Luke 12:47–48).

The lost do have degrees of light. Some have never heard the Gospel. In North America or Britain, you can walk into most bookstores and pick up a Bible. But in many countries they have never even heard of the Bible. The Lord, the wise Judge, will take that into account. As for the saved, for those of us who know better and have been taught, it won't be a pretty sight. I pray that every one of us will focus on the task of being ready—prepared for anything, prepared for God to do something unexpected in our midst. The unexpected arrival may be the second coming of Jesus. May it happen soon!

Chapter 20

The Parable of the Barren Fig Tree

> A man had a fig tree, planted in his vineyard, and he went to look for fruit on it, but did not find any.
>
> Luke 13:6

Fig trees were very prominent in ancient Israel, and they are still prominent there today. They are referred to throughout the Bible in both the gospels and the Old Testament. Good fig trees usually produce fruit after three years, sometimes for ten months of the year. In this chapter we will look at the parable of the barren fig tree found in Luke 13:1–9, keeping in mind two additional texts: Matthew 24:32–35 and Matthew 21:18–22.

In Matthew 24, Jesus told His disciples to "learn this lesson from the fig tree: As soon as its twigs get tender and its leaves come out, you know that summer is near" (Mathew 24:32).

In Matthew 21, it was the fig tree that was the focus of attention when Jesus symbolically cursed it, saying, " 'May you never bear fruit again!' Immediately the tree withered" (Matthew 21:19). This latter statement of Jesus signified the fact that the judgment of Israel had already begun. As we are going to see, the fig tree was used as a metaphor for the people of Israel.

In Luke 13:1–9, Jesus told a short parable after having warned people that they should take the opportunity to repent now, before anything happens to them that would cause it to be too late. He told the story of a man who owned a vineyard and had planted a fig tree in it. For three years he kept on inspecting it, hoping to find some fruit, but there was none. Eventually he became frustrated and ordered it to be cut down by the man who tended his vineyard for him. The vineyard manager, however, appealed and asked that the tree be spared for just one more year.

One could assume that the tree was six years old, because such a tree wasn't expected to bear fruit until it was at least three years old. The owner wanted to have it dug up and destroyed, but his servant stepped in with a request to spare the tree.

Why Is This Parable Important?

First, we can see in this parable the incredible patience of God. God is like the owner of this vineyard who was upset with the fig tree. God was upset with Israel. He had warned Israel again and again, sending them one prophet after another, until now they were on the brink of being destroyed. That is why Jesus gave this parable about an "owner" looking for fruit—the owner was ultimately the only one who could be persuaded to postpone his judgment. It shows the patience of God.

Second, this parable highlights the impending judgment of God. The purpose of a fig tree was to bear fruit, and the purpose of Israel was to show obedience to God. The purpose of the Church today is to bear fruit. The purpose of the individual Christian's life is also to bear fruit. Having introduced Himself as "the true vine" and His Father as the "gardener," Jesus had also said, "He cuts off every branch in me that bears no fruit" (John 15:2).

Jesus continued by underlining the fact that "if anyone does not remain in me, he is like a branch that is thrown away and withers; such branches are picked up, thrown into the fire and burned" (John 15:6).

This is the judgment of God. This parable also shows that God may rescind His will if He so chooses. The servant in the fig tree parable stepped in and asked his master if he could make a suggestion: "Leave it alone for one more year, and I'll dig around it and fertilize it. If it bears fruit next year, fine! If not, then cut it down" (Luke 13:8–9).

Jesus gave this parable to show that God can be persuaded to change His mind. There are two truths here that are parallel and that appear to contradict each other. There are Bible verses that say, "God will not relent; He will not change His mind; He is always the same" (see Numbers 23:9; 1 Samuel 15:29; Psalm 110:4). But there are also cases in which God relents. Take the case of the king of Nineveh. When the king heard that God was going to destroy his city, he called for a national fast in order to plead with God:

> "Who knows? God may yet relent and with compassion turn from his fierce anger so that we will not perish." When God saw what they did and how they turned from their evil ways, he had compassion on them and did not bring upon them the destruction he had threatened.
>
> Jonah 3:9–10

There is another interesting example of this in 1 Kings 21. We are told that there was never a man like Ahab who sold himself to do evil in the eyes of the Lord; yet when Elijah warned Ahab, the king put on sackcloth, fasted and went around meekly (1 Kings 21:25–27). Then the word of the Lord came back to Elijah, "Have you noticed how Ahab has humbled himself before me? Because he has humbled himself, I will not bring this disaster in his day" (1 Kings 21:29). Extraordinary! Wicked though Ahab was!

It could be that you are in a situation and you think, *It is all over. There is nothing to do but endure the worst.* Listen, if Ahab could go to God on his knees, it shows the extent to which God can show compassion. That is why, in this text, Jesus encouraged everyone, no matter who they are, to repent and seek God. Jesus said, "Unless you repent, you too will all perish" (Luke 13:3).

We know that repentance, like faith, is the gift of God (Romans 2:4; Acts 11:18). And it is a great gift. If God has given you repentance, thank Him for it. The worst possible scenario is when you don't hear Him speak anymore and nobody can reach you.

This parable establishes the fact that God has a right to see spiritual life and fruitfulness in our lives, because when there is no fruit, God will cut down the tree. Jesus said to the Church, "You are the salt of the earth" (Matthew 5:13). Later He said, "Let your light shine before men, that they may see your good deeds and praise your Father in heaven" (Matthew 5:16).

He has a right to see spiritual life and fruitfulness in us. However, God's patience has a limit for He has said, "My Spirit will not contend with man forever, for he is mortal" (Genesis 6:3). Moses was told that although God maintains His love for thousands, "Yet he does not leave the guilty unpunished" (Exodus 34:7).

There comes a time when God says, "Enough is enough." Do you need to hear this word? I have tried over the years to let the Scriptures speak what they will. I don't take a problem to the Bible and say, *Lord, give me something to say that will be relevant.* I always try to begin with whatever the text is, believing that the Lord will have present those He wants to hear it. So please be open to what the Lord wants to say to you throughout this chapter.

Finally, this parable is important because it teaches that repentance is the only way to avert the judgment of God. If Ahab—the most wicked king in anyone's memory—could humble himself, then God is most certainly gracious. Therefore, when you are convicted that you need to repent of something, receive it, act on it and thank the Lord for His faithfulness to you.

The Context of the Parable

Let's look a little more closely at the context in which Jesus was speaking this message. First we will look at some false assumptions that Jesus was addressing and then at some factual assumptions that Jesus took for granted.

False Assumptions

We are told that some people went to Jesus and told Him about some Galileans whose blood Pilate had mixed with their sacrifices (Luke 13:1). It becomes obvious from Jesus' response that these people were assuming the Galileans in question were very wicked people and had therefore received an awful judgment. Jesus knew what they were thinking and why they had brought up the issue, so He said to them, "Do you think that these Galileans were worse sinners than all the other Galileans because they suffered this way?" (Luke 13:2).

The first false assumption is that accidents only happen to evil people and are a sign of divine judgment. That was the assumption underlying this story. However, some time previously Pontius Pilate had sent Roman soldiers into the Temple, which was a sacrilegious thing to do. He did it when some Galileans were offering their sacrifices; these Galileans had been killed, and their blood had been mixed with the sacrifice. The assumption was that these Galileans must have been vile sinners or this would not have happened to them. Jesus brought up the story of another eighteen people who had died when the tower of Siloam fell on them (obviously a recent incident in Jerusalem). "Do you think they were more guilty than all the others living in Jerusalem? I tell you, no! But unless you repent, you too will all perish" (Luke 13:4–5).

The second false assumption, by implication, is that some people don't need to repent because they are honorable, decent, good people who live upstanding lives, don't hurt anybody, pay their bills and are nice. Since bad things don't happen to people like that (they thought), it follows that such people don't need to repent.

Factual Assumptions

There are some factual assumptions that Jesus made when speaking to those present. The first is that bad things happen to good people and good things happen to bad people. Jesus was saying something that agrees with the words of the book of Ecclesiastes: "In this meaningless life of mine I have seen both of these: a righteous man perishing in his righteousness, and a wicked man living long in his wickedness" (Ecclesiastes 7:15).

The writer also said, "There is something else meaningless that occurs on earth: righteous men who get what the wicked deserve, and wicked men who get what the righteous deserve" (Ecclesiastes 8:14). And, "I have seen something else under the sun: The race is not to the swift or the battle to the strong, nor does food come to the wise or wealth to the brilliant or favor to the learned; but time and chance happen to them all" (Ecclesiastes 9:11).

The second factual assumption Jesus made was that everyone needs to repent. That was a forthright thing to say to this group of people who obviously considered themselves "good," blessed and without a need to repent. But Jesus said, "Unless you repent, you also will perish." He was saying that even to those who are apparently the most righteous. None of us can say that we have no need to repent. If we do, it shows that we are blind, that we have no objectivity about ourselves and that God has kept us from seeing ourselves as we are. If you say, "I haven't done anything wrong," it means that God isn't even granting you the privilege of repentance. Even the most righteous need to repent and even those who have suffered greatly need to repent. Don't look at someone who's handicapped, or can't see, or who can't hear, or is bedridden and so on, and say, "Well, they'll go to heaven because they have suffered so much." Sorry!

"Unless you repent, you too will all perish" (Luke 13:3). Jesus says that to everyone. God commands all men everywhere to repent.

The third factual assumption is the reference to eternal punishment in verses 3 and 5. Jesus said it twice. *Perishing* is a word that is used interchangeably with *eternal punishment* throughout the New Testament. The people who were questioning Jesus wanted to talk through these philosophical issues with Him. They were looking for answers about why some people suffer. Almost certainly they were not intending to get into a conversation with Jesus that might expose their own sins. But Jesus cut right through this idle philosophical and theological speculation and came to the heart of the matter. "Except that you repent, you will perish." He spoke to the heart. Jesus preached as a dying man to dying men. People have often asked me, "R. T., why do you make so much of this issue of eternal punishment? This is a peripheral issue." I always respond, "But wait a minute, what if it is true? What if there is a hell? If there is a hell, it is not peripheral after all, is it?"

Characters of the Parable

What do the different people of this parable signify? Most scholars agree on the following.

The owner of the vineyard refers to God the Father. The vineyard, or the fig tree, refers to the nation of Israel. The servant who said, "Wait one more year," represents the intercession of God's Messiah, the Lord Jesus. The owner of the vineyard, God the Father, owns everything and has a special interest in His covenant people. God has a right to look for fruit in them, and He also has the right to judge them. If He decides, "For three years I have been coming to look for fruit on this fig tree; I haven't found any so I will have it cut it down!" then He has the right to do just that. He could have overruled the servant but He chose not to.

The man who took care of the vineyard, then, is the mediator, the intercessor. He is the one who steps in and says, "Sir, leave it alone for one more year," and offers to dig around it and fertilize it. Be careful, then, if you are a fence straddler—you do not have the right to sit in judgment, as God may be on the brink of saying, "Enough!" You may have been spared until now because the Lord is behind the scenes, crying, "Wait, wait, wait!" interceding on your behalf. That is the role of a mediator, to stand in the breach between God and man. Jesus pleads on our behalf with the Father.

Look at the account in Matthew 21 when Jesus cursed the fig tree. The disciples marveled that it withered so quickly. Usually you can cut a tree down and the leaves will not wither for a few more days. But this withering occurred in just a matter of hours. Jesus was sending a signal that the judgment had already begun to take place. He had already entered the city on Palm Sunday and had wept over it, and now judgment had come upon the nation of Israel.

The Lord Jesus intercedes on behalf of the fruitless people of God. There is a fourfold application to this.

- The first is regarding the nation of Israel. Jesus was giving a last opportunity in this parable for Israel to repent. In a word, the coming of Christ gave the people of Israel their last chance. Jesus went to Jerusalem, back to Galilee, then back to Jerusalem and back to Galilee again. Yet all they wanted to do was kill Him. They did not realize that He was giving them one last chance.
- The second application is to the Church—the new Israel. God expects the Church to bear fruit. The first church addressed in Revelation 2 is the church at Ephesus—the center of much divine

activity. Something had happened, and they had abandoned their first love. Jesus said, "Remember the height from which you have fallen! Repent and do the things you did at first" (Revelation 2:5).

God has a right to say that to the Church. Jesus intercedes on our behalf.

- This teaching is also relevant to anyone who is not yet saved. Unless you repent you will perish—don't sit on the fence. Have you nailed your colors to the mast? His Spirit will not contend with man forever (Genesis 6:3).
- The final application is to Christians who develop hardness of hearing at a spiritual level. This is what happened to the church to which the letter to the Hebrews was addressed. They had become hard of hearing. The author said, "You don't realize that it is going to get worse and worse until you are not going to hear at all, and there will be no repentance" (see Hebrews 6:4–6). Listen! Repentance is the most precious thing for a Christian. When the Holy Spirit identifies something of which you need to repent, be grateful and thank Him. When God puts His finger on something in your life, take it with both hands.

Many years ago I died a thousand deaths when God spoke to me. I had a desire to be a scholar and a theologian and to make my impact on the scholarly world, but God said, "Let somebody else do that. I am not asking you to do what they can do." He called me instead to Westminster Chapel and to be an evangelist. It was an awful moment. I thought, *What about the reputation of the Chapel, Lord? The Chapel has such a good reputation. It is going to change, and they are not going to like it.* God said, "Leave that to Me."

Don't be afraid of what others will think of you when you enter the role to which God calls you. When you stand before God, what they think will mean nothing.

Cautions of the Parable

For the nation of Israel this was history in the making. When Jesus approached Jerusalem and saw the city, He wept over it (Luke 19:41–42). He said, "If you, even you, had only known on this day what would bring you peace—but now it is hidden from your eyes" (Luke 19:42).

The third year had come for the tree and there was intercession, but now it was over. Now the fig tree had withered. Jesus wept. Repeatedly Jesus had told Israel that God was going to go to another nation—to the

Gentiles (see Acts 13:46; Acts 19), but they didn't listen. The caution for the Church is to stick with the motto of the Reformation—"the Church reformed but always reforming." This is why God has had to raise up new denominations and movements over the years.

This parable also cautions us to remember that God is looking for fruit in our lives. What is the fruit that God looks for? Three things: *righteousness* (see Philippians 1:10–11), *reformation* (which means producing fruit by being continually transformed—see Matthew 3:8) and *repentance* (which means turning away ever more from our previously sinful ways and being changed from glory to glory—see 2 Corinthians 3:18). It is the same thing as saying the Church should be reformed but always reforming.

Luke 13:6–9 shows that God is patient. Let me put it to you like this. If you come to a place where you no longer hear God speak, where you are not being renewed into repentance and you have backpedaled spiritually, God doesn't just cut you off. This parable shows that before a person gets into a state where he or she becomes unreachable, God is very, very patient. You don't lapse easily into a Hebrews 6:4–6 situation where it is impossible to be renewed again into repentance. It only occurs after the Father has been very patient and the Son has stepped in and interceded, saying, "Please wait one more year. Watch what I do and if you see repentance then, fine. But if not then cut them off" (Luke 13:8–9).

Challenges of the Parable

First, is it possible that the Gentile world is on the verge of seeing a reversal of what happened in Jesus' day? Paul said, "But they were broken off because of unbelief, and you stand by faith" (Romans 11:20). Paul was speaking about the olive branch, which refers to Israel. He was speaking to Gentiles who "stand by faith." Paul continued:

> Do not be arrogant, but be afraid. For if God did not spare the natural branches [Israel], he will not spare you either. Consider therefore the kindness and sternness of God: sternness to those who fell, but kindness to you, provided that you continue in his kindness. Otherwise, you also will be cut off. And if they do not persist in unbelief, they will be grafted in, for God is able to graft them in again.
>
> Romans 11:20–23

In other words, although God turned to the Gentiles, there will come a time (if I understand Romans 11 correctly) when God will turn back to

Israel. For the patriarchs' sake, He is not finished with Israel after all. Now that does not mean that no Gentiles will be saved during this time, because when God turned to the Gentiles some Jews were still saved—although they were few. When the reversal comes again, there will be a mass turning to God by Israel. To those of us who have heard the Gospel a great deal, God will say, "You have had a long time." That is the first challenge.

Second, is it possible that God will give up on the Church as we know it and turn to a people we would never have dreamed of? Remember Samuel went to the house of Jesse and the anointing was on the one person that no one would have considered—little David. David was insignificant, pushed behind the door, underestimated by his father and his brothers. Could God ever do that again?

Finally, the last challenge is for those who have maybe heard a great deal of teaching in their lives, and because of that, sometimes try to rationalize what God is saying or even dismiss it altogether. We must not become spiritually hard of hearing; we must be ever open to what God's Spirit is saying to us and then listen and obey. We must live in a frame of mind that allows for continual, ongoing repentance—not carrying around guilt but being open to the correction of the Spirit. If we do this, then we will never live in fear of being unfruitful and needing to be cut down by God.

Chapter 21

The Parable of the Vineyard

"These men who were hired last worked only one hour," they said, "and you have made them equal to us who have borne the burden of the work and the heat of the day."

Matthew 20:12

All of the parables of Jesus had an element of shock to them, but the effect of this one would probably have left the people more stunned than any parable they had heard so far. The parable speaks of a group of workers who were hired to do a job. Some worked for a long time, while others came in at the eleventh hour, yet they were all paid the same amount. The workers who were hired first thought they would be paid more than those who came later, but they weren't.

Jesus Himself taught elsewhere that a worker deserves his wages (see Luke 10:7). We know that God notices when people don't treat their employees right: "Look! The wages you failed to pay the workmen who mowed your fields are crying out against you. The cries of the harvesters have reached the ears of the Lord Almighty" (James 5:4). God knows when we are not being paid what we deserve. Yet here is a parable that seems to contradict that idea.

In Jesus' time, a working day might have been as long as twelve hours. Manual workers would often have worked from dawn till dusk. We know that the people in the parable who began working at dawn agreed to work for one denarius—the standard pay at that time. But then more people came in at the third hour (around nine o'clock in the morning), and they agreed to receive whatever was right—that is the way it was put (Matthew 20:4–5). At noon some more arrived. At three o'clock still others came, and they also agreed to be paid whatever was right. Then at five o'clock, which would have been the eleventh hour if they stopped at six o'clock, the owner of the vineyard went out and found still more people standing around and he asked them, "'Why have you been standing here all day long doing nothing?' 'Because no one has hired us,' they answered. He said to them, 'You also go and work in my vineyard'" (Matthew 20:6–7).

Despite the differing starting times, when they were paid, all the workers received the same wage. Naturally, this seems unfair to us, and it would seem logical that those who had worked the longest should get paid the most—or at least those who worked the least should receive a bit less. The workers in the parable grumbled about the situation but were rebuked by the vineyard owner, who got the last word. He pointed out that each man had agreed to work for the stated wage, and that it was his right as the owner to pay each man the same if he wished to. Then he cut to the heart of the matter: "Are you envious because I am generous? . . . The last will be first, and the first will be last" (Matthew 20:15–16).

A Sovereign God

Jesus did not give this parable in order to teach us about economics. This is not God's view on how a nation should be run. Neither does the parable teach about equality, although we all have equal standing before God. The topic is not efficiency—as if those who came in at the last hour somehow got more done and were entitled to a relatively higher wage. What this parable is teaching are the principles of the Kingdom of heaven (Matthew 20:1). We see here that God's ways are different than ours.

" 'For my thoughts are not your thoughts, neither are your ways my ways,' declares the LORD. 'As the heavens are higher than the earth, so are my ways higher than your ways and my thoughts than your thoughts' " (Isaiah 55:8–9).

The parable is about God' sovereignty. He has the right to do what He wants with His resources. In fact, Kingdom rewards depend only on His sovereign grace. The anointing comes by grace alone. God said to Moses many years before, "I will have mercy on whom I will have mercy, and I will have compassion on whom I will have compassion" (Exodus 33:19).

Why Is This Parable Important?

This parable teaches that we must learn to live within our anointing and not look over our shoulders, asking, "Well, what about him? What about her?" We all have an anointing. Not everyone in the Body of Christ will be used by God in the same way. We shouldn't look at those with a higher profile and desire to function in their role. This is exactly what happened to Simon Peter when Jesus told him how he was going to die. Peter asked, "Well, if this is the way I am going to die, what about him?" (He was referring to John.) Jesus said, "If I want him to remain alive until I return, what is that to you? You must follow me" (John 21:22).

We all have a particular inheritance, and we all have our anointing. You may wish you had the anointing of another person, or you may even wish you *were* another person. Perhaps you wish you had lived in another day or that you had a different job. This parable is about living within the gifting God has given you and not looking over your shoulder.

This parable is also about the Gospel of grace. It shows the sheer, outrageous grace of God. We are all saved by God's grace, as Paul wrote: "For it is by grace you have been saved, through faith—and this not from yourselves, it is the gift of God—not by works, so that no one can boast" (Ephesians 2:8–9).

This means that the greatest sinner who may have lived the most wicked life can be forgiven by God and be acquitted of his sins, just the same as a child who comes to the Lord without having had much opportunity to sin. God could take an Adolf Hitler or an Al Capone and convert them as easily as converting a six-year-old boy. He can convert anyone because in one stroke the blood of Christ washes away all our sins. A person who receives Christ on their deathbed will go to heaven just as quickly as one who has been serving the Lord faithfully for sixty years. The scandal of the New Testament is that a person can live a righteous life—be moral, upright, highly respected and so forth, and yet still end up in hell. Sometimes when I used to walk around Westminster Abbey in London and think of all the people who are honored there, I would wonder, *Where they are now? What if they are in hell?* Yet the most wicked person can receive the Lord and then go straight to heaven.

Interpretations of the Parable

There are various ways in which this parable may be applied. I am going to give several examples, but there are more than these. Take, for example, the way in which God chooses to use His servants for various tasks. You and I may bear the heat of the day having worked in God's vineyard for years and years, then some "unknown" person turns up and God uses them for a much more prestigious task than ours! God can do that. Look, for instance, at Saul of Tarsus. Imagine how sore Peter, James and John must have felt about him—suddenly appearing on the scene and yet rising so quickly to a very high profile in the Church. It must have really gotten their goat.

Paul was one who came in at the eleventh hour. The disciples had worked hard—they had followed Jesus for three years, and they had been spoon-fed His teaching. Then Paul, born with a silver spoon in his mouth (which probably made matters worse), who had sat at the feet of the famous teacher Gamaliel, got saved and was used by God to write two-thirds of the New Testament. Those of us who think we have labored hard and done everything God told us to do need to be aware that God could raise up somebody else for whatever task He has in mind.

The second way the parable can be applied is to those who experience revival. Perhaps you belong to a church that has prayed faithfully for revival to come for years and years, and yet has never seen a move of God. Then perhaps a recently established neighboring church begins to pray, and within a month the Spirit is poured out in revival. You may hear about it and think, *Is there no justice in this world?* God says, "Look, I will have mercy on whom I will have mercy, and I will be gracious to whom I will be gracious." He can do that.

The third way this parable can be applied is to those who experience the unusual. I remember the first time I saw Jennifer Rees-Larcombe. She was in a wheelchair and had been in that condition for years and years. My heart went out to her, but she gave her testimony about how she was serving the Lord. In the meantime she had every person you could imagine to pray for her. Every person who claimed to have the gift of healing anointed her with oil and laid hands on her, and then some charismatic Christian who had been converted for just one month prayed for her and she was healed. She is walking today. God can do that!

This parable can also be applied to those who get in on what God suddenly decides to do. Here is an example. Imagine your church has been praying for revival. One day it breaks out, and everyone rejoices. A week or two later, crowds begin to flock into your church. They get in on what is happening, even though they had no part in praying for it to come about. They didn't toil in prayer alongside you, but nevertheless they are getting all the benefit of the move of God. It would be tempting for any long-standing member to think, *Who are these people? They don't deserve to get in on this—we are the ones who have waited for this!* If revival does come to your church, I can assure you that that *will* happen. Like it or not, other people will get in on the act.

Another way this parable can be applied is to our rewards in heaven. There are those who have been Christians for years who could, at the end of the day, be saved only by fire. This is because although they have been Christians for years (i.e. they began by building on the right foundation), their superstructure was erected not with gold, silver and precious stones but with wood, hay and stubble. They are saved but only by fire, which means they will have no reward. Then there are those who have been converted for only a short period of time but who will get a reward in heaven. You can say that it's not fair, but that is exactly what the workers said in the parable (Matthew 20:11–12). I expect there will be people in heaven who get a reward whom I didn't think would get anything. And there will be people in heaven saved by fire whom I thought would have a reward.

Last, we are *all* like the eleventh-hour person sooner or later and in one way or another. Perhaps you always read this parable and think of someone else coming in at the eleventh hour. I want you to know, *you* will most certainly be seen that way by somebody else. Many of us know what it is to reap what we didn't sow. If you ever think, *Well, I didn't actually deserve that,* you are an eleventh-hour person too—never forget it.

The Gift of a Job

"For the kingdom of heaven is like a landowner who went out early in the morning to hire men to work in his vineyard. He agreed to pay them a denarius for the day and sent them into his vineyard" (Matthew 20:1–2).

The ability to work and earn or create wealth is actually a gift from God. God desires to bless us with the ability to work. The parable tells us that the vineyard owner went out into the marketplace at the third hour and saw some people standing around. He encouraged them to work in his vineyard, and they did. Later he went out and did the same thing again, three more times! It was a free offer. No one was obliged to accept the offer of work. It was an indiscriminate offer to anyone who was willing to work for a denarius. That is the way it is with the Gospel. It is offered to everyone, regardless of who they are. "For God so loved the world that he gave his one and only Son, that whoever believes in him shall not perish but have eternal life" (John 3:16).

The opportunity to work for money is a gift from God. "Every good and perfect gift is from above, coming down from the Father of the heavenly lights, who does not change like shifting shadows" (James 1:17).

If you have a job, be thankful. Be thankful for any financial opportunity that will help you through, and don't be angry when someone who doesn't work as hard as you gets paid more. Remember, "godliness with contentment is great gain" (1 Timothy 6:6). "For the love of money is a root of all kinds of evil. Some people, eager for money, have wandered from the faith and pierced themselves with many griefs" (1 Timothy 6:10).

It could be that you have been very happy with your job until you found out that somebody else in an equivalent role is making more money than you are. Suddenly you find that you are not that happy with the job anymore. Be careful about that attitude. Be thankful that you are able to have a job at all.

The gift of a job refers also to having a fruitful occupation. Some people love their work; others hate it. If you like your job, be thankful for that. Be thankful that you have a fruitful occupation. It may not make you rich, but if you enjoy your work, it makes a huge difference. Be thankful because there are many who are very unhappy with their lot.

In Jesus' parable, the workers agreed to a certain wage and so they were obliged to keep the agreement. Similarly, if you have agreed to a certain wage for the job that you do, then you too are obliged to keep your agreement and not complain. Be thankful and be content.

Once I listed all the things that I would do differently and the things that I would do the same if I were able to have all my years in ministry again. One thing I would do differently is to have the courage from day one to be myself and accept the way that God made me. You can't imagine the inferiority complex I had in the early days as a person from the hills of Kentucky coming into the pulpit of Westminster Chapel—I just couldn't deal with it. If I could turn the clock back, I would say, *God, You made me this way so I believe I can do the job.* The point is that we all need to be content with how God deals with us and others and not be discontent. We need to accept the anointing God gives us and be thankful. That gratitude may just result in an increased anointing and an increased responsibility since God loves and rewards gratitude.

Greed and Jealousy

"He agreed to pay them a denarius for the day and sent them into his vineyard" (Matthew 20:2).

Notice that the first group of workers did not complain about the original deal. They agreed to work for a denarius, and they were blessed to get it. They didn't say, "Hey, I'm not going to work for a measly denarius." Neither did those who came in later give any hint of an argument about working for a denarius. They readily agreed to it, yet the next thing you know they are angry. "So when those came who were hired first, they expected to receive more" (Matthew 20:10).

These workers were accusing the landowner. Can you imagine arguing like that with God? Imagine yourself receiving the great news of a pay raise. Let's say you get a ten percent raise, and you can't wait to tell someone because you are so thrilled. Then another person comes up to you and says, "Today I got a fifty percent raise!" Now you are suddenly not as happy—but you should be. Greed and jealousy—that is what the workers in the vineyard were feeling. But the landowner overruled their complaint.

Envy

> Friend, I am not being unfair to you. Didn't you agree to work for a denarius? Take your pay and go. I want to give the man who was hired last the same as I gave you. Don't I have the right to do what I want with my own money? Or are you envious because I am generous?
>
> Matthew 20:13–15

Envy was the cause of the first murder in human history. And envy will cause you to lose your peace more effectively than anything else. You can be sailing along, walking in the Spirit, praising the Lord and feeling good, when you hear of a friend who has been incredibly blessed. Suddenly you feel a surge of jealousy, and it causes you to lose your peace.

Equality

"'These men who were hired last worked only one hour,' they said, 'and you have made them equal to us who have borne the burden of the work in the heat of the day'" (Matthew 20:12).

These men, the complainers, thought they were a cut above those who had gotten in at five o'clock in the evening. Some of us, if we are not careful, will feel this way too because we have been very faithful and have worked hard. It is easy to develop a self-righteous spirit and think, even unconsciously, that you are a cut above others.

Energy

Look at verse 12 again. I will paraphrase it: "These men were hired at the eleventh hour, and you have made them equal to us who worked through the heat of the day. We were out there slaving at high noon when the sun was beating down. These men arrived at five o'clock when it is cool and yet they get the same amount!" Those who were hired first thing in the morning believed that because they had expended more energy, they should be more greatly rewarded.

Grace and Justice

This parable calls for grace and justice. The workers were given a job—that is grace. They must have felt very fortunate, or they wouldn't have agreed to it. When God has given us work to do, we feel blessed. It is a high honor to be chosen and to be given an anointing to work in God's vineyard. But they were not only given a job; they were also given justice. "The workers who were hired about the eleventh hour came and each received a denarius. . . . When those came who were hired first . . . each of them also received a denarius" (Matthew 20:9–10).

You may say, "How is justice served when people come in at the eleventh hour and get paid the same amount?" This is the way in which God can be just and merciful at the same time. Justice means that we deserve to be punished. Mercy means that God doesn't want to punish us. But when Jesus died on the cross, His blood satisfied divine justice, so now God can save those who come in at the eleventh hour just as quickly as those who have been converted for most of their lives.

Judgment

Finally, the workers are given a judgment. The landowner said, "Take your pay and go. If I want to give the same amount to somebody who has arrived in the last five minutes I can do that. Don't I have a right to do what I want with my money?" (Matthew 20:14–15). That is judgment. God can do what He wants with each of us.

> Who are you, O man, to talk back to God? Shall what is formed say to him who formed it, "Why did you make me like this?" Does not the potter have the right to make out of the same lump of clay some pottery for noble purposes and some for common use?
>
> Romans 9:20–21

God says, "I will have mercy on whom I will have mercy" (Exodus 33:19). God can do what He wants with His fallen creation, because His judgment is right. This parable is about the grace of God and how He sovereignly bestows it upon different people in different ways. Ultimately God decides. My duty and yours is to let God be God.

Chapter 22

The Parable of the Pompous Guest

When he noticed how the guests picked the places of honor at the table, he told them this parable.

Luke 14:7

Many of Jesus' parables contained an element of shock; this one, however, suggests His sense of humor. I can't imagine Jesus ever laughing at anyone in a malicious way, but He did love to poke fun at pompous people. I guarantee that had you been present during the Sermon on the Mount when Jesus described people who announce with trumpets when they are going to give money in order to be honored by men (Matthew 6:2), you would have heard a terrific ripple of laughter in the crowd.

This parable is told in Luke 14:7–14. Jesus was visiting at the house of one of the leaders of the Pharisees "to eat bread on the Sabbath" (Luke 14:1). The first thing we notice is that Jesus' power of observation is revealed. We read, "When he noticed how the guests picked the places of honor at the table, he told them this parable" (Luke 14:7).

Would you have noticed that? Jesus did. He never missed a thing then, and He never misses anything today either. He knows when we are hurt over the way someone has spoken to us, or when we have spoken curtly to somebody else. He knows if you have pressures at home because of a marital situation. He notices every single thing.

Jesus noticed that people were taking the most honored places at the table for themselves. Many scholars believe that Jesus *was* the guest of honor on this occasion. Possibly this prominent Pharisee himself could have been the person of honor, and Jesus was just one of the guests. Whichever is the case, Jesus noticed those who rushed up to the head of the table. In those days, the seating would have been arranged in a U-shape, with the main guest seated at the center. The farther away from the center you got, the lower the place of honor. Everyone wanted to sit next to the person at the center.

The Incident of the Parable

It is rather surprising that Jesus was the guest of a prominent Pharisee at all, given that He often either poked fun at the Pharisees or made caustic comments about the way in which they conducted themselves. You may also find it surprising that He accepted an invitation from a leader of the Pharisees, when He is better known for associating with the poor and with sinners. The truth is that Jesus reached people at every conceivable level.

The Purpose of the Parable

The purpose of the parable is to teach us how to receive true and valid honor here on earth. Do you crave recognition? People will do strange things to be noticed. God is not opposed to our being honored, providing it is done in His way and in His time. There is an honor that comes from God alone (John 12:43), and the way to get that, Jesus said, is not to rush to the top of the table (the place of highest honor) but to take the lowest seat. Then you will be invited to come up to a higher position (Luke 14:10–11). That is God's way of doing it.

The parable also shows us how to avoid unnecessary embarrassment. We all value our self-esteem. Nobody enjoys being embarrassed, and Jesus kindly shows us how we can spare ourselves unnecessary humiliation. He was saying, "Play it safe—go to the lowest place and you will spare yourself embarrassment." It is a practical word.

The purpose of the parable is also to show us how we can be guaranteed a reward at the judgment seat of Christ. Let me tell you how *not* to get that reward. Don't bother inviting the president to have supper with you! Even if he was to accept, Jesus said, "Don't do it that way." Instead, Jesus said, "Invite the poor, the crippled, the lame, the blind, and you will be blessed. Although they cannot repay you, you will be repaid at the resurrection of the righteous" (Luke 14:13–14).

Why Is This Parable Important?

Jesus spoke of a type of class system that will always exist in society. There are some people who will always be regarded as more important than others. To have a classless society is impossible. Human nature will always be the same—we all want to be seen with the most important people. It gives us prestige. Even Jesus, when He said that we should always consider that someone more distinguished has been invited to the table, was admitting that there will always be levels of prestige.

The parable indicates that nobody outgrows the possibility of wanting to feel important or of wanting to avoid embarrassment. Jesus was being realistic. He understands human nature like nobody else. Like it or not, we are all conscious of what others think of us— anyone who says he is totally dead to that is a liar. If I weren't conscious of what other people think, I wouldn't bother to wear a tie in the pulpit; I would preach in my pajamas and my bedroom slippers. But I do care a little about how others view me.

We also learn that God clearly approves of a person being openly honored in the way that occurs in this parable. He wants us to take the lowest place, because when we are then called to move up, it is both ourselves and God who are honored. God isn't jealous when we are given honor—He gets the glory too. The question is, do we only want to receive the honor of men, or are we are willing to see what God can do when He alone orchestrates things? We can have a hand in cooperating with God in this, and the best way to do it, Jesus said, is by taking the lowest place.

Arthur Blessitt was invited to be the chief speaker at a Jesus rally some years ago in Washington, D.C. The organizers heard that Arthur was going to visit a particular church in Virginia that was a bit "doubtful" in their eyes because it was a little "over the top" in the things of the Spirit. The conference leaders asked him not to go to this particular church, or they would have to cancel his rally invitation. However, Arthur wanted to go, and he simply said to me, "If you start running, where do you stop?" He decided to go ahead and visit the church, assuming that it meant his invitation to speak at the rally would be made void. However, when he later turned up at the rally, carrying his wooden cross as he always did, the place went wild. When the people saw him arriving, they began to yell and cheer enthusiastically. Frankly, the organizers had no choice but to invite him up onto the platform to speak as originally planned. God can do this in His sovereignty—just when you aren't trying to gain any kind of recognition, God decides to honor you.

Bear in mind that there is a subtle danger in applying this word. There are those who will say, "Oh well, I always take the lowest place— glory to God, I am just a humble servant," and yet they don't really mean it. They are trying to "play the game" instead of being genuine; what they are doing is actually false humility. Have you ever noticed a person who doesn't really have a posh accent but tries to claim they do?

I tell you even a hick from the hills of Kentucky can see through that! It is so obvious. Jesus does not want us to have false humility. Don't be pretentiously unpretentious! Jesus is not after that—He wants us to sincerely desire the glory of God.

A Pompous Assumption

The pompous assumption of this parable is that it is important to be seen in a place of honor, even if you don't deserve it. It is like someone who drives a Bentley but can't really afford it. They get their kicks from people thinking they *can* afford it. It is also like those who refer to famous people whom they don't really know, but they name-drop all the same. People like this are often sensitive to being found out. What would those people who chose the places of honor at the table have said if the host had approached them and said, "Look, I'm sorry about this, but you are going to have to sit over there instead"? It would have been very embarrassing, and they would suddenly look very unimportant.

Dale Carnegie, who wrote the book *How to Win Friends and Influence People,* said that the strongest urge in people is the desire to feel important. No one is denying that; in fact, Jesus was admitting it. It is in all of us. The people Jesus described here, however, are ones who don't see the folly of promoting themselves.

The "pompous assumption" of this parable may also be applied to salvation, to those who don't see the folly of self-effort and who think they can be saved by their good works. It can also be applied to those who don't see the folly of self-exaltation as far as appearance is concerned. They want instantaneous recognition, and they don't realize that the honor is temporary. They don't stop to think that ten minutes later or ten days later, people may forget about them. They just live for the "now" moment and to enjoy a little bit of glory. We can liken this to this occasion when Absalom built a monument to himself (2 Samuel 18:18).

Could anything be any more ridiculous? Absalom was afraid he wouldn't be noticed or remembered. Now he is remembered, and it is with pity! Is that the way you want to be remembered? The Bible says, "Let another praise you, and not your own mouth" (Proverbs 27:2).

Prudent Advice

Jesus gave prudent advice in this parable. I am tempted to call it pragmatic advice. It is very practical and is, by the way, a rare moment because Jesus doesn't always give explicit, practical advice. People were always coming to Him, saying, "What would You do about this?" and He wouldn't get involved. He grasped this opportunity, though, with both hands. As I said above, God gives hints rather than directions and often that is true, generally speaking. But here Jesus gave explicit advice, telling us what to do and what not to do.

First, He said not to go to the place of honor. "When someone invites you to a wedding feast, do not take the place of honor, for a person more distinguished than you may have been invited" (Luke 14:8).

In heaven we will all be conscious that we don't deserve to be there. God puts us there anyway. The person who is saved is the one who humbles himself and recognizes that he is a sinner and has fallen short of the glory of God. He prays, *God, be merciful to me a sinner.* He humbles himself. Maybe there was a time when that person thought his good works would help him, but now he sees that that is not the case. So he climbs down and pleads for the mercy and blood of Jesus.

"He who humbles himself will be exalted" (Luke 14:11). That is the way to be saved. It takes humility. Likewise, if you seek a place of honor, there will inevitably be a double humiliation. First, you will be embarrassed in front of everybody because you are asked to move and sit someplace else. Then you find that the next few places are already taken, so you have to go all the way down to the end. Perhaps someone comes and sees you sitting in the lowest place and says, "What are you doing here? I thought I saw you up there." So you are humiliated twice. Jesus said that is the way it will be (Luke 14:9).

The Unveiling of Honor

I think this parable gives us a further hint, in case we needed it, that the judgment of Christ will happen in the open for everyone to see. You will find out whether so-and-so is real or a sham. You will find out whether I am really a man of God or a fraud. There will be no arguing at that time. Varying degrees of honor will be unveiled, as well as varying degrees of humiliation. You see, Jesus said, "You will be repaid at the resurrection of the righteous" (Luke 14:14).

What happens at the resurrection of the righteous? We will all stand before the judgment seat of Christ. The apostle Paul said, "For we must all appear before the judgment seat of Christ, that each one may receive what is due him for the things done while in the body, whether good or bad" (2 Corinthians 5:10).

At that time all will be revealed, and everyone will know what you and I are really like. You can hide now, and no one really knows what you are like, but at that time it will all be out in the open. This parable gives a preview of what it will be like at the judgment seat of Christ. Honor and humiliation will be out in the open. Those who are saved by fire will all be known. This is why Jesus said, "For there is nothing hidden that will not be disclosed, and nothing concealed that will not be known or brought out into the open" (Luke 8:17).

Anything that is not covered by the blood of Jesus will be out for all to see. The truth about our relationship with God will be plain. It will be better for all of us if we lower our voices and look to take the lowest seat. Play it safe: Don't murmur and don't complain. Take this prudent advice from Jesus. Don't try to make any overblown claims; don't look for instant recognition or for people to honor you.

The Host

Taking the lowest place means a willingness to wait and let God do the judging. What is promised if you wait? Jesus said:

> When you are invited take the lowest place, so that when your host comes, he will say to you, "Friend, move up to a better place." Then you will be honored in the presence of all your fellow guests. For everyone who exalts himself will be humbled, and he who humbles himself will be exalted.
>
> Luke 14:10–11

If you hold back and don't try to promote yourself, you will be honored in front of everybody. It will be a lot better that way; it is certainly a lot better than humiliation. The host is a type of God the Father. The promise is that God will find you—your host will find you. That gift that you have and that you are afraid is not going to be recognized—God will find you and use it. Perhaps you have an ability that you think nobody knows about—God knows about it. How will anybody find out about it? God has a way.

We are so afraid that we won't be noticed and that we won't be honored, but God knows what each of us can do. He will find you. In the meantime, take the lowest seat and don't exalt yourself. God is the host in this parable, and nothing is hidden from Him. He loves to honor those who wait and don't try to raise a finger to exalt themselves.

Guaranteed Justice

Jesus said, "Everyone who exalts himself will be humbled" (Luke 14:11).

Have you been exalting yourself? Have you been pushing your name forward? Have you been trying to get someone to pull strings for you? Don't do it. If God has chosen you for a specific task, then no one will be able to prevent you from being promoted into that position. Don't make the mistake of thinking that you have to strive to promote yourself there. If God wants you to be exalted, He will exalt you. If you are supposed to have a particular job in your church, God will find you. If God wants you to be in a particular place, He will put you there. Luke 14:11 is a precautionary axiom, a self-evident truth. Jesus is warning us—if you exalt yourself, you will be abased. Those who build their own empire, protect their own name, run ahead of God, walk over the underdog and seek to vindicate themselves will be brought down.

We should note that Jesus wasn't really saying anything new in this parable, because in Proverbs 25 we read, "Do not exalt yourself in the king's presence, and do not claim a place among great men; it is better for him to say to you, 'Come up here,' than for him to humiliate you before a nobleman" (Proverbs 25:6–7).

Notice that Jesus didn't give any indication of how long we will have to wait. It may be that the justice you get will be on earth, but it will certainly be there at the judgment seat of Christ, when everything will be out in the open.

Guaranteed Joy

"And he who humbles himself will be exalted" (Luke 14:11).

Being exalted will give us great pleasure. We read in Philippians:

> God exalted him [Jesus] to the highest place and gave him the name that is above every name, that at the name of Jesus every knee should bow, in heaven and on earth and under the earth, and every tongue confess that Jesus Christ is Lord, to the glory of God the Father.
>
> Philippians 2:9

Have you ever wondered whether Jesus liked that? He did. I am convinced that it must have helped Him to endure His terrible humiliation before Pilate and Herod. Throughout all that He suffered and the awful shame of the cross, He knew of the reward that was coming, and He said, "I'll wait for it." He didn't wag His finger at Pilate or Herod; He didn't even open His mouth. He didn't do anything that would counteract the joy that was set before Him. Do you know that God wants to do that with you and me? He says, "Your attitude should be the same as that of Christ Jesus" (Philippians 2:5).

Guaranteed joy comes when God exalts us, either on earth or at the judgment, but we must first humble ourselves before God. There are four things that I would like us to notice about humbling ourselves.

Humiliation

First, it is a *voluntary* humiliation. It is accomplished by choice, by an act of the will. Second, it is a *valiant* humiliation because it takes great courage; it takes the willingness to lose face, to wait on God's time and to be misunderstood in the meantime. That was exactly what happened to Jesus on the cross. If there is a need to explain or defend yourself and say, "Now let me tell you exactly what was happening here," then God may say, "I would have vindicated you, but you just had to do it yourself." It takes courage. Third, it is a *valuable* humiliation because it puts you in good stead, and the end is worth waiting for. And fourth, it is a *victorious* humiliation because the result is absolutely guaranteed. It is an axiom: He who humbles himself *will* be exalted.

A Practical Application

There is one final thing about this parable. Jesus gave a practical application. He spoke to the host—the prominent Pharisee:

> When you give a luncheon or dinner, do not invite your friends, your brothers or relatives, or your rich neighbors; if you do, they may invite you back and so you will be repaid. But when you give a banquet, invite the poor, the crippled, the lame, the blind, and you will be blessed. Although they cannot repay you, you will be repaid at the resurrection of the righteous.
>
> Luke 14:12–14

This was a serious put-down to the host who had invited Jesus. How can we apply Jesus' words? Jesus gave some very straightforward, practical advice: "Don't throw parties for all your rich friends who are more than able to honor you in return. Instead, have a banquet for the poor, the crippled, the lame, the blind ... you will be blessed because they cannot repay you." You will only be able to do this when you have no need to prove anything. The greatest liberty in life is having nothing to prove.

Let me give a different example. Say we have been praying for a person to be healed and we hastily (and rather unwisely) declare that they are healed before we are really sure. That is like going to the top of the table. What if it turns out two days later that they weren't healed? Take the lower seat—if they have been healed, it will come out later. The point is, don't make exaggerated claims. Take the route of humility instead.

Jesus applied His own parable. He was teaching us not to try to build up our own reputation by being seen with the great and the good. Instead be a friend to the poor, to those who have no reputation and cannot increase your prestige. That way God will give you a blessing. You may get that blessing immediately—perhaps you will find that you just feel very good inside. But when you choose as a friend someone who can't repay you, or you decide to be seen with those who are not going to help your reputation, it is a guaranteed blessing—if not here, then certainly at the resurrection of the righteous.

Jesus was saying three things. First, your reward will be spiritual and not material. Second, your reward is eternal and not temporary. And third, your reward is from God and not from man.

So what is our responsibility? To bless those who cannot bless us back, to befriend those who cannot befriend us and to give to those who cannot pay us back. Spend time with those who have nothing but time on their hands. Jesus was saying this to the Pharisee who invited Him; He was no respecter of persons. What are you doing now that can only be rewarded on judgment day?

Chapter 23

The Parable of the Great Banquet

A certain man was preparing a great banquet and invited many guests.
Luke 14:16

This parable from Luke 14:15–24 is similar to, though not the same as, the parable of the wedding banquet in Matthew 22 (which we will look at in the next chapter). The parable of the great banquet follows directly from the parable of the pompous guest. You will remember that Jesus was a guest at the table of a prominent Pharisee, possibly even the honored guest. He has just taught the lesson that those who exalt themselves will be humbled and those who humble themselves will be exalted (Luke 14:11). Jesus also encouraged people to invite to their banquets those who are disenfranchised or vulnerable—those who could not repay the favor. He said that those who look after the poor in such a way will be repaid "at the resurrection of the righteous" (Luke 14:14).

Then, as they were seated at the table, someone spoke up and said, "Blessed is the man who will eat at the feast in the kingdom of God" (Luke 14:15).

We are not exactly sure what this man had in mind when he spoke out. Maybe it was just a throwaway comment, or perhaps he was speaking under the inspiration of the Spirit. Either way, Jesus seized upon this statement, took it seriously and gave this parable by way of reply.

Jesus told the story of a man who threw a great banquet and invited many guests to come and join him. When it was time for the dinner, he sent out his servant to tell those who were invited to come, because the banquet was ready. However, one after another, the guests made excuses as to why they could no longer come to the banquet. When the servant reported back, the master of the house was furious. He ordered the servant, "Go out quickly into the streets and alleys of the town and bring in here the poor, the crippled, the blind and the lame" (Luke 14:21).

The servant did this and later had to go out and do the same again before his master's house was finally full. The master then swore that none of those who were invited at the beginning would taste even a bite of his supper.

Jesus said that because the people who had been invited gave lame excuses rather than coming to the banquet, the host then invited the very kind of people whom He had recommended in the previous parable—the poor, the crippled, the lame and the blind.

How can we interpret this parable? Remember the context in which Jesus was speaking. The wealthy host who did the inviting clearly refers to God the Father. The servant who announced that the feast was ready refers to those who preach the Word. Those who made excuses stand primarily for the Jews—to whom the Gospel was initially offered—and those who eventually came to the banquet were the Gentiles. Finally, the oath in verse 24 was God's declaration to those who reject His offer.

Why Is This Parable Important?

The Honor of God

This parable is primarily concerned with the honor of God. God's desire is that we honor Him by honoring His Son. The words, "so that my house will be full" (Luke 14:23) show that appearances do matter to God. It wouldn't have looked good, when this banquet was given, for no one to show up. Everyone would have laughed at the host and said, "Did you hear what happened?" Like it or not, appearances do matter to God.

God's Wrath

The parable gives us a glimpse of God's wrath. Just look at the feeble excuses in Luke 14:18–21 that the guests gave for not turning up. One man had just bought a field and wanted to go and see it. Another had just bought five yoke of oxen and wanted to try them out. A third couldn't come because he had just gotten married. In his anger, the host turned to those who *would* be grateful. He was angry toward those who had rejected the invitation but as a result showed mercy to those who would never normally have received an invitation like this. They chose to come because they wanted to—and they were grateful.

When Jesus gave the oath at the end of the parable (Luke 14:24), it is reminiscent of God's words to the Israelites: "Not one of you will enter the land I swore with uplifted hand to make your home, except Caleb son of Jephunneh and Joshua son of Nun" (Numbers 14:30).

After that, the Israelites repented of their grumbling against the Lord and said they would go to the land the Lord had promised. But Moses warned them, "Do not go up, because the LORD is not with you. You will be defeated by your enemies" (Numbers 14:42). They went anyway, and their enemies cut them down, because when God says you won't get something, it means you won't get it. The same was happening here when Jesus said, "I tell you, not one of those men who were invited will get a taste of my banquet" (Luke 14:24).

Fulfillment of the Old Testament

The words of Jesus in verses 16 and 17 provide an amazing illustration of what was soon happen to Him. In verse 16 He said, "A certain man was preparing a great banquet" (Luke 14:16). This is a picture of the Father God bringing to an end the whole Old Testament era in anticipation of the day when Jesus would come. The following phrase, "Come, for everything is now ready" (Luke 14:17) brings to mind Jesus' words, "It is finished," on the cross. The words were prophetic, showing that Jesus was *the fulfillment* of the Old Testament. The message we preach today is that everything is now ready. Jesus has died on the cross and His blood has satisfied divine justice. It is a finished work.

Our Excuses

Jesus' teaching in this parable once again contains astute observations regarding human nature. Jesus implied that the "guests" who changed their minds about attending the banquet didn't give the real reasons why they wouldn't attend. Instead they had trumped-up excuses. It is as if they didn't realize that the master of the banquet could see right through their excuses—but he does. It is the same with us. When God calls people to salvation, maybe through a preacher or an evangelist, they can come up with every excuse under the sun as to why they cannot respond at this time. They don't realize that they are not rejecting the invitation of men but of God Himself. They give their excuses, perhaps even a theological rationale, to cover up the real reason that they don't want to accept the invitation.

The Importance of Evangelism

This parable demonstrates the vital role of evangelism in God's Kingdom. When he was told there was still room at the table, the master told his servant, "Go out to the roads and country lanes and *make them* come in, so that my house will be full" (Luke 14:23, emphasis added). The King James Version says, "*Compel* them to come in, that my house may be filled" (Luke 14:23, emphasis added).

These words show us our commission and the importance of evangelism. When the Lord called me to be a personal evangelist and to begin an outreach ministry in London, I nearly died a thousand deaths. I thought, *I do my job. I stand in the pulpit every week, and I follow in the tradition of making the Sunday evening services evangelistic. Very few ministers do that week after week after week.* But God said, "Go out into the streets!" My pride was shattered, and I was out of my comfort zone—I had aspired to be a theologian! But God wanted me to go out to the "roads and country lanes" (Luke 14:23) and do my best to "bring them in." I had modest success, but I never looked back.

The Danger of Rejecting God's Plan

Jesus shows us the danger of rejecting what God wants to do—and the danger of rejecting the Gospel. The oath of the master was that not one of those who had rejected the invitation would get a taste of the banquet. For those who have heard the Gospel but have never received the Lord or confessed their sins, time is running out. You cannot say forever, "One day I will make that commitment, but not today," for God says, "My Spirit will not contend with man forever, for he is mortal" (Genesis 6:3).

This parable may also be interpreted as showing the danger of rejecting the Holy Spirit. Being open to the moving of God's Spirit is not an option we can just take or leave. The danger is that if we do not respond to the guidance of God's Spirit, God will raise up people to take our place—people who will really honor Him as He desires. It breaks my heart to see this happen.

The Importance of Gratitude

Again, we can see the importance of gratitude and the danger of ingratitude. God is looking for a grateful people. The poor, the lame and the blind never dreamed of getting into a banquet such as this. Those who filled the room knew they were unworthy, but they were very glad to be there. Those who said they would come, and then when the time came rejected the offer, showed ingratitude to God. God hates ingratitude and presumption. Those who were initially invited were just like the Pharisee whom Jesus had gone to have dinner with.

God's elect is made up of all kinds of people, including those who are indeed blind, poor, crippled and lame, but who have been compelled to come in by our loving heavenly Father. God is determined that His house will be full—even if it is populated by people who have benefited because others were foolish enough to reject His invitation. The Gospel reached us Gentiles only after the Jews rejected the Messiah. They are the ones who had the Gospel coming to them first. This is why Jesus gave the parable with the Pharisee listening.

God's Plan A

The parable shows that what appears to be "plan B" is really God's "plan A." The Jews rejected Christ, and God turned to the Gentiles— that was the plan B. But those Gentiles who were saved had been chosen from the foundation of the world. It is a paradox. It turns out that it was plan A after all. Peter described Jesus as "a stone that causes men to stumble and a rock that makes them fall" (1 Peter 2:8).

He said of the Jews, "They stumble because they disobey the message—which is also what they were destined for" (1 Peter 2:8).

God's elect have been chosen from the foundation of the world, so those who rejected Jesus actually did not take God by surprise. Neither do those who reject Him today take Him by surprise. What appears to be God's plan B in fact turns out to be His plan A.

A Privileged Invitation

Remember that Jesus told this parable in response to a statement: "Blessed is the man who will eat at the feast in the kingdom of God" (Luke 14:15).

Notice how this unknown person got so excited at the banquet table. This person realized what a privilege it would be to be invited to the Lord's banquet. This word *blessed,* as you probably know, means "happy." Those who are destined to partake in God's banquet are happy indeed.

I recently found an even a better translation for the word *blessed.* One Greek scholar says that it also means "congratulations." Imagine that in the context of the Beatitudes—"congratulations" to the poor in spirit; "congratulations" if you suffer persecution. Here we have "congratulations" to the man who will eat at the feast in the Kingdom of God. It is a privilege—the unknown guest was right.

The Purpose of the Invitation

The purpose of the invitation was "so that my house will be full" (Luke 14:23). Have you ever decided to have a big meal or a big party, and you think, *I wonder if anybody will come?* Unless you are the queen of England, or the president, or someone very famous, you may have worried if people would come. I don't suppose the Queen paces up and down before a banquet wondering to herself, *Will anyone turn up?* People don't tend to say no to a sovereign. But when people like you and me who are not so important decide to arrange a big event, we wonder whether anyone will come.

If you invite someone to attend an important event and they say no, it could be a little humiliating, but it is worse when they say yes at first and then later find an excuse not to come, as happened in the parable. Numbers do matter to God. Throughout the Bible we see many instances where God takes careful note of numbers. For instance, Luke recorded on the Day of Pentecost that three thousand were converted (Acts 2:41). Later he wrote in Acts 4:4 that five thousand were converted. Finally, in Revelation we read, "I looked, and behold, a great multitude which no one could number, of all nations" (Revelation 7:9, NKJV).

This is a significant verse. It shows us that, in the end, there will be a vast multitude of people in heaven, because God wants His house to be full. We won't need to worry about there not being enough people in heaven to bring honor and glory to the Son of God. It will be one great banquet and a time of worship when countless millions will be praising the Lamb.

The Passing Up of the Invitation

It amazes me how the people in the parable came up with their poor excuses.

> The first said, "I have just bought a field, and I must go and see it. Please excuse me." Another said, "I have just bought five yoke of oxen, and I'm on my way to try them out. Please excuse me." Still another said, "I just got married, so I can't come."
>
> Luke 14:18–20

The impoliteness! They had obviously already agreed that they would come. It is like that parable where Jesus said, "There was a man who had two sons. He went to the first and said, 'Son, go and work today in the vineyard.' 'I will not,' he answered, but later he changed his mind and went" (Matthew 21:28–29). Then the father asked the second son to go. "He answered, 'I will, sir,' but he did not go" (Matthew 21:30).

In the parable of the great banquet, there are those who said yes, and then when everything was ready, they said, "Sorry, we just can't make it." Jesus wants us to know that it is not only impolite, but it is impudent. Impudence is the height of impertinence, and it was an insult to the host. The definition of an insult is to speak or act in a way that hurts the feelings or pride of another person and arouses his anger. In some cases, it may be that the insult was *intended* to hurt this man. That is why Jesus said, "Not one of those men who were invited will get a taste of my banquet" (Luke 14:24).

God Hates Ingratitude

I have tried to teach over the years that God loves gratitude and that He hates ingratitude. But gratitude must be taught. The people of Israel were utterly without excuse. They could read in the Scriptures how much God loves gratitude. The Psalms are literally full of exhortations to give thanks. "*Give thanks* to the LORD, for he is good. His love endures forever" (Psalm 136:1, emphasis added). "Let them *give thanks* to the LORD for his unfailing love and his wonderful deeds for men" (Psalm 107:21, emphasis added).

Israel was not a grateful people. And God responded, "I revealed myself to those who did not ask for me; I was found by those who did not seek me. To a nation that did not call on my name, I said, 'Here am I, here am I' " (Isaiah 65:1).

This passage was referring to the Gentiles, those who would be brought in to attend God's banquet after the first invitation had been refused. Again God said through Isaiah, "All day long I have held out my hands to an obstinate people, who walk in ways not good, pursuing their own imaginations" (Isaiah 65:2).

God described His chosen people as "obstinate." This prophecy looked forward to the Jews' rejection of Jesus as Messiah. They were "obstinate" because they were entrenched in their old ways of thinking and weren't prepared to receive anything new. The refusal to take what God offers in the way He gives it, whether salvation or the Holy Spirit, is summed up by the word *ingratitude*.

The Irony of the Parable

The irony in this parable is God's simultaneous anger and mercy. He was angry toward those who refused His mercy—those who were first given an invitation. But He was merciful toward those who never expected to receive an invitation, to those who never dreamed that they would even be invited. "Consider therefore the kindness and sternness of God: sternness to those who fell, but kindness to you, provided that you continue in his kindness" (Romans 11:22).

His mercy is toward the Gentiles, who in Jesus' day didn't have a chance because they were regarded as the scum of the earth. In ancient Israel, every male Jew prayed three things every day—he thanked God that he wasn't a woman, he thanked God that he wasn't a dog and he thanked God that he wasn't a Gentile. But now the Gentiles were blessed—to the Gentiles God says, "Congratulations."

The impetus to evangelize with zeal springs from this act of God's mercy. God stirs us to action and says to us, "*Compel* them to come in, that my house may be filled" (Luke 14:23, KJV, emphasis added). And then God judges those who rejected His kind invitation: "I tell you, not one of those men who were invited will get a taste of my banquet" (Luke 14:24).

It is an important postscript on the event that God remembers those who are grateful and those who are not. When Jesus healed ten lepers, Luke recorded that only one returned to say thank you. "He threw himself at Jesus' feet and thanked him—and he was a Samaritan" (Luke 17:16). Jesus' comment was, "Were not all ten cleansed? Where are the other nine? Was no one found to return and give praise to God except this foreigner?" (Luke 17:17–18).

So God turned from Israel. What had happened in ancient Israel (when God swore that the grumbling Israelites wouldn't enter the Promised Land—see Numbers 14:30) is paralleled by Hebrews 6:4 and 6: "It is impossible for those who have once been enlightened . . . if they fall away, to be brought back to repentance."

It is so important to accept God's invitation—to come to Him in humility and repentance—that I can hardly underline it enough. If God told me that He was taking me home to heaven before sundown today, I would spend my remaining time urging everyone I came across to seek His face on bended knee, to be sincere in prayer and receive His invitation and then to live with a grateful heart. Maybe reading this today you will be convicted of any ingratitude you have allowed into your life and say, "Thank You, Lord, for giving me this 'wake-up' call. I am truly grateful for all You have done for me." Amen.

Chapter 24

The Parable of the Wedding Banquet

> The kingdom of heaven is like a king who prepared a wedding banquet
> for his son.
>
> Matthew 22:2

The parable of the wedding banquet is similar to the parable of the
great banquet discussed in the previous chapter. Some of the applications we saw then overlap with this parable, but they are different
enough to deserve separate treatment. The similarities can be summar-
ized as follows: In Luke's parable of the great banquet, the main
reference was to a "certain man." In this parable, found in Matthew,
the reference is to a king. In Luke the meal was a great supper, but here
it is a wedding banquet for the king's son. In Luke, the invited guests
only made excuses, but in this parable they refuse to come and even
turn violent. In Luke, the guests who refused to come were passed over,
but in Matthew they are destroyed. The most striking *difference* is that
the Matthew account contains a description of a person who arrives at
the wedding banquet inappropriately dressed and is subsequently
punished.

The parable teaches us five main things. First, it speaks of the fact
that God invited the Jews to His messianic banquet. It agrees with
Paul's words in Romans: "I am not ashamed of the gospel, because it is
the power of God for the salvation of everyone who believes: *first for the
Jew, then for the Gentile*" (Romans 1:16, emphasis added).

Second, since the first invitation was rejected by the Jews, a second
one was given (Matthew 22:4). Jesus was giving a prophetic word to
show what would happen after the Spirit came down at Pentecost. The
apostles were the ones to give this second invitation, but the Jews only
rejected it and began to persecute them. Martyrdom ensued.

Third, we see that God's retribution was to pass over the ancient Jews
and call the Gentiles to Himself. Paul said that the Lord hardened the
hearts of the Jews: "God gave them a spirit of stupor, eyes so that they
could not see and ears so that they could not hear, to this very day"

(Romans 11:8). Over the centuries it has been exceedingly difficult to communicate the Gospel to Jewish people because of the hardening that came upon them. Paul said, "Israel has experienced a hardening in part until the full number of the Gentiles has come in" (Romans 11:25).

The fourth thing we see is that God's invitation to the Gentiles is conditional. Though the invitation went first to the Jews, it didn't mean that every one of them could accept the invitation to attend the wedding banquet. The same is true of the Gentiles. It seems that a person still had to meet certain conditions in order to be able to attend the banquet. This is illustrated by the attendee who was discovered to be inappropriately dressed. Jesus was saying that the invitation was based on the condition of faith. The condition was that they *believed.* Faith counts as righteousness: "It is the power of God for the salvation of everyone who believes" (Romans 1:16). The one who managed to get into the wedding hall was like those who get into the church without being converted—they do not have the proper attire. They are not covered by Christ's righteousness.

The fifth thing that we learn in this parable is that those who believe are *chosen.* Jesus added a PS to the end of this parable. He said that "many are invited, but few are chosen" (Matthew 22:14).

Why Is This Parable Important?

First and foremost, this parable reminds us of God's plan. It reminds us of the fact that He began with the Jews, and later, because of their unresponsiveness to Him, He turned to the Gentiles. Those of us who are Gentiles should be thankful that, belatedly, we have been invited to the banquet. We Gentiles became the beneficiaries of covenant mercy after Israel said no to Jesus Christ the Messiah.

The parable also revealed Jesus' prophetic gift. Through this parable He prophesied the rejection of the Gospel by the Jews, how they would turn on the very ones who gave the invitations. The first invitation was Jesus' own ministry: "Come to Me, all you who labor and are heavy laden, and I will give you rest" (Matthew 11:28, NKJV).

Jesus said this to the Jews. The second invitation was given by the apostles who preached the Gospel after the Day of Pentecost. Many of those New Testament believers gave Israel another opportunity. But there were still many Jews who rejected it. Jesus wanted us to know that nothing takes God by surprise. At the end of this parable He said, "Many are called, but few are chosen" (Matthew 22:14, NKJV).

Peter described Jesus as " 'a stone that causes men to stumble and a rock that makes them fall.' They stumble because they disobey the message—which is also what they were destined for" (1 Peter 2:8).

So we can conclude from this that those who rejected the Gospel were destined to do so. Jesus was saying, "Don't be surprised." When both invitations have been rejected, God goes looking for others.

"So the servants went out into the streets and gathered all the people they could find, both good and bad, and the wedding hall was filled with guests" (Matthew 22:10). This means that God's elect were all saved, and they are made up of both good and bad people. "Good" does not mean morally righteous and without need of a Savior. Jesus was simply referring here to upstanding people. "Bad" refers to the scum of the earth. In other words, it doesn't matter whether you are a beggar, a tramp or a millionaire, whether you drive a Rolls Royce or are homeless. God wants His wedding hall to be full; this is why the servants went out and gathered anyone and everyone. God's elect are made up of every tribe, kindred, tongue and nation *and* of the ungodly (Romans 4:5).

However, the parable makes the important point that some get into the Church without warrant. "When the king came in to see the guests, he noticed a man there who was not wearing wedding clothes. 'Friend,' he asked, 'how did you get in here without wedding clothes?' The man was speechless" (Matthew 22:11–12).

So it wasn't enough to be invited or to be a Gentile. You were still required to have the right clothing, that is, the robe of righteousness given to you by the blood of Jesus. This clothing comes when you transfer your trust to what Jesus did for you on the cross and say, "I have no hope of getting to heaven but by the blood of Jesus. My hope is built on nothing less than Jesus' blood and righteousness."

Those in the church who are not saved will be found out eventually because Jesus said the man was speechless. This hints at the final judgment. Jesus said, "Many will say to me on that day, 'Lord, Lord, did we not prophesy in your name, and in your name drive out demons and perform many miracles?' Then I will tell them plainly, 'I never knew you. Away from me, you evildoers!' " (Matthew 7:22–23).

This parable also refers to hell and to eternal punishment. "Then the king told the attendants, 'Tie him hand and foot, and throw him outside, into the darkness, where there will be weeping and gnashing of teeth' " (Matthew 22:13).

When I was a boy, we once went to Mammoth Cave in western Kentucky. It was several hundred feet into the ground, and the guide said, "I am going to turn out the lights and in one minute we will turn them back on." You never saw such darkness. You couldn't see your hand in front of your face, and after fifteen seconds everyone was ready for the lights to come back on. It was the longest minute you can imagine. Hell will be like that. If you reject the offer of the Gospel and choose darkness rather than accept Jesus as your Lord and Savior, you will get utter darkness. There will be weeping and gnashing of teeth.

Jesus concluded the parable by saying that many are invited but few are chosen. Although we Gentiles are God's "plan B," we were also chosen from the foundation of the world. Don't try to figure out predestination; you just have to accept it. God has made us worthy.

I was looking recently at a photo of myself with the former British Prime Minister Margaret Thatcher. It happened that I was given some time with her at a certain event, and then later they brought in the vice president of the United States, America's ambassador to England, the chief justice of the Supreme Court and two other famous dignitaries. All these people got to do was shake her hand, yet somehow I had managed to spend some time talking to her! Then they took a photo and said they wanted me in it—I was in the front row. I felt like a fraud, but they said, "No, we want you there." This is the way it will be when we get to heaven. We will see all the people who were invited and we will think, *Me? How did I get in?* But God says, "Yes, you." We are saved by the sheer grace of God. We did nothing to deserve it.

There are five further main elements to the parable that I will examine in turn—rejection, revenge, righteousness, retribution and revelation.

Rejection

"He sent his servants to those who had been invited to the banquet to tell them to come, but they refused to come. . . . They paid no attention and went off—one to his field, another to his business. The rest seized his servants, mistreated them and killed them" (Matthew 22:3, 5–6).

Jesus was preaching the Kingdom of heaven to the Jews. He chose twelve disciples—all of whom were Jews. The one hundred twenty people in the Upper Room on the Day of Pentecost were all Jews. Three thousand were converted on the Day of Pentecost, every single one of them a Jew. It began to look as though Jesus had gotten it wrong. Revival had come, and Judaism was gradually turning to Jesus. But this apparent overnight success didn't last. In Acts 4, after the first great miracle in the early Church, the Jews became disturbed about the teaching of Jesus' being raised from the dead, and they seized Peter and John and put them in jail until the next day. Then "they called them in again and commanded them not to speak or teach at all in the name of Jesus" (Acts 4:18).

Then in Acts 8 we are told that a great persecution broke out against the Church. Saul also continued his persecution of the believers. This was the fulfillment of Jesus' parable—when the second invitation came, the Jews turned on the very servants who did the inviting and violence broke out.

Revenge

"The king was enraged. He sent his army and destroyed those murderers and burned their city" (Matthew 22:7).

We read that the king was furious and set about to wreak revenge on those who had so callously treated his servants. The Bible reveals three ways in which God wrought His revenge upon Israel for their rejection—through jealousy, justice and judgment.

Jealousy

We read about how God used jealousy in Romans: "I will make you envious by those who are not a nation" (Romans 10:19). "Salvation has come to the Gentiles to make Israel envious" (Romans 11:11).

I wonder if you have realized that jealousy is sometimes a judgment upon you. Let me put it this way. Do you know what it is when somebody who really gets your goat seems to be doing really well, and you think, *Who are they to be blessed?* Inwardly you are upset. The trouble is that most of us will never admit that this is jealousy. Jealousy is the sort of thing you can see in other people every single time, but you can never see in yourself. The Jews' jealousy, when they saw others turning to Christ, was the judgment of God upon them—they were filled with envy. Jealousy is a painful thing. It would have been painful for the Jews to see God turning to Gentiles.

Some years ago I saw something for the first time in the passage in which Paul had the privilege of addressing the Jews in Jerusalem. The crowds listened to Paul until he remarked, "Then the Lord said to me, 'Go; I will send you far away to the Gentiles'" (Acts 22:21). The Jewish response was, "They raised their voices and shouted, 'Rid the earth of him! He's not fit to live!'" (Acts 22:22).

That's what really got them—the idea that God would turn to the Gentiles. Similarly, whenever God comes in revival, there will be those who are jealous. They will say, "It is not real revival, because if it were really the genuine thing, it wouldn't be happening to *them*—it would be happening to us." Whenever you feel a bit jealous, consider that it could be God's judgment on *you*.

Justice

Justice means an absence of mercy. Do you know the difference between grace and mercy? Grace is getting what you don't deserve. Mercy is not getting what you do deserve. We all deserve God's justice. Likewise, God, seeing the Jewish response, said, "If they want justice, that's what they'll get." From that moment on, being a Jew was no great advantage because they would get justice. The idea that Jews get a second chance just because they are Jews is nonsense. At present they get justice.

Judgment

The reality of judgment is an inability to see and to believe. Throughout the book of Acts, we see God reaching out to the Jews. But then, "Paul and Barnabas answered them boldly: 'We had to speak the word of God to you first. Since you reject it and do not consider yourselves worthy of eternal life, we now turn to the Gentiles'" (Acts 13:46).

We see it again in Corinth where Paul was rejected. He said to them, "Your blood be on your own heads! I am clear of my responsibility. From now on I will go to the Gentiles" (Acts 18:6).

The point is that all of this was predestined. The Spirit came down on the disciples for the preaching of the Gospel to the Jews, but they turned against the preachers and martyrdom began. Stephen and James were killed. So God said, "I will judge them." That is, He gave them an inability to see and believe. It is the worst thing that can happen to a person, not to be able to see God at work. Do you think that if anybody can recognize the hand of God it is you? I worry about those who have heard the Gospel so frequently that they let it go. They may find that one day they are *unable* to believe. Those who *won't* see eventually find they *can't* see and then God turns to others.

Righteousness

I want us to look here at the person who came in without a wedding garment. He was indicative of those who are not clothed in righteousness.

"But when the king came in to see the guests, he noticed a man there who was not wearing wedding clothes. 'Friend,' he asked, 'how did you get in here without wedding clothes?' The man was speechless" (Matthew 22:11–12).

Speechless! It shows that some people will inevitably get into the church without actually being converted. You may say, "Why would anybody want to come to church if they are not saved?" For some reason they do. In fact, the little epistle of Jude was written for just this reason. Jude says, "Certain men whose condemnation was written about long ago have secretly slipped in among you" (Jude 4).

In other words, such people have been predestined to slip into the church "illegally." They are described as godless men, and they enter through the back door to become members of the church—they do it without receiving the Gospel.

When I see some of the preaching that is televised throughout America, I wonder whether some of those preachers fall into this category. Some of their preaching is a perversion of the Gospel. There is sometimes no respect at all in this teaching for the main reason Jesus died on the cross. It relates only to what Christianity can *do for you* and appeals to a person's sense of prosperity. Well, such people do get into the church, but one day they will be exposed. Getting into the wedding hall without proper wedding clothes is like joining the church without being truly saved. Each of us needs the true righteousness, the righteousness that we receive by faith. If you say, "I am going to start doing better; I am going to turn over a new leaf. From now on here is what I am going to do . . ." then you are just as lost as ever. You only receive righteousness when you see that you are lost and that Jesus paid your debt on the cross.

Retribution

Retribution is punishment. "The king told the attendants, 'Tie him hand and foot, and throw him [the one who was speechless] outside, into the darkness, where there will be weeping and gnashing of teeth'" (Matthew 22:13).

He Was Found Out
When the king asked this man how he had gotten into the wedding banquet, the man was speechless. Paul says that the purpose of the revelation of the gospels is that every mouth may be stopped (Romans 3:19). As long as you keep arguing back to God, your mouth has not been stopped. Only when you become speechless will you see that you

have no hope unless you receive the mercy of God, and by then it might be too late for you to be saved. "Speechless" needs to happen to you now—otherwise it will happen to you at the judgment. Remember, if God were to say to you, and He might, "Why should I let you into My heaven?", what would you say? This man was found out.

He Was Forced

"Tie him hand and foot, and throw him outside" (Matthew 22:13).

A story I have told before finds its origin in this very parable. Here is how it came about. When I was a boy, one Sunday morning I was called out of the Sunday school class and someone told me, "The preacher wants to see you." I thought I was in trouble, and I tried to think of anything I might have done wrong that morning. But the preacher, an eighty-year-old man named Dr. W. M. Tidwell, only said he was going to be preaching in the eleven o'clock service on the parable of the wedding banquet and would I be willing to help dramatize it. At the appropriate moment, I was to come in and sit on a chair, and he would call out certain people to bind my hands and feet and carry me out. He was doing this for everybody to see what it is like when a person is tied up, as happened in the parable. I can't say I understood everything that was happening, but I understood a bit. There was great power in that service. Everyone talked about it afterward. They said it was very moving to see.

Have you heard the phrase, "God doesn't send anybody to hell; you send yourself there"? I want you to know that God takes full responsibility for sending people to hell. In today's church we tend to try to make God look good. But God *will* send you to hell. He is the king who says, "Tie him hand and foot and throw him outside into the darkness."

He Was Forsaken

The man who was cast out by the king was condemned to *separation*. In hell you will not have your friends, you will not have your relatives, you will not have your wife and you will not have your husband. You will not have any company. I heard somebody say recently, "Well, if I go to hell, I am going to have a lot of company." It will not be like that! It will be everlasting loneliness. It will mean separation, solitude and suffering. There will be weeping and gnashing of teeth.

Revelation

Finally, Jesus' parable gives us revelation. What is revealed? It is God's plan, God's purpose and God's predestination. We have already said that God's plan B turns out to be His plan A. We Gentiles have been chosen from the foundation of the world. So what is God's purpose?

The invitation is given to everybody, but God gives faith to those who are chosen. The only way you can believe is if God enables you to believe. You can't even take the credit for believing, because it is a work of the Spirit. It is due to sovereign grace.

"As many as had been appointed to eternal life believed" (Acts 13:48, NKJV). There is only one word for it—it is predestination. Jesus said, "You did not choose me, but I chose you" (John 15:16).

"All things have been committed to me by my Father. No one knows the Son except the Father, and no one knows the Father except the Son and those to whom the Son chooses to reveal him" (Matthew 11:27).

Jesus is the One who chooses. This means we had all better appeal to Him for mercy. None of us knows how much time we have left on earth, and so we need to turn to God while He may be found. The result of rejecting the Gospel is judgment. Those who refuse to see eventually will not be able to see and become as blind as Israel did.

Chapter 25

The Parables of the Lost Sheep and the Lost Coin

In the same way there will be more rejoicing in heaven over one sinner who repents than over ninety-nine righteous persons who do not need to repent.

Luke 15:7

Luke 15 is famous for three parables: the parable of the lost sheep, the parable of the lost coin and the parable of the lost son. Luke, probably more than any of the other gospels, shows Christ's love for the sinner. In Luke in particular, a sinner is usually seen as an object of sovereign grace. One Puritan put it like this: "The sinner is a sacred thing; the Holy Ghost hath made him so."

There is a theme running through the Bible that God is for the underdog. Have you watched everyone else excel while you lag behind? Do you know how it feels to be rejected by a parent, a teacher or a colleague? I want you to know that Jesus knows where you are and your situation gets His attention. The more you are rejected, the more you get the attention of Jesus. The more people look down on you, the more Jesus will look at you. This is a fact.

"A bruised reed he will not break, and a smoldering wick he will not snuff out" (Matthew 12:20). If you are bruised, Jesus knows about it.

In this chapter we will look at two parables, the parable of the lost sheep and the parable of the lost coin, because the two are virtually identical in meaning.

The parable of the lost sheep was easily understood by Jesus' audience because Galilee was largely a rural farming community. Jesus spoke about a shepherd who had one hundred sheep in his care. One of the sheep had wandered off and gotten lost, so the shepherd left the 99 remaining ones alone and went off to look for it. When he found the lost sheep, he was so delighted that he called for a celebration. Jesus immediately gave the central application of the parable, saying, "I tell you that in the same way there will be more rejoicing in heaven over one sinner who repents than over ninety-nine righteous persons who do not need to repent" (Luke 15:7).

This does not mean that there will be those people who never need to repent. The "ninety-nine persons" refers rather to those in the Church who are already walking in obedience.

Immediately following this parable, Jesus told a second one with a similar meaning to underline His point. In the parable of the lost coin, He told the story of a woman who had ten silver coins but lost one of them. Jesus pointed out that the woman lit a lamp and swept through the entire house until the coin was found. When she eventually found the coin, she called her friends and neighbors together and celebrated. Then Jesus said, "In the same way, I tell you, there is rejoicing in the presence of the angels of God over one sinner who repents" (Luke 15:10).

In this second parable, Jesus was almost certainly referring to this woman's bridal headdress (Luke 15:8). Historians report that in ancient times it was a common custom for ten coins to be placed inside bridal headdresses. If a girl lost one of the coins from her headdress, no doubt she would be very concerned until she retrieved it.

The Meaning of the Two Parables

The overwhelming message of these two parables is that *God loves sinners.* The lost sheep and the lost coin symbolize those who are help-less—being found is not something they can arrange for themselves.

Second, we learn that sinners are like sheep. God often refers to His people as sheep: "May the God of peace, who through the blood of the eternal covenant brought back from the dead our Lord Jesus, that great Shepherd of the sheep" (Hebrews 13:20). "For you were like sheep going astray, but now you have returned to the Shepherd and Overseer of your souls" (1 Peter 2:25). "He tends his flock like a shepherd: He gathers the lambs in his arms and carries them close to his heart; he gently leads those that have young" (Isaiah 40:11).

Best known of all perhaps is the following verse: "We all, like sheep, have gone astray, each of us has turned to his own way; and the LORD has laid on him the iniquity of us all" (Isaiah 53:6).

Third, we notice that when the sheep are lost, God looks for them and doesn't give up until He finds them. What is the theology behind that? There are two kinds of "lost sheep" for which God looks. First of all, we see the doctrine of election and effectual calling come into play. This means that if a person "belongs" to God because He has predestined them to belong to Him, even though they may not have been converted yet, it is as if they are one of God's sheep already. There are those out in the world of whom God says, "They are mine, and I will call them in due time." St. Augustine said, "God loves every person as if there was no one else to love." God goes after those lost sheep as if no one else existed, until He finds them and gathers them in. The second type of lost sheep is the Christian who has fallen into sin, wandered from the fold and then is later brought home. It shows God's tenderness towards the backslider.

Whether you apply the parable to the person not yet converted or to the converted person who is brought back, a celebration is called for. When the newly converted are brought to repentance, all heaven rejoices, and when a backslider returns, again, all heaven rejoices.

The fourth point that these passages teach is that heaven and the angels notice what is happening on the earth. This is an interesting point—how much do they actually *know* in heaven? Hebrews 12:1 says we are surrounded by a great cloud of witnesses. Many people believe this is saying that there are galleries filled with people, already in heaven, who look down and see what is happening on the earth and are cheering and rooting for us. Some good Bible interpreters take that view. What we can learn from these parables is that Jesus is saying those in heaven do know some of what is going on down here.

Last, the only slight difference between the two parables is that Jesus used the analogy of a sheep that wanders off in the first parable, and a coin—an inanimate object—in the second. In either case, they are helpless and need to be found because they cannot do it themselves. Likewise God doesn't give up until He finds the one He is after—until He completes the number of the elect.

Why Are These Parables Important?

A Magnet for Sinners

The context in which Jesus told these parables is very interesting. Luke 15 begins by saying that tax collectors and "sinners" were gathering around Jesus to hear what He had to say. This clearly offended the smug, self-righteous "religious" people who were also there. Does it shock you that the Pharisees and teachers of the law muttered against Jesus for this? "This man welcomes sinners and eats with them" (Luke 15:2).

But that's the way Jesus was. How would you have felt if you saw people who were known to be sinners and generally not "nice people" attracted to Jesus like a magnet? And He welcomed them! Did you know that whenever God starts a new work, almost always it begins with the scum of the earth? The rich and famous and the righteous in the Church usually want nothing to do with it. They say, "Let somebody else reach those people."

Years ago there lived a couple in Nottingham, England, by the names of William and Catherine Booth. Their minister was quite happy when they brought an unconverted person into the church from time to time. But as the number of visitors increased, the minister noticed that the type of people William and Catherine Booth were bringing in did not do a lot to make that church look prestigious. The numbers increased until there were a couple of dozen. The pastor of the church asked if they could all sit together and not mix with the others. William Booth said, "Sure, we will all stay together." But the numbers began to grow until they outnumbered everybody else. Those who were outnumbered resented the type of people that were being brought in. William and Catherine Booth eventually decided to move across town where for the first time they unfurled a banner reading "Blood & Fire," and the Salvation Army was born.

One of the quickest ways you can grieve the Holy Spirit is to behave like those described above who were outnumbered. It would be awful if someone came into our churches because they were desperate to hear the Gospel and were made to feel unwelcome. The sinner is a sacred thing—the Holy Spirit has made him so.

He Finds Us
Second, this is an important word because it is relevant to everyone— we have all been lost, and God sees our helplessness. "For He knows our frame; He remembers that we are dust" (Psalm 103:14, NKJV).

If we are lost, God doesn't give up until He finds us, whether we happen to be His elect and hear His call to salvation, or whether we are a backslider. All of us have all been backsliders to some degree. You don't have to behave in a scandalous way that brings the Church into disrepute to be a backslider. If your heart is cold, then your very presence in a service grieves the Holy Spirit. If you are bitter and think you are a cut above the rest, then you are in a backslidden state that will keep the Spirit from working. The point is that whether we are "sheep" or "coins," God sees our helplessness.

The Importance of Repentance
Third, these parables show the importance of repentance. "I tell you that in the same way there will be more rejoicing in heaven over one

sinner who repents than over ninety-nine righteous persons who do not need to repent" (Luke 15:7).

In case you thought it was just a throwaway comment, Jesus said it again: "In the same way, I tell you, there is rejoicing in the presence of the angels of God over one sinner who repents" (Luke 15:10).

I have heard people say, "I think I should go into pubs or bars and witness." That's fine until you start drinking and find you want to show that you can fit in. If you say you are a Christian, I guarantee you they will pull you down. Do you know what was so attractive about Jesus? It was that He was different. He didn't have to act like He was one of them. The truth is that He was sinless, and yet the sinners still felt welcome around Him. So remember, in all our witnessing, it is repentance that must take place sooner or later. The word *repentance* comes from the Greek word *metanoia* meaning "change of mind." It is not a theological word; it just means "change of mind." Some say it means agreeing with God. Some say it means, "I was wrong." It certainly means to be sorry, and the proof that you are sorry is that you make a U-turn.

The One Who Searches
The emphasis in these passages is not on the one who is lost but on the One who is searching. The lost are Jesus' property. How wonderful that David the psalmist could see how he and God had actually reversed roles. He was a shepherd, but he said:

> The LORD is my Shepherd;
> I shall not want.
> He makes me to lie down in green pastures;
> He leads me beside the still waters.
> He restores my soul;
> He leads me in the paths of righteousness
> For His name's sake.
>
> Yea, though I walk through the valley of the shadow of death,
> I will fear no evil;
> For You are with me;
> Your rod and Your staff, they comfort me.
> You prepare a table before me in the presence of my enemies;
> You anoint my head with oil;
> My cup runs over.
> Surely goodness and mercy shall follow me
> All the days of my life;
> And I will dwell in the house of the LORD
> Forever.
>
> (Psalm 23:1–6, NKJV)

The stress in both parables is on the One who is searching. The lost are Jesus' property. Is He looking for you? If He is, then He is hurting over you right now. Notice that in these parables, it is the shepherd and the woman who do all the suffering. The shepherd suffered because his sheep was lost. The woman suffered because she lost a valuable coin. When we grieve the Spirit, normally we feel nothing—He is the one who suffers. Repentance begins when we start to feel what God is feeling; then we become truly sorry. In that moment when we first go astray, the action we take seems the right thing to do. We justify it. There is no pain and no awareness of grief. But repentance is when at long last you feel what the Lord has been feeling, and you agree with Him.

The Context of the Parable

A closer examination of the context of the parable reveals three main points, which I summarize as the attraction, the accusation and the admission.

The Attraction

"Now the tax collectors and 'sinners' were all gathering around to hear him. But the Pharisees and the teachers of the law muttered, 'This man welcomes sinners and eats with them'" (Luke 15:1–2).

Jesus was like a magnet to sinners. What kind of people do we attract to ourselves? If there is something about my life and my demeanor that does not send a signal to others that I would care for them, love them and accept them, then there is something seriously wrong with me. The Church must be a hospital that helps those who are sick, not a courtroom where we judge the guilty.

The Accusation

"This man welcomes sinners and eats with them" (Luke 15:2).

To the Pharisees this was a dead giveaway that Jesus was no good. They used this scenario as a reason to reject Jesus.

The Admission

Of course, Jesus pleaded guilty to this charge by giving three parables, one after another, all saying the same thing. The parable of the lost sheep, the parable of the lost coin and the parable of the lost or Prodigal Son (which we will look at in the next chapter) were His answer to the charge.

Did you ever think about the fact that it took courage for Jesus to do this? It must have taken a lot of courage to welcome people whose reputation and appearance offended the Pharisees. I wonder how William Booth felt when the people who wanted to come to church with him were the type of people that the minister was unhappy about. I remember when I first went out on the streets of London to evangelize. I was so full of enthusiasm that nothing could have stopped me. But it wasn't very long before I began to realize that the type of people who were receiving the Lord were not merchant bankers and members of the House of Lords. Realizing what I had really signed up for, I then had to make a recommitment to evangelism. When the people who were saved on the streets started coming into the church, there were those who muttered, "Do you realize the kind of people they are bringing in?" People actually said that. I remember somebody coming in to see me and saying, "The 'quality' people in the church [that was the actual phrase they used] are unhappy with what is going on in the Chapel." The underlying cause of the complaint was that these "undesirable" people would have no money to contribute to the running of the church, and therefore, the "quality" people would effectively be subsidizing them. I found the inference absolutely astonishing!

My own ministry seems to have been characterized by people who are unhappy with what is going on at any given time! There never seems to have been a time when there wasn't somebody saying that kind of thing. In response to that particular person, I said, "Let's give it six months. If it turns out that God is not with us, I will resign. I don't want to stay where I am not wanted. I didn't try to get into this church and I am not going to try and keep it, so we are not turning back." I made a deal to review the situation after Easter. Easter came, and I had to send for this person. He hadn't changed his opinion, but interestingly, church offerings were actually up and God was clearly with us.

The moment we start worrying about issues like this, we risk losing the anointing. Paradoxically, unity is never achieved by trying to achieve unity but by keeping your eyes on Jesus. If I offend people by pursuing the cause of the Gospel, then I offend people. I always seek to recall how Jesus welcomed all kinds of people and did things that offended the upstanding people.

> The Pharisees and the teachers of the law who belonged to their sect complained to his disciples, "Why do you eat and drink with tax collectors and 'sinners'?" Jesus answered them, "It is not the healthy who need a

doctor, but the sick. I have not come to call the righteous, but sinners to repentance."

Luke 5:30–31

For John the Baptist came neither eating bread not drinking wine, and you say, "He has a demon." The Son of Man came eating and drinking, and you say, "Here is a glutton and a drunkard, a friend of tax collectors and 'sinners.'"

Luke 7:33–34

Part of being like Jesus is having the courage to let people hurt your reputation. The only thing that would have taken more courage than this was when Jesus actually made some of them His disciples. Matthew, for example, was a tax collector. To appoint a tax collector to a position of authority or ministry would have been seen as the most outrageous, scandalous behavior. If you had been around in those days, whose side would you have been on? Well, Jesus' answer to the condemnation was these three parables. Instead of accepting their condemnation, He just turned their accusation on its head.

We Are Like Sheep

It is helpful to look more closely into Jesus' use of the analogy of sheep—which is indeed a recurring theme in Scripture. A number of years ago, I asked my old friend Douglas MacMillan, a preacher and a former shepherd, about sheep. He began talking, and I wrote down everything he said.

The first thing he mentioned was that the basic habit of a sheep is to wander and go astray. They always think the grass is greener on the other side of the fence. Also, because they have a herding instinct, they have a tendency to gather together in a group. If one does go astray, something is badly wrong with that sheep—it is acting out of character.

Sheep are known to be stubborn—they want their own way—and Douglas added that they are stupid. You can't teach sheep a trick. Even cattle don't need a shepherd, but sheep frequently wander into dangerous areas and then get stuck. They cannot care for themselves like other animals. They have no thought of what is coming next—no thought of the future. Doesn't that resemble the backslider? He doesn't realize that someday will be payday. Instead he lives for immediate gratification and does what feels right at the time. He doesn't bother to weigh the consequences or think that he is going to have to live with himself somewhere down the road.

Douglas mentioned one more thing. He said that a sheep yearns for authority and guidance. Jesus knows that about all of us. David, a shepherd, viewed himself as a sheep; he knew that he needed God's guidance very badly, which is why he wrote the words, "The LORD is my shepherd" (Psalm 23:1).

The Shepherd's Love

Not only does God welcome sinners, He doesn't give up until He finds them, and He goes to where they are. He doesn't give up until they return to Him.

The Bible says that God's sheep know His voice (John 10:16). Arthur Blessitt said that when he walked across the Sahara Desert, he saw four or five different shepherds with their sheep. The shepherd would just say one word, and his sheep would follow him. No one else's sheep followed him. That's amazing! What Jesus was saying here is, "I will call them, and they will come." Have you ever noticed the legacy Jesus left? Not only does He welcome sinners, but He died for them too. As Paul said, "While we were still sinners, Christ died for us" (Romans 5:8).

It shows the care of Jesus. Notice Jesus' loving care in the following verse: "And when he finds it, he joyfully puts it on his shoulders and goes home" (Luke 15:5–6).

I remember some years ago I was feeling very discouraged. At the upcoming Sunday service, we were due to share in the Lord's Supper together. The day before the service, I had decided that we would sing the hymn, "The King of Love My Shepherd Is." I will never forget the impact of the words, "perverse and foolish oft I strayed, but yet in love he sought me, and on his shoulders gently laid, and home rejoicing brought me." At that time I felt I needed to be carried, and God in His grace lifted my spirit. That's what Jesus was showing in this parable—when He finds us, He carries us home.

Rejoicing and Restoration

Let's take a moment to look briefly at the contrast between the lost sheep and the lost coin. As we said, both were lost, but the sheep was alive while the coin was an inanimate object. Finding the sheep caused rejoicing in heaven, while finding the coin brought about rejoicing in the presence of the angels. The sheep wandered, but the coin was lost due to someone's carelessness. Could it be that the Lord was giving a hint here about the responsibility of the Church to care for those around it? We are accountable to one another. Am I my brother's keeper? The answer is a resounding yes. Although they were lost for different reasons, the good news is that both the sheep and the coin were found.

Many years ago I heard a preacher by the name of Sam Sparks tell of a person who had been prayed for by his mother. The mother died, and a year or two later this man came to the Lord and wanted to know more than anything else that his mother knew he was saved. He said that the Lord gave him this verse: "There is rejoicing in the presence of the angels" (Luke 15:10). He said it didn't necessarily mean that the angels were rejoicing, but that rejoicing is occurring in the presence of the angels. Where was his mother? In the presence of the angels. The man took this as evidence that his mother knew he had been saved. I am not completely sure of the theology of that, but it was a blessing to him.

What we do know from this parable is that when that lost sheep was found, the shepherd was relieved. This is implied in Luke 15:5–6. The woman also was relieved (Luke 15:9)—it is possible that those ten coins in the headband were her life savings. To lose one was to lose a lot of money. We also know that there is rejoicing, whether it is over the person initially converted or the person who has been restored. Perhaps people in heaven know when others are saved. Certainly the angels know. If you have never been converted and you now come to Christ, I want you to know that all heaven rejoices.

I used to drive home to Nashville on a Sunday night from Palmer, Tennessee, and would turn on the radio and hear Billy Graham. In those days, George Beverley Shea sang the same song every week. It went something like this:

> I've wandered far away from God,
> Now I'm coming home.
> The paths of sin too long I've trod,
> Lord, I'm coming home.
> I've wasted many precious years,
> Now I'm coming home.
> I now repent with bitter tears,
> Lord, I'm coming home.
> Coming home, coming home, never more to roam.
> Open wide Thine arms of love, Lord, I'm coming home.

So Jesus pleaded guilty as a man who welcomed sinners and ate with them. Jesus said, "Suppose a man has a hundred sheep and loses one of them, what does he do? He goes after it." That means there is hope for you and for me. To the person who has never been converted, Jesus is seeking you. To the backslider He is saying, "Come home."

Chapter 26

The Parable of the Prodigal Son

> The father said to his servants . . . "Let's have a feast and celebrate. For this son of mine was dead and is alive again; he was lost and is found."
>
> Luke 15:22–24

This parable has been called the pearl or the crown of all of Jesus' parables. Somebody once referred to it as the Gospel within the Gospel. Someone else has observed that there is no equal to it in all literature. There is certainly no more powerful picture of a forgiving God, nor of the motivation that lay behind Jesus' ministry. Like the parable of the lost sheep, this parable is set in a context where tax collectors and sinners were gathering around to hear Jesus. At the same time, the Pharisees and teachers of the law were muttering, "This man welcomes sinners and eats with them" (Luke 15:2).

Dare I say that this parable describes every single one of us to some degree? For my first series at Westminster Chapel, more than 25 years ago, I preached on the topic of Jonah, and many people asked why. I said, "Because I am a Jonah—I know what it is like to run away from what God has told me to do. I know what it is like to be swallowed up by a big fish and to cry out, *Lord, give me another chance!*" It is the same with the Prodigal Son. I might add that it is also the same with his older brother, but we will look at that in more detail in the next chapter.

The Father's Love

In this parable, the younger son of a wealthy father asked for his inheritance ahead of time. Instead of investing the money or starting a business, he went to a distant country and squandered it on wild living. Why the father decided to give him the inheritance in advance we don't know. Presumably the father thought he would take the money and invest it. The son, however, soon ran out of money and reached the lowest of the low. He got a job feeding pigs and was so hungry that he actually became jealous of the food that the pigs were eating. We are told that no one gave him anything (Luke 15:16). Perhaps you know what it is to move far away from God, feel destitute and then find that no one will help you. The son finally came to his senses and realized what he had left back home. He sat down and began to rehearse a little speech: "Father, I have sinned against heaven and against you. I am no longer worthy to be called your son; make me like one of your hired men" (Luke 15:18–19).

Then he headed home, intending to plead for mercy in the hope that his father will "employ" him. From a distance, though, his father saw him and was filled with compassion. He ran to his son, threw his arms around him and kissed him. The Prodigal Son gave his rehearsed speech, but the father's response was not to take his son back as a servant but to throw an extravagant celebration heralding the return of his son. It is wonderful to think that a father would love a son so much.

Jesus wants us to know that this is the way our heavenly Father loves us, even when we backslide. That is the main theme of this parable. If you pushed it, you might be able to say that the parable is also about God's elect who have not yet been called, but generally it is aimed at those "prodigals" who belong to God and yet have slipped back into sinful ways. This means the person to whom the parable refers is already saved—a Christian who has fallen into sin. The question most people ask is, "When a person backslides, do they cease to be a child of God? Do they cease to be a Christian? Are they now lost in the sense that they would go to hell if they died in that state?" We will look at those questions later. The parable deals also with the slavery of sin and the consequences of sin.

The previous two parables—the lost sheep and the lost coin—dealt with entities that could not fend or think for themselves. But in this parable Jesus was referring to a human being who could think and who eventually came to his senses (Luke 15:17). The King James Version puts it this way: "he came to himself." We are going to see that this backslider returned and was loved by his father.

The Father's love is described in Jeremiah:

The Lord appeared to us in the past, saying:

> "I have loved you with an everlasting love;
> I have drawn you with loving-kindness.

> I will build you up again
>   and you will be rebuilt, O Virgin Israel.
> Again you will take up your tambourines
>   and go out to dance with the joyful."
>   Jeremiah 31:3–4

Celebration marks the end of all of these three parables in Luke: first, rejoicing in heaven; second, rejoicing among the angels; and in this parable, the rejoicing of the father. It shows how our heavenly Father feels when someone comes back to Him. Can you recall a time when you were sorry for your sins; you confessed them; you trusted only the blood of Jesus and you were given a new life and a new destiny? God put His Holy Spirit in you, you began to read your Bible and everything was different. Then at some point temptation came. It could have been temptation of the world, of the flesh or to be famous; it could have been the temptation to make money, to be seen with this or that person. You thought, *This is not going to do any harm,* so you went out and did certain things, never dreaming that it would bring you to such a low point—but it did. If that is you, allow God to give you a tap on the shoulder. I want you to know that the only person who will be happier than you when you come back is the Father Himself.

Why Is This Parable Important?

This parable shows the tenderness of God: "You have heard of Job's perseverance and have seen what the Lord finally brought about. The Lord is full of compassion and mercy" (James 5:11). The King James Version says that He is "very pitiful, and of tender mercy" (James 5:11).

Second, the parable shows the folly of sin. To choose to go out into the world and wander away from God is the most stupid and irrational thing a person can do; but we do it, don't we? It doesn't add up, and it doesn't make sense. This parable shows the slavery and the folly of sin—how every time you backslide you end up regretting it. Jonah learned this in the belly of the fish. He cried out to God, saying, "It just isn't worth it!" (Jonah 2:1–10).

Most of us have a story to tell of how we have wandered away and come back. And most of us can testify that it just isn't worth it. If you are among those who have been spared going out into the world and listening to the devil, attracted by the lure of sin and temptation, fame and money, power and sex, then listen: If you wander, eventually you will come to the place where no one will give you anything.

Third, this parable does, thankfully, teach the doctrine of "once saved, always saved." This shows more than anything that we are loved with an everlasting love. As in the words of the hymn: "O love that wilt not let me go." I have talked to people who have backslidden in the past and have come back to the Lord. They all said, "I tried to get away from God, but He wouldn't let me. I knew then that I was loved." That is what God is saying in this parable. He doesn't point the finger at you and moralize and say, "How dare you do that?" He doesn't make you feel guilty by asking why you did whatever you did. This is the way earthly parents are. Instead He is tender—like the father in the parable, He sees you coming before you see Him.

Did you know God sees Himself as being married to the backslider? There is an interesting verse in Jeremiah: " 'Return, faithless people,' declares the LORD, 'for I am your husband. I will choose you—one from a town and two from a clan—and bring you to Zion' " (Jeremiah 3:14).

God is saying, "I won't let you go."

Last, the greatest thing about this parable is that it shows how our restoration is recorded with great festivity and dignity. By the way, that is the way the Church should feel. When you see somebody coming back, don't say, "Where have you been?" but rather exclaim, "Oh, it is wonderful to see you!" and embrace them. People like this already feel guilty, and they will already have heard moralizing words. It is time for the Church to say, "Thank God—it is wonderful to see you!" If you are one of those who has wandered, I want you to know that God is waiting to welcome you back. The one who is restored gives God as much joy, honor and pleasure as the one who is first converted.

Traceable Folly

The foolishness of the Prodigal Son can be traced to one thing.

"The younger one said to his father, 'Father, give me my share of the estate.' So he [the father] divided his property between them" (Luke 15:12).

His request revealed the young man's impatience. He couldn't even wait until his father died; he wanted his inheritance right then. His insistence betrayed his folly—an inheritance is something one should wait for at least until the loved one dies.

What was the father's response? First, acquiescence. We are not told how the father felt about releasing the inheritance to his son, but nevertheless he agreed to do it. In fact, he divided his property between his two sons so that the elder son received his share at the same time.

This part of the parable is very difficult. Why did the father do it? Let us look at an analogy. Do you believe that God Himself would do this? Remember that one of the rules for interpreting parables is that you cannot necessarily find a biblical parallel for every detail you see. Is this one such point that we would not want to apply? Would our heavenly Father really do this? Would He give us what isn't good for us? Actually, I believe that we *can* apply this part of the parable, because I believe that the answer to that question is sometimes yes. Look at this haunting verse in Psalm 106: "He gave them what they asked for, but sent a wasting disease upon them" (Psalm 106:15). The King James Version says, "He gave them their request; but sent leanness into their soul" (Psalm 106:15, KJV).

What this means is that sometimes God finally says, "Okay, I have said no, but if you keep asking, then you are going to get it." Perhaps you can look back on a time when people were giving you all kinds of warnings: "Be careful," or, "Are you sure you want to do that?" In a multitude of counsel there is safety. I wouldn't take all the money in the world in exchange for the kind of counsel I get from friends. God has blessed my wife, Louise, and me with unusual friends. You couldn't begin to imagine how such friends have ministered to us and encouraged us in our ministry and how many times they have warned me and said things that others wouldn't dare say to me. "Faithful are the wounds of a friend" (Proverbs 27:6, NKJV).

You must know what it is to have somebody say to you, "Are you *sure* you want to do that?" Maybe that is what the father in the parable said to his son, yet because of the son's absolute insistence he gave in. Dr. Martyn Lloyd-Jones once said to me, "The worst thing that can happen to a man is for him to succeed before he is ready." If you have longed for success in a certain area and it hasn't come, be thankful for it. It could be that one day you will be very glad you didn't get what you asked for, unlike the Prodigal Son.

Tragic Failure

Not long after that, the younger son got together all he had, set off for a distant country and there squandered his wealth in wild living. After he had spent everything, there was a severe famine in that whole country, and he began to be in need. So he went and hired himself out to a citizen of that country, who sent him to his fields to feed pigs. He longed to fill his stomach with the pods that the pigs were eating, but no one gave him anything.

Luke 15:13–16

We should thank God when He does not grant our request. Listen to this word from James 4:3. "When you ask, you do not receive, because you ask with wrong motives, that you may spend what you get on your pleasures."

If you do what God tells you to do, He'll give you everything you ought to have. If you say, "But I want more than that," then beware. The downward spiral in this parable begins in Luke 15:13. The son took "all he had" and set off for a distant land. Instead of wisely investing his money, he wandered. He ended up in a foreign land, far from home, and the next thing we know he was wasting his inheritance—squandering his wealth on worldliness or wild living. If you wonder what "wild living" looks like, it is explained in verse 30. The elder brother said, "this son of yours who has squandered your property with prostitutes" (Luke 15:30).

Most of this young man's money was spent on buying sex. Have you ever been tempted to do that? It is only a matter of time before you have an opportunity, and you will be sorry if you do. If you are already thinking of something you might do, or maybe you are about to get involved in, then stop now. Break it off!

You may say, "It is too late"—not so. God wouldn't let you read this just to make you feel guilty. He is saying, "Stop it!" If you are involved in any kind of lifestyle that is not honoring to God, then stop it. Break it off!

It gets worse for this son because he spent *everything* he had (Luke 15:14). Then his circumstances deteriorated further as famine broke out in the land. It is very interesting to see how things outside his control conspired against him. God is sovereign, and everything that happens in the world is under His control. It is amazing how God can make world events touch your life. After the famine, of course, there was great want. We are told that this son began to be in great need and finally decided to get a job.

"So he went and hired himself out to a citizen of that country, who sent him to his fields to feed pigs" (Luke 15:15). This was the only job he could get. It shows his desperation and his disgrace. The son then became wistful. "He longed to fill his stomach with the pods that the pigs were eating, but no one gave him anything" (Luke 15:16).

Finally, he began to feel completely worthless. No one would help him. If this has happened to you, it is God's way of sending a signal to you that He is behind it all. It comes as that lack of success, the things that are not happening for you, the time running out until you are at rock bottom. You think God has left you. Oh no—God is trying to get your attention!

Transparent Feelings

The son's and the father's feelings about this situation were vividly described by Jesus. They show how far down we have to go before we wake up and realize what has happened and how wretched our existence has become.

Honesty

The son came to his senses and said, "How many of my father's hired men have food to spare, and here I am starving to death!" (Luke 15:17).

At last he was developing some objectivity about himself. It took a bad experience, but thank God, it got his attention.

Homesickness

The son eventually realized that he needed to go home. Perhaps you know what it is to have Christian parents, but you have wandered off. I can tell you, people with a Christian heritage who wander off begin to appreciate their Christian background sooner or later. Maybe you grew up in a Christian home and think, *Boy, I had to have Christians for parents!* One day you will say, "I didn't realize how blessed I was." You can trust those parents who know their Bibles and who love the Lord.

Humility

The son, now realizing the gravity of his misdeeds, decided that he must confess what he had done to his father and ask for his forgiveness. "I will set out and go back to my father and say to him: 'Father, I have sinned against heaven and against you'" (Luke 15:18).

After making this confession, he had determined that he would ask his father to employ him on the same basis as one of the servants. His declaration was, "I am no longer worthy to be called your son; make me like one of your hired men" (Luke 15:19).

He was so eager now to be reunited with his father, and yet so ashamed, that he was thinking of things he could say that would put the matter into perspective. To become a slave to his father seemed an appropriate response for him to make.

The son became determined to return to his father, and so he got up and set out for his father's house. If you have wandered from the right path, this is what you have to do too. You may have reached the place where you are sorry, and you think, *How can I possibly approach God?* I tell you, make a decision—be determined to do what God tells you to do today. Say no to the way you have been living.

Total Forgiveness

Remember that total forgiveness takes place when you forgive someone without them having to apologize. Total forgiveness is not when you say, "Well, let them repent, let them say they're sorry, let them come back and eat humble pie, and then I think I could forgive them." Most of us are like that. You don't have to be a Christian to do that. The Bible says, "A gentle answer turns away wrath" (Proverbs 15:1).

You could make most people happy if you apologized in an appropriate way for some wrong you had caused. It doesn't take much grace to be nice to a person who is genuinely sorry for the wrong they have caused. Total forgiveness takes place when you forgive them while they still don't think they have done anything wrong. You could put most people I have had to forgive under a lie detector, and they would not be aware that they had done anything at all. It wouldn't do for me to say, "I forgive you," to those people because it would be inappropriate. They would say, "For what?" You may think we should expect people to repent before we forgive them, but did Jesus demand that at Calvary? No. Jesus' response was not, "When you are sorry for what you have done, I am going to pray for you." Instead He said, "Father, forgive them."

When the Prodigal Son was on his way home, the father saw him before he saw the father. This shows God's initiative. Through this God says to us, "Despite all that has happened, I love you."

Then came the confession. As soon as the father ran to him, threw his arms around him and kissed his son, the son might have thought, *Oh, I won't have to repeat that speech now; I've got what I wanted.* But no. This man was genuinely repentant. He confessed even though he sensed his father's love. Maybe that is what you need to do. You need to say, *God, I am sorry; I am so sorry.*

The Celebration

Then came the celebration. The father showed his acceptance, his affection and even his authority—his response was to give his son authority again in the family.

"The father said to his servants, 'Quick! Bring the best robe and put it on him. Put a ring on his finger and sandals on his feet. Bring the fattened calf and kill it. Let's have a feast and celebrate' " (Luke 15:22–23).

This is how much God is pleased when one who is saved and has backslidden returns. God is saying to *you,* "Come home." There will be true festivity and restoration. The restoration is one of righteousness. You will start living for the Lord again and will give dignity to the robe of righteousness that Jesus gives you. The reason for the rejoicing is this: "This son of mine was dead and is alive again; he was lost and is found" (Luke 15:24).

The father never expected to see his son again. He was lost. But now that he had been found, they began to celebrate.

One final point—a theological question. For the Christian who gets his inheritance at the beginning and then squanders it, what is left? I can tell you, King David blew it big time when he sinned with Bathsheba and then killed her husband, Uriah. That was squandering his inheritance. David came to terms with the fact that perhaps life on earth wouldn't be like it had been, but he knew that he would still have a reward in heaven. From then on, his focus turned to building up treasure in heaven, and as a result God began to use him here on earth far beyond his expectations. He wrote more psalms. God wasn't finished with him. And He is not finished with you.

Chapter 27

The Parable of the Older Brother

Look! All these years I've been slaving for you.
Luke 15:29

The parable of the older brother is really "part two" of the parable of the prodigal son. We saw in the previous chapter that the younger of two sons demanded his inheritance early from his father and went away and squandered it all. Later he returned, intent on begging for forgiveness, and was readily welcomed back by his father. We discover in Jesus' parable that there was an older brother also. The text implies that the older brother was a good son and had never caused his father any trouble. He was probably what James Dobson would call a *compliant* child. He had never really done anything wrong in his life. Because of his younger brother's actions, he too received his inheritance early, though the Bible does not reveal how he felt about that. We are told, however, how he felt when he heard the news secondhand that there was a celebration going on because his wayward younger brother had returned. What should have been good news to the older brother is actually bad news. He became angry and refused to even go to the celebration.

In life it is always easier to find somebody to weep with you than it is to find somebody to rejoice with you. Paul said, "Rejoice with those who rejoice, and weep with those who weep" (Romans 12:15, NKJV).

If the Prodigal Son had come back weeping and then the father had rejected him, I am sure the older brother would have gone up to him, put his arm around him and commiserated with him. Instead, he found it impossible to rejoice along with his father. His father came to him and pleaded with him to come and join the celebration, but the older brother only rebuked his father, saying, "Look! All these years I've been slaving for you" (Luke 15:29).

Slaving? the father must have thought. *Is that the way you looked at it?*

[I] never disobeyed your orders. Yet you never gave me even a young goat so I could celebrate with my friends. But when this son of yours [notice he doesn't call him his brother] who has squandered your property with prostitutes comes home, you kill the fattened calf for him!

Luke 15:29–30

Jesus gave the father the last word: " 'My son,' the father said, 'you are always with me, and everything I have is yours. But we had to celebrate and be glad, because this brother of yours was dead and is alive again; he was lost and is found' " (Luke 15:31–32).

This second part of the parable was aimed squarely at a specific audience that Jesus had in mind: the Pharisees. Like many of the other parables in Luke's gospel, this one was set in the light of the Pharisees' charge that Jesus "welcomed sinners." The Pharisees had no appreciation of the Father's love and no sympathy for a profligate sinner. They resented the Prodigal Son being totally forgiven, so Jesus sent them a signal at the end of the parable that they were acting like a jealous older brother who was angry and refused to join in the celebration.

The Meaning of the Parable

The parable shows the awkward position of the father. He loved both sons equally and wanted them to love each other. It is a reminder that we are all in the family of God. The truth is that our heavenly Father loves us all equally, and we put Him in an awkward position when we fall out with one another. He is the perfect parent, unlike Jacob who was a miserable failure as a parent and showed partiality toward Joseph, and unlike David who was Israel's greatest king but an absentee father. Our heavenly Father is the perfect parent who loves "older brothers" as much as much as He loves "younger brothers." God loves every person the same. It doesn't matter whether you have a high profile in the church or a more important job than somebody else. It doesn't matter whether you have higher education or whether you are illiterate. God loves us all the same.

This parable gives us a hint of how the Father is grieved when His children aren't speaking to each other. Is there anybody to whom you are not speaking? Have you any idea how much this grieves the Holy Spirit? It is highly unlikely that you will ever have the kind of relationship with God you ought to have until you put other relationships right or get over your bitterness.

The older brother in the parable thought that he should have been loved more than the younger because of his continued hard work and obedience. We may think that way too, but God is incredibly impartial. Those who have "been around" for a while often take themselves too seriously, as the Pharisees did. This parable is much like the parable of the vineyard in which those who worked all day long were happy with the wage they got until they found out that somebody else who hadn't worked as hard got the same amount. In the same way, the father's acceptance of the younger brother, despite his behavior, "got the goat" of the older sibling.

Older Christians, sadly, often react this way. If you have been a Christian for a few years, be careful—this is a weakness that we all have. Many of us need to learn from this parable. We need to guard against having an older brother mentality. God loves all of His children the same.

The Importance of the Parable

Self-Righteousness

It is so important for us to learn from this parable because it reveals just how easy it is for us to become self-righteous. There are two basic ways of displeasing our heavenly Father. One is by committing scandalous sin and the other is by becoming self-righteous. This parable shows how self-righteous we are. Maybe you identify with the Prodigal Son? I certainly do. But can you identify with the older brother? I must admit, I see myself in both. I know what it is to be a Jonah. I also know what it is to become self-righteous and take myself too seriously. The Prodigal Son and the older brother are mirrored in the book of Jonah. The first two chapters of Jonah reflect the Prodigal Son as Jonah goes to a foreign country, eventually "coming to his senses" in the belly of a fish. In the next two chapters Jonah behaves like the older brother, becoming angry that God would bring revival to the Ninevites and cause him to lose face. This is how the older brother felt when the young Prodigal returned. It reveals his self-righteousness.

Revealed Sin

Second, this parable is important because it shows how conditions and circumstances reveal sin in us that we did not know was there. In other words, you may think you are very godly until you face a situation that reveals to you what you are really like.

My old friend Rolfe Barnard used to say, "The reason that there are as many Josephs as there are is because they haven't run into Potiphar's wife yet." It may well be that you have been spared that sort of sin, but you don't know what it is to have the kind of temptation that another person has had. In the same way, maybe you are not the Prodigal Son who went into a distant country and blew it—but God has another way of showing you what you are like. The parable of the Prodigal Son and the older brother is partly aimed at revealing how circumstances and conditions bring out in us sin that we never dreamed was there. God's way of letting you grow is to let you see what you are really like.

Jealousy

Third, this parable is important because the sin that it demonstrates is *jealousy*. This is a sin that we will all deny until our dying day unless we are caught. It's the easiest sin to see in another person and the hardest sin to see in yourself. It is embarrassing to admit that you are jealous.

In the parable of the vineyard that I referred to earlier, nobody would have complained if the workers who arrived at the end of the day were paid in proportion to the time they had worked. It is the fact that they received the same amount that caused jealousy to emerge in those who had worked all day long. It is the circumstance we encounter that causes jealousy to surface in us. Don't say you are not a jealous person. Don't make me laugh!

Many of the parables of Jesus were given to reveal to us what we are really like. Our sense of fairness is never keener than when someone else is receiving special recognition. We wouldn't naturally have known the older brother was a jealous person, but because of the circumstances he was put in, it came out. Never forget that jealousy is what led to the first murder in human history. Later, King Saul became so jealous that he was more threatened by David, who was only a teenager at the time, than he was by the Philistines (1 Samuel 18 and 19). That is how jealousy can get out of hand and how a Christian can become so jealous and enraged that they would rather see that person out of the picture completely than see the lost won to Christ.

Jealousy may not bring scandal like the flagrant sin of the Prodigal, but in God's sight it is just as bad. God hated the sin that surfaced in the older brother as much as He hated the profligate lifestyle of the younger brother. The truth is that when we become angry or annoyed, we should stop and ask ourselves if there is any chance we could be jealous. When a person is given recognition and you catch yourself thinking, *Why them?* ask yourself if it could be jealousy. Believe me, it is! You can stay prim and proper in your pew and you can think you are godly, but the right circumstances will reveal to you what you really are.

Circumstances That Bring About Sin

This parable gives us some useful insights in the conditions and circumstances that bring about sin. This is relevant for all of us.

The Suppressing of Sin

Suppressing sin is just what the younger brother didn't do—he suppressed nothing; he held nothing back. When he went to that far country, he went all out—enjoyed sex, good food, spent all his money and then hit rock bottom. He was at the bottom of the heap in a foreign country. But God loved him right there.

As for the older brother, you would never have guessed that there was a volcano inside him. As long as nothing stirs you up, you may get the deluded feeling that you have spiritual victory. I have gone for weeks and months without losing my temper or giving in to any temptation. I have looked in the mirror and thought, *We are really getting there!* But when this happens, it is probably because conditions have been made easy for you. Perhaps you have sufficient income so that you don't have to worry about finances—you don't need to fall flat on your face before God and say, "How am I going to make it through the day when I don't even have money to buy my next meal?" But as long as money is coming in, you see people out on the street and wonder why they don't just get a job! You don't realize that this is self-righteous, judgmental thinking. You go on thinking that there is nothing wrong with you at all—but God heard it, and the angels blushed! "If we claim to be without sin, we deceive ourselves and the truth is not in us" (1 John 1:8).

Maybe God is allowing you to go through a period of time when sin isn't showing itself and as a result you feel good about yourself. Remember that one day the Lord had a conversation with Satan and said, "Have you considered my servant Job?" (Job 1:8).

Imagine the Lord saying, "What about Bert? He hasn't been challenged too much lately. What about Bill? What about David?" What if suddenly God said, "Yes, I want to do a work of grace in their hearts—they haven't realized what is present in their hearts and they ought to know. They ought to know what I have been forgiving them of. They ought to know the extent of the grace they have been enjoying."

The Surfacing of Sin

> The older brother became angry and refused to go in. So his father went out and pleaded with him. But he answered his father, "Look! All these

years I've been slaving for you and never disobeyed your orders. Yet you never gave me even a young goat so I could celebrate with my friends. But when this son of yours who has squandered your property with prostitutes comes home, you kill the fattened calf for him!"

Luke 15:28–30

There was sin in the heart of the older brother already. It only needed the right circumstances to come about in order for it to surface. There are two things that cause sin to "surface." The first of these is what I call the *underlying cause*—theologians call it *original sin*. "All have sinned and fall short of the glory of God" (Romans 3:23). David said, "In sin my mother conceived me" (Psalm 51:5, NKJV).

Then there is the *precipitating cause*—certain circumstances and conditions that cause sin to surface. In the case of the older brother, he heard the music and saw the dancing. He thought, *Great! This is going to be a lot of fun!* But then he discovered that the celebration was for his sinful little brother, and he couldn't handle it. We can only suppress sin for so long—until God allows something to happen that causes it to surface.

The Surprise of Sin

Circumstances and the sin that follows reveal all kinds of attitudes that we didn't know were there. We may say things we didn't think we would ever say. I was brought up in a denomination where it was taught that you would eventually reach a place in your walk with God where you no longer sinned. I remember when I was a boy they would use the following text to illustrate this: "In all this, Job did not sin" (Job 1:22). It is amazing how people can be selective with the verses they want.

I remember some years later I read through the whole book of Job. It is a hard book to understand. One of my regrets is the fact that I never really preached through the book of Job in public. One thing has kept me from doing it. There was a Puritan by the name of Joseph Carroll who started out with a congregation of five thousand. He went through the book of Job and finished it fifty years later with a congregation of fifty. I could see how that might happen!

But in reading through the book of Job, I came to chapter 13 where Job said, "How many wrongs and sins have I committed? Show me my offense and my sin" (Job 13:23).

Later he said, "I will never admit you are in the right; till I die, I will not deny my integrity. I will maintain my righteousness and never let go of it" (Job 27:5–6).

When his friends began to see that he was getting riled, he shouted at them, "miserable comforters are you all!" (Job 16:2).

One of the lessons we learn from the book of Job is that God wanted Job to see how self-righteous he was and how such sin does not please Him. The story does have a good ending because we find later that Job said, "I am unworthy—how can I reply to you? I put my hand over my mouth" (Job 40:4). He had become aware how inherently sinful he was.

Maybe you are surprised at yourself. You say, "I can't believe I said that; I didn't think I was like that." But circumstances and conditions can cause any of us to behave in a way we wouldn't want anyone else to see. If you are honest, it has no doubt already happened to you.

The Contrast between the Two Brothers

In the case of the younger brother, we see the sorrow and slavery of sin. He went out and got a job feeding pigs. "He longed to fill his stomach with the pods that the pigs were eating, but no one gave him anything" (Luke 15:16). He was full of shame and regret over his sin. He had been made a fool of, and he was in bondage.

In the older brother we see the subtlety of sin. He was angry and self-righteous. He too was in slavery—the slavery of service. He said, "Look! All these years I've been slaving for you" (Luke 15:29).

The father clearly didn't know he felt this way. This older son let his father know that all his obedience, all his compliance, was in reality—slavery. Neither the slavery of sin nor the subtlety of sin makes God happy. Do you feel like that? Maybe you have faithfully served your church for years, then one day you say, "I have *slaved* for this place." Oh, really? Is that the way you have looked at it? All this time others had thought it was all godly sacrifice, but underneath you are angry! It's as though you had only served because you wanted recognition. Nobody wants to see such an attitude.

The older brother had the nerve actually to rebuke his father. Are you, underneath, actually angry with God? Do you think, *How dare He do this to me? How dare He let this happen to me?* The older brother was jealous and judgmental—it was he who brought up the matter of prostitutes; we wouldn't have known otherwise. He spilled the beans. Perhaps you know something about somebody that you think everyone else ought to know. Or maybe, just beneath the surface, you are angry that people don't know the truth about how you have been treated and the things you have endured. You think such things ought to be made known.

I had somebody talk to me recently about a book I was writing. He asked if I was going to reveal certain things and I said, "No." He thought some of these issues should have been made known, but would it have brought honor and glory to God? No.

The Brothers' Security

The security of the younger son was revealed when he returned home. "The father said to his servants, 'Quick! Bring the best robe and put it on him. Put a ring on his finger and sandals on his feet. Bring the fattened calf and kill it. Let's have a feast and celebrate'" (Luke 15:22–23).

Yet the older son was just as secure. "'My son,' the father said, 'you are always with me, and everything I have is yours'" (Luke 15:31).

This doesn't mean that the older son would retain his inheritance in the Kingdom of God. Probably the quickest way to lose your reward in heaven is through uncontrolled anger, uncontrolled jealousy, self-righteousness that is not put in check, self-pity or by taking yourself too seriously. All these things can cause us to lose our reward in heaven. This is why God's initial response is to chasten us for the way we are behaving—He doesn't want us to lose our reward unnecessarily.

What does Jesus want us to conclude from the parable of the Prodigal Son and that of the older brother? First, that He loves sinners. Second, that He hates self-righteousness. Jesus' point in bringing the parable of the older brother into the parable of the Prodigal Son was to enable the Jews to see themselves as the older brother. Jesus wanted them to see what they were really like. Maybe you too need to see what you are like. Self-righteous people often become jealous when they see that God is willing to forgive others of great sin, scandalous sin, sexual sin—*just like that!* But when you resent that forgiveness, you attack the blood of Jesus. I want you to know that one drop of the blood of Jesus washes away all sin, never mind how deeply you have sinned. For you to become self-righteous about your life means that you need to be forgiven just as much as the younger brother who squandered everything.

The parable gave the father the final word: "Everything I have is yours. But we had to celebrate and be glad, because this brother of yours was dead and is alive again; he was lost and is found" (Luke 15:31–32).

The unsung hero of this parable is the father. He loved his children, and he embraced them both. He was put in an awkward situation, but he tried to reconcile them, and he loved both with a deep, unconditional love. If you see a little bit of the older brother in yourself, remember that you need to repent just as much as the younger brother. Your sin is as heinous in God's sight as the younger brother's sin.

Chapter 28

The Parable of the Shrewd Manager

> Whoever can be trusted with very little can also be trusted with much, and whoever is dishonest with very little will also be dishonest with much.
>
> Luke 16:10

The insights that one can draw from this parable are both profound and exciting. At the same time it is one of the most difficult parables of all to understand. It has taken me forty years to begin to grasp what the parable is teaching, and I have talked about it with many great Bible teachers and theologians. What makes it so difficult is that fact that Jesus seems to be condoning dishonesty.

The parable depicts an incompetent manager, perhaps like an estate agent, whose job it was to collect rent but who was accused of wasting his boss's possessions. His boss was calling for him to give account of his actions. The manager realized that he had been unfaithful and had made mistakes. He also realized that he was not cut out for manual work and he didn't want to lose his current job. He decided that the best way to handle the situation was to take immediate action, which, he hoped, would safeguard his future.

First Corinthians 4:2 tells us that every steward is required to be faithful. This word is relevant for anyone who feels they have blown it. If you know you have been stupid and you are ashamed, or you think maybe you are going to be fired, then this word is for you.

This manager was not actually fired, but he was called to give account of himself. He realized the fact that he had been called to account meant there was hope—he was being given a little bit of time. In those days a manager would have been aware that his boss could have thrown him in jail. So he said to himself, *Maybe this is a warning; and if I handle myself correctly, it may not mean the end.* Whenever God gives a warning like this to us, it is because there is still time for mercy.

The action the manager took was to make a deal with all his boss's debtors. At present, he still had the authority to do this because the debtors did not know that he was in trouble with his boss. He reduced everyone's debt by a significant amount, presumably in return for them paying up more quickly. The manager hoped that by doing this, the debtors would be kind to him in the event of him being fired. It turns out, though, that his actions made his boss look very generous, and the end result was that his boss was pleased and commended the manager for acting shrewdly.

The Meaning of the Parable

Let me begin with a story. In the last century, Henry Ford went from Detroit, Michigan, to Dublin to trace his ancestry. It was a fact-finding mission. A person who was a fund-raiser for an old people's home went to Henry Ford while he was there and asked if he would contribute a thousand dollars to the old people's home. Henry Ford wrote out a check for a thousand dollars. That was a lot of money at that time. In the newspaper the next day, an article appeared saying that the great Henry Ford of America had contributed fifty thousand dollars to an old people's home. The following day the very shrewd fund-raiser went to Henry Ford and said, "Look, you can either give me another forty-nine thousand dollars or I will go to the newspaper and say, 'Oh, there was a mistake—he only gave a thousand dollars.'" Henry Ford gave the other forty-nine thousand dollars, but he did add one condition—that a Scripture motto would be placed over the door of the old people's home. They agreed. The motto read, "I was a stranger and you took me in."

That story contains a hint about the meaning of this parable. The shrewd manager who collected the rent knew that his boss, the land-owner, was likely to honor the deal that he made with the customers who owed money, so he put his boss on the spot. The boss would not have looked good if he rejected the deal the manager had made, so he went along with it. The rich boss was seen as being merciful, which made him look really good, and the manager saved his own skin. He may even have kept his job, but he certainly endeared himself to the customers.

The manager who pulled this off said to himself, *If I don't get my job back, then I can go to all those people and tell them that I am the one who canceled their debt and they will receive me* (Luke 16:3–4). And Jesus said, "For the people of this world are more shrewd in dealing with their own kind than are the people of the light" (Luke 16:8).

The shrewd manager, then, was like the people of the world, not the children of light, because he understood his boss. The Pharisees and teachers of the law couldn't understand God since they despised sinners. Jesus was not commending dishonesty in this parable. Instead He was trying to get His disciples to see the analogy. The shrewd manager made his boss look good. Jesus wants the children of light to make God look good. We have a responsibility to make God look good.

The Context of the Parable

The context of this parable goes all the way back to Luke 15. Because it had been so long since the Pharisees and teachers of the law muttered about Jesus sitting with sinners, we forget that Luke has been relating a string of parables. First there was the parable of the lost sheep, then the lost coin and then the two sons. The only difference with this parable is that it was given to the disciples, whereas the previous ones in Luke 15 were given to the Pharisees.

The "children of the light" refers to the Jews who had forgotten what God was really like and could only think self-righteously. They had forgotten the following: "He knows how we are formed, he remembers that we are dust" (Psalm 103:14). And, "As far as the east is from the west, so far has he removed our transgressions from us" (Psalm 103:12). And, "As a father pities his children, so the LORD pities those who fear Him" (Psalm 103:13, NKJV).

Jesus wanted God to be known as One who loves sinners. As He told this parable, He was still responding to the accusations of the Pharisees that He spent too much time in the company of sinners and undesirable people.

In the parable we see a manager who had blown it and it looked as if he were finished, but he had the presence of mind to know that his boss, who was basically a generous person, would want to look good in the eyes of everybody. He took full advantage of what he believed to be true about his boss. Jesus was saying, "The trouble is that the children of light forget this about God"—it is, sadly, true to this very day.

Most people's biggest problem in living the Christian life is really to believe that God loves them. All we think of is what we have done wrong. Our mind-set and our frame of reference for what God is like are usually based upon our earthly parents. Whether we had good or bad parents makes no difference—all our parents had their flaws, and our image of God as Father is distorted in some way as a result. Our negative concepts of God have left us in a place where we find it hard to imagine how much He loves us. The Pharisees had almost completely forgotten what God was like, and yet so much in the Old Testament shows that God is a God of mercy and that He is gracious.

Why Is This Parable Important?

God's Mercy

Rather than condoning dishonesty, Jesus was asking why it is, if a shrewd manager could know the heart of his boss, that we, the children of our heavenly Father, can't see how merciful God is. Members of the family should be the first to affirm God's mercy. The Jews in those days had lost touch with the tenderness of God. The children of this world do better in their own realm and with their own kind than God's people seem to do in their understanding of Him. We need to learn that our heavenly Father has a very soft heart and is full of tender mercy.

Let me ask, are you like that manager who blew it? Have you let God down? Do you feel that judgment is hanging over your head, that time has run out on you and that there is just no hope for you? Be like this shrewd manager who still had a little presence of mind. A child of God may blow it but can still have the presence of mind to think, *Wait a minute; God is merciful—He sent His Son to die for our sins.* We can plead the blood—never forget that. However foolish you have been, however stupid, however unworthy, you can cling to the cross and your heavenly Father will say, "Well done." When we do this, we put God on the spot because He has decreed that all those who come to the cross He will save. This parable was given to the disciples so that they could understand what their heavenly Father was like. Do you see your heavenly Father as being this gracious? Do you have difficulty believing that God loves you?

It all comes down to a fundamental belief in the Gospel. Either Jesus paid our debt on the cross or He didn't. Either the blood satisfies God's heart and justice or it doesn't.

God's Reputation

This parable is important because God wants us to believe in His love just as the shrewd manager believed his boss would be pleased. By cutting a deal with those debtors, the rich boss would be made to look merciful. This would help his reputation. God cares about His reputation and about His honor, and He wants to be seen as the merciful sovereign He is. The rich landowner was seen here in a light in which the debtors had never before seen him—as being tender, loving and compassionate. The debtors gained an admiration for him that they had never had before. So the boss was obliged to treat gently and graciously the manager who had helped him in this way.

Reminding God of His Word

As Christians we let God down. I recently heard of a pastor who said to his congregation, "If you really knew me, you wouldn't come to hear me preach. And if I really knew you, I wouldn't let you in." We have all let God down; we are all capable of blowing away our inheritance—but there is a way forward. It is to call attention to God's honor. Do you know that this is exactly what Moses did? When God said, "I am going to destroy the people of Israel. I am going to destroy the whole nation and start all over with you," Moses said, "No, You can't do that, Lord, because Your name is at stake—Your honor is at stake. They are going to say back in Egypt that You weren't able to deliver Your people" (see Exodus 32:9–14).

John Calvin said, "The greatest way to pray is to remind God of His own Word and His own honor—you get to Him." I know how one day, years ago, I said to our son, T. R., "Sorry, T. R., we are not going to be able to do that." T. R. said, "Dad, you promised! You gave your word." I tell you I moved heaven and earth to make sure I kept my word to my son.

Charles Spurgeon said, "If I go to hell, I will go to hell trusting the blood of Jesus." Nobody goes to hell trusting in the blood of Jesus! God always keeps His Word. This parable is about how to show that you believe in God's mercy—by reminding Him of His Word. You know that God will come through for you at the end of the day. More than anything else God loves the fact that we know we can touch His heart. This parable shows that even an unworthy person still knows how to get God's attention because he understands God's true heart. Is this the kind of view of God that you have? If you have this kind of view of God, then you see your heavenly Father the way that Jesus wants you to see Him. So if you think there is no hope for you, you are wrong. Go back to the heavenly Father on bended knee and ask for mercy.

Characteristics of the Manager

What were the characteristics of this shrewd manager?

His Intent

The intent of the manager was to save his own skin. The ancient rabbis understood wisdom as being, in part, how to preserve oneself. When you know you have blown it and you still have a vestige of wisdom, you can say, "I remember that I can ask God for mercy and plead Jesus' blood." The manager knew how he could impress his boss, and he did.

His Impertinence
The manager supposedly had the authority to propose the deal to all those who owed money, because they didn't yet know that he was about to be fired. He was impertinent enough to put his boss on the spot by making him look good!

His Intelligence
The manager was praised for his intelligence (Luke 16:8)—shrewd actions that revealed the fact that he understood his boss's character. God is pleased with us when we cry out to Him for mercy, because it shows that we recognize what He is like. If you are able to see this about God, then you see something that many theologians who have studied the Bible have missed in practice—you know that He is rich in mercy. "Let us therefore come boldly to the throne of grace, that we may obtain mercy and find grace to help in time of need" (Hebrews 4:16, NKJV).

Belief in His Love

Some years ago I began reading 1 John 4:16 every morning. It refers to relying on the love God has for us. The King James Version reads, "We have known and believed the love." We can always rely on God's love. Some of us (myself included) have an overscrupulous conscience. We worry about this and that, and we don't want to grieve the Lord. I have learned just to believe in His love and to know that whatever failings there may have been in me as a minister, whatever things I would do differently the second time around—they are covered by His love. I know if I could turn back the clock, I would have tried to be a better husband and a better father. But what does one do? All you can do is plead for God's mercy, and God says, "That will do nicely."

David was described as a man after God's own heart, but he blew it—big time. He slept with another man's wife and then tried to cover up his sin through murder. He felt horrible. Do you know the first thing he did when he turned to the Lord? He cried out for mercy. "Have mercy on me, O God, according to your unfailing love" (Psalm 51:1).

Have you ever reached a place where the only thing left to ask God for is mercy? Maybe prior to this you tried to strike a deal with Him— "Lord, You know how good I have been—You owe me one." God will look down from heaven and say, "Really?!" He knows us inside out. But when you ask Him for mercy, He loves to grant it. That is something the children of God tend to forget, just as the Jews did. Do you believe He loves you? Do you believe He *really* loves you? God wants you to believe that.

Rewards in Heaven

This parable also has eschatological implications. It refers to the future, to the end times. We know that it refers not to lost people but to Christians, because Jesus taught this parable specifically to His disciples. I have preached a lot on rewards, but what we have in this passage is altogether different from anything else I have seen in the Bible. It not only shows a different way of achieving a reward in heaven—it also shows something of what that reward is.

Jesus introduced this topic with some intriguing words: "I tell you, use worldly wealth to gain friends for yourselves, so that when it is gone, you will be welcomed into eternal dwellings" (Luke 16:9).

Jesus made this further application to show that life on earth is not all there is. He brought up the subject of death and made His audience ponder what would happen when life was over and they wanted to be welcomed into eternal dwellings. How we live here on earth will determine the kind of welcome we receive in heaven. Second Peter 1:11 says we may receive a rich welcome, but it isn't given to all. We might wish that it was, but it isn't. Peter wrote:

> Add to your faith virtue, to virtue knowledge, to knowledge self-control, to self-control perseverance, to perseverance godliness, to godliness brotherly kindness, and to brotherly kindness love.... For so an entrance will be supplied to you abundantly into the everlasting kingdom of our Lord and Savior Jesus Christ.
>
> 2 Peter 1:5–7, 11, NKJV

Peter said that our personal life needs to be godly so that we will receive a rich welcome in heaven. Jesus said something similar in this parable—He spoke about how we handle money.

When was the last time you heard a sermon that said your reward in heaven will be determined somewhat, perhaps largely, by how you handle money? How we live will sooner or later be reflected in how we handle money—our own and that of other people's. This in turn will either please or displease our heavenly Father. So the next time you begin to take money out of the bank or you write a check, ask yourself, "Is this going to please the Lord?"

When you go to work, how you spend your time (because you are being paid) provides an example of how you handle another person's money. Do you go to work on time or do you arrive late and leave early, expecting to be paid the same? That is misuse of another person's money. Are you faithful on the job because you are being paid? That is good use of another person's money. Apparently in the days of the old Soviet Union, Christians made an impact on their employers because they were noticed as being willing to do a day's work and could be trusted not to steal things.

Wisdom in Finances

It is possible that Jesus spoke more about finances than about any other subject in the Bible. Jesus said, "I tell you, use worldly wealth to gain friends for yourselves" (Luke 16:9). He was advocating the responsible handling of our money. How we handle money will be an indication of how we will cope with greater responsibility, which Jesus referred to as "true riches." "So if you have not been trustworthy in handling worldly wealth, who will trust you with true riches?" (Luke 16:11).

You are being tested when you are not aware of it, to see whether you can be trusted with greater responsibility. Are you praying for a greater anointing? Be aware that you are being tested to see whether you can be trusted with a greater anointing. Here is a verse that I have possibly quoted more than any other. I call this principle the cornerstone of reliability: "He that is faithful in that which is least is faithful also in much" (Luke 16:10, KJV). The New International Version says it like this: "Whoever can be trusted with very little can also be trusted with much, and whoever is dishonest with very little will also be dishonest with much" (Luke 16:10).

Jesus went on to say, "If you have not been trustworthy with someone else's property, who will give you property of your own?" (Luke 16:12).

This does *not mean* that we can buy our way to heaven! "For it is by grace you have been saved, through faith—and this not from yourselves, it is the gift of God—not by works, so that no one can boast" (Ephesians 2:8–9).

This is affirmed in Isaiah where we read: "Come, all you who are thirsty, come to the waters; and you who have no money, come, buy and eat! Come, buy wine and milk without money and without cost" (Isaiah 55:1).

Neither can we buy our reward in heaven. Our reward will not be related in volume to the amount of money we gave to the Lord while we were on earth. What will count is the attitude of heart we had when dealing with money. To get a reward because of how much money we gave would be to miss the point. Jesus used the analogy of the shrewd manager to show that we please our Father by using wisdom and being trustworthy in the way we use money. This wisdom comes only from the Holy Spirit.

The Testing of the Lord

Your daily life is a test as to whether you can be trusted with more. Maybe you want a raise in pay or a better job? Maybe you aspire to a position of leadership? As Christians we must realize that God does the promoting. As the psalmist put it, "I choose the appointed time; it is I who judge uprightly.... No one from the east or the west or from the desert can exalt a man. But it is God who judges: He brings one down, he exalts another" (Psalm 75:2, 6–7).

Choosing a path of honesty in the whole of life puts you in a good place for the promotion of the Lord. You may not realize that you are being tested, but God is watching.

Contrast between the Realms

Jesus referred in the parable to two realms—the earthly realm and the eternal realm (Luke 16:9). In the earthly realm we need money to live. The way we use it will affect our relationship with God and our relationships with others, as usually we are paid by someone with whom we have a hierarchical relationship. In the earthly realm money will come to an end: "For we brought nothing into the world, and we can take nothing out of it" (1 Timothy 6:7).

What about in the eternal realm? We need to know that this life is not all there is and that there is continuity between this life and the life to come. How we live here below will determine not only our welcome in heaven but also what we will be doing in heaven and the responsibility we will have there. You may not believe in the theology of "once saved, always saved" as I do, but you must certainly believe "once in heaven, always in heaven." How we live throughout eternity will be determined by what happens in the temporal life God gives us here on earth. If that ever begins to grip you, it will have a major effect on your life. If you come to a place where you agree with Paul that we must give an account of the things done in the body whether good or bad (2 Corinthians 5:10), then you have to accept that these things determine our status throughout eternity.

The Cornerstone of Reliability

This is the verse that I always refer to as *the cornerstone of reliability:* "Whoever can be trusted with very little can also be trusted with much, and whoever is dishonest with very little will also be dishonest with much" (Luke 16:10).

An Unconscious Test

Very possibly we are unaware of the implications of our daily decisions because we just don't realize that God sees all we do and hears all we say. When you are dealing with temptation, God is watching you. He knows whether you are walking in the light. I can tell you that God does give us responsibility in proportion to our obedience in the smaller things.

A Uniform Test

The testing of God in regard to our trustworthiness is a uniform test—it does not vary from person to person or alter according to personal circumstances. We often make excuses based on our circumstances. For instance, we say to ourselves, *I would tithe if I had more money.* You wouldn't. *I would pray more if I had a different job.* You wouldn't. *I would go to church if things were different.* No, you wouldn't. *I would be faithful in my marriage if I had a different wife!* No, you wouldn't! *If I had a more interesting job, I would be more responsible and trustworthy.* "Wrong," said Jesus. "He that is faithful in that which is least is faithful also in much" (Luke 16:10, KJV).

I quote from Joseph Soame: "What a man does with his responsibility here will substantially affect his situation in eternity. The manner in which our eternal future is determined is by the way we discharge our duties here on earth." Joseph Soame connects this to Luke 19:17: "'Well done, my good servant!' his master replied. 'Because you have been trustworthy in a very small matter, take charge of ten cities'" (Luke 19:17).

The Ultimate Test

One day God will make His final judgment. All our pleading at that time will be useless. You may say, "But, Lord, you forgot what I did." But the Lord will say, "I don't know you" (Matthew 7:23).

Comparison between Riches

"So if you have not been trustworthy in handling worldly wealth, who will trust you with true riches?" (Luke 16:11).

It is important to note that Jesus was not talking here about being rich. When He used the phrase "worldly wealth," He was not merely speaking to the wealthy—He was referring to all of us. He was teaching about how all of us handle our earthly resources. Earthly wealth is temporal in any case. It can be with us one moment and gone the next. Remember how quickly the twin towers fell in New York City—it took only one hour. That symbol of capitalism and wealth was gone in an instant. The stock market can plummet overnight. These things do not indicate true wealth—they are only temporal. So what is true wealth? It is what the apostle Paul called the "unsearchable riches of Christ" (Ephesians 3:8). Paul also said, "I consider that our present sufferings are not worth comparing with the glory that will be revealed in us" (Romans 8:18).

The Continuity of Responsibility

Whether it is with property or possessions, he that can be trusted with little can also be trusted with much (Luke 16:10). Nothing on earth belongs to us. We are entrusted with earthly things in order to test our stewardship. Our administration of earthly things is God's barometer of our faithfulness to Him.

According to this parable, your reward in heaven will be greater responsibility, and it will remain yours throughout eternity. That is a long time to have responsibility, and it is all based on how we behaved here in this temporal realm. If we fail the test, we will not be given responsibility in heaven. So there will be a continuity of responsibility between the present age and the age to come. This is what Jesus meant by true riches. To quote Joseph Soame again, "With this we have come full circle, back to the issue of the final purpose of God with mankind, which is to put us in charge over all creation."

So the degree to which we have proved ourselves responsible in this present age will be the degree to which we are given responsibility in the age to come. How does that fit your theology for a reward in heaven? Maybe it will be a star in your crown, maybe it will be a better mansion, but according to Jesus it is a measure of responsibility. Don't forget that the apostle Paul said that we will judge angels (1 Corinthians 6:3). We are going to be given responsibility, but there will be some in heaven with no reward—those who are saved by fire (1 Corinthians 3:15).

The Condition for the Reward

Watch everything in your life in the here and now. We must all stand before the judgment seat of Christ someday and give an account of the things we have done in our life. It does not have to do just with money; that is only the emphasis of this particular parable. Everything that is going to happen on the other side is being determined right now. The apostle Paul was given just a glimpse of the judgment seat of Christ and he said, "Knowing, therefore, the terror of the Lord, we persuade men" (2 Corinthians 5:11, NKJV).

In fact, to Paul it was so important that he said, "I discipline my body and bring it into subjection, lest, when I have preached to others, I myself should become disqualified" (1 Corinthians 9:27, NKJV).

It is all based on our faithfulness here below. What if you feel you have blown it? You know you are going to go to heaven, but you say, "I am not going to get a reward." That is the purpose of this parable! I don't care what you have done or how deeply you have sinned, God isn't allowing you to read this just to make you feel guilty. There is hope. The manager in this parable blew it big time, but in the end he pulled something off and he probably even kept his job. That's speculation, but we do know that he was commended for what he did.

So even if you are a King David and you think the outlook is totally bleak because you have completely blown it, you can begin now to improve your situation by pleading for mercy. Then all you need to say is, "From this day forward I will walk in the light."

Chapter 29

The Parable of the Rich Man and Lazarus

> There was a rich man who was dressed in purple and fine linen and lived in luxury every day. At his gate was laid a beggar named Lazarus.
>
> Luke 16:19

A Loser in Life

The parable of the rich man and Lazarus, found in Luke 16:19–31, is a picture of a loser in life and a winner in death. The parable tells the story of Lazarus, a beggar who was covered in sores and who laid at the gate of a rich man, longing to eat the scraps that fell from the rich man's table. We don't know whether he had a family, who his parents were or whether he had brothers and sisters. The Bible implies that there was nothing attractive about his appearance and that the only company he kept was stray dogs. He probably welcomed the dogs because they kept him company and brought him physical relief: "the dogs came and licked his sores" (Luke 16:21).

We read that the rich man, on the other hand, "was dressed in purple and fine linen and lived in luxury every day" (Luke 16:19).

Probably everyone knew Lazarus's name. He was a permanent fixture at the gate. A person like this was usually referred to by his first name. He was in a state so low that he probably didn't even indulge in the usual fantasies that people have about living a better life. Lazarus wouldn't have fantasized about a beautiful girl suddenly taking notice of him, or about wearing fine clothes or about shopping at Harrods or Bloomingdales. He knew that his earthly status was wretched and that there was no prospect of it improving.

It is likely that Lazarus had no qualifications, and even if he had, he would have been excluded from most places of work because of his medical condition. His occupation was begging. I daresay that having

284

to beg no longer stung his pride as it had in the early days, as he surely had given up any hope of independence or self-respect years ago. When do you suppose it happened? Perhaps he dropped out of school? Perhaps his girlfriend jilted him? Perhaps his parents died when he was young and he was thrust out into the world alone? Dr. Clyde Narramore says, "every person is worth understanding." Here was a beggar with no future; his permanent place was at the rich man's gate. The King James Version says that he was "laid" at the gate—somebody must have brought him there and picked him up at the end of each day. The rich man's dustbin provided Lazarus with his daily diet. He longed, we are told, to eat the crumbs that fell from the rich man's table. Perhaps the rich man dropped him a coin once in a while. This is what I mean when I say Lazarus was a loser in life.

But one day Lazarus died. It is not likely that his obituary was carried in the regular death notices of the time. He was too unimportant for that. Neither is it likely that his passing occupied anything but the most superficial of conversations in the rich man's house—maybe an offhand comment like, "I wonder who will be rummaging through the dustbin now?" Or maybe someone said, "Perhaps there won't be all those dogs hanging around now." The rich man would not miss Lazarus, that's for sure. It's not likely that many mourned his passing at the funeral, if he had one. We don't know how he spent his last day. We don't know how he spent his last hour or who saw him or what he saw just before he died, but we do know what Lazarus saw the moment he breathed his last: He saw angels.

Lazarus witnessed a sight lovelier and more magnificent than the rich man's gate and more beautiful than all the well-to-do people who entered the rich man's house. These angels weren't coming along to drop Lazarus a coin—they were coming for him! Maybe his first inclination was to reach out a hand because that was his habit in life. Perhaps when he saw them he expected them to rush on by, but they didn't. Maybe he thought, *Who are they coming for?* and then he began to realize—they were coming for him.

Never had Lazarus known such treatment, such attention, such honor—he had probably never seen an angel before. But they would have put him at ease. The angels would have treated Lazarus with a dignity and respect that even the rich man never received and that they as angels would never receive either. They regarded themselves as honored to have the privilege of escorting Lazarus to Abraham's side. "Abraham's side" was a nickname for where Jesus is now. Sometimes it is called paradise. It is the immediate presence of God, which means an end to suffering, pain and indignity. It was all over. Lazarus was a loser in life but a winner in death.

A Loser in Death

Sometime later, the rich man died and was buried. (It doesn't say that Lazarus was buried; who knows what they did with his body.) Maybe the rich man had a stately funeral, perhaps in the equivalent of Westminster Abbey or another great cathedral. Dignitaries, ambassadors and journalists may have been present. Perhaps a famous clergyman read an eloquent sermon. Perhaps many important people made statements about the rich man. Perhaps they spoke of his vast influence and his unusual talents. Maybe he had a bronze coffin. But there was one thing the mourners at this ornate funeral wouldn't have known or believed: "In hell, where he was in torment, he looked up and saw Abraham far away, with Lazarus by his side" (Luke 16:23).

At the very moment when all those reverent statements were being made about the rich man, he couldn't have cared less since he was in hell.

Do you know where you will go when you die? Do you know for certain that if you were to die today, you would go to heaven? Do you realize that when three thousand people were suddenly killed in the World Trade Center, all of them went immediately either to heaven or to hell?

Why Is This Parable Important?

The context of this parable goes all the way back to Luke 15 and the Pharisees' accusation that Jesus spent too much time with sinners. You could say the theme of this parable is that God is for the underdog. It is better to be a winner in death than a winner in life and a loser in death. Are you a happy person? Do you have a good life? Are you making a bit of money? Are you worried about the stock market right now? Are you worried about the possibility of a terrorist attack?

This parable is important because there are only two final destinies—heaven and hell—and there is nothing in between. You may say, "I thought we went to purgatory?" I wish that were true, but if such a place as purgatory did exist, the Bible would have taught it. Purgatory is a tradition that came about just a few hundred years ago because it sounds better than hell. We need to know that if we died today we would go to heaven, because eternity will last a long time.

Don't be a fool. When people die they go straight to heaven or to hell. Immediately. If you are saved and you die, you go to be with the Lord right then. There are many great stories of saints who died and caught a glimpse of glory in their last moments. Jonathan Edwards was at the deathbed of David Brainerd, who would have been his son-in-law had he lived. He said that the moment Brainerd died, the glory of the Lord just came into the room and then rose up.

Another reason this parable is important is because it gives us an insight into how people end up in heaven or in hell. Social status has nothing to do with it. You can be rich and go to heaven and poor and go to hell—the opposite of what happened here. The important factor is the state of a person's heart. Reading between the lines of the parable, we can conclude that Lazarus feared God, but the rich man did not.

Some years ago I read a book by the founder of the Salvation Army, William Booth, called *God's Hell*. William Booth tells of the first time the Salvation Army had an undergraduate class. He addressed the graduates, "Brothers and sisters, I feel that perhaps I should apologize for having to keep you here for two years to teach you how to be a soul winner." He said it would have been better if they could have spent five minutes in hell, because "then we could just turn you loose."

The German philosopher Ludwig Feuerbach said that God is nothing more than man's projection on the backdrop of the universe. He says man wants to believe there is a heaven out there so he can believe that he will be taken care of when he dies. But given that kind of reasoning, who would have thought up hell?

Discussing hell is not my favorite topic, but the Bible teaches it is real, and so we must face the issue. Jesus had more to say about hell than anyone else. You may say, "I believe in heaven, but I don't believe in hell." But logically, if there is no such place as hell, then you have no right to believe in heaven. The Bible has much more to say about hell than heaven.

This passage also teaches that hell is a place of conscious punishment, not annihilation. That is the reason for the following illustration. "Father Abraham, have pity on me and send Lazarus to dip the tip of his finger in water and cool my tongue, because I am in agony in this fire" (Luke 16:24).

The fire did not annihilate the rich man.

The Place of Hell

I have reason to believe that I preach on hell more than most. In fact, hearing preaching on hell today is pretty rare. Jesus was keen to show us that both heaven and hell are places that actually exist. When we speak of hell, we are not talking about a state of mind. I have had people say to me, "Oh, I believe in hell. This is it—hell on earth." Life on earth is not hell, however difficult it may be. You may have lived through an awful lot of suffering, but neither is that hell. Hell is a specific place, and it is a place of torment (Luke 16:23).

Preparation for Hell

This passage teaches us about the preparation for hell. How do you prepare for hell? The answer is to live only in the present. The rich man lived in luxury every day. You may not live in luxury now, but perhaps you would if you could. Maybe you spend money on the lottery because you have an aspiration about how you would like to live. The way to prepare for hell is to live to suit yourself; do your own thing; show contempt for those going to heaven—laugh at them. Ignore those who bring the message of the Gospel—that is how to prepare for hell.

Prayer in Hell

The parable also shows how people pray when they are in hell. For 25 years I have tried to encourage people to pray. About every six months I will mention the prayer meeting and ten more people will turn up on that day; then it is back to normal the following week. Do you know where the most fervent prayer meeting is going on right now? This is not funny—it is in hell. They are praying in hell. Do you know what they are asking God for? Mercy. The New International Version says that the rich man prayed for "pity"; the King James Version says he prayed for "mercy" (Luke 16:24).

What is mercy? It is what you ask for when you have no bargaining power. When you are at rock bottom and there is no way to bargain, you pray for mercy. That's the way they are in hell—they pray for mercy, but tragically it is too late. Those who ask for mercy in this life are the only ones who go to heaven. After that it is too late.

Prevention of Hell

How do we avoid hell? "By becoming a beggar now," as one person put it. My old friend Rolfe Barnard, who is now in heaven, said, "Only beggars will be saved." The trouble with many people who profess to be Christians is that they really think they are doing God some kind of a favor. If they do something good like putting money in the offering, they think, *Well, God, I hope You are noticing.* Heaven is a place where only beggars will be found—those who realized how worthless and bankrupt their lives on earth really were and cried out to God for mercy—like the leper who came to Jesus after He had finished His Sermon on the Mount and pleaded, "Lord, if you are willing, you can make me clean" (Matthew 8:2).

There was no snapping of the fingers: "This is what You have got to do for me, Lord." This leper knew his place. He was saying, "Lord, You don't have to; I know You don't have to—but would You? Please, if You will, make me clean." That is the way to be saved.

The Punishment of Hell

In hell you will have all of your senses. The rich man "called out" to father Abraham (Luke 16:24). This was Jesus' way of saying that you will have your senses. You will be able to feel, touch, hear and see. You will have your memory in hell because in the parable Abraham spoke to the rich man and said, "Son, remember that in your lifetime you received your good things, while Lazarus received bad things, but now he is comforted here and you are in agony" (Luke 16:25).

End of story. If only one could take out the memory. One of the things that will make hell, hell, is your memory. If only you could forget.

The Purpose of Hell

The purpose of hell is summed up in one word—*punishment.* There are various degrees of judgment that God exercises as appropriate. Sometimes there is what I call gracious judgment, when God steps in and, although your behavior is awful, He gives you a hint so you can do something about it. It is a wake-up call. Then there is retributive judgment. With this there is no wake-up call; it is too late. When this comes it is all over. You keep thinking, *No, this can't be the end. No, no, this is not the end surely?* But it is. Although the rich man cried out for mercy and pity, none was forthcoming. Abraham continued in response to the rich man's plea, "And besides all this, between us and you a great chasm has been fixed" (Luke 16:26).

The Perpetuity of Hell

The awful reality is that no one can rescue you from hell however much they may want to. You can never get out. "A great chasm has been fixed, so that those who want to go from here to you cannot, nor can anyone cross over from there to us" (Luke 16:26).

Jesus made this very clear. But while we are on earth, you can still make the crossover from death into life. God punishes sin in two ways—either by the blood of Jesus or in the fires of hell. The fires of hell never satisfy the justice of God—ever; they just keep burning. The inhabitants of hell keep reaching out for justice but they never make it. The wonderful news is that two thousand years ago, on Good Friday, the blood of Jesus paid the price for all our sin now and forever if we only trust in Him. The blood of Jesus totally satisfies God's justice.

The Proof of Hell

The Bible is the only authority on the proof of hell. If you don't believe what the Word of God says about the existence of hell, then you won't believe anyone. If you were so unfortunate as to be condemned to hell, there would be no use crying out, "I believe in hell now! I see that it is real! Please forgive me for not believing You when I was alive. Have mercy!" It will be too late for that. Those who escape the terror of hell are those who trusted in God's Word while they were alive. Heaven is made up of people who just believed in His Word. Why would anyone believe in the Bible? We are enabled to believe by the power of the Holy Spirit when we open our hearts to God. Calvin called it the "internal testimony of the Holy Spirit." That is how we can know that the Bible is true.

Having realized that hell did indeed exist, the rich man wanted Lazarus to be sent back into this life to warn his brothers because they didn't believe that there was a hell. The rich man reasoned that, "If Lazarus is raised from the dead and he goes to my five brothers then they will believe." But "Abraham replied, 'They have Moses and the Prophets; let them listen to them'" (Luke 16:29).

"That's not enough!" the rich man protested. Abraham, however, spoke the truth when he replied, "If they do not listen to Moses and the Prophets, they will not be convinced even if someone rises from the dead" (Luke 16:31).

It is interesting that in this parable we never find out the rich man's name, but we do know the name of the one who went to heaven.

Remember that God knows your name. "This is what the LORD says—he who created you, O Jacob, he who formed you, O Israel: 'Fear not, for I have redeemed you; I have summoned you by name; you are mine'" (Isaiah 43:1).

The disciples said, "Lord, even the demons submit to us in your name" (Luke 10:17). But Jesus said, "Are you excited about that? Let me tell you what ought to excite you...."

"Rejoice that your names are written in heaven" (Luke 10:20).

Is you name written in the book of God's Kingdom? If you are sure it is, then you can rejoice. If you are unsure, then call on God's mercy without delay.

Chapter 30

The Parable of the Persistent Widow

Yet because this widow keeps bothering me, I will see that she gets
justice, so that she won't eventually wear me out.

Luke 18:5

The parable of the persistent widow is one of my favorite parables. I
love it because the bottom line is basically, "Never ever give up
praying." The parable is Jesus' way of letting us know that God does
not always answer prayer immediately. Sometimes He will wait a good
while. Sometimes He might wait years.

Some of the parables are hard to interpret, but this one was made
easy for us, since Jesus introduced it by revealing the point of the
parable: "Then Jesus told his disciples a parable to show them that they
should always pray and not give up" (Luke 18:1).

How much do you pray? I remember asking my dad four or five years
ago how it was that he prayed so much, because my earliest memory
was seeing him on his knees for half an hour each day before he went to
work. He was not in full-time Christian ministry, but he still prayed for
thirty minutes a day. My stepmother, Abby, has told me that after he
retired he would spend an hour or two in prayer each day. One time
when they were on a trip, she decided to count his requests. She was
driving, and he began to pray through his prayer list. She said she lost
count after 345 items. That's my dad!

Do you know the average minister in Britain and America spends an
average of four minutes a day in prayer? And we wonder why the
Church is so powerless! Could it be that this explains why you too are
powerless? My dad's reason for praying was very simple—his pastor,
Gene Phillips, told him to pray for thirty minutes a day and he did.
How much do you pray?

The Widow's Request

This parable is about an insensitive man who was in a position of power and kept denying a widow's request on a matter that was obviously very important to her: "Grant me justice against my adversary," she pleaded (Luke 18:3).

We can't be certain whether Jesus was making up a story or recounting a real-life situation of which He was aware. Whichever it was, He endorsed implicitly our asking God for anything we want. Sometimes people are a little embarrassed to talk about what they pray for. I wouldn't want you to know about some of the things I ask the Lord for because you would probably laugh at me. You would probably say, "I wouldn't bother the Lord with that!" Well, I do because Proverbs says, "In all your ways acknowledge Him, and He shall direct your paths" (Proverbs 3:6, NKJV).

I pray about everything. Everything!

On the surface, the widow's request seems rather selfish. But Jesus said that that is what she asked, and she just kept it up. She didn't give up when the man seemed indifferent, and eventually one day he said, "I am going to get rid of her and give her what she wants." It wasn't because he cared about her; it was actually because he was annoyed (Luke 18:3–4). She didn't mind at all—she got what she wanted. Then Jesus made the application. If an unloving judge who doesn't care about the situation finally said yes, how much more will our loving heavenly Father say yes to His elect—His chosen ones who keep crying out to Him day and night (Luke 18:7). So that is the point. Here was a situation in the secular world in which an insensitive judge finally granted a request; but we have a loving heavenly Father who would not withhold anything good from us—how much more will He grant our requests!

Why Is This Parable Important?

The Importance of Prayer

This parable talks about the importance of prayer. How important is prayer to you? Prayers that are read aloud can be very inspiring, and God can use liturgy powerfully, but that is not what I mean. How much do you *actually* pray, that is, have a two-way conversation with God? The business writer Stephen Covey famously said, "No one ever says on their deathbed, 'I wish I had spent more time in the office.'" Do you say, "One day I am going to start praying more"? Do you spend a minimum of thirty minutes a day alone with God? There will be no praying in heaven.

I will tell you something that used to hurt me. I was driving in my car one Monday morning, and the Holy Spirit changed my life. I am sure it was the baptism of the Spirit because the centrality of the Gospel was revealed to me. I thought I had discovered something new. I saw election, predestination and "once saved, always saved" in seconds. I thought I was the first since the apostle Paul to see it. Less than a year later I left my Nazarene church and found my way into Baptist ranks where they were all "five-point Calvinists," and to a large degree they accepted me. They were a little suspicious, and they were cessationists. They didn't believe what had happened to me in the car could happen, but they kind of put it to one side because my doctrine was acceptable to them. The one thing that hurt me, apart from their minimizing my experience, was that these people didn't pray. They didn't have prayer lives. They would read Spurgeon's sermons but that was about it. The importance of prayer was something I wanted to contribute to the spiritual life of Westminster Chapel. That is the first thing about this parable: It shows the importance of prayer.

Perseverance in Prayer

The parable is an implicit acknowledgment that God does not always answer prayer immediately. Why else would such a parable be necessary? If God answered prayer the first day you asked Him, you wouldn't have to encourage people to pray. Everyone would want to pray. It would be like buying a ticket to the lottery and winning every time. What's more, everyone would become Christians. They would say, "This has worked—this is a great thing!" But the God of the Bible is sovereign, and He wants to see if we love Him; one reason He doesn't answer our prayers immediately is because He wants us to keep spending time with Him.

These words of Jesus are an encouragement not to give up. If God doesn't answer prayer, He has a reason, but don't stop asking. Have you lived long enough to thank God for unanswered prayer? Have you lived long enough to thank Him for a closed door? The encouragement to pray and not to give up is a theme throughout the gospel of Luke and the book of Acts. This was obviously an important theme to Luke. He recorded another story in which Jesus made an identical point.

> Suppose one of you has a friend, and he goes to him at midnight and says, "Friend, lend me three loaves of bread, because a friend of mine on a

journey has come to me, and I have nothing to set before him." Then the one inside answers, "Don't bother me. The door is already locked, and my children are with me in bed. I can't get up and give you anything." I tell you, though he will not get up and give him the bread because he is his friend, yet because of the man's boldness he will get up and give him as much as he needs. So I say to you: Ask and it will be given to you; seek and you will find; knock and the door will be opened to you. For everyone who asks receives; he who seeks finds; and to him who knocks, the door will be opened.

Luke 11:5–10

The context of the parable of the persistent widow discussed wanting more of God. The context of the above passage is the Sermon on the Mount in which Jesus was talking about being hungry for the Kingdom of heaven. Jesus added:

Which of you fathers, if your son asks for a fish, will give him a snake instead? Or if he asks for an egg, will give him a scorpion? If you then, though you are evil, know how to give good gifts to your children, how much more will your Father in heaven give the Holy Spirit to those who ask him!

Luke 11:11–13

This parable is also important because it is *proof* that God answers prayer. I have a prayer list on which I have now started writing down answers to prayer so that I can thank God for them. I have made it a habit to thank Him for answered prayer. I will thank Him again and again for days and weeks after He has answered a prayer because I am so grateful. Maybe you are praying for a baby? Maybe you are praying for a loved one to be saved? Maybe you are praying for revival? Maybe you are praying for a raise in pay or a different job? Maybe you are praying for a husband or a wife? Jesus says, "Don't stop." Ask for anything you want and until He says no, just keep on praying.

Waiting in Faith

This parable ends with a warning about not being ready for answered prayer; it could also be interpreted as being a warning about not being ready for the Second Coming. My grandma used to say, "Say what you mean, and mean what you say." Be careful when you ask the Lord for something. Don't ask Him unless you really want it. If He hears your request and gives it to you when you don't want it anymore, you might be a little embarrassed. It may not be today or tomorrow, but it will come and then you will find out how much you really meant it.

Zechariah and Elizabeth prayed for a son, but after a few years they just tore up that prayer request. Twenty-five or thirty years later it would seem, Gabriel appeared to Zechariah and said, "Your prayer has been heard." Zechariah didn't have a clue what Gabriel was talking about! Gabriel said, "You and your wife, Elizabeth, prayed for a son." Zechariah thought, *Oh, that prayer. Well, there must be some mistake. Have you had a look at my wife lately?* Now I can think of nothing more stupid than arguing with Gabriel. If Gabriel showed up and said something to me, I would believe it. The point is, however, that even though Zechariah had forgotten he had prayed that prayer, it was still answered.

A Warrant for Answered Prayer

Praying in His Will

"This is the confidence we have in approaching God: that if we ask anything according to his will, he hears us" (1 John 5:14).

The warrant or guarantee for answered prayer is simply this: You find out what the will of God is in a situation and then pray it back to Him, knowing He will answer your prayer positively. You may say, "Well, that doesn't sound like much fun. It means I have got to pray in the will of God in order for my prayer to be answered." That's true. There is one exception to this—the situation in which a person doesn't like God's will and persists in asking for something different. Eventually, to teach you the error of your ways, God may just grant such a request. If this ever happens to you, I guarantee you will be sorry. "And He gave them their request, but sent leanness into their soul" (Psalm 106:15, NKJV).

I can tell you now that if God says, "No, this is not what I want for you," you should accept it—don't argue, because "no good thing will He withhold from those who walk uprightly" (Psalm 84:11, NKJV).

If God is saying no to something you want, then believe it is right. One day you will be thankful. John continued, "And if we know that he hears us—whatever we ask—we know that we have what we asked of him" (1 John 5:15).

That is a big "if." We don't always know that He hears us. Maybe you are so spiritual that every time you pray in the will of God you know it. I don't. Zechariah didn't, and neither did Paul, for he said, "The Spirit helps us in our weakness. We do not know what we ought to pray for, but the Spirit himself intercedes for us with groans that words cannot express" (Romans 8:26).

I think there is a case to be made for this referring to speaking in tongues. When you pray in tongues, you don't know what you are saying. I pray in tongues. I was sharing with someone recently as we were enjoying a time of fellowship in East Africa on the edge of the Indian Ocean. I said, "Here is a phrase that comes up often when I pray in tongues—does it sound like any language you have heard?" This man thought perhaps it was a Semitic language. I would love to know what I say when I pray in tongues, but I don't.

If you don't agree that Paul was referring here to speaking in tongues, then perhaps it simply refers to groaning, "O Lord, please hear me." The point is that Paul didn't always know what he needed to pray for. He said, "I don't know, but the Spirit helps me in my weakness."

"And he who searches our hearts knows the mind of the Spirit, because the Spirit intercedes for the saints in accordance with God's will" (Romans 8:27).

If you knew what you were saying in the Spirit, then you would know God's will. I don't always know whether I am praying in the will of God, but I keep on praying. I continue to pray for revival to come, and until God tells me it is *not* coming, I will continue to pray.

The Shape of Answered Prayer

Jesus revealed another principle of prayer through this parable, and this is the scary part. The shape that answered prayer takes is determined by our readiness at the time to receive the answer and whether we are still praying for that request. You can't say, when God finally answers your prayer, "Oh, I don't think I am interested in that now." If you had told Zechariah while he was praying for Elizabeth to conceive that when the answer to prayer arrived he would *not* be thrilled by it, I am sure that he would not have believed you. Yet he eventually ceased praying about it and was shocked and unprepared when the answer to prayer came. Before Gabriel returned to heaven, he had an unpleasant duty. Because Zechariah was found in unbelief, he was struck dumb by the angel until the baby was born.

Some people would like to suggest that unbelief aborts the prayer process. Wrong! Zechariah had years of stored-up unbelief, but his prayer was answered. Why? Any prayer prayed in the will of God will be answered (1 John 5:14). What ought to have been Zechariah's finest hour came under a cloud. You can imagine people all over the Judean hillsides saying, "Zechariah, this is wonderful! Congratulations! You must be so happy that Elizabeth is going to have a baby." But Zechariah couldn't reply.

The Witness for Answered Prayer

"Have faith in God [the Greek reads, "Have the faith of God"]. . . . I tell you, whatever you ask for in prayer, believe that you have received it, and it will be yours" (Mark 11:22, 24).

One of the most marvelous experiences you can have is to receive the assurance that your prayer will be answered before it actually happens. I am grateful that this has happened to me a few times. It's not an everyday occurrence, but there are certain prayer requests that I know will be fulfilled. How do I know? I just *know* that I *know*. The Spirit is an immediate witness; He comes in and reveals to you in your spirit that something will happen, and you know that it's as good as done. Then all you need to do is wait for the answer to materialize. It doesn't happen to me all the time, and it didn't happen to Zechariah. It doesn't mean you are unspiritual if it doesn't happen at all. Sometimes God gives you this assurance, and sometimes He doesn't.

A Warning about Answered Prayer

"When the Son of Man comes, will he find faith on the earth?" (Luke 18:8).

Jesus ended His parable by making an interesting comment. Why did He make this statement on the end of a parable about prayer? Was He changing the subject to mention the Second Coming? Was He making an eschatological statement? I think He was referring to the Second Coming, but I also think He was referring to answered prayer. I think His point is that when He does return, He wants to find you believing that He is going to answer your prayer. He doesn't want to find that you have said to yourself, *Oh, I gave up on that one years ago.* The Lord says, "You asked for it, so I have given it." You can't say, "Oh, but that was then, and this is now."

Remember that the encouragement not to give up praying is a theme throughout the gospel of Luke that continues right through Acts. Let me show you how it comes out later in Luke.

> As [Jesus] approached Jerusalem and saw the city, he wept over it and said, "If you, even you, had only known on this day what would bring you peace—but now it is hidden from your eyes. The days will come upon you when your enemies will build an embankment against you and encircle you and hem you in on every side. They will dash you to the ground, you and the children within your walls. They will not leave one stone on another, because you did not recognize the time of God's coming to you."
> Luke 19:41–44

In the synagogues throughout Palestine and Judea, they prayed, "Oh that thou wouldest rend the heavens, that thou wouldest come down" (Isaiah 64:1, KJV). But when God came down, they weren't ready; they didn't recognize Him. This is a great illustration of how any prayer prayed in the will of God gets answered, but the shape that it takes is determined by our readiness at the time. Also, the very person who asks for God to act may not be the one who gets to enjoy His answer.

Zechariah wasn't ready for the answer to his prayer, and judgment came upon him. When you talk to God, say what you mean and mean what you say. Then when He is ready to answer, He will find you praying. It is put like this in Isaiah: "Lo, this is our God; we have waited for him" (Isaiah 25:9, KJV).

What a wonderful moment!

There was a man back in Ashland, Kentucky, who, along with another couple, wanted to start a church in the southern part of the town. People laughed at them. I remember when they had up to eleven people they rented a garage. People said, "Did you hear about the group in South Ashland? They got eleven people last week!" But those eleven people prayed that God would give them a church.

The man whose vision it was to start the church fell out with some of the townspeople. He didn't get his way, and he left angrily. Then he had marriage difficulties.

A few years later the most beautiful church was erected in that part of Ashland. They brought in the general superintendent of that denomination to preach the dedication address. The church seated four hundred. The place was packed, and cars had to be parked two blocks away. The man whose original vision it was to have the church wasn't even welcome. They said he just drove by, looked at the building and kept on going. But his prayer was answered.

Are you ready for answered prayer? It is a severe warning. When the Son of Man comes, will He find you waiting and living in faith? I would urge you today to go back to that old prayer request and say, "Lord, thank You for the warning." I mean it. Say, "Lord, please do it; I want to be ready—don't let me miss what could be the basis for my greatest enjoyment."

Never Give Up

The message of this parable is, don't give up. Take this verse seriously and go back to your old requests. Remember it can be something as big as praying for revival or it can be something as simple as "give me justice against my adversary."

I was preaching at the garden tomb in Israel about fifteen years ago when a couple came up to me and said, "Do you recognize us?" I said, "No." They said, "Well, we are from Edinburgh, and you preached a sermon at our church about being ready for answered prayer and told us to go back to asking for what we had given up on. We had always prayed that we would get to go to Israel one day and we had given up. So we started praying again that we would get to Israel, and here we are—and of all things, you are here too!" It was just a little touch of God—it made them happy, and it made me happy.

Don't give up on whatever it is. One of the reasons God doesn't answer immediately is to see whether you are serious about it. He is serious about answered prayer. Any prayer prayed in the will of God will be answered. Now if God says no, then accept it; it will be because He has a better idea. However, until He says no—don't give up!

Chapter 31

The Parable of the Two Men Praying

God, have mercy on me, a sinner.
Luke 18:13

Immediately following the parable of the persistent widow, which encourages us to pray and keep on praying, Jesus told a parable about how *not* to pray. If you are intent on offending God, Jesus said, then pray like this! It is therefore also a parable in which we can learn how to pray if we want to endear ourselves to Him.

The parable told of two men who went up to the temple to pray. One was a Pharisee and the other a tax collector. The Pharisee, being supremely confident of his standing before God (and also extremely self-righteous), prayed loudly about the strength of his religious convictions and about all he did to honor God. The tax collector, however, stood at a distance, head bowed, and simply muttered, "God, have mercy on me, a sinner." Jesus said the tax collector, rather than the Pharisee, was the one who went home "justified before God."

The reason? "For everyone who exalts himself will be humbled, and he who humbles himself will be exalted" (Luke 18:14).

Into which category would you fit? If you have a sense of your own sin and shame, then this is a most encouraging parable for you. But if you are repulsed by the thought of being "a sinner" and you are quite happy about yourself; if you feel that you would be comfortable with being judged by your own personal righteousness at the judgment seat of God—then you are not going to like this chapter at all!

It is very interesting that this comes as part of a long succession of parables that Jesus gave in response to the Pharisees' accusation that He kept company with sinners. The very ones who the righteous people of Jerusalem thought God would reject were the ones He accepted. In the parable of the rich man and Lazarus, God was on the side of Lazarus. In the parable of the persistent widow, God was on the side of the widow.

302   The Complete Guide to the Parables

Here in this parable we have perhaps the boldest example of how the religious people of the day could reject Jesus and still feel good about it. This parable went against the popular view of piety and righteousness. It is equally the boldest example of how Jesus' theology agrees with that of the apostle Paul.

Jesus was the first to teach *justification by faith alone;* we can see this in the Sermon on the Mount. But here Jesus taught very boldly that we are justified before God not by our works *but because of His grace.* This parable will show you how to become a Christian.

The Paradox of the Parable

The paradox of this parable is this: A good man is described, but he is entirely wrong; a bad man is also described, and he is entirely justified.

"The Pharisee stood up and prayed about himself: 'God, I thank you that I am not like other men—robbers, evildoers, adulterers—or even like this tax collector. I fast twice a week and give a tenth of all I get'" (Luke 18:11–12). It turns out that this person, whom you would call a good man, was categorically rejected by God despite his many pious acts.

The "bad" guy, the tax collector, stood at a distance and we read that "he would not even look up to heaven, but beat his breast and said, 'God, have mercy on me, a sinner'" (Luke 18:13). Jesus then said, "I tell you that this man, rather than the other, went home justified before God" (Luke 18:14).

Jesus chose a Pharisee, the most popular and pious type of person of that day, as the bad guy. The Pharisees were a religious sect among Judaism. The Pharisees' hero was Ezra—the book of Ezra tells us all about love for the law. The name "Pharisee" comes from a word that means "to separate," because they thought they were separate from other people—a cut above the rest. In spirit their successors are still alive today—some are in churches; they are not necessarily Jews. But in actual, natural succession, their literal successors exist also. We would probably see some of them today at the Western Wall in Jerusalem—dressing in the same way, not shaving their beards, wearing the right kind of clothes and so on. They regard themselves as a cut above all the others. Jesus was the first to see through people like this. He said, "Everything they do is done for men to see" (Matthew 23:5).

In other words, "they do what they do so that people will admire their piety and godliness."

What about the tax collector? Jesus chose as the good guy a person who was hated by all the Jews. He was the lowest you could get and still be a Jew, because as a tax collector you were seen as being on the side of Rome. All tax collectors were viewed as traitors because they worked for the hated Romans. They were almost certainly less than honest, and they regularly took bribes. Yet this was the man who went home completely justified before God.

The Purpose of the Parable

As with the last parable, we are told from the beginning why Jesus taught it. Luke wrote, "To some who were confident of their own righteousness and looked down on everybody else, Jesus told this parable" (Luke 18:9).

He might have said, "Here is a parable to show you how to be saved," because the parable does do that. But instead Luke said that it was aimed at "righteous" people. Do you know any "righteous" people? People who look at you with a straight face and say, "I haven't done anything wrong"? Perhaps you feel quite confident that when you stand before God, He will say, "Come on in because you have tried to live the kind of life that you thought would please Me." Some people really think they have done nothing that would disqualify them from going to heaven. The purpose of this parable is to reveal to people that they are lost, so that if they died right now, as they are, they would go to hell.

Confident of His Own Righteousness

Jesus said that the Pharisee was confident of his own righteousness. In other words, he felt good about his righteousness. Are you like that? This is the most precarious state to be in on earth. It is a scary position in which to be. If that's you, perhaps God in His mercy is allowing you to read this as a wake-up call. I will tell you another thing: Being confident of your own righteousness is a dead giveaway that Satan has performed surgery on you. Paul wrote, "The god of this age has blinded the minds of unbelievers" (2 Corinthians 4:4).

Do you wonder why people aren't Christians? They have been under the scalpel of the devil. He has performed an operation on them to make them blind to the glory of Jesus. Consequently they are also blind to their own inner condition. If you ever see yourself as God sees you, and you recognize that you are vile and wretched in His eyes without the covering of Jesus' righteousness, then it is a good sign. It means that the Holy Spirit is undoing the work of the devil and allowing you to see yourself as you are. You could be a brilliant person with a high IQ on a natural level and yet still be blind to a sense of sin. But the Bible says, "If we claim to be without sin, we deceive ourselves and the truth is not in us" (1 John 1:8).

He Looked Down on Others

The Christian is someone who knows he has no right to look down on others because he is what he is only by the grace of God. There are two ways you can fall into sin. First, there is scandalous sin (and here the Christian should say, "That could happen to me, so I am not going to judge"), and then there is the kind of sin where we are not aware that we have fallen. About this instance Paul wrote, "Brothers, if someone is caught in a sin, you who are spiritual should restore him gently. But watch yourself, or you also may be tempted" (Galatians 6:1).

The hardest person on earth to talk to is a person who doesn't think that they have done anything wrong. But even then we shouldn't look down on them because it could happen to any one of us. The Pharisees looked down on everybody. At the end of this parable, Jesus said, "For everyone who exalts himself will be humbled, and he who humbles himself will be exalted" (Luke 18:14).

Remember also that James wrote, "God opposes the proud but gives grace to the humble" (James 4:6).

Listen to this word from Proverbs:

> There are six things the LORD hates,
>   seven that are detestable to him:
>   *haughty eyes,*
>   a lying tongue,
>   hands that shed innocent blood,
>   a heart that devises wicked schemes,
>   feet that are quick to rush into evil,
>   a false witness who pours out lies
>   and a man who stirs up dissension among brothers.
>   Proverbs 6:16–19, emphasis added

God doesn't like any of these things, but pride is first on the list. Also, "The LORD detests all the proud of heart. Be sure of this: They will not go unpunished" (Proverbs 16:5).

The purpose of the parable is to give a wake-up call to people who feel good about themselves.

Similarities between the Two Men

The parable compares the Pharisee and the tax collector. They had three things in common. First, they both stand to pray (Luke 18:11, 13). Second, they both address God directly. The Pharisee said, "God, I thank you that I am not like other men" (Luke 18:11). And the tax collector said, "God, have mercy on me, a sinner" (Luke 18:13).

Finally, they both wanted to be heard by God—they wanted to somehow reach His heart. That is the purpose of prayer, after all—to reach God. There is no greater power than the power of God. Perhaps you want to reach somebody influential so you can influence *them* to do something for you. Usually highly influential people are unreachable, but it is not that way with God. When you want to reach God, there is a way to do it.

Differences between the Two Men

The Pharisee was self-justifying. We are told that he stood up and prayed about himself. The Greek could be read as "he prayed *to* himself"; scholars are unsure whether it reads he prayed "to" himself or "about" himself, but the point is that although he may have addressed his prayer to God, he focused entirely on himself. It is a dead giveaway that he had no concept of the nature of God. He actually thought that God was going to like his talking like this.

He began, "God, I thank you . . . " That is at least a good start—always thank God whenever you can—but then he said, "I thank you that I am not like other men" (Luke 18:11).

In that moment the Father turned His face away. Don't ever say that. Don't ever feel good about yourself because you know someone who is worse than you in terms of morality or wickedness. You may say, "Well, I am not perfect, but I am no Saddam Hussein." When you begin to compare yourself with other people, you can always find someone who is worse than you in some way. The Pharisee focused upon himself and compared himself to four kinds of people: "robbers, evildoers, adulterers—or even like this tax collector" (Luke 18:11).

The funny thing is that although the tax collector stood far off, the Pharisee still saw him and said, "God, I want to thank You that I am not like him." And God was supposed to say, "Oh, good, that's wonderful"? The Pharisee actually thought he was endearing himself to God. It is easy for a person to be so self-deceived that he fancies himself talking to God and thinks that God is talking back to him.

I was recently speaking to a friend in Fitzgerald, Georgia, who made a throwaway comment. I don't think he knew what he was saying, but I got out my pen and wrote it down because it is only about once a year that I get an insight like this. He said, "If God tells you something and you don't like it, pray again and you might get a different answer—Balaam did." He is right. But that wasn't good! Too many of us, when we don't like what God has said, just keep talking—which Balaam did. God initially said to Balaam, "Have nothing to do with these men" (Numbers 22:12). But when the men showed up, Balaam said, "Sit down and let me find out what God wants." God had already told him. Balaam kept talking when God had *already* answered. Not good.

I fear that there are some people to whom God has spoken who didn't like what they heard; and now they just hear what they want to hear and have become utterly deceived. The Pharisee compared himself with others, and it made him feel good because he actually thought he had communion with God. He believed that—right in the middle of his comfort zone. But the tax collector accused himself. He stood at a distance because he didn't feel worthy to go near a Pharisee— he knew his place. He believed that the Pharisee was a cut above him because everybody thought that the Pharisees were truly righteous people.

There are people who give you the impression that they are godly when they are not. They may have the profile, and there may be things about them that give you the impression they are close to God, but it is those who say "I am nothing" who really know His presence. That was the tax collector. He stood far off, couldn't even look up to heaven and beat his breast. Who said tax collectors never felt guilty about their lifestyles?

Unseen Work of the Spirit

Jesus was saying, "Don't think they don't know what they are doing." There are a lot of people who are involved in things that are not right, and you think they don't know what they are doing wrong. But the Holy Spirit can work on a person in a way you never thought possible. That is why we should pray for someone like Osama Bin Laden. Do you realize what it would mean if someone like that were converted? Talk about catching a big fish! I wish that Christians everywhere would pray for that man—and love him. It could almost mean the reconciliation of the world if that man was converted. There is no person more strategic. You may think that people like this don't feel any guilt, but even when Saul of Tarsus was struck down by the power of God, God said to him, "It is hard for you to kick against the goads" (Acts 26:14).

God knew that Saul was fighting with his convicted conscience all along. Saul had never forgotten the sight of seeing Stephen before the council with his face shining like an angel. Neither had he forgotten the stoning of Stephen when he heard Stephen say, "Lord, do not hold this sin against them" (Acts 7:60).

Saul of Tarsus couldn't get away from that memory. You wouldn't have known it while he was killing Christians, but God knew it. Maybe the people for whom you are praying seem wicked and unreachable, but God may be at work—don't give up praying for them.

Righteousness of the Pharisee

A Respectable Righteousness
The Pharisee had a respectable righteousness. Never doubt that. No one was condemning the Pharisee because he didn't rob banks and commit adultery. He fasted—in fact he fasted twice a week—and he tithed. There is nothing wrong with that. I wish that everybody would tithe. This man was not being condemned for fasting and tithing.

A Rejected Righteousness
But here is the scandal of the Gospel: Seemingly "righteous" people go to hell. Christ died for the ungodly—He justifies them and they go to heaven. "For it is by grace you have been saved, through faith—and this not from yourselves, it is the gift of God—not by works, so that no one can boast" (Ephesians 2:8). Isaiah said to God, "All our righteous acts are like filthy rags" (Isaiah 64:6).

That is the way you will see yourself when you are under the searchlight of God. Why is our righteousness rejected? Because it competes with God's way of doing things. The sacrificial system in the Old Testament pointed people to the cross. It showed them that they couldn't save themselves.

Righteousness of the Tax Collector

A Remote Righteousness
The tax collector had a remote righteousness that was the opposite of the Pharisee's. The tax collector had no righteousness of his own, and there was nothing about him that would have made you think, *This*

man is going to go to heaven one day. He stood far off because he was spiritually bankrupt and he knew it. Are you aware of being spiritually bankrupt? Do you know that in yourself you have nothing? This was the state of the tax collector.

A Received Righteousness

Something was going on between God and the tax collector that the Pharisee wouldn't have known about. In his prayer the tax collector pleaded for mercy. It shows that he knew all about the sacrificial system of the Old Testament. He uses the verb form of the word *mercy seat* from the Greek word *elasterion.* The same word is found in Hebrews 9:2–3. The verb form is *elaskomi.* What the tax collector was saying was, "God, be merciful to me because of the mercy seat." The common Greek word for *mercy* in the New Testament is *helios:* "Let us therefore come boldly to the throne of grace, that we may obtain *mercy*" (Hebrews 4:16, NKJV, emphasis added).

The tax collector asked God for mercy, and he knew that God could give or withhold it as He chose.

David Brainerd became angry with God as he read the Bible and began to understand that God demanded a perfect righteousness that he knew he couldn't produce. This made him angry. He realized that God required faith, and he couldn't produce that either. Then he realized that God could give faith or withhold it, and that too made him angry. He saw next that God could save him or damn him, and so he sulked until one day he humbled himself and asked God to save him and have mercy upon him—and God did. David Brainerd was a godly man, and the glory of the Lord came into the room when he died.

Jonathan Edwards published Brainerd's journal.[1] When John Wesley read it, he said, "Let all our people read this." The life and diary of David Brainerd was said to have put more people on the mission field than any other body of literature until recent times. Here was a man who quarreled with God because he thought his righteousness should count. But eventually he humbled himself and accepted God's grace.

When this tax collector said, "God, be merciful," he used a word that is also found in Hebrews 2:17 and is translated "reconciliation" by the King James Version. The same word is translated in 1 John 2:2 and 1 John 4:10 as "propitiation." It is an old-fashioned word that shows that the blood of Jesus satisfied the justice of God. This is the way the tax collector prayed—pleading for the mercy seat to cry out to God on his behalf. He knew that he had nothing in himself.

I mentioned earlier that this parable shows us how to become a Christian. The tax collector's prayer is the nearest you get in the Bible to what we call the "sinner's prayer." If you want to become a Christian, this is how to pray: "God, have mercy on me, a sinner" (Luke 18:13).

Jesus made the point that it was the tax collector rather than the Pharisee who went home justified before God because "everyone who exalts himself will be humbled" (Luke 18:14). When will this occur? When it is too late—before God at the judgment seat of Christ.

"And he who humbles himself will be exalted" (Luke 18:14). When? Right now—if you humble yourself and plead for mercy, then God will save you.

A Legal Righteousness

We could say that the righteousness of the tax collector was a *forensic* righteousness. This is a word used in law enforcement that means that *legally* the tax collector was righteous. A received righteousness is a legal righteousness because it comes through the cross of Christ. Jesus said, "I tell you that this man, rather than the other, went home justified before God" (Luke 18:14).

If you had looked at the tax collector, you wouldn't have found a thing that made you think he was righteous; but his righteousness was legal before God. This is what Martin Luther saw in the sixteenth century that turned the world upside down. He saw that before God this justification by faith was a forensic righteousness because we trust not in ourselves but in God's mercy. What people say or think about you is irrelevant. You may have people pointing the finger at you and declaring that you are not a Christian. There wasn't a hint, as this tax collector beat his breast, that he was doing business with God. Yet he was the one who got through to God. He was the one who was heard. His righteousness was faultless because God provided it on his behalf. It was provided by Jesus' blood—and His was a faultless sacrifice. This parable gives the basic Gospel message and shows us how to be heard by God. Do you need to hear this message? May God help you to see it and be saved while there is still time.

Chapter 32

The Parable of the Ten Minas

> A man of noble birth went to a distant country to have himself appointed king and then to return.
>
> Luke 19:12

The parable of the ten minas overlaps with the parable of the talents, which we will look at in the next chapter, although they each have distinct meanings. This is the third parable in a row in which Jesus introduced the reason for the parable: "While they were listening to this, he went on to tell them a parable, because he was near Jerusalem and the people thought that the kingdom of God was going to appear at once" (Luke 19:11).

It lets us know that Jesus always knew what the people were thinking.

This parable shows the kindness of the Lord and how He lets us down gently when He sees we have a false expectancy. I could write a book on that one point alone, but let me just say this much. Jesus knew what they were thinking, and instead of hitting them right between the eyes, He gave them a parable. The parable was to give them time to think and to see where they were wrong in their view of the Kingdom. The people who heard Jesus were convinced that He was the One for whom they had been waiting, and they were right. But they were also convinced that the Kingdom of God would be both political and material, and that it was immediately at hand. In this they were wrong.

It is amazing how we can be so right in some things and so wrong in others. When we are right about one thing, we often assume that the same Lord who gave us that insight must have given us equally clear insight about other things. However, we may be absolutely correct in one area of doctrine and yet completely adrift in another. The Jews were right that Jesus was the Messiah, and they were right to believe He was the One they were looking for, but they were wrong in their view of the Kingdom of God. So convinced were they that they were right in their understanding of the Kingdom, that every time they heard Jesus, they heard only what they wanted to hear.

I have seen this in my own ministry. People can listen to you, and the whole time they believe you are speaking about one thing when you are really speaking about something entirely different. It is easy to absorb what you hear someone else say through the filter of your own prejudices. Similarly, these people around Jesus believed that at any moment Jesus was going to unveil His glory, show Himself to be a Moses, a David or another Solomon and put to shame the Roman soldiers who guarded the area. It was what they desired to happen so much that they did not consider any other alternative.

How easy it is when you want something a great deal to look in the Bible for a verse as confirmation—and to find it! It is amazing how we find ways to get what we want. You may ask God to give you a verse, and if you don't like what you get, you just open your Bible and point to another one until finally you get what you want. You may say, "The Lord told me that I was going to marry this person. . . . The Lord told me I was going to be this or that. . . ." When it comes to our theology, we have often decided *what* we want to believe. It is an amazing gift to be able to stand apart from yourself and say, "This is what the Bible teaches." We should not look to what we like but to what it actually says.

Jesus knew what people were thinking about the Kingdom. The sad thing is that the disciples didn't understand even when they heard this parable. Even after Jesus was raised from the dead, the first question they asked when they got some time on their own with Him was, "Lord, are you at this time going to restore the kingdom to Israel?" (Acts 1:6).

It was still on their minds; they just couldn't think any other way. It is a reminder to us that we can be so sure we are right about something—we can be absolutely convinced—and yet be dead wrong.

The parable of the ten minas tells of a man of noble birth who was traveling to another country to be appointed king. He called his ten servants to him and gave each of them a *mina* (the equivalent of about three months' wages), telling them to "put the money to work" while he was away. When he returned, each of the servants had to account for how they had invested the money. Most of them made more money for their master, except one, who hid his mina away in a cloth rather than investing it. The master was furious and took the mina away from the man, giving it instead to the servant who had made the most money.

Waiting in Faith

I once preached on the Mount of Olives. It sounds like a pompous thing to say, but I can tell you that it was to a grand total of two people! God had awakened me the night before and told me what I was to say on the Mount of Olives to Alan Bell and Lyndon Bowring. I had been studying this parable, knowing that I was going to preach on it when I got back; and I saw how the parable fit with the rest of Luke about being ready—and about what happens if you are not ready.

"If we ask anything according to his will, he hears us" (1 John 5:14).

As we have previously noted, Zechariah and Elizabeth prayed for a son and God said yes. When the "yes" came, however, Zechariah wasn't ready. Similarly, at the end of the parable of the persistent widow, Jesus posed the question, "When the Son of Man comes, will he find faith on the earth?" (Luke 18:8). He was referring not just to His Second Coming but also to God stepping in and answering prayer. Will you be found believing when the answer comes?

Likewise, in Luke 19, as Jesus approached Jerusalem and saw the city, He wept over it, saying:

> If you, even you, had only known on this day what would bring you peace—but now it is hidden from your eyes [in other words, the Lord came but they weren't ready]. The days will come upon you when your enemies will build an embankment against you and encircle you and hem you in on every side. They will dash you to the ground, you and the children within your walls. They will not leave one stone on another, because you did not recognize the time of God's coming to you.
>
> Luke 19:42–44

The Lord Jesus knew that He would be rejected when He wept over the city of Jerusalem. He said, "If you had only known that this belongs to you" (Luke 19:42). Perhaps He would weep today for some of us if God did send the fire and we were not ready. That is the very point of this parable.

Responsibility in the Waiting Time

Jesus knew that people were thinking that the Kingdom of God was going to come suddenly, and He wanted to let them down gently in light of their false expectancy. He gave them this parable to help them see that it would be a while—a long while perhaps. He also gave the parable to get them, if possible, to reassess their view of the Kingdom.

Jesus was not surprised when the Jews rejected Him as their king. He knew He would be rejected, and He used the parable to illustrate this.

He started out by saying, "A man of noble birth went to a distant country to have himself appointed king and then to return" (Luke 19:12).

The kings of Israel, from Herod on, had to go to Rome to gain permission from Caesar to rule as the king. Everyone in that day would have understood that the nobleman had a right to become a king, but that he had to go to a distant country to receive his kingdom. The nobleman was Jesus. He would be going to a distant country to be made King. That distant country was heaven, and He would be made King by His Father. Now this presupposed that He would die on a cross, be raised from the dead and would ascend to the right hand of God. When Jesus ascended to heaven and was welcomed back by the Father and the angels, He was made King. He was made King the moment He sat down at the right hand of the Father. This is why Peter could preach, "God has made this Jesus, whom you crucified, both Lord and Christ" (Acts 2:36).

As the parable unfolded, Jesus was made King, but His subjects, the Jews, did not accept Him. "But his subjects hated him and sent a delegation after him to say, 'We don't want this man to be our king'" (Luke 19:14).

However, as Luke 19:12 says, He was made King and would, there-fore, be returning as King. In the meantime He gave the Church a mission. "So he called ten of his servants and gave them ten minas. 'Put this money to work,' he said, 'until I come back'" (Luke 19:13).

The main point of the parable is that the king wants his servants to use his money openly and faithfully, because shortly he is going to return. There may be a delay, but he'll be back. The King James Version says, "He called his ten servants, and delivered them ten pounds, and said unto them, Occupy till I come" (Luke 19:13).

Those words, "Occupy till I come" have given many preachers over the centuries numerous sermons to preach. The New International Version simplifies it, saying, "Put this money to work ... until I come back" (Luke 19:13).

In Greek the words really were just, "occupy until I come." His servants were to carry out the king's order. The master did come back (Luke 19:15) and immediately he said, "Let me know how you have done." The first servant's mina had earned ten more. He was praised, and because he had been trustworthy in this very small matter, he was given charge of ten cities. The second servant's mina had earned five more. He was praised and given charge of five cities. The third servant had kept his mina hidden. He said, "I was afraid of you, because you are a hard man. You take out what you did not put in and reap what you did not sow" (Luke 19:21).

> His master replied, "I will judge you by your own words, you wicked servant! You knew, did you, that I am a hard man, taking out what I did not put in, and reaping what I did not sow? Why then didn't you put my money on deposit, so that when I came back, I could have collected it with interest?"
>
> Luke 19:22–23

The king took away this servant's mina and gave it to the one who already had ten because, as Jesus said, "To everyone who has, more will be given, but as for the one who has nothing, even what he has will be taken away" (Luke 19:26).

It just goes to show that if we are not ready, God will take the anointing that we have away from us and give it to a person who already has a great anointing. You may not like it, but that is what the King has a right to do.

The Possibilities of the Parable

There are various interpretations of this parable, all of which are valid. This is one of those parables that can be interpreted in more than one way, and all of them are right. I will explain what I mean.

The Coming of the Spirit

The parable could easily refer to the initial descent of the Holy Spirit on the Church at Pentecost. The Spirit came down ten days after Jesus was made King in heaven. When the Spirit came down, Peter announced, "God has made this Jesus, whom you crucified, both Lord and Christ" (Acts 2:36).

He had already been made King in heaven. One might wonder how many of those who thought they followed Jesus were ready for that news? Over five hundred people at once saw Jesus alive after His death (1 Corinthians 15:6). And almost certainly that is how many were there when Jesus said, "Stay in the city until you have been clothed with power from on high" (Luke 24:49).

The disciples received this word from Jesus and immediately started praying. Perhaps they prayed every day, perhaps all night. I am speculating and I can't prove this, but here is what I think could have happened. Just before they got to the tenth day, there would have been some who said, "Look, as you know, Pentecost is coming up tomorrow, and there will be a lot of old friends we haven't seen since last year; we'll be back the day after tomorrow. We're going to give tomorrow a miss. You all keep praying." I am sure several said that. So when Pentecost arrived, there were then only one hundred twenty people praying when the Spirit came down. How would those who had left have felt?

When God Hides His Face

There is a second way this parable can be interpreted.

"Truly you are a God who hides himself" (Isaiah 45:15).

I don't understand it, but God does hide Himself. God left Hezekiah to test him and to see what was in his heart (2 Chronicles 32:31). It is a peculiarity, that is the best word I can give for it, but God does this. You can sometimes sense His presence very powerfully and you say, "Oh, this is wonderful—I'll never doubt You again, Lord." Then the next day He just doesn't seem to be there—then maybe the day after that, and the day after that, until you think, *What have I done? Did I grieve the Holy Spirit? Why has He left?* And you think that maybe the Lord isn't going to show up anymore.

This was what happened in ancient Israel. Moses slipped away and went up to the top of Mount Sinai, and everybody said, "We don't know where he has gone; we don't even know if he is coming back." And they began to do awful things.

It shows that we must be ready at all times, and that we must wait faithfully for God to show His face according to His will. Jesus wept over Jerusalem because they didn't know the time of their visitation (Luke 19:41).

The Second Coming of Jesus

Luke 19:13 says the king is coming back. Jesus is coming back soon. People ask how I dare say that I think Jesus is really coming soon. When I first started preaching 45 or 50 years ago, I preached a lot on eschatology, and my dad warned me about it. He said, "Son, the man you were named after, R. T. Williams, used to say, 'Young men, stay away from the subject of prophecy and eschatology. Let the older men do that, because that way they won't be around to see their mistakes.'" Well, I'm old and I'm telling you, I would *not* be surprised to be alive when He comes. He is coming soon. To those who doubt the promise of His coming, I would say, just look at the Scriptures. We've heard it and heard it and heard it, and now I am saying it again. I want to be *ready*.

When we get to heaven, we are not going to be sitting around twiddling our thumbs. Life will go on, and people who said, "Oh, I don't care about rewards in heaven—I just want to get to heaven," won't think that then. You see, the one whose mina earned ten more was given charge of ten cities—that was his reward; and the one whose mina earned five more was given charge of five cities.

There will be some who will be saved by fire at the judgment seat of Christ. They will get to heaven, but as one escaping through the flames. They won't be receiving a great reward in addition to getting into heaven. There will also be retributive judgment for those who rejected the Kingdom altogether. "But those enemies of mine who did not want me to be a king over them—bring them here and kill them in front of me" (Luke 19:27).

It will happen.

Preparation

How do we live so that we can be sure we won't be ashamed? Jesus isn't telling us that we have got to wake up every day believing that that is the day He will come back. He doesn't expect me to step into the pulpit and say, "Today I know revival is going to come." After a while we would all become demoralized with this. God is not unreasonable. How then do we live to ensure that when He does come, whether it is through the coming of the Spirit, an end to the hiding of His face, revival or the Second Coming, that we won't be ashamed? How can we live in such a manner that we will be found ready when He does show up?

Graciousness

This means that each day you let anyone and everyone off the hook. You may be able to throw the book at them and point the finger, but you don't. You remain gracious. You can't know when He is going to come. If you make exceptions, He may come at an hour when you are found unbelieving. None of us knows the day or the hour. Jesus said that even the Son doesn't know—only the Father. Even the angels don't know. You are not expected to know, but you are expected to remain gracious. You are expected to forgive totally all those around you.

Gentleness

This one puts me to shame. I have deacons who pray for me every day that I will be gentle. That is a major thing for me—it is almost like praying for Lazarus to be raised from the dead. But I pray and ask Him to make me gentle. I also ask my closest friends to do the same. Lyndon Bowring prays every day that I will be gentle. I have a prayer covenant with Colin Dye from Kensington Temple—he prays every day that I will be gentle. I want to be found gentle, not stern or losing my temper even when it may seem justified. You know that when we lose our temper it always seems right to us at the time, but later we realize we were wrong.

Gratitude

I want to be found showing gratitude—thanking Him for every little thing and missing nothing if I can help it. I want to be found thanking God; I want to be grateful for His goodness. Our daughter Melissa recently came back to the Lord, for which I thank Him several times a day. I want to be found grateful.

Generosity

I want to be found to be generous. When it comes to finances I give God everything He has said belongs to Him. I want to be found guileless—believing and faithful. It doesn't mean I have to be perfect, but it does mean I am walking in all the light that God has given me. This is how we must live. Then we won't be ashamed when the Lord turns up. And if that turning up should be the manifestation of His glory and not the Second Coming, it will mean an increased anointing, an increased responsibility. Are we ready for that? Are we ready for answered prayer? Are we ready for the coming of the Spirit? Are we ready for the Second Coming?

Chapter 33

The Parable of the Talents

The kingdom of heaven will be like a man going on a journey.
Matthew 25:14

In the parable of the talents, Jesus told the story of a man who embarked on a journey. Before he left, he called together his servants and entrusted varying amounts of money to them. He gave to them according to their ability. When the master returned, he called his servants together and asked them to report back on how they had invested his money. Like the parable of the ten minas, most of the servants had done well—except one, who buried his talent in the ground to hide it. The master was furious with this servant and took the talent away from him, giving it to the servant with the most money. The lazy servant was then cast out of his master's presence.

The Greek word *talanta* means money. It is not used in this parable in the way we use the word *talent* today—as a gift or ability. This parable is very similar to the parable of the ten minas, but it is subtly different. In ancient times a *talanta* was a large sum of money. In the parable of the ten minas, a mina was a comparatively small amount—perhaps three months' wages. But a talent would have been well over $100,000 by today's standards.

In Luke's account of the parable of the ten minas, each person was given the same amount (Luke 19:13). But in the parable of the talents, each was given according to his *ability* (Matthew 25:15). Some were given five talents, some two and another one. In Luke's parable of the minas, the focus was on the unexpected nature of the master's return. But in the parable of the talents, the focus was on the responsibility and accountability of the servants. In Luke the focus is on *faithfulness* as opposed to self-indulgence. In the parable of the talents, the focus is on *work* and *productivity* as opposed to being lazy.

Is this parable about finances since the word *talent* means money?

Perhaps. Does it refer to the gifts of the Holy Spirit? Some say so. Others connect it to God's calling and one's natural abilities. But the key to understanding it is that each servant was given *according to* his ability. My own view is that it refers to the anointing. The "talent" refers to one's measure of responsibility in using a skill that God has already given by common grace.

We can say that *responsibility + skill = anointing.* We are entrusted with a responsibility *according to* our level of skill. Not everyone is given the same responsibility. This is because not all have the same level of skill. Skill refers to what you have already, although even that comes from God. When God gives a responsibility (a talent), He takes into account the amount of common grace He has already given to you.

All people, even unsaved, have been given a measure of common grace. That is why we call it "common" grace, because it is given to everybody. This is why Albert Einstein could have an IQ of 212. Men like Shakespeare and Churchill also had enormous ability, but there is no evidence they were Christians. If such a person becomes a Christian, they would be a "five-talent" person—a higher level of responsibility would be given to them. Some, because of God's common grace, are given greater *responsibility* (talents) in an area because He has already endowed them with *ability.* How do you know what your anointing is? Well, this parable gives us a hint. If you have been given a lot of natural ability in a certain area, then do not be surprised if God gives you great responsibility to use it for His glory.

However, Paul advises us, "By the grace given me I say to every one of you: Do not think of yourself more highly than you ought, but rather think of yourself with sober judgment, in accordance with the measure of faith God has given you" (Romans 12:3). Because, Jesus said, "From everyone who has been given much, much will be demanded; and from the one who has been entrusted with much, much more will be asked" (Luke 12:48).

God knows what we can do. He will never promote a person to a level at which they would be incompetent. In the world people are promoted to their level of incompetence. Somebody in the office who should have been sweeping floors is made a manager. Or a person says, "I want this job because it will pay more and I will have more prestige," and he gets it. But then his marriage breaks down, and he gets high blood pressure and can't cope. People promote others to a level of incompetence, but God never does it. To whom much is given, much will be required. Responsibility (one's God-given talent) plus skill equals one's anointing. Some have a greater anointing than others.

God gives responsibility according to our ability—and our capacity to grasp it.

Living within Our Anointing

To live within our anointing, we must know the limit of that anointing. This can be very humbling. It is a delicate thing to have to tell someone who believes they are called to preach that they do not have that ability, or to tell someone who has written a poem that they are no Wordsworth. I have had people come up and say, "God has given me this song. Would you get the worship group to sing it?" And you hear it and you think, *Oh, dear me.* You don't want to hurt the person's feelings. This is one of the hardest things on earth. I do not pretend to be like some great preachers—Campbell-Morgan or Martyn Lloyd-Jones—I live within my anointing. That is rule number one.

The Potential to Use or Abuse Our Anointing

We all have the potential to use or abuse our anointing. We could equally say, to abuse or double our anointing. We will look at four key areas with regard to this point.

The Origin of the Anointing

▶ *The calling.*
In the parable, the master called his servants and entrusted his property to them (Matthew 25:14). The origin of the anointing is that God does the calling. This probably doesn't refer to the initial calling of the Spirit in a person's life, but it could mean that. I rather suspect it refers to God's specific calling or mission, His plan for your life, which varies from individual to individual. We do not all have the same calling. Not everyone is called to be a missionary. Not everyone is called to be a lawyer or a doctor.

▶ *The conferring of the anointing.*
"To one he gave five talents of money, to another two talents, to another one talent, each according to his ability" (Matthew 25:15). The responsibility is conferred in varying degrees. To some he gave five talents—a high measure of responsibility—to some two and to another one.

► *The caliber of the anointing.*

God never promotes us to the level of our incompetence, and He is careful to follow that in every aspect of our lives. "No temptation has seized you except what is common to man" (1 Corinthians 10:13). The word *temptation* comes from the same Greek word that means *trial*. God is faithful. He will not let you be tried beyond what you can bear. It is also true of all God's commands. If God gives you a command, He will give you the grace to fulfill it. He will never ask you to do what you cannot do, but He will give you the strength. We are all, therefore, without excuse. To whom much is given, from them much will be required.

If you are really honest with yourself, you will know what abilities you have. You know there are certain things you can do. You may say, "Well, my gift isn't going to be worth very much because there is no demand for it." But think of Joseph, the man who became prime minister of Egypt. What kind of training did he have for that job? If he had gone into an employment agency and they asked him to list his skills, he would have said, "Well, I can interpret dreams." A person like that would leave, saying, "There is no way I can be used by the Lord." You may not think that your particular gift is of much use, but it is. We cannot assume that the parable is saying that if you are a "single-talent" person, you need to bury it. No! A person who only has one talent to invest can still double it or triple it. Likewise, a very gifted "five-talent" person is capable of burying those talents in the ground and letting them go to waste. Jesus was not saying that you are fixed in your mode. God gives us all a responsibility, and we can all do what He wants us to do.

If you will humbly but honestly recognize your own skill and then be open to God's tap on the shoulder, who knows how He will use you. But if you do have some considerable ability and choose to live in bitterness because the world hasn't recognized you, you will be like those of whom Jesus says, "Throw that worthless servant outside, into the darkness, where there will be weeping and gnashing of teeth" (Matthew 25:30).

The Ownership of Our Anointing

Who do you suppose owns our anointing? The Lord. Now there is a sense in which we can say, "This is *my* anointing." I may refer to "my church," but really it is God's church. Jesus said, "It will be like a man going on a journey, who called his servants and entrusted *his* property to them." Later he said, "Well then, you should have put *my* money on deposit" (see Matthew 25:14, 27, emphasis added).

The money never belonged to the person to whom it was entrusted. There are four things I want us to see about the ownership of the anointing.

▶ *It is on loan.*

God has loaned you your anointing. We have been entrusted with the Holy Spirit, and that means that we must see our own anointing as being on loan from the Lord. It is not mine; it is His. In the same way, we have been bought with a price. We are not our own; we were bought with the blood of Christ.

▶ *The limit of the anointing.*

Some of us have been given five talents; some have been given two talents; some one. But God knew before He gave the one that you would be the one to whom He would give it. You may say, "Well, I feel pretty awful; all I got was the one talent." It's OK. You have the opportunity to get the same reward in heaven as the ones with two and five talents. What is required is that we are faithful. All of us have the same calling in this sense. Those who were faithful received the same commendation from their master. So the person with the two talents won't be able to say, "Oh, if only I had been given five in the first place, now I could have ten." Listen!

> The man who had received the five talents brought the other five. "Master," he said, "you entrusted me with five talents. See, I have gained five more." His master replied, "Well done, good and faithful servant! You have been faithful with a few things; I will put you in charge of many things. Come and share your master's happiness!" The man with the two talents also came. "Master," he said, "you entrusted me with two talents; see, I have gained two more." His master replied, "Well done, good and faithful servant! You have been faithful with a few things; I will put you in charge of many things. Come and share your master's happiness!"
>
> Matthew 25:20–23

It is interesting that the faithful servants all received the same commendation from their master. Even though they had been responsible for varying amounts of money, the master commended them all the same, because they had all been faithful with a little. Live within the limits of the "loan" of your anointing. Be faithful, and you will have the same commendation as the one who has more responsibility.

▶ *Levels of the anointing.*

There is an implicit hint that God will double our anointing in the same way that the five-talent man was given ten, the two had four and so on. This is a promise that goes back to Isaiah 61. We are told, "Instead of their shame my people will receive a double portion, and instead of disgrace they will rejoice in their inheritance" (Isaiah 61:7).

This is what Elisha wanted from Elijah, and he got it. God may do that for any of us. While the reward is not guaranteed until the end, God may not wait until the end to double the anointing, assuming that you have been faithful with the level of anointing already given. If this is your attitude, one day, overnight, God may double your anointing.

▶ *Loss of the anointing.*

It is so sad when this happens.

"The man who had received the one talent went off, dug a hole in the ground and hid his master's money" (Matthew 25:18).

Listen! "God did not give us a spirit of timidity, but a spirit of power, of love and of self-discipline" (2 Timothy 1:7).

The man in the parable was afraid and then justified what he had done. Those who hide their talents, don't walk in the light and don't take the responsibility, think that they can outtalk God when the showdown comes.

" 'Master,' he said, 'I knew that you are a hard man, harvesting where you have not sown and gathering where you have not scattered seed. So I was afraid [he justifies himself] and went out and hid your talent in the ground' " (Matthew 25:24–25).

The reply came:

> You wicked, lazy servant! So you knew that I harvest where I have not sown and gather where I have not scattered seed? Well then, you should have put my money on deposit with the bankers, so that when I returned I would have received it back with interest. Take the talent from him and give it to the one who has the ten talents.
>
> Matthew 25:26–28

It is amazing how those who have a high level of responsibility are given more to do because somebody else out there wouldn't do what God told *them* to do. My dad used to say, "If you want something done, ask a busy person to do it." Ask the person who just doesn't have time—they'll get it done all the same.

So what was the fate of this servant? The master said, "Throw that worthless servant outside, into the darkness, where there will be weeping and gnashing of teeth" (Matthew 25:30).

Did he lose his salvation? No. This parable is not talking about salvation but about one's inheritance. It is saying that there will be saved people who will gnash their teeth because they have lost their anointing and their reward.

The person with the five talents didn't automatically double his. The five-talent guy was capable of blowing it, just as the one-talent servant could have doubled his anointing. There have been people in the ministry with the highest profile who have blown it and are now out of the ministry. They were five-talent people. We must live in such a way as to avoid losing our anointing on earth and our reward in heaven. Hence the words, "You wicked, lazy servant! So you *knew* that I harvest where I have not sown" (Matthew 25:26, emphasis added).

Here Jesus was talking to people who *know* the teaching on the sovereignty of God. It is amazing to me how those who are the most theologically articulate are often the least involved when it comes to getting out the Gospel. God gave them the first opportunity, but they said, "Ah, but I believe in the sovereignty of God. I am not going to be seen out on the streets saving the nonelect and bringing them to a profession of faith." They justify themselves. They may lose their anointing and their reward at the judgment seat of Christ.

The Operation of the Anointing

This parable shows us how the anointing works—*works* being the operative word. Salvation is by grace, but the parable of the talents is about works. The writer of Hebrews said, "Let us . . . make every effort to enter that rest" (Hebrews 4:11). How do we work to enter this rest?

▶ *We labor in love.*

The first key to doubling your anointing is living in total forgiveness for what people have done to you. You wipe the slate clean. Next time you start to accuse somebody of something, remember that you would like a double anointing. Just don't do it, so that the Spirit is not grieved and you don't lose your anointing. Turn the other cheek when someone says something that is not very nice.

▶ *We labor in the anointing.*

This can also mean to labor in leadership. There are levels of leadership. For example, let us say the five-talent person is a high-powered lawyer or a businessman in the city who has considerable skills and acumen and is able to make a lot of money. Yet at church, he is a one-talent person. I know wealthy people and high-powered people who all week long tell people what to do. Then they come to church and sit under the Gospel and hear their minister. They may not have much to do in the church, but they are faithful. It is possible to have five talents in the world and one talent in church, or it is possible to have two talents in the church and five talents in the world.

What about the person who is really busy in the work of the church, but the job they do in the world is not that high-powered? The person like this should not be angry or jealous—accept what you have; come to terms with the limit of your anointing. You can't be everything. A person can have five talents at church and one talent at work and that person, if he or she will be true to their anointing, will be the best employee in the building. You are the one your employer can trust. The best testimony at work is to be loyal and faithful in your job.

▶ *We labor in learning.*
The issue of what knowledge we have is important. The lazy servant said, "I knew you are a hard man, harvesting where you have not sown" (Matthew 25:24).

How does God measure how we have used our talents? We are judged by two things: what we know and how we use what we know. Some of us grasp things more quickly than others. Some people possess more ambition to learn than others. There is an interesting verse in Philemon in which Paul wrote, "I pray that you may be active in sharing your faith, so that you will have a full understanding of every good thing we have in Christ" (Philemon 6).

Paul said that it is possible to have learned all about the faith and yet not be active in sharing it. You may know your Bible and your theology, but if you are not active in sharing your faith, you will never gain a full understanding of "every good thing we have in Christ." Second Peter says the same thing: "Add to knowledge, self-control; and to self-control, perseverance; and to perseverance, godliness. If you possess these qualities in increasing measure, they will keep you from being ineffective and unproductive in your *knowledge*" (2 Peter 1:6, 8, emphasis added).

It is vital that we apply what we have learned. This means walking in the light, it means becoming obedient to what God is telling us to do and sooner or later it means getting out of your comfort zone.

▶ *Lethargy and the anointing.*

The master said, "You wicked, lazy servant!" (Matthew 25:26). So many people who are theologically apt would not dare be out on the streets talking to others about the Gospel. They would be afraid of seeing someone make a profession of faith—perhaps because they would not know what to do with that person afterward! Remember though that the master said to the servant, "You have been faithful with a few things; I will put you in charge of many things" (Matthew 25:23).

When the Spirit speaks, we must listen and act. However great or small the thing is, all we must do is obey and do our part. What happens after that is God's responsibility.

Salvation is by grace, but the anointing comes through struggle. We read that "The man who had received the one talent went off, dug a hole in the ground and hid his master's money" (Matthew 25:18).

This man lapsed in his anointing. He was guilty of hiding and "hedging" his anointing. He said, "I knew that you are a hard man, harvesting where you have not sown. . . . I was afraid and went out and hid your talent in the ground" (Matthew 25:24–25).

Hedging is protecting oneself against a loss. It is a defense mechanism to avoid pain or responsibility. It is a justification for what we didn't do. "I was afraid so I hid the talent in the ground." Hiding is avoiding responsibility, playing it safe. This servant didn't labor under his anointing.

Obstruction of the Anointing

This is the confession of the learned person: "I know, you harvest where you haven't sown." But this servant was lazy: "You wicked, lazy servant!" (Matthew 25:26). He is the loser: "Take the talent from him and give it to the one who has the ten talents" (Matthew 25:28).

There is that expression, "Some are winners and some are losers." In God's economy, you have to *choose* to be a loser, you have to choose to obstruct your anointing, and this man was liable. Jesus said, "Throw that worthless servant outside ... where there will be weeping and gnashing of teeth" (Matthew 25:30).

It was condemnation. This is what the servant should have done: "You should have put my money on deposit with the bankers" (Matthew 25:27).

We don't like to be told what we should have done, especially when it is too late. That is part of the condemnation. If you lose your anointing, it will be painful and lonely. Don't worry about the opinions of other people. Don't let them cause you to act in a way that obstructs your anointing or causes you not to accept the responsibility God has given to you. Believe in the sovereignty of God, but accept the responsibilities He gives you as if it all depended upon you. Take your anointing seriously and seek to safeguard it.

Chapter 34

The Parable of the Ten Virgins

The kingdom of heaven will be like ten virgins who ... went out to meet the bridegroom.

Matthew 25:1

For many years the parable of the ten virgins has been one of my favorites. It is set in an eschatological context and was told to alert us to the fact that Jesus is coming back very soon. The parable describes ten virgins who took their lamps and went out to meet the bridegroom. Five were wise because they took extra oil for their lamps along with them, but five were foolish because they didn't take extra oil. The bridegroom was a long time coming, and so they fell asleep waiting. At midnight there came a cry, "Here's the bridegroom! Come out to meet him!" The five wise virgins could do so immediately, but the foolish ones could not, since they had used up their oil and didn't have any more. They had to go out and buy more oil, but by the time they returned, the bridegroom's banquet was underway and the doors were closed. The moral of the parable is, "keep watch, because you do not know the day or the hour" (Matthew 25:13).

Many years ago I had an insight into this parable. I had always thought that the term *midnight* indicated when Jesus would come back. I had heard many preachers talk about the present time being "five minutes to midnight." But the Greek word translated here as *midnight* simply means "the middle of the night." The point I want to make is that there was an interval between the cry, "Behold, the bridegroom is coming!" (Matthew 25:6, NKJV) and His actual arrival. In parallel to this I believe that there will be a widespread awakening of the Church just before the return of Christ. The call will go out that He is returning, and we will see a revival occur. I wouldn't build my whole eschatology on that verse, but it certainly fits.

It is important to remember that the context of this parable is a continuation of the thoughts expressed in Matthew 24 that deal with the end times. After speaking of the last days, Jesus went on to introduce this parable, "At that time the kingdom of heaven will be like ten virgins who took their lamps and went out to meet the bridegroom" (Matthew 25:1).

So we are talking about how it will be in the very last days, just before the Second Coming. It is important to make a distinction here between the *last days* and the *very last days*. According to Hebrews 1:2, we are in the last days, and 1 John also talks about our being in the "last days." But the *very last days,* I believe, refers to the last generation before the Second Coming. I am not saying we are necessarily in that generation, but I would not be surprised if we are.

This particular parable is important because it is a reminder that Jesus is coming again and probably coming very soon. It is so wonderful to know that He is coming back. It also shows us that nothing surprises God, because Jesus was prophesying that the Church would be asleep, generally speaking, in the last days. The curious thing about this parable is that the bride is never mentioned. Instead it talks about "ten virgins." I think what Jesus was trying to do was to symbolize what will be a mixed Church. It doesn't take God by surprise that the Church is sleeping, and I think we would have to agree that generally this is an accurate description of the Church in our present day.

The parable also shows a basis for last-day ministries. Let me explain what I mean by that. I believe that the midnight cry will usher in an awakening of the Church that will result in a great awakening. People in Israel will turn in large numbers to the Lord. The Islamic world will be affected. It will be a momentous time. But sadly, there will be those in the Church who will not get in on it, because they are like the "foolish virgins" who took no oil with them—they are unprepared and asleep. I cannot imagine anything sadder than to be part of the Church and yet miss out when this glorious thing happens.

One of the most striking images of this parable is the need to have oil in your vessel. Oil is prophetically seen as the Holy Spirit. Jesus was implying that there would be those in the last days who would realize their great need of the Holy Spirit, but there would be those who take Him for granted. The parable emphasizes the importance of being ready for Jesus to come and having to stand before Him on the day of judgment. The issue is not whether you are saved or lost in this parable but whether you will receive a reward. I think there is an intentional ambiguity here—two meanings are intended. There is certainly an evangelistic appeal for any unsaved person to see the need for being "ready." But parallel to that is an appeal to the Church to awaken.

The Wedding Context

There is strong matrimonial imagery in this parable. Jesus was speaking of a wedding—an Oriental or particularly a Middle-Eastern wedding in ancient times. Jesus' hearers would have understood the context of His remarks well.

The wedding took place in the house of the bridegroom—not in a church building, cathedral or registry office. Sometimes the wedding would take the form of a seven-day celebration. At a specific time the bridegroom would come to get his bride from her house. The bride would never know exactly when the bridegroom would arrive at her house. There would be young ladies who were friends of the bride (that is why they are called "virgins" in the parable) who were unmarried and would accompany the bridal couple from the house of the bride to the house of the groom. There would be a procession in the streets. Everyone in the procession would be very expectant and would carry their own burning torches. Without a torch you were seen as a gate-crasher and had no right to be there. Festivities would last several hours and sometimes, as mentioned, up to seven days. Because the exact time of the bridegroom's arrival was uncertain, the bride was expected to be ready to leave at any moment. Often the bridegroom would come in the middle of the night!

The lamps in question would have been oil-fed lamps whose rags would need a periodic dousing with oil to keep them burning. Those who were prudent would bring along a flask with an additional oil supply so that their lamps would always be burning. The fact that Jesus said the bridegroom was a long time coming told His listeners that His second coming could be a long time away. Notice what it says in Habakkuk:

> Write down the revelation and make it plain on tablets so that a herald may run with it. For the revelation awaits an appointed time; it speaks of the end and will not prove false. Though it linger, wait for it; it will certainly come and will not delay.
>
> Habakkuk 2:2–3

Jesus was implying that the tarrying, the waiting for the Bridegroom, would be a long time. Indeed it has been over two thousand years to this day. There have been those who have said that Mussolini was the Antichrist, then Stalin or Khrushchev, and some have even said that the scar on Gorbachev's forehead could have been the mark of the beast! Remember only one thing: Eventually Jesus is coming back. The very last days are going to come. Those who ask, "Where is the promise of His coming? I have heard it all my life," are those whom Peter called scoffers (2 Peter 3:3). So be careful that in your speech you don't become cynical and a "scoffer."

There is an assumption in the parable about the people of God being the Bride of Christ. This is referred to in many places throughout Scripture. In 2 Corinthians Paul wrote, "I am jealous for you with a godly jealousy. I promised you to one husband, to Christ, so that I might present you as a pure virgin to him" (2 Corinthians 11:2).

Here is what John said while on the Isle of Patmos: "I saw the Holy City, the new Jerusalem, coming down out of heaven from God, prepared as a bride beautifully dressed for her husband" (Revelation 21:2).

Now the Church is seen as the Bride of Christ, and in case you didn't realize it, we are not married yet. We are only engaged. I love the point that Charles Carrin made, that the gifts of the Spirit are the engagement ring of the Bride. We are waiting for the day when the marriage will take place—that will be at the Second Coming. You and I are waiting for the Bridegroom to come.

A Mixed Church

Jesus said that five of the virgins were foolish and five were wise. There are those who would say that this means half of the people in the Church are not really saved. But I must point out that the foolish virgins said, "Give us some of your oil; our lamps are going out" (Matthew 25:8). They did have oil—the Holy Spirit. The parable is not referring to unsaved people. Like it or not, in the best of times the Church has always had those with varying degrees of expectancy, maturity and spirituality. We might wish that all Christians were equally prudent, equally possessing the full measure of the Spirit, but that is not the way it is. Paul had to rebuke the Corinthian church, which had been born in revival. He called them carnal, fleshly and worldly. He didn't say they were not saved. He never questioned that. As a matter of fact, Galatians 5:4 says, "you have fallen from grace," which gives ammunition to some who don't know the context and say that people can lose their salvation. It is not saying that at all. It is referring to how a Christian can slip back and not enjoy what is really his or hers. The Church that Jesus describes is mixed—both spiritual and carnal, strong and weak, mature and immature. Jesus' simple categorization was "wise" and "foolish."

I happen to believe that what happened on 11th September 2001 was the initiation of the midnight cry—a precursor to it. It may take a while before it begins to add up, but it will not be long until the messengers of God are going to have great power to preach this message concerning the very last days. Then the Church will be awakened and the condition you are in, wise or foolish, will be revealed.

Misguided Christians

"The foolish ones took their lamps but did not take any oil with them" (Matthew 25:3).

Imagine taking a lamp with you but not taking sufficient oil. What would it mean? You have what appears to be needed, but you don't have enough oil to keep the lamp burning. Have you made provision for yourself to make sure your lamp will stay burning? How much praying do you plan to do this year? What kind of Bible reading plan do you have for the year? How deep is your commitment? Or do you think, *Oh, I will be fine, thank you very much.* If so, then I say to you with the deepest respect, you are a fool!

"The heart is deceitful above all things and beyond cure. Who can understand it?" (Jeremiah 17:9).

Do not trust yourself so much that you say, "I am going to be fine." Do you dare to go out into your day without having spent thirty minutes on your knees? Do you make sure that your Bible reading is done, even if nothing else happens that day? When the midnight cry comes, you won't be thinking, *Well, I was always on time for work, and I got that pay raise I really wanted. I got that opportunity that meant so much.* Do you realize how much these things will mean to you then? Never think that you are the one who is going to be okay. Make provision.

The wise virgins took oil in jars. The foolish took their lamps but did not take any oil with them. This is like having the Word without the Spirit; it is like the Scriptures without the power of God. We know that oil in the Bible is often used to symbolize the Holy Spirit. Sometimes the Holy Spirit is symbolized by fire—as on the Day of Pentecost—but fire comes from oil. If there is not enough oil, then there will be no fire.

What do we know about fools from the Bible? A fool was one who wouldn't listen to correction: "The way of a fool seems right to him, but a wise man listens to advice" (Proverbs 12:15). And, "do not speak to a fool, for he will scorn the wisdom of your words" (Proverbs 23:9).

A fool does not listen to correction. He is unteachable. But there is something else about a fool. He will be found out eventually. Here is an awful verse:

> Those who oppose him [the man of God] he must gently instruct, in the hope that God will grant them repentance leading them to a knowledge of the truth, and that they will come to their senses and escape from the trap of the devil, who has taken them captive to do his will.
>
> 2 Timothy 2:25–26

The wise are open to correction and discipline, but the foolish are not. Paul wrote about the "trap of the devil." He was encouraging people to be open to correction and to put things right quickly. He recognized that if you don't deal with problems quickly—whether it is bitterness, anger, hurt feelings or something else—then the devil will ride in on that. If you have any kind of weakness and you don't make provision to protect yourself, the devil can find a way into your life because of that. Be open to correction and be prepared.

Mature Christians

"The wise, however, took oil in jars along with their lamps" (Matthew 25:4).

A wise person listens. The proof that you are wise is that you listen (Proverbs 1:5). If someone says, "Can I have a word with you?" you listen.

A wise person also accepts a rebuke: "Do not rebuke a mocker or he will hate you; rebuke a wise man and he will love you" (Proverbs 9:8).

Sometimes the most difficult thing in the world is to approach a person who has been overtaken by a fault, when that person doesn't see the fault. Let me ask you a question. Do you think there are people who would love to say something to you, but no one can get near you? Maybe someone has already tried, and you wouldn't listen. Another person may have tried and you said you were fine. If two or three people who know you and like you are saying the same thing, you need to take it seriously—they may be right. The proof that you are wise is that you love it if someone tells you the truth: "Faithful are the wounds of a friend" (Proverbs 27:6, NKJV). Desire correction. We should want to get it right. When you are defensive—that is a bad sign.

This verse (Matthew 25:4) indicates that a mature Christian knows not to proceed without the Spirit. They will ensure that they have an adequate supply of oil. We are told that the wise took oil in jars along with their lamps, because they wanted to be sure.

Have you come to appreciate how precious the Holy Spirit is? Are you at the place where you would never want to grieve Him or to quench His ability to work in your life? On my prayer list for the year 2002, I wrote my desire to become hypersensitive to the Holy Spirit. I tend by nature to be hypersensitive. I have a fragile ego. I like a compliment, and I don't like criticism. I get my feelings hurt easily. These aren't great things, but I *want* to be that way when it comes to the Holy Spirit. I want to be able to tell when He gets hurt. Paul wrote in Ephesians 4:30, "Do not grieve the Holy Spirit of God." The word *grieve* comes from the Greek word that means to get your feelings hurt. The Holy Spirit is a Person. He gets His feelings hurt. I want to know the Holy Spirit so well that when He gets His feelings hurt, I can feel it as soon as it happens.

A Miserable Condition

"The bridegroom was a long time in coming, and they all became drowsy and fell asleep" (Matthew 25:5).

This seems to be prophetic, as if Jesus was saying to the Church that when He returns they will be spiritually asleep. There are three things to note about sleeping—you could call them three characteristics of backsliding. We are told: "There is a way that seems right to a man, but in the end it leads to death" (Proverbs 14:12).

You Don't Realize You Are Asleep
First, you do not know that you have been asleep until you wake up.

You Do Things You Wouldn't Do When Awake
When you are asleep, you dream of things that wouldn't cross your mind if you were awake. Have you ever woken up saying, "Thank God that was a dream!"? When you dream, you sometimes do things that you wouldn't do when awake. And so when you are spiritually asleep, you do things you wouldn't do if you were spiritually awake. It begins very easily. You make an exception: "I won't pray today because God knows how busy I am, and I have got to make it to this appointment on time." Can I quote to you Martin Luther's journal? "Have a very busy day today. Must not spend two hours, but three in prayer." He reckoned that by spending more time in prayer, he would get more done.

How is it that you always manage to see your favorite TV program, but you have trouble making time to pray? It is a lot easier to watch

Frasier than it is to read your Bible. You may say, "It's a lot more fun too." I know what you mean by that. Sometimes reading the Bible is not inspiring. But there are things that you do because they are right. I don't always feel led to pray, but I do it! I don't always feel like reading my Bible, but I do it! I don't want to think what I would be like if I didn't. You don't know that you are asleep until you wake up and think, *I can't believe I have done this. I have let my life get into this mess. I have been doing things I said I would never do.*

You Dislike the Sound of the Alarm

When you are asleep and someone tries to say something to you, you generally mutter, "Leave me alone!" Jesus said: "You say, 'I am rich; I have acquired wealth and do not need a thing.' But you do not realize that you are wretched, pitiful, poor, blind and naked" (Revelation 3:17).

Why were the virgins sleeping? Perhaps they had been impatient that things weren't happening fast enough. This is often the reason that people backslide. They say, "Well, I prayed, and God didn't answer my prayer." And then they conclude that "God doesn't really love me." "I have had this prophetic word, and it hasn't happened yet." Jesus said He was coming; He hasn't come yet.

I would urge you to decide, no matter how long He takes in answering your prayer, no matter how long you must wait for that word that was given to be fulfilled, *not* to give up. Keep oil in your vessel. Don't let the fire go out.

The Midnight Cry

In the middle of the night came an unexpected word (Matthew 25:6). It was an urgent warning, an unmistakable wake-up call because, would you believe it, all the virgins woke up and trimmed their lamps.

Some Will Lose Their Reward

If the five foolish virgins were backsliders and unprepared Christians, did they lose their salvation? After all, we read that after the bridegroom arrived, "The virgins who were ready went in with him to the wedding banquet. And the door was shut" (Matthew 25:10).

Then the foolish virgins turned up and cried out, "Open the door for us!" But the stern reply was, "I tell you the truth, I don't know you" (Matthew 25:11–12). Only the wise virgins made it into the marriage celebration. The question is, were they the only ones saved? Were the foolish virgins eternally lost? If so, that disproves the teaching of once saved, always saved.

We have said that Jesus often told parables that had an intentional ambiguity. The ambiguity is usually that there is a general as well as a specific meaning to the parable. The general meaning here is simply to be ready for the Second Coming of Jesus. The specific meaning shows that the foolish virgins are those who will miss out on what has been planned for them—the celebration of the Marriage Supper of the Lamb. It is a description of those who will be saved by fire (1 Corinthians 3:14–15). They will lose their reward. In a way, they will miss out on what could have been theirs. The Marriage Supper of the Lamb is described in the book of Revelation. The parable of the ten virgins is primarily eschatological, but it also describes those who miss out on what could be theirs.

It is interesting that the bride is never mentioned in this parable, only the virgins. The reason, I believe, is as follows: All the redeemed make up the Bride of Christ and all the redeemed will be glorified. But there will be things that some people miss out on, and they are going to wish they had been more faithful. Jesus was wanting to show, as He did again and again in the parables of the Kingdom of heaven, what it is going to be like for Christians who take for granted the responsibility that is theirs.

Why is it that there are so many people for whom their Christianity is a faith that makes them comfortable? How many Christians have never led a soul to Christ? Don't sit back comfortably and rationalize the position you have chosen to take.

This parable could even be symbolic of revival. When the Church is awakened, those who did not have oil are in real trouble and don't get to enjoy the revival. Someone once said to me, "You are afraid that revival is going to come, and I am going to miss out on it, aren't you?" I said yes. And I believe that. This parable is designed to wake you up.

An Unexpected Word

The midnight cry was an unexpected word. There are three key points concerning this.

A Providence of Extraordinary Proportions

Due to the providence of the grace of God, something will happen to wake up the Church prior to Jesus' return. How is this going to happen in the 21st century? It will almost certainly involve more than the exhortation to "go out and meet the bridegroom." It must be something that will be undergirded by a providence of extraordinary proportions. This is why I believe that world shake-ups like September 11th play a part in paving the way for the Gospel. Such events shake both the saved and the unsaved.

I don't think that this midnight cry has fully happened yet. It is my view that the next thing to take place on God's calendar is an outpouring of the Spirit in such power and in such measure that preachers will have power beyond anything that they have ever known. That hasn't happened yet. Since September 11th, people around the world are already sinking back into their lethargy. Perhaps in America they are more awake than in other countries because this incident happened in America.

A Proclamation with an Extraordinary Perspective
Look at what happened many hundreds of years ago between Isaac and Ishmael. The prophecies that were given to each of them are quite amazing in a present-day context. Look at the rivalry that has lasted over the years between the Jews and the Arabs. In the sixth century Mohammed came, and the emergence of Islam and then the Arabs actually had a theological basis for standing together. I believe that this ancient rivalry will increase in fervor in these very last days, and we will see a depth of hostility like we have never seen before. All that has already happened is only the beginning, and this will provide the context for the Spirit of God to be poured out on His messengers. This is a providence of extraordinary proportions. It will result in preaching with an extraordinary power—a proclamation of the Gospel with an extraordinary perspective. Jesus is coming soon—go out to meet Him!

The Need for Discipline

The 1950s were, for me, an era in which I had visions. One time I saw the following regarding this parable. The midnight cry came, and when it did, it made people believe the truth whom you would never have thought would believe it. Witnessing this, I thought to myself, *These people are believing this!* Yet I could go out onto the streets the next weekend and shout, "The Bridegroom is coming! Go out to meet Him!" and the people would just laugh at me, because that is not the way it is at the moment. Yet something will take place that will touch the atheists, infidels and agnostics of this world, and church members who have never been converted and church members who have been converted but are asleep—*all* are going to wake up!

When the midnight cry fully comes, I believe that Christians will have an increased authority to preach the Gospel. I anticipate, if I am alive, that I will have an authority that I haven't had before.

Matthew 25:7 says, "Then all the virgins woke up and trimmed their lamps" (Matthew 25:7). It was a sense of moral consciousness—a sudden realization of duty and a return to discipline. The trouble with many Christians today is that they are not disciplined. You may manage to get to work on time, but you read your Bible only if it is convenient and if you can get up on time. You make sure that your bills are paid, but for some reason, praying—well, you have good intentions to get around to it. You are disciplined when it comes to your wallet, your pocketbook and anything that concerns your lifestyle. But when it comes to spiritual things, you have no discipline. Jesus was giving us this parable to challenge us. What has the Christian faith done to change your life and your lifestyle? How disciplined are you?

Why is it that a person can say genuinely one day, *Lord, You know I love You,* but the next day temptation comes and they give right in to it? Why? No discipline. Jesus said to the church at Ephesus, "You have forsaken your first love" (Revelation 2:4). You have *lost* your first love. Can you remember that time when Jesus was so special to you, so real and so precious? You say, "Well, it's not quite like it was, but you know, God understands that I'm busy." And you know what Jesus said? "Remember the height from which you have fallen! Repent and do the things you did at first. If you do not repent, I will come to you and remove your lampstand from its place" (Revelation 2:5).

What that means is God will raise up somebody else to do what you wouldn't do. Don't allow that to happen.

If the Church of England had been all that it was supposed to have been in the eighteenth century, there never would have been a Methodist Church. If the Methodist Church had been all that it was supposed to be in the nineteenth century, there never would have been a Salvation Army. God raises up those who will do the work. I decided a long time ago that I would say, *Lord, don't go to somebody else. Here am I—send me.* We need a restoration of devotion.

The Bridegroom Tarries

This is a melancholy confession: "The foolish ones said to the wise, 'Give us some of your oil; our lamps are going out' " (Matthew 25:8).

There are things we need to learn from this. The foolish ones' folly was exposed, but not *until* the bridegroom returned. Some people, someday, will be found out. At the moment, we can wear masks of respectability and keep up the good appearance, but when the Bridegroom returns, everything will be out in the open. It is an interesting point to me that had the bridegroom come sooner, the foolish virgins would not have been found out, because there was a time when everybody had oil. It was because the bridegroom tarried that some didn't turn out to be all that they thought they would be.

There was a time when, had the Bridegroom come, you yourself might have received a reward, because at that moment your lamp *was* trimmed and burning bright—you were on fire for the Lord. If only the Bridegroom had come then. But He tarried, and you cooled off.

Perhaps one reason God delays His coming is to let everyone see what we are really like. Think of the person who prays, and God doesn't answer their prayers in the first week, so they give up. They say, "Well, I prayed about it, and I didn't get an answer. God must not care about me." Yet there are other people who, three years later, are still praying—six years later still praying—that is what I'm talking about. God delays, just to see how deep our devotion really is. Many have an enthusiastic beginning, but when God hides His face and things don't happen, people start to give up. If this is you, then God is graciously nudging you and saying, "Don't harden your heart."

The sad fact is there was no change in the virgins' spiritual condition after the midnight cry. It was then too late. Maybe now you will admit your lamp is going out. It is amazing how we will, in a time when we have no other choice, be unashamed of the Lord. At last the virgins confessed to their real condition. They pleaded for help with the wise who were Spirit-filled. "Give us some of your oil, pray for us—we've blown it." I predict that that is going to happen in the Church. Some of us who have been unreachable, unteachable and inflexible will then say, "I need help." But it will be too late.

There is still time to cross over and not be a foolish virgin who will one day be found out. Until the fullness of the midnight cry, there is still time. "Watch out that you do not lose what you have worked for" (2 John 8).

Makeshift Counsel

" 'No,' they replied, 'there may not be enough for both us and you. Instead, go to those who sell oil and buy some for yourselves' " (Matthew 25:9).

The wise were put on the spot. The truth is they only had enough for themselves, because they themselves had also been asleep. They had become drowsy. So their makeshift counsel was, "Go to those who sell oil and buy some for yourselves." In other words, do what you can under the circumstances. The wise virgins who took extra oil for their vessels were unable to help the foolish ones. It could be that you want to help those who have blown it, but you say, "I have just enough by the grace of God. I don't deserve it myself, but I don't know what to say to you." And while all this is going on, the Lord returns: "While they were on their way to buy the oil, the bridegroom arrived. The virgins who were ready went in with him to the wedding banquet. And the door was shut" (Matthew 25:10).

This is the actual moment of the Second Coming. The midnight cry and the actual coming of the bridegroom were separated by a period of time—how much time we don't know. But when the midnight cry becomes apparent to everybody—it could be today, it could be tomorrow, it could be in the next year or two—it isn't going to be long before the Second Coming itself.

> They will see the Son of Man coming on the clouds of the sky, with power and great glory. And he will send his angels with a loud trumpet call, and they will gather his elect from the four winds, from one end of the heavens to the other.
>
> Matthew 24:30–31

Are you ready for that moment?

Then came the marriage celebration. The virgins who were ready went in with the bridegroom to the wedding banquet. Until then we, the Church, are just engaged to be married. In the Bible, an engagement was permanent. You didn't break engagements. If you did, it was as serious as getting a divorce. That is why Joseph was thinking that he would have to divorce Mary when he discovered she was pregnant—even though they were only engaged.

Although God will never break the engagement, there will be those who will be found sleeping and will miss out on so much that could have been theirs. Seek the Lord while He may be found. If God is speaking to you, it could be that you can still cross over. For the era ahead, you can be on the front row as it were.

"Later the others also came. 'Sir! Sir!' they said. 'Open the door for us!' But he replied, 'I tell you the truth, I don't know you'" (Matthew 25:11–12).

This describes those who are going to miss the coming, and there will be nothing they can do because it is then too late. The result is a merciless closure. Jesus ended the parable with what I can only call the major conclusion: "Therefore keep watch, because you do not know the day or the hour" (Matthew 25:13).

What are you to do in the meantime? Today if you hear His voice, don't harden your heart (Hebrews 3:15). If the Holy Spirit is dealing with you, thank Him. Return to your first love. Return to discipline. Let this word be the wake-up call. The internal chastening of the Lord (the two-edged sword—Hebrews 4:12) is the best way to have your problems solved. God speaks, and you say, "Lord, You have been patient with me, and I have waited too long, but I've got the message now—thank You."

Chapter 35

The Parable of the Sheep
and the Goats

Come, you who are blessed by my Father; take your inheritance, the
kingdom prepared for you since the creation of the world.

Matthew 25:34

This is the final parable in this book and, as far as we know, was the last
of Jesus' parables. Certainly it is the last major one in the gospel of
Matthew. It is a parable that reveals the judgment seat of Christ and
therefore has an eschatological context. We saw in the parable of the
ten virgins a revelation of a great awakening and then the second
coming of Jesus. In the parable of the talents, we saw how faithfulness
is rewarded at the judgment seat of Christ. In the parable of the sheep
and the goats, however, the setting is more general. It gives not a
distinction merely between the saved and the lost—it gives a distinction between the saved who have a reward and the lost. This is a point
that is overlooked by nearly every Bible commentary and biblical
scholar. But to miss this point is to play right into the hands of those
who say that this proves that we are saved by good works. The parable is
a reminder that all will stand before the judgment seat of Christ to give
an account of the things done while they were on earth, whether those
deeds be good or bad.

Some would question whether this is a parable at all, because it
begins, "When the Son of Man comes in his glory" (Matthew 25:31). In
other words it sounds more like a prophecy or a factual account. But as
we continue to read, we find that it is a mixture—there is parabolic
language along with factual details about the Second Coming. This is
the way Jesus chose to describe final justice. As I have said about so
many of the parables, this is not an easy one—don't ever say Jesus was
simple. So why is this one difficult?

For one thing, it speaks of a literal judgment of the nations. We are
told, "All the nations will be gathered before him" (Matthew 25:32).

Does this mean that the United States will be judged as a nation? Will Russia be judged as a nation? Now there is a problem. Will a nation be judged on its merits today, or will it be judged by its history? Rather than judging "Russia," will God judge "the Soviet Union"? Or "Czarist Russia"? It is difficult to interpret this statement of Jesus.

It is also difficult because a superficial reading of the parable would suggest that one goes to heaven or to hell on the basis of whether or not he feeds the poor or gives to the hungry and those who are in prison. We are told that those who are on His left (the goats) He will reject, while those who are saved (the sheep) He will welcome (Matthew 25:34, 41). But it is not quite that simple. It is showing a distinction between the lost and the saved who have a reward, because to the sheep Jesus said, "Come, you who are blessed by my Father; take your inheritance, the kingdom prepared for you since the creation of the world" (Matthew 25:34).

Inheritance is a word almost always used in the Bible with reference to a "reward." That is why it is about the *rewarded* saved and the lost. If it referred to the way of salvation, it would mean only those who feed the poor and visit people in prison will go to heaven, while those who don't will go to hell. If you see the parable as referring to saved people who have had their inheritance given to them, it changes everything.

Why Is This Parable Important?

The parable reveals, and only in this parable is it explained, why God created hell in the first place. Have you ever wondered? We are told, "Depart from me, you who are cursed, into the eternal fire prepared for the devil and his angels" (Matthew 25:41).

Hell was originally made for Satan and those who fell with him. We do not know how many angels fell. If you take Revelation 12 to refer to the revolt of Satan in heaven, then maybe one-third of the angels fell, but that is a bit speculative. What we do know is that Satan tried to recruit every angel in heaven to revolt against God, and he succeeded with some. The reason God created hell was for the devil and his angels.

This parable is also a reminder that it was God who created hell. Don't let anybody say to you that you make your own hell. I know what people mean by that. You can be a fool and choose the way of darkness rather than the way of light, and you can make your own bed in hell. But you need to remember that hell was God's idea.

The German philosopher Feuerbach said that God is nothing more than man's projection upon the backdrop of the universe. He said that man wants to believe that there is a God out there who will give him heaven when he dies; that man has created a kind of figure that will give him some kind of peace. Well, given that logic, who would have thought of hell? There is nothing more horrible and nothing more horrendous; there is nothing more awful. There is nothing good or nice about it. Man would not have thought of this. Hell was God's idea.

The parable reminds us that God doesn't forget what we have done. We so often *do* forget. I recently wrote a book called *Thanking God* to remind us that God wants to be thanked. Count your blessings—name them one by one; it will surprise you what the Lord has done. We tend to forget, and so we need to make ourselves remember. But God doesn't need to make Himself remember—He reminds us that He knows what He has done for us. He also knows what we have done.

"God is not unjust; he will not forget your work and the love you have shown him as you have helped his people and continue to help them" (Hebrews 6:10).

God sees it all. This parable is a reminder to us that God remembers. But it is also a reminder that in hell you will have your memory. Abraham said to the rich man, in the parable of the rich man and Lazarus, "Son, remember that in your lifetime you received your good things" (Luke 16:25).

There is another thing about this parable that is important. It is a further indication that hell is eternal just as heaven is eternal. Now we are quite happy for heaven to be eternal, but many people are not happy that hell will be eternal. This parable concludes with the words of Jesus: "They will go away to eternal punishment, but the righteous to eternal life" (Matthew 25:46).

Heaven and hell are equally parallel, equally perpetual. We do not have the right to be selective and say, "I believe in heaven and that it will last forever, but I don't believe in hell." But if there is no hell, there is no heaven. Here it is as clear as it can possibly be—some will go away to eternal punishment and some (the righteous) to eternal life.

Professor David Gooding—a world-class Greek scholar—from Queens University, Belfast, showed me that in the Greek it literally reads, "They will go away to eternal punishing." Those who believe in annihilation say, "It is eternal punishment because it is eternal—it is over." They think the unsaved will be annihilated. But the Greek literally reads "eternal punishing."

I wish it weren't so. I don't like having to talk about this in the last parable. But this parable also shows us how true it is that Jesus is the

Alpha and the Omega. That means He had the first word, and He will have the last word. He is the judge in all of this.

"When the Son of Man comes in his glory, and all the angels with him, *he* will sit on his throne in heavenly glory" (Matthew 25:31, emphasis mine).

And so, "The King will reply, 'I tell you the truth, whatever you did for one of the least of these brothers of mine, you did for me'" (Matthew 25:40). And, "Whatever you did not do for one of the least of these, you did not do for me" (Matthew 25:45).

Jesus will have the last word.

The Judge

His Power

In Matthew 24:30, Jesus is referred to as the Son of Man, which is an echo of the words of Daniel (see Daniel 7:13).

> They will see the Son of Man coming on the clouds of the sky, with power and great glory. And he will send his angels with a loud trumpet call, and they will gather his elect from the four winds, from one end of the heavens to the other.
>
> Matthew 24:30–31

The King of glory is coming a second time, and then he will be a Judge.

"Behold, He is coming with clouds, and every eye will see Him, even they who pierced Him. And all the tribes of the earth will mourn because of Him" (Revelation 1:7, NKJV).

What took place in New York City on September 11, 2001, is virtually nothing compared to the wailing and the gnashing of teeth that will occur when He comes in His glory. Never has there been such a display of power.

"All the nations will be gathered before him, and he will separate the people one from another" (Matthew 25:32).

His Posture

"When the Son of Man comes in his glory, and all the angels with him, he will sit on his throne" (Matthew 25:31).

Do you realize what you and I will be doing? We will be standing. This can be consistently seen through the New Testament. Every time it mentions the judgment, we are standing. The multitudes stand, but Jesus will sit. In ancient times the posture of sitting was one of authority. Jesus taught the Sermon on the Mount from a sitting position. Pontius

Pilate did not give his decree of judgment until he sat. So we read, "I saw a great white throne and him who was seated on it" (Revelation 20:11).

We shall stand. He will sit.

His Province

"All the nations will be gathered before him" (Matthew 25:32).

The Greek word for *nations* here is *ethnos,* which really just means "peoples," so it could be a mistake to read the word *nations* into it in a technical sense. Therefore it should not necessarily be understood to mean the nations or governments of the world, although God may well gather them before Him in some way. Perhaps He has been doing that for centuries, for the truth is, He has always controlled nations; He puts one down and exalts another (Psalm 75:7). The nations to Him are just a drop in a bucket (Isaiah 40:15). The wicked shall be sent to hell, as well as all the nations that forget God (Psalm 9:17). But this passage in Matthew 25 is probably to be understood as referring to every kindred, tribe, tongue, race, village, province, every accent, every dialect—*all* the people of the world will stand before Him. The sea will give up its dead (Revelation 20:13). You and I will be there. Every single person who has ever lived will be there. Adolf Hitler will be there; Saddam Hussein will be there; Fidel Castro will be there; Mussolini will be there; the ancient wicked emperors of Rome will be there.

How will the nations be gathered? They will be summoned. It won't be a polite invitation on a card, saying, "His Majesty, King Jesus, graciously invites you to appear before His throne of glory." We are told in the book of Revelation that they will do everything within their power to escape it. It was a sight to behold, said John in Revelation 6:15:

> Then the kings of the earth, the princes, the generals, the rich, the mighty, and every slave and every free man hid in caves and among the rocks of the mountains. They called to the mountains and the rocks, "Fall on us and hide us from the face of him who sits on the throne and from the wrath of the Lamb!"
>
> Revelation 6:15–16

Every slave and every freeman—this includes the poor. Don't think because you are poor you are going to be exempt. Don't think because you have had it hard in life you will be exempt. *Every* freeman and *every* person hidden in the caves and among the rocks will be summoned. The summons will fill people so full of dread that they will want to kill themselves, if that were possible, but it will be too late.

"For the great day of their wrath has come, and who can stand?" (Revelation 6:17).

His Prerogative

We are told that Jesus will do the separating (Matthew 25:32–33). He has a right to do this in advance of the sentencing, or even in advance of the hearing of people's cases. If you want a chance to plead your case, you will probably have plenty of time, because we are told that having been given the sentence, the people began to try to change the mind of the Judge (Matthew 25:44). But "The Lord knows those who are his" (2 Timothy 2:19).

This is why as soon as the saved die they go straight to heaven. God doesn't have to think twice and say, "Now, let me see, did this person believe in Me? Will someone just get Me the record and let Me see? Where do we send him, heaven or hell?"

The Lord knows those who are His, and He will separate people on the basis of what He already knows. It will be an awful moment. Friends will be separated from friends, never to see them again; loved ones will be separated from loved ones, never to see them again. People you know will be taken from where you are, and you will find yourself standing beside people that you don't know. And those who are taken from you, you will never be with again. That is the Judge's prerogative.

His Procedure

In Matthew 25:34, the king addresses not those who are saved but those who are saved and have an inheritance. Jesus didn't deal, in this parable, with those who are saved by fire. He did that in the parable of the ten virgins and in the parable of the talents. In this particular parable, He immediately affirmed those who had an inheritance. At that moment, receiving your reward will mean everything to you. Of course, it is far better to be saved by fire than to go into the everlasting fire. The apostle Paul said, "I beat my body and make it my slave so that after I have preached to others, I myself will not be disqualified for the prize" (1 Corinthians 9:27).

The procedure of separation begins in verse 34. Jesus will address those on His right, "Take your inheritance, the kingdom prepared for you since the creation of the world" (Matthew 25:34). All that we are going to have has been planned for us—it is not an afterthought.

To those on His left, He will say, "Depart from me, you who are cursed, into the eternal fire prepared for the devil and his angels" (Matthew 25:41).

Do you know why they are called cursed? It is because they bear their own sins. Jesus has already borne the sins of the saved, but those who will not trust in what He did on the cross will bear their own sins—and they are called cursed.

The Justice

The Strategy of Judgment

The strategy shows why the people were separated. To those on His right, Jesus will say:

> I was hungry and you gave me something to eat, I was thirsty and you gave me something to drink, I was a stranger and you invited me in, I needed clothes and you clothed me, I was sick and you looked after me, I was in prison and you came to visit me.
>
> Matthew 25:35–36

To those on His left, He will say:

> I was hungry and you gave me nothing to eat, I was thirsty and you gave me nothing to drink, I was a stranger and you did not invite me in, I needed clothes and you did not clothe me, I was sick and in prison and you did not look after me.
>
> Matthew 25:42–43

And so the strategy of the judgment is simply to show why they have been separated. There will be those who say, "I want to be on that side," and He will explain why they are where they are. Sadly, you won't be able to cross over. The great gulf will be fixed, and you won't be able to cross from one side to the other. There will be no destinies changed then. I tell you, "Now is the time of God's favor, now is the day of salvation" (2 Corinthians 6:2).

Don't harden your heart.

The Standard of Judgment

What do you suppose the standard of judgment is? Based on this parable, it is how people have treated the Church.

"'Lord, when did we see you hungry ... and did not help you?' He will reply, '... whatever you did not do for one of the least of these, you did not do for me'" (Matthew 25:44–45).

The standard is the way you look after the Church of God, the way you care for the people of God and the way in which you deal with other Christians. Those who were saved were those who cared about the Church and fellow Christians. *They* are the ones with the inheritance. Those who were lost showed contempt for the Church of God and for Christians; that is the standard of judgment.

The Surprise of Judgment

Look at verses 37 and 44—there will be surprise on both sides. Both those with an inheritance and those who are eternally lost will be surprised. Rewarded Christians are unaware that they have done anything great. They have taken seriously the words of Jesus and they have only done their duty (Luke 17:10). They weren't expecting a reward. Jesus said, "Don't let your right hand know what your left hand is doing" (Matthew 6:3). The lost, on the other hand, are unaware that they have done anything wrong. They saw no need to care for the Church or the people of God. The implication is that had they known, they would have acted differently. They didn't realize that it would have been Jesus they were serving.

A minister from Colorado was invited to go to Calcutta a number of years ago and do some work with Mother Teresa. At the end of a day of ministering to the poor, she had a question for him. "Did you see Jesus today?"

I can guarantee you that if Her Majesty the Queen had a tire puncture in her limousine in front of your house, you would be out there like a shot doing anything you could to take care of her. You would invite her in; you would feed her; you would do whatever you could to look after her. Jesus was saying, "You ought to see *Me* behind needy people." In life we should strive to be consistent in the way we treat others—to give equal time to the tramp and to someone who is middle class. Do all you can because you never know whom you are reaching.

Martin Luther said, "When I get to heaven I expect three surprises: those who will be in heaven that I didn't expect to be there; and those missing that I thought *would* be there. But the greatest surprise will be that I am there myself." I expect that when we get to heaven we will be surprised to see who gets a reward, and we will be surprised to see who was saved by fire. But the greatest surprise for all of us will be that God remembers everything *we* have done. He knows all that you have been through. He knows if you dignified a trial. He knows whether you totally forgave. He knows whether you can do something without grumbling. He knows whether you can do something without asking for credit. He will credit you then.

The Sense of Judgment

Some people say, "Judge me by my actions." They want to be judged by their works. They will be! The judgment will reveal how selfish and defensive and self-righteous people are. Jesus didn't give a total rationale for judgment in this parable, but He gave a hint that God is aware of everything. He knows how people hate Him; He knows how He has been accused. The most maligned person in the history of the world is God. God is aware of how man charges Him with the ills of the world. In one stroke God will declare His justice and clear His name.

The Sentencing of Judgment

From the moment He conceived the plan of redemption, God also planned our inheritance. Think of the book of Ezekiel. It contains the detailed plans that God had for Israel. Those plans concerning the Temple have now been done away with (otherwise, in waiting for their fulfillment, we would all still be making blood sacrifices). The Temple in Ezekiel simply shows what God *would have* done for Israel. Nothing could be more painful than for you to find out what you might have been and what the Lord envisioned for you. But you said, "No, I have got to have my own way—sex, drink, pleasure...." One of the things that will make hell hell will be realizing how things might have been instead.

The reward in hell will be retribution (Matthew 25:41). According to this verse, hell cannot mean annihilation. If this were the case, why would the fire need to be everlasting? If it annihilates, everything would be burned up. Annihilation never entered God's mind. I wish it had. I would prefer it. Those who believe in annihilation, sadly, present to an unbeliever a theological rationale on a silver platter—what non-Christians already want to believe, that when you die your consciousness ends and that's it.

We are even told that Satan won't be annihilated: "The devil, who deceived them, was thrown into the lake of burning sulphur, where the beast and the false prophet had been thrown. They will be tormented day and night for ever and ever" (Revelation 20:10).

Finally, Jesus said, "Then they will go away to eternal punishment, but the righteous to eternal life" (Matthew 25:46).

Those are sobering words with which to end the last chapter of this book. I only know that they are the words of Jesus. I think we must all remember this verse from Genesis: "Will not the Judge of all the earth do right?" (Genesis 18:25).

Amen.

Notes

Chapter 9

1. Arthur Blessitt has carried a twelve-foot cross around with him since 1969, on a journey that so far has taken him through 300 nations and some 36,067 miles. Source: www.blessitt.com

Chapter 13

1. Story posted on Tony Campolo's web site: www.tonycampolo.org.

Chapter 31

1. Philip E. Haward, Jonathan Edwards (editor), David Brainerd (editor), *The Life and Diary of David Brainerd, second edition* (Grand Rapids: Baker, 1989).

R. T. Kendall spent 25 years pastoring the historic Westminster Chapel in London, England, as successor to G. Campbell Morgan and Martyn Lloyd-Jones. In early 2002 he moved back to his native America, where he makes his home with his wife, Louise. He is currently ministering throughout North America as part of the Word, Spirit and Power Team, along with Jack Taylor and Charles Carrin. Kendall is the author of numerous books, including *Total Forgiveness, The Anointing* and *The Sensitivity of the Spirit.*